European Food Regulation after Enlargement

Nijhoff International Trade Law Series

VOLUME 9

The titles published in this series are listed at brill.nl/nint

European Food Regulation after Enlargement

Facing the Challenges of Diversity

By
Karolina Żurek

MARTINUS NIJHOFF PUBLISHERS

LEIDEN • BOSTON
2012

This book is printed on acid-free paper.

Library of Congress Cataloging-in-Publication Data

Zurek, Karolina.
European food regulation after enlargement : facing the challenges of diversity / by Karolina Zurek.
p. cm.
Includes bibliographical references and index.
ISBN-13: 978-90-04-19584-4
ISBN-10: 90-04-19584-X
1. Food—Europe—Safety measures. 2. Food industry and trade—Europe—Safety measures. 3. Food industry and trade—Government policy—Europe. 4. Food law and legislation—Europe. I. Title.
HD9000.6.Z87 2012
363.19'2561094—dc23
2011034382

ISBN 978 90 04 19584 4

CONTENTS

SUMMARY

This book aims to present a critical legal perspective on the current direction of European Union (EU) food safety regulation. Through an analysis of three regulatory mechanisms—*mutual recognition*, *scientific risk regulation* and *standardisation*—combined with a study of the evolution of food legislation in the EU, I seek to show how the current framework fails to face new challenges, such as the globalisation of world trade and the last two enlargements. In particular, the volume focuses upon the case of a newly acceded EU member state, namely Poland. The main argument is that an enlarged and more diversified Europe must not disregard the numerous socio-economic implications of market regulation. If not properly acknowledged and reflected in the regulatory scheme, the mismatch between market regulation and socio-economic factors can lead to a kind of gradual disembedding of the regulatory framework. This is of critical importance as the EU project is not only tasked with securing greater European *homogeneity*, but also with preserving unique European *diversity*—in the field of food as well as in other aspects. I am thus suggesting that the existing regulatory approach can be opened up to include a wider set of relevant socio-economic implications, allowing for protection of diversity while aiming for greater homogeneity and unity. The legal system for the regulation of food can be rebalanced to become more flexible and responsive by shifting the use of existing regulatory mechanisms, in order to diversify regulatory intervention. First, this would require improvement of application of the *risk analysis* model, in order to guarantee inclusion of valid socio-economic concerns in the decision-making process. Second, it would also entail reliance on managed *mutual recognition* in those areas where protection of diversity does not collide with protection of consumers (for example, where either longstanding trust has been available or national codes have provided sufficient safety guarantees), and where consequently imposition of strict *standardisation* is not necessary. Largely due to legitimate concerns with crisis, but also with economic considerations, the regulatory framework for food in Europe has generated a bias in favor of homogeneity and unity, turning against diversity and leading to unforeseen and unintended consequences. This book argues that this need not be so.

ACKNOWLEDGEMENTS

A number of people have contributed to making this book possible.

I owe the greatest gratitude to my academic mentor, Professor Christian Joerges. Christian has been a true 'Doktorvater' of my project throughout its entire duration. His trust in this project has taken it further that I would have dared to imagine. It is largely thanks to his encouragement, support and patience that all those ideas of mine could be gathered and organised in this volume.

It would be impossible to thank all the people who have shaped and sustained my interest in European matters. Their comments and discussions have helped me to clarify my thoughts and make this text better. My special gratitude goes to Stanisław Biernat, Marise Cremona, Kerry Rittich, Joanna Szychowska, Ellen Vos and Robert Wai. I am also particularly grateful to Mads Andenas, editor of Martinus Nijhoff Series in International Trade Law, for his comments and the overall supervision of publication of this book.

On a more personal note, I would like to thank my family and friends for their constant help and support.

CHAPTER ONE

INTRODUCTION

1. On Food and Europe—Introductory Remarks

This book is basically about two things: 'food' and 'Europe', and the relationship between them. However, the book also seeks to track the determining and highly influential role of 'law' in shaping that relationship, with regard to cultural diversity, *trade*, and the social expectations to which they are subject. In the following, I will take a closer look at how food and Europe relate to these three different paradigms and how legal regulation structures this relationship.

1.1. *Food*

1.1.1. *Food and (Agri)culture*

Food is undeniably one of the most crucial elements of our existence. Food defines us as humans, both physiologically as well as culturally, socially and in many other ways. Food can make you sick. Food can make you well. Food can cause wars. Food can win wars. Food can make you love (after all, the way to a man's heart is through his stomach, as proverbial wisdom teaches us). We identify ourselves through our food; thus, we refer to ourselves as vegetarians, meat-eaters or green. We think of ourselves as slow-food believers, fast-food lovers or five-element diet practitioners. We identify societies and nations through their foods. Without a moment's hesitation, we match Italians with their pasta, Germans with sausages and sauerkraut, and the French with escargots. Most of all, however, we all acknowledge that when it comes to food we are all different. It is true that we all need to eat in order to stay alive, but what we eat and how we do it is very individual. It is shaped by our upbringing, our social and economic situation, our geographic and climatic conditions, as well as by the culture and traditions we grew up with. From this point of view, we are indeed all different.

Food is tied to the land. Thus, agriculture and food must be viewed in conjunction, and any other approach would not only be illogical but also unnatural. Throughout the centuries, generations of men and women have produced and consumed food in accordance with the natural cycle of the seasons of the year, within the limits of geographical conditions imposed, often according to the knowledge handed down through the generations, but sometimes also through experimentation and invention caused by necessity as well as opportunity.

However, modern methods of production and distribution, as well as the modern flexible patterns of life, have tended to blur the link between what we produce and what we consume. This is due to many and various reasons, among which I will mention only industrialisation, urbanisation, improvement of techniques of storage and transport, development of new technologies, and the spreading of information that comes from natural human curiosity. The existence of natural links between food, agriculture and culture, however, is crucial for any understanding of problems dealt with in this volume.

1.1.1.1. *On Food, Its Roots and Its Rooting Out*

In traditional societies, the principal occupation of people was the production of their own food. The overlapping of food production and local culture was, therefore, obvious and far-reaching. Food defined culture, traditions, social roles and the concept of belonging to a certain community. Food's historical importance illustrates its personal nature and its meaning for individuals and social groups. The socio-cultural role of food in human lives and societies is undeniable, and it relates not only to survival and social patterns but also to religion, medicine and security. It has to be acknowledged, though, that the ways in which these functions of food were retained and developed in various societies can differ greatly. Cultural preferences and attitudes towards what food is appropriate and safe, have over time, been expressed in the ways in which societies have regulated these matters.[1]

Food production in today's developed world is probably more closely linked to technology and business than to any kind of tradition, but in most developing countries the old patterns have remained vital, although the economic reliance of those countries on the export of agricultural products is gradually affecting the situation.[2] Speedy industrialisation, development of new technologies, improvements in means of transport and progress in the area of food processing have changed the landscape, and are taking food further and further away from its source. It is not only that people no longer know the producer, or where the food came from and how it was grown and processed, but also they are often simply not interested. As changes in production and work patterns in the industrialised world were followed by overall changes in people's ways of life, the need for new types of food has begun to emerge. This might explain the extraordinary career of highly processed 'convenience food' and 'fast food', both of which have provided an answer to the needs of modern families that value time and money more highly than nutrition and taste. At

[1] F van Waarden, 'Taste, Traditions, Transactions, and Trust: The Public and Private Regulation of Food' in C Ansell and D Vogel (eds.), *What's the Beef? The Contested Governance of European Food Safety* (The MIT Press, Cambridge MA 2006) 37–42.

[2] Compare MA Echols, *Food Safety and the WTO. The Interplay of Culture, Science and Technology* (Kluwer Law International, The Hague 2001) 28–31.

the same time, highly processed food has responded to the needs of producers as well. This has been the case especially in the US, where the overproduction of semi-processed food components needed a good way of dispatch.[3] A subtle, but important consequence of this development is a gradual 'de-socialisation' of food, which implies the reduction of everyday food consumption from being a form of socializing to being simply a method of sustaining energy levels.[4]

Expanding big multinational companies have taken over most of the international food trade. Being capable of buying food at very low prices, transporting it across vast and sometimes ridiculously circumvented distances, and yet remain able to compete with local producers in serving the needs of poorer consumers. The last but definitely not the least element of this 'cultural revolution' in the food sector has been the emergence of genetic engineering and its use in food production. Genetic engineering, in simple terms, is a process of manipulating genes undertaken outside the organism's natural reproductive process, with the aim of introducing new characteristics or attributes, such as higher resistance, novel traits or increased productivity. Food produced by genetic modification has been around since the 1990s and has always been a source of controversy. Some see it as a hope for the developing world and an answer to global hunger. Others oppose genetic engineering in food due to its potential for unforeseen consequences for consumers as well as for the environment and biodiversity.

1.1.1.2. *On Pace and Power*

Although some societies have kept their traditional views, in many industrialised and developed countries it has taken a harsh wake-up call to turn attention towards the problems of these new food-production processes. It was often in connection with food scandals, highlighted life threats and terrifying reports on adverse effects on health that people started to consider 'the old ways' and give their attention again to what they eat. Over the last two decades, this movement has strengthened and has been popularised enough for me to dare to call it a trend. People have again started to consider the provenance of their food, as well as the societal and environmental aspects of farming and food production. As a consequence, all these issues have been brought back to the fore and onto the socio-political agenda. Having reviewed the most interesting and influential of the current social movements focusing

[3] Among the extensive American and international literature on food scams and manipulations of both public opinion on nutritional choices and food quality, as well as governmental decisions on the food business, see e.g. M Nestle, *Food Politics. How the Food Industry Influences Nutrition and Health* (California Studies in Food and Culture, University of California Press, Berkeley 2002); T Lang and M Heasman, *Food Wars. The Global Battle for Mouths, Minds and Markets* (Earthscan, London 2004); ME Lien and B Nerlich (eds.), *The Politics of Food* (Berg, Oxford 2004).

[4] F Fernandez-Armesto, *Food: A History* (Macmillan, London 2001) particularly 22, where the author poetically claims that 'the loneliness of the fast-food eater is uncivilizing'.

on food issues, I have observed two major streams of development. One can be described as 'consumeristic': it concentrates on issues of food safety and quality, changing consumption patterns and conscious consumption. The second wave of social movement, which can be called 'productionistic', concentrates on the supply side of the food chain and promotes the preservation of small-scale farming and traditional local farming patterns over the transformations forced by globalisation and free trade expansion.

With regard to the consumerist stream, it is interesting to observe that in NGOs' manifestos, efforts towards food safety have been supplemented by claims for its quality. Nevertheless, although part of it was an effect of social movements, such as the slow-food movement,[5] it has translated into governmental and intergovernmental agendas. As a consequence, a considerable proportion of this development is an effect of conscious governmental or supranational actions, such as quality labelling systems[6] or organic farming[7] regulations in the EU.

Another important cultural aspect of contemporary food is the development of new consumption patterns. In many developed countries, consumers are no longer simply following the basic logic of cost-efficiency, but instead are pursuing a much more complex purchasing scheme, informed by multiple concerns and interests. As a result, contemporary markets have to learn to respond to the 'conscious consumer' or the 'green consumer', who does not simply consume, but makes a point of consuming a specially chosen product. This 'conscious consumer' believes that his or her choice makes a difference and embodies his or her rights as a citizen and as a human being.[8] Modern consumption, therefore, turns out to be a phenomenon far too complex to be analysed solely by recourse to economic rationality.

The second wave of social activism that has to do with food issues is focused upon the societal and environmental aspects of farming and food production. Movements such as the people's food sovereignty[9] aim to develop a food and

[5] For more on the slow-food movement and its activities, see <http://www.slowfood.com>.

[6] See Council Regulation (EC) 510/2006 of 20 March 2006 on the protection of geographical indications and designations of origin for agricultural products and foodstuffs [2006] OJ L 93 and Council Regulation (EC) 509/2006 of 20 March 2006 on agricultural products and foodstuffs as traditional specialities guaranteed [2006] OJ L 93.

[7] Council Regulation (EEC) 2092/91 of 24 June 1991 on organic production of agricultural products and indications referring thereto in agricultural products and foodstuffs, [1991] OJ L 198 and Commission (EC) 'Proposal for a Council Regulation on organic production and labelling of organic products', COM (2005) 671 final, 21 December 2005.

[8] Compare M Everson and Ch Joerges, 'Consumer Citizenship in Postnational Constellations?, (2006) EUI Working Paper LAW No.2006/47, 7; see also G Trumbull, *Consumer Capitalism. Politics, Product Markets, and Firm Strategy in France and Germany* (Cornell University Press, Ithaca and London, 2006) 161–178.

[9] See, for example, the manifesto of LaVia Campesina as well as PM Rosset, *Food is Different. Why We Must Get the WTO out of Agriculture* (The Global Issues Series, Zed Books Ltd, London & New York 2006).

agriculture system that offers rural people in each country the opportunity to work and live in the countryside, thus conserving rural environments and rural-based cultural and culinary traditions, based on sustainable long-term management of natural resources. Representatives of this 'productionistic' stream warn that if present trends towards free trade in food—framed as 'free trade' for other products—continue, the accompanying land concentration and industrialisation of agriculture will make it impossible to achieve social or ecological sustainability, and will be detrimental to lives of peasants, rural women and small farmers, who make up more than half of the world's population.[10] In Europe, similar ideas are declared by the European Farmers' Co-ordination (CPE), which demonstrates that similar concerns are not foreign to the old continent either.

All in all, we seem to be observing the first sparks of social development towards a re-rooting of food issues, in both the production and the consumption senses. Slowly but steadily, they are gathering attention of the public, the media and the authorities. Moreover, however, they remind us of what used to be and what should have remained close to our hearts, but what, in the rush of days and the race for progress, we sometimes seem to forget. Food is important and special. Not only because we eat and need it, but also because it is such an important part of our identity: who we are, how we are and what we care for.

1.1.2. *Food and Trade*

> From Ghana cocoa is imported into Europe, America and the Soviet Union; in turn French cube sugar, Portuguese Sardines, Italian tomato paste, American corn, are virtually "staples" of the Ghanaian urban diet, while Yugoslav tractors, Bulgarian wine, Chinese bicycles and Polish conserves have been prominent elements in the recent repertoire of imported consumer goods.[11]

The quotation with which I decided to begin this section on food and trade was chosen because it illustrates two important developments in international trade in food. It shows, on the one hand, how enormous food trade is in size and influence, and how it encourages the changing of consumption patterns in both the developed and the developing world, making them interlinked and interdependent. On the other hand, however, it puts sardines and tractors in the same league, illustrating how very little significance is given to the specificity of food products.

The food industry is the single largest manufacturing sector in the EU in terms of turnover, added value and employment, and its share in the sector continues to grow. The total turnover in the year 2008 amounted to €965 billion, which represents 12.9% of the manufacturing sector, and which makes it the

---

[10] Ibid 6–14 and 106.

[11] J Goody, *Cooking, Cuisine and Class. A Study in Comparative Sociology* (Themes in the Social Science, Cambridge University Press, Cambridge 1982) 2.

largest manufacturing sector in the EU. Food employs about 4.4 million people and is organised through almost 310,000 companies, which makes the sector the leading employer in the EU (13.5%). It also purchases and processes 70% of the European agricultural production. The EU was a net exporter of food products in 2008, with export value of €58 billion, which contributes to a positive trade balance of over €1.1 billion.

The EU thus plays a major role in world trade in food products. It is the world's largest exporter and the second-largest importer of food products worldwide, excluding intra-EU trade. This export volume amounts to 20.8% of the world share, while import volume represents 18% of the world share.[12]

In order to paint a more complete picture, international trade statistics valid for global exchange have to be taken into consideration as well. According to WTO estimates, the value of the world merchandise export of agricultural products amounted to US$945 billion in 2006, which constituted 8% of the total world merchandise trade. Consequently, exports of agricultural products increased by 11% in nominal terms. Within that category, the volume of food export represented 80% of all agricultural exports, expanding by 10%.[13]

In contrast to the view of food as culture, current rules of world trade treat food no differently than they treat an automobile or a computer.[14] The system is constructed so that it restrains the ability of states to use safety concerns as an alleged reason for protective trade measures or to impose local safety concerns on international trade. As a result, the international trade system presents a scientific and economic, rather than a social, approach to food, and pushes towards a uniform and standardised determination of what is fit to sell, and what is safe or hazardous.[15] The situation is slightly different in cases where food is regulated through the perspective of its link with agriculture, but the need for recognition of the complex (agri)cultural aspects of food is still overlooked in contemporary trade regulation, or alternatively, if it is subordinate to the pure agricultural regulations, it is rather misdirected.

However, due to its economic potential as well as its particular sensitivity to consumer safety, the food market is among the most heavily regulated both in Europe and elsewhere. The augmentation of global food trade governance and

---

[12] All numbers and figures used in this fragment are taken from the EUROSTAT sources available at: <http://epp.eurostat.ec.europa.eu/portal/page/portal/eurostat/home> accessed 25 May 2011, as well as from a brochure of the CIIA (Confederation des Industries Agro-Alimentaires de l'UE), 'CIAA Annual Report 2009', available at <http://www.ciaa.be/asp/documents/brochures_form.asp?doc_id=75> accessed 25 May 2011 and 'The EU Food and Drink (F&D) Industry in Figures', available at <http://www.ciaa.be/documents/brochures/CIAA%20key%20figures%20bookmarkV6.pdf> accessed 25 May 2011.

[13] Figures quoted after the WTO report, 'International Trade Statistics 2007', available at: <http://www.wto.org/english/res_e/statis_e/its2007_e/its07_toc_e.htm> accessed 25 May 2011.

[14] MA Echols, *Food Safety and the WTO* ... (n 2) 41.

[15] Ibid 42.

regulation can be traced back to the Uruguay Round of the GATT, which concluded in 1994. As the declaration launching the negotiations[16] recognised that one of its objectives was the minimisation of the adverse effects that sanitary and phyto-sanitary regulations and barriers can have on trade in agriculture, the negotiations produced a new Agreement on the Application of Sanitary and Phyto-sanitary Measures (the SPS Agreement), which laid down rules for measures targeting selected risks to animal, plant and human life and health. At the same time, the code of standards was revised, resulting in the WTO Technical Barriers to Trade Agreement (the TBT Agreement). The package was completed by the new Agreement on Trade-Related Aspects of Intellectual Property Rights (the TRIPS Agreement), which included rules for the protection of geographical indications of origin of certain agricultural and food products.[17] These new trade measures were strengthened by the accompanying establishment of a new dispute-settlement mechanism, which was designed to ensure that the new rules were effective.

The GATT/WTO core regulatory framework is surrounded by a constellation of multilateral agreements, which include provisions applying to agricultural food production and trade.[18] Even more importantly, however, the system also relies on various technical agreements, as well as on international organisations that develop technical standards to facilitate the implementation of these agreements. Among those institutions, three bodies functioning under the auspices of the SPS Agreement require special mention, as they have a particular relevance for the food sector. They are (1) the World Organization for Animal Health, previously L'Office International des Epizooties (OIE), which is in charge of measures relating to animal and human health, (2) the International Plant Protection Convention (IPPC), which is in charge of plant health measures, and (3) the Codex Alimentarius Commission (CAC), in charge of food-safety standards. The standards of these three rule-developing organisations were given special recognition, creating a presumption of compliance with the provisions of the Agreement.

This has been a very short and simplified description, and it has not taken into account many multilateral, regional and bilateral trade agreements that involve agricultural and food trade measures. Nevertheless, the rules and standards set out in the agreements mentioned, which are upheld and negotiated

[16] The Punta del Este Ministerial Declaration of 1986.

[17] For a good summary, see T Josling, D Roberts, D Orden, *Food Regulation and Trade: Toward a Safe and Open Global System* (Institute for International Economics, Washington DC 2004) 35–63.

[18] For example, the Convention on International Trade in Endangered Species of Wild Fauna and Flora (CITES) and the Convention on Biological Diversity (CBD).

through these institutions, constitute the multinational governance framework for the production, distribution and consumption of food worldwide.[19]

1.1.3. *Safe Food*

Traditionally, people determined food safety through their personal experience and the experience of their communities. They knew where their food came from, how it was produced and how it should be prepared, in order to minimize potential harmful consequences. There was, therefore, little demand for safety regulations.[20] As trade developed and the distance from the farm to the table grew, the need for intervention arose and patterns of safety regulation started to develop, making up for the loss of personal and social control. Even these days, however, the food safety convictions debated internationally still reflect traditional approaches to production methods and the different opinions that societies have about them.[21] What constitutes an acceptable level of safety for one society, nation, group or individual is sometimes far from acceptable for another. Looking for a common denominator in international safety regulation is a difficult exercise. On the one hand, this is due to the immense delicacy—even intimacy—of this socially and culturally determined issue. On the other hand, however, it is also due to the enormous pressure of the economic forces behind food trade, which affect regulation and influence rulemaking. Hence, debate is not only about the question of 'what is safe?', but also the questions of 'how safe is safe enough?' and 'who is privileged to decide what is safe?' Establishing an acceptable level of food safety is the result of negotiations between 'food and culture' and 'food and trade', or, again, between what is socially and culturally acceptable and what is demanded by the market. Hence, finally, all comes down to the question: how much are we willing—or should we be willing—to pay for the safety of our daily bread?

1.2. *Europe*

1.2.1. *Europe as Unity—Or Diversity?*

The 1950s integration of Europe, heavily wounded by the terrible experiences of the Second World War and afraid of history's tendency to repeat itself, demanded a strong foundation. Although the integration project concentrated

---

[19] Compare T Josling et al., (n 17) 39–61.

[20] MA Echols, *Food Safety and the WTO* … (n 2) 30.

[21] Let me just give two examples of transnational trade conflicts, where convictions about safety of production methods reflect different traditions and attitudes towards food production: namely, the WTO disputes between the Old and the New World over the use of hormones in beef, and over the acceptance of genetically modified organisms; these will be further discussed later in this volume.

on economics and market-building, it needed something more to back up that agenda. The ideological foundations of European integration go back to the end of the seventeenth century.[22] Their new application in the post-war context, however, was concentrated on ideas of reconciliation and reconsolidation, as well as on the creation of a conflict-preventing spirit of togetherness and cooperation.

The concepts of reconciliation and integration have an inbuilt assumption of variety as a point of departure. In that context, integration implies that this variety, although it is undoubtedly there, can be managed to an extent that allows smooth coexistence and fruitful cooperation. It allows for a certain degree of diversification, but it sets out clear and unified rules with regard to matters of fundamental importance. However, 'even in a Europe in which the historical record seems to have made large segments of the political public relatively immune to the temptations of an untamed nationalism, to be "united in diversity" requires much more than a combination of goodwill and skilful constitutional engineering, if the motto is not to be taken only as a simple rhetoric formula'.[23]

With varying degrees of awareness of this aspect of the problem, the EU has embarked on a project of unifying in diversity. At the initial stage of integration, cutting the integrating market off from the realm of the social and cultural, which was left to the member states, made the whole exercise somewhat easier. Speaking of diversity in abstracto without really dealing with all its problems, has allowed Europe to keep its slogan on demonstration signs while keeping it off its bill. The Treaty of Maastricht, together with the progress of the enlargement process and ideas of cohesion, moved diversity a little closer to appearing on the political agenda, not only because Maastricht made a promise of much more than just market integration, but also because differences between welfare Sweden and impoverished post-communist Greece were difficult to overlook if 'unity' was supposed to be taken seriously.

With each and every enlargement of the EU, diversity increased and intensified, with the last two—in 2004 and 2007—being a case in point. Accepting a group of central and eastern European countries and two Balkan states, all marked by the heavy legacy of their communist past and their accompanying deep economic, social and cultural baggage, probably changed the architecture and the landscape of the EU more than anything before.

Diversity is a category often applied when comparing economic situations, modes of organizing societies, and traditions in different European states. Nevertheless, the most frequent reference is to cultural diversity, with particular regard to language, customs, ethnicity and religion. Although it might be well known in

---

[22] D Urwin, *The Community of Europe: A History of European Integration* (2nd edn Longman, London 1995).

[23] PA Kraus, 'Legitimacy, Democracy and Diversity in the European Union' (2006) 8 *International Journal of Multicultural Societies*, 203, 205.

a general sense, contemporary regulatory discourse does not seem to take fully into account that 'diversity' does not come in separate packages: biodiversity, for example—as it has evolved throughout the millennia—does not only rely upon 'natural' processes. In fact, there are several more aspects of diversity: social diversity, economic diversity, cultural diversity and political diversity. Although these often work in different spheres and directions, they are interlinked in such a way that an external influence on any one of them (whether it is regulatory or 'merely' economic) will invariably have an impact on the others. How do we reconcile regulation of all those different types of diversities? Which of them can we really manage by regulation? The current trends of European integration and trade regulation, as well as the power structure it has installed, do not always appear to acknowledge these linkages. This, perhaps paradoxically, can lead to contradictory effects in the form of economic inefficiency.

The EU has, since its early days, developed a range of legal and administrative mechanisms to deal with diversity, which are both structural and rather *ad hoc*. Among them we can distinguish techniques that deal with diversity by eradicating it, and other methods that, on the contrary, aim at preserving it, when diversity is considered an asset rather than a liability. One regulatory technique, which will be given special attention in this volume, is a mechanism of mutual recognition. It will be analysed in detail in the following chapter. For the remainder, I will simply list and briefly describe some of the most interesting examples.

Probably the most advanced regulatory strategy for dealing with diversity is a mechanism of 'closer cooperation', which was introduced in the Treaty of Amsterdam. It allows some states to progress with their integration processes despite not all members being ready to follow. The Treaty of Nice renamed and repackaged this as 'enhanced cooperation', but the idea remained the same.[24] The initial aims of the mechanism were to circumvent blockages caused by the unanimity voting in the Council, and thus acquire the capacity to create new sub-groupings, such as the Eurozone and the Schengen Area. Under the provisions of Article 20 TEU (ex Article 43),[25] a group of member states which intend to establish enhanced cooperation between themselves may do so with the use of institutions, procedures and mechanisms of the Treaties, as long as a set of conditions is met. The proposed cooperation must, among other things, be aimed at furthering the objectives of the EU, must respect the *acquis*, must remain within the Treaty limits of EU activity and must not fall within its exclusive competences. Furthermore, it should not undermine the internal

---

[24] For more on enhanced cooperation and the changes prescribed in the Lisbon Treaty in EPC, see Egmont and CEPS Joint Study, 'The Treaty of Lisbon: Implementing the Institutional Innovations', November 2007, 99–119.

[25] New numbering as introduced by the Treaty of Lisbon will be used in the present text. Old numbers will be provided in brackets for clarity and reference.

market or economic and social cohesion, must not constitute a trade barrier, discrimination or distortion of competition, must involve a minimum of eight states, must respect the rights of those states which do not participate, and must remain open to all other member states. Enhanced cooperation should only be used as a last resort, where the Council has established that the objectives cannot reasonably be achieved otherwise by the entire EU. Although the Nice conditions made the actual use of the method more feasible and operational, its use remains rather limited. Strictly speaking, it has been used more as a threat than as an opportunity.[26] There were a number of attempts to initiate closer cooperation but none was adopted. On the other hand, there have been existing forms of flexibility implemented, although not within the exact enhanced cooperation scheme: one is the Schengen Agreement and the measures building upon it, in which the United-Kingdom, Ireland and/or Denmark do not participate. All in all, however, the idea of managing flexibility by closer cooperation has, so far, remained limited in its efficiency and its impact on both the EU as well as on European diversity in general.

On the other side of the regulatory spectrum, with the development of structural, regional and cohesion policy, a set of tools has been created that aims at managing diversity by diminishing it. Here, legal measures and financial instruments are meant to lead to adjustment rather than acceptance. Financial assistance should give 'slower' states or less developed and unprivileged regions an opportunity to catch up, and should gradually reduce the discrepancies between them.

Cohesion policy received the protection of the Treaties with the adoption of the Single European Act in 1986. Articles 174–178 of the Treaty on the Functioning of the European Union (TFEU)[27] (ex Articles 158–162 TEC) lay down that the Union should promote harmonious development overall, and strengthen economic and social cohesion by reducing development disparities between the regions. This concept is based on the assumption that redistribution between richer and poorer regions in Europe is necessary in order to balance the effects of the progress of economic integration. European regional policy is designed to further economic and social cohesion and to reduce the gap between the development levels of the various regions. Regional policy helps to finance

[26] See, for example, S Kurbas, J De Clerck-Sachsse, JI Torreblanca, G Ricard-Nihoul, 'From Threat to Opportunity: Making Flexible Integration Work', (2004) EPIN Working Paper, No. 15/2006; F Dehousse, W Coussens, G Grevi, 'Integrating Europe. Multiple Speeds—One Direction?' (2004) EPC Working Paper No. 9/2004; E Philippart and M Sie Dhian Ho, 'From Uniformity to Flexibility. The Management of Diversity and its Impact on the EU System of Governance', in G de Burca and J Scott (eds), *Constitutional Change in the EU From Uniformity to Flexibility* (Hart Publishing, Oxford 2000) 319–325.

[27] As renamed by the Treaty of Lisbon. The abbreviation TFEU will be used throughout the text.

concrete projects for regions, towns and their inhabitants. The whole regional policy is in line with the priorities set by the EU in its Lisbon strategy: growth and jobs. The policy is meant to contribute to three major objectives: convergence, regional competitiveness and employment, as well as to European territorial cooperation. Putting it shortly, and simplifying it a little, the objective of convergence has as its rationale the promotion of growth-enhancing factors leading to conversion of the least-developed states and regions; the regional competitiveness and employment objective aims to strengthen competitiveness and attractiveness, as well as employment; while the European territorial cooperation objective intends to strengthen cross-border cooperation through joint local and regional initiatives. In the period 2007–2013, cohesion policy will benefit from 35.7% of the total EU budget, which amounts to approximately €347.41 billion. Out of this sum, 81.54% will be devoted to convergence, 15.95% will be spent on regional competitiveness and employment, and 2.52% is planned for European territorial cooperation.[28] This new wave of cohesion programs will be administered, implemented and evaluated according to a new legal basis consisting of five regulations adopted by the Council and the European Parliament in July 2006.[29]

Probably the main problem with the cohesion policy is uncertainty about its performance, as well as its far-fetched perspective, which requires a long waiting period before noticeable results arrive, combined with immediate and quite considerable spending by contributors. At the same time, structural policy presupposes the existence of a certain level of solidarity between the contributing and the benefitting states, which may at times also be questionable. Its effectiveness in solving integration problems will, thus, depend on 'the urgency of achieving results, the availability of resources and the readiness of member states to converge and Europeanise'.[30] In my view, another important aspect of the efficiency of the cohesion policy in coping with diversity is that it can only deal with selected types of diversity—those of a strong economic nature. Moreover, it is probable that other types of diversity, including those

[28] Facts and figures taken from the Inforegio website <http://ec.europa.eu/regional_policy/index_en.htm> accessed 27 May 2011.

[29] Council Regulation (EC) 1083/2006 of 11 July 2006 laying down general provisions on the European Regional Development Fund, the European Social Fund and the Cohesion Fund and repealing Regulation 1260/1999 [2006] OJ L 210/25; Regulation (EC) 1080/2006 of the European Parliament and of the Council of 5 July 2006 on the European Regional Development Fund and repealing Regulation 1783/1999 [2006] OJ L 210/1; Regulation (EC) 1081/2006 of the European Parliament and of the Council of 5 July 2006 on the European Social Fund and repealing Regulation 1784/1999/EC [2006] OJ L 210/12; Council Regulation (EC) 1084/2006 of 11 July 2006 establishing a Cohesion Fund and repealing Regulation 1164/94 [2006] OJ L 210/79; Regulation (EC) 1082/2006 of the European Parliament and of the Council of 5 July 2006 on a European grouping of territorial cooperation (EGTC) [2006] OJ L 210/19.

[30] E Philippart, M Sie Dhian Ho, 'From Uniformity to Flexibility ...' (n 26) 316–317.

which are considered worth retaining, will suffer as a side effect of cohesion programs.

The final diversity-handling device I will mention here is the possibility for the member states to make reservations with regard to the *acquis*. Although it sounds like an assault against the core idea of the common market, it is possible for the member states to introduce temporary or permanent derogations from harmonised market provisions. The catalogue of options is, however, rather limited. One important example is the possibility to notify derogations towards harmonised measures on the basis of Article 114(4–10) TFEU (ex Article 95(4–10) TEC). Article 114(4) allows a member state, after the introduction of a harmonised measure, to maintain national provisions on the grounds of major needs referred to in Article 36 (ex Article 30 TEC), or relating to protection of the environment or the working environment. Article 114(5), on the other hand, establishes the possibility for a member state, after adoption of a harmonised measure, to introduce national provisions based on new scientific evidence relating to the protection of the environment or the working environment on the grounds of a problem specific to that state that arises after the adoption of the harmonised measure. Further on in the Article, detailed provisions for notification and justification, as well as review by the Commission, are prescribed. While Article 114(4) can be read mainly as a provision complementary to that of Article 36 in cases where a harmonisation measure has already been adopted, Article 114(5) is an interesting novelty introduced in Amsterdam, which allows member states to take a national legislative measure against the harmonising *acquis*. As long as the requirement of new scientific evidence is clear and its application has a history and practice in international trade regulation, the second condition for using Article 114(5) can be treated as a particular EU-diversity-type of clause, as it requires the existence of a problem specific to the member state that applies it. This reference to a specific national problem clearly implies the awareness and acknowledgement by the European regulator (at least in theory) that some particularities exist in EU member states which may be serious enough to justify exceptions from the common provisions that harmonise internal market conditions. Naturally, it remains questionable how much of this specificity the Commission will be ready to accept, and how stringently the conditions will be reviewed, and it can be expected that practical application of this exception will meet with stringent scrutiny and may turn out to have little practical impact. Nevertheless, the regulatory rationale of Article 114(5), and the theoretical existence of the possibility it delivers, seem to admit the existence of a problem as well as of the need for regulatory mechanisms to manage it. Thus, there is no question that European nations are diverse. The question is how much of this 'diversity' can be accepted for Europe's 'unity' to remain functional.

1.2.2. *Europe as a Market*

> Markets are a social institution, and their continued existence is predicated on the perception that their processes and outcomes are legitimate. As Karl Polanyi (1944) pointed out more than 50 years ago, the international market is the only market that is not regulated by an overarching political authority. Consequently, transactions undertaken in the international marketplace carry the least inherent legitimacy. This in itself is an ongoing source of tension between globalization and society. The problem becomes much worse when segments of society are perceived as having broken their links with their local communities and become footloose. Institutions that lose their legitimacy can no longer function, and markets are no different.[31]

Since its very beginning, the European integration project was thought of as a common-market-building exercise. Market rationale was, therefore, the most important driving force behind the integration activities undertaken on the basis of the founding Treaty. The 'single market', or the 'internal market', in simplified terms, stands for the freedom of movement of goods, people, services and capital. On a more practical level, the single market means the possibility for EU citizens to live, work, provide and receive services, and do business throughout the EU, and to benefit from the ability to buy and sell a variety of competitively priced goods without national barriers or obstacles. One of the four freedoms that receives particular attention in my work, and which will therefore receive more emphasis here, is the freedom of movement of goods.

Let me now provide some figures on European market and trade in goods, which will be followed by a short simplified description of the regulation of the common market for goods. According to the information provided by the European Commission, the GDP of the EU's single market is steadily growing. With the enlargements to 27 countries, has become the largest GDP of any economy in the world, approximately US$1.2 trillion in 2005. During the ten years following the completion of the single market program in 1993, the internal market increased the EU's GDP by €223 billion, which accounts for 2.2% of EU GDP. Employment grew by 1.4%, providing an extra 2.75 million jobs. Internally, trade between EU countries accounts for two-thirds of all EU trade, and it is vital to the economies of all member states. In 2005 it accounted for over half of all trade in each of the 25 countries, and in some cases amounted to around 80%. Internationally, the EU is the main exporter in the world and the second-largest importer. Its

[31] D Rodrik, *Has Globalization Gone Too Far?* (Institute for International Economics, Washington DC 1997) 71.

trade balance for 2006 was, however, negative, amounting to a deficit of €193 billion.[32]

The category of 'goods' includes a wide variety of products covering conventional goods, as well as energy, industrial products, agricultural products, foodstuffs and others. According to the Treaty, goods are able to circulate freely around the EU, without being subjected to any duties, fees or discriminatory taxation, or to any additional or excessive approval procedures, tests or other restrictions. Member states are only allowed to restrict the free movement of goods in exceptional cases, which particularly involve the protection of public health, the environment or consumers, and in introducing such restrictions they have to observe the principle of proportionality. As products that are potentially subject to such issues are usually the most problematic, the EU has adopted legislation to harmonise production conditions for the single market, in order to manage the risks and to ensure legal certainty. In the areas where conditions were not harmonised, the provisions of Articles 34–36 TFEU (ex Articles 28–30 TEC) apply, which forbid discriminatory barriers to trade, except in special circumstances. In those areas, trade relies on the mutual recognition principle, under which products legally manufactured or marketed in one member state can, in principle, move freely throughout the EU. Around 75% of intra-Community trade is in goods, half of which is covered by harmonised regulations, while the other half exists in the non-harmonised sector, which either is regulated by national technical regulations or is not specifically regulated at all. The Commission monitors the application of the principles of free movement of goods and intervenes in the case of a breach. The Commission's supervision, along with the jurisdiction of the European Court of Justice, constitutes important factors in the development of regulations of trade in goods on the internal market.

Another important introductory point to be made is that European trade regulation does not happen in a vacuum. The EU, along with all its member states, is a regular participant in the global market, and is thus subject to international trade regulations. This has far-reaching consequences for the content and the implementation of trade legislation and adds a new twist to the relationship between the EU administration and its member states. Conducting relationships with the global partners, and executing decisions taken by and for the EU and its member states, creates a new dynamic in their relations. The consequences of participating in international trade agreements include obligations to observe internationally set standards, to acknowledge decisions of global

[32] Facts and figures gathered from the European Commission, Single market for goods—Information pack 2008, available at: <http://ec.europa.eu/enterprise/regulation/goods/index_en.htm> accessed 25 May 2011, as well as on the websites of DG Enterprise and DG Internal Market.

dispute settlement bodies, and to ensure their enforcement both by the EU and by all EU member states. As recent developments show, this is not always an easy task. Hence, the EU, with its specific governance structure and its factual diversity, is not always the easiest partner to deal with.

The external influence aspect is, of course, an important issue, but it must be strongly emphasized that it is primarily internal tensions and visions that have shaped the common market since the beginning of the integration project. It should be remembered that this project is constantly developing and will probably never be regarded as finished and settled once and for all. As time goes by, the leading direction of development, as well as the focus of discussions and disagreements, evolves. Although the single market program itself was to be completed in 1992, the building of the internal market is still continuing. The initial focus on purely economic aspects of the process, however, has transformed considerably, and although the economic concern is still central, the internal market is now conceptualised much more broadly. The new concept tries to include non-economic, or not purely economic, aspects—such as environmental policy, social welfare or consumer protection—in the thinking of the internal market, and to promote them as relevant and influential factors of market-building and integration policy. This conscious discursive exercise, clearly reflected in various policy papers and declaratory documents,[33] was intended to countervail criticism against the EU, which claimed that market integration had negative consequences for welfare and social protection in member states. It managed, however, to produce rather opposite effects when translated to the adoption of concrete legislative measures. Some non-economic aspects of the market have been promoted more successfully and have become reality, while others, in particular the more sensitive ones, have largely remained merely an object of the declaratory papers.

One particular problem in this context, which raises specific concerns in my work, is the inherent lack of cohesion between the integration of the common market and its impact on the economically weaker states, which in the long run translates into a lack of coherence between the economic and the social spheres of market regulation. As Dehousse points out, this problem, which is at the heart of my work, is particularly difficult, as 'it cannot be allayed by derogatory measures alone', and 'if the Community does not find a way to offer some compensation to those countries which feel they have more to lose, market

[33] See for example, the Communication from the Commission, Action Plan for the Single Market, SEC (97) 1 final, Presidency Conclusions, Lisbon European Council, 23 and 24 March 2000, 100/1/00, <http://www.consilium.europa.eu/ueDocs/cms_Data/docs/pressData/en/ec/00100-r1.en0.htm> accessed 25 May 2011; Presidency Conclusions, Nice European Council Meeting, 7, 8 and 9 December 2000, SN 400/1/00, <http://www.consilium.europa.eu/ueDocs/cms_Data/docs/pressData/en/ec/00400-r1.%20ann.en0.htm> accessed 25 May 2011.

integration could be severely hampered'.[34] Hence, finding the right balance between the building of the single market and the need to cope with structural imbalances, as well as to find appropriate legal and regulatory forms and the redistributive means to do it, will be of paramount importance in the near future of the Union. Will Europe prove to be a polity or just an economy? Will it try to align social concerns with its market-development policies, or will the 'indissoluble link between economic performance and social progress' promised by the Nice Council[35] remain a void declaration?

1.2.3. *Europe as a Polity*

This introductory section concludes with a reference to yet another unfinished paradigm switch in the European integration story—the switch from the common-market rationale to the 'Social Europe' project. Many of the concerns raised in this book are reflected in that debate, which illustrates the complicated relationship between the economic and social spheres of integration.

1.2.3.1. *From 'Common Market' to 'Social Europe'*

The distinction between the two separate (and quite antithetic) public-policy paradigms of the common market and Social Europe was often characterised by reference to the competing visions of the neoliberals and of the supporters of some form of regulated capitalism.[36] Put simply, the issue is the difference in emphasis each system puts on various policy problems, such as individual and collective responsibility for general welfare, the production and distribution of wealth, and the means of directing market energy for the advancement of self- and societal interest.[37] In Europe, the shift from the one policy orientation to the other was visible more in the alteration of this emphasis on policy objectives than in the rise of new ones. The priorities of post-war integration attempts focused on questions of economic recovery and social protection by the prevention of possible future military conflicts. At this initial stage, economic integration was itself both the means and the end.[38] Social concerns were left to be dealt with at the national level, and this attitude encountered very little criticism. In the second half of the 1980s, however, when the European project

---

[34] R Dehousse, 'Completing the Internal Market: Institutional Constraints and Challenges', in R Bieber, R Dehousse, J Pinder, J Weiler (eds.), *1992: One European Market?* (Nomos, Baden-Baden 1988) 336.

[35] Presidency Conclusions, Nice European Council Meeting (n 33) par 13.

[36] L Hooghe and G Marks, 'The Making of a Polity: The Struggle over European Integration' [1997] 1 No. 4 *European Integration Online Papers* <http://eiop.or.at/eiop/texte/1997-004a.htm> accessed 25 May 2011, 3.

[37] M Carson, *From Common Market to Social Europe? Paradigm Shift and Institutional Change in European Policy on Food, Asbestos and Chemicals, and Gender Equality* (Acta Universitatis Stockholmiensis, Stockholm Studies in Sociology, 2004) 12.

[38] Ibid 12.

was supposed to be given a new direction and new dynamics by the introduction of the single-market program, the question of Community social policy entered the agenda. Partly due to the social consequences of the deregulation process, which was an important component of the internal-market program, and partly due to the unsatisfactory results of regulation at the national level, stronger demands for active intervention by the EU emerged, in an effort to establish the necessary balance between market and social concerns.[39]

Similar concerns have been raised by European academics, and their theoretical concepts, which I will describe in the following section, might now serve as a source of support for the political agenda-builders, providing various visions of how to undertake the reunification of the economic and social spheres of European integration.

1.2.3.2. *The 'European Social Model' Debated*

The concept of the 'European Social Model', announced by Jacques Delors in the beginning of the 1990s, does not correspond to the reality of European integration even now, but it is definitely a relevant normative vision to be considered. Describing the phenomenon of 'Social Europe', F. W. Scharpf[40] refers to it as to a 'road not taken'. During the negotiations of the Treaty of Rome in 1956, the French Prime Minister, Guy Mollet, tried to condition the integration of industrial markets by the harmonisation of social regulations and fiscal burdens, but there was no political will for such a commitment among the other states' representatives. This led to the 'political decoupling' of economic integration and social-protection matters, with the latter remaining under national discretion. Such a distinction remained crucial and consequential until the Treaty of Maastricht. The situation allowed economic policy rhetoric to dominate the European agenda and led to the asymmetrical development of two aspects, economic and social, of the integration process. The establishment by the Court of Justice of the doctrine of direct effect and supremacy strengthened this decoupling by confirming the precedence of the supranationally constitutionalised economic law and the subordination of social issues. At the same time, the progress of economic integration was gradually reducing the possibility for member states to sustain their own individual policy goals and realise their national social policies. The 'negative integration' strategy, which aimed at abolishing not only tariff barriers and quantitative restrictions on imports, but also all other cross-border and internal measures of equivalent effect, deprived member states of their power to protect national producers against foreign competitors, as they could no longer provide national entrepreneurs with a

[39] Ibid 13–14.

[40] FW Scharpf, 'The European Social Model: Coping with the Challenges of Diversity' (2002) 40 *Journal of Common Market Studies* 645–670.

supportive regulatory environment or tax regime. On the one hand, this gave producers the right to shop around for the most attractive location for their business, but, on the other, it increased regulatory competition among member states and had far-reaching consequences for their national regulatory systems. The creation of the single market constrained member states in their provision of subsidy policies, and consequently led to the privatisation and deregulation of wide range of infrastructure services and facilities, which had previously been either directly or indirectly provided by the state. Those changes, although beneficial for economic efficiency and, in the longer run, for European consumers, seriously affected the ability of member states to sustain their employment levels and their social policy instruments. Furthermore, the establishment of the monetary union ended national control of interest and exchange rates, which until then had remained the last resort of their macroeconomic policy for employment-increasing strategies. Consequently, as a result of the kind of 'negative integration' that was experienced in connection with the common-market-building program, member states lost their freedom to pursue policies that aimed at attaining non-economic goals.[41] The only exception from this general trend was the Common Agricultural Policy, in which the integration process went much further; both economic integration and the social concerns caused by it were dealt with at the European level.[42]

It came as no surprise that some states and various interest groups tried to advocate the 'European Social Model' and the re-establishment of 'constitutional parallelism of economic ('market-making') and social-protection ('market-correcting') interests and policy purposes that had existed at the national level before the take-off of economic integration'.[43] Less obvious, however, was the question of how the proud notion of the European Social Model was to be understood? Most generally, it was understood to refer to the European experience of simultaneously promoting sustainable economic growth and social cohesion.[44] It was first officially defined in 1994 by the European Commission in its 'White Paper on Social Policy', in which it is referred to as a set of common values: the commitment to democracy, personal freedom, social dialogue, equal opportunities for all, adequate social security, and solidarity with the weaker individuals in society.[45]

---

41 FW Scharpf, 'Democratic Legitimacy under Conditions of Regulatory Competition: Why Europe Differs from the United States' in K Nicolaidis and R Howse (eds), *The Federal Vision. Legitimacy and Levels of Governance in the United States and the European Union* (Oxford University Press, New York 2001) 359–362.

42 FW Scharpf, 'The European Social Model ...' (n 40) 646–648.

43 Ibid 649.

44 M Jepsen, AS Pascual, 'The European Social Model: An Exercise in Deconstruction' (2005) 15 *Journal of European Social Policy* 231–245.

45 Commission (EC), White Paper: European Social Policy—A Way Forward for the Union COM (94) 333 final, 27 July 1994.

Such equality of social and economic integration patterns could be achieved either through European social programs or through the harmonisation of national social-protection systems. However, it has to be borne in mind—and European policy-makers were well aware of it—that common solutions in the social-protection field can be very difficult to achieve, as differences among national systems and institutional structures, and long-rooted traditions of social policy-making, will be there in competition.[46] That is why many academics look for solutions to the dilemma by directing attention to new forms of governance that allow for a high degree of differentiation in synchronized activities. Hopes for the successful integration of 'Social Europe' in the area of employment and social welfare were directed towards the New Governance project, and especially to the mechanism of the Open Method of Co-ordination (OMC).[47] The OMC was seen by many as a sort of middle way between the national and the European spheres, providing an acceptable platform for gradual reintegration of the decoupled realms—the economic and the social aspects of market integration. This solution, however, does not seem to provide a sufficient answer to my major questions, mostly due to the internal constraints of the method itself—specifically, its high degree of voluntarism, which can be a virtue in some cases but can also be extremely problematic when redistributive responsibilities emerge. As far as the use of the OMC is concerned, the main emphasis of the literature advocating this form of governance is on the phenomenon of mutual information exchange and mutual learning, as well as on the voluntarism of joining the initiatives to an extent that is feasible for individual participants, giving them the possibility to retain traditional differences in approach or apparatus.[48] The OMC is much

[46] On variety of social models in Europe, see A Sapir, 'Globalization and the Reform of European Social Models', (2006) 44 *Journal of Common Market Studies* 369–390.

[47] FW Scharpf, 'The European Social Model ...' (n 40); C Offe, 'The European Model of "Social" Capitalism. Can it Survive European Integration?' (2003) 11 *Journal of Political Philosophy* 437–469; J Zeitlin, 'Social Europe and Experimentalist Governance: Towards a New Constitutional Compromise?' in G de Burca (ed), *EU Law and the Welfare State. In search of Solidarity* (Oxford University Press, Oxford 2005) 213–241; DM Trubek and LG Trubek, 'Hard and Soft Law in the Construction of Social Europe: the Role of the Open Method of Co-ordination' (2005) 11 *European Law Journal* 343–364; S Fredman, 'Transformation or Dilution: Fundamental Rights in the EU Social Space', (2006) 12 *European Law Journal* 41–60; E Szyszczak, 'Social Policy in the Post-Nice Era' in A Arnull and D Wincott (eds), *Accountability and Legitimacy in the European Union* (Oxford University Press, Oxford 2002) 330–344.

[48] For a more extensive analysis of the OMC, see MJ Rodrigues, 'The Open Method of Coordination as a New Governance Tool' in M Telo (ed), *L'Evoluzione della Governance Europea*, (2001) special issue of 'Europa/Europe', Rome, No. 2–3, 2001, 96–107; C de la Porte, 'Is the Open Method of Coordination Appropriate for Organising Activities at European level in Sensitive Policy Areas?', (2002) 8 *European Law Journal* 38; D Hodson and I Maher, 'The Open Method as a New Mode of Governance: The Case of Soft Economic Policy Coordination', (2001) 39 *Journal of Common Market Studies* 719; D Chalmers and M Lodge, *The Open Method of Co-ordination and the European Welfare State* (2003) CARR Discussion Papers 11.

weaker, however, when it comes to features that seem to be necessary for effective redistribution, such as a long term, a hard law based, stable involvement, as well as a genuine commitment in both policy and financial terms. For such project to be successful, hardly any degree of voluntarism or differentiation would be acceptable. As Scharpf observes when referring to the limits of the OMC:

> … the selection of policy goals confirms the expectation that, under the constitutional priority of European law, policies promoted through the open method of co-ordination must avoid all challenges to *acquis* of the internal market and monetary union. Even when responding to OMC guidelines, therefore, Member States continue to operate under exactly the same legal and economic constraints of economic integration which limit their policy choices when they are acting individually.[49]

Such a presentation of the method's limitation leads me to question its usefulness for the introduction of any redistributive mechanisms, as it is difficult to imagine introducing such an instrument without shaking the core of the internal market *acquis*, as well as the national economic constraints. Even Scharpf himself, although he advocates the new governance option, notices that a hard law is necessary in order to achieve a balance between the economic and the social. He notes, at the same time, that 'at the present stage of economic integration, the aspirations of "Social Europe" can no longer be realized through purely national solutions'.[50] There is a clear need for a European social law, in order to provide some sort of legal counterweight to the European regulations on the internal market and competition, and to marshal individual member states to adjust to the common regime.[51]

One more observation seems relevant in the context of the proposal of realisation of the Social Europe project through new methods of governance, although it is connected more with the method than the substance of the issue. When deliberating democratisation through new participatory forms of governance, it often seems that ideas are formulated with regard to the 'old Europe', and without much account being taken of the practical differences in new member states. Obstacles—such as the difficulty of access to modern electronic communication and, even more so, language barriers—cannot be disregarded when one treats new governance as a democracy-enhancing mechanism. It must be noted that the vast majority of websites inviting public participation, consultation and other forms of direct inclusion are not available in 'new' European languages. In some new member states, the *acquis*

[49] FW Scharpf, 'The European Social Model …' (n 40) 655.
[50] Ibid 662.
[51] This is probably the reason Scharpf accepts a kind of mixed solution, with a minimum of harmonization directives and differentiation in implementation.

has not yet been entirely translated. Taking these observations as a point of departure, it seems difficult to talk about equal democratic rights of public participation and new forms of legitimisation. It can be assumed that, for citizens of new member states, new governance initiatives will not be able to provide an appropriate answer to the European democracy deficit for years to come. This makes me think that it would be more in the interest of new members to focus on strengthening their old representative procedures, as their delegates in the European institutions are the only thing their citizens can rely on. From their point of view, further democratisation and judicialisation of the good old 'Community method' might actually have more practical relevance than the development of new forms of direct inclusion, which they have very little ability to engage in anyway. A final remark that can be made here is that even though the prospect of European enlargement was one of the incentives behind the new governance prospect at the time of its launching,[52] it seems that its democratic relevance was actually weakened by the accession of new states. It will probably be decades before new methods of governance will have much practical significance in the new members' societies and have much impact on their feelings of democratic inclusiveness.

1.2.3.3. *Left to the Judges and the Markets?*

This concluding section opens with questions. The first is borrowed from Leibfried:[53] is social policy in Europe really only left to the judges and the markets? And if it is, is it possible and desirable to change it?

The current situation, after the failure of the reform of the European Constitution, generates a rather pessimistic impression. Working towards the Constitutional Treaty was seen by many as a starting point for much-needed positive action in the social sphere. Many have claimed that the project of the European Constitution can only succeed if it introduces a 'European social model'.[54] Not having lived up to this expectation, and having failed to come into force at all, the European Constitution project could be interpreted as a defeat of aspirations for Social Europe, and a great discouragement to its promoters.

In the absence of the greatly expected amendment, and with an unclear idea of the future direction of events, it seems important to ask how the shape of 'the

[52] Commission (EC), European Governance. A White Paper COM (2001) 428 final, 25 July 2001.

[53] S Leibfried, 'Social Policy. Left to the Judges and the Markets?' in H Wallace, W Wallace and MA Pollack (eds), *Policy-Making in the European Union* (Fifth Edition Oxford University Press, Oxford 2005) 243.

[54] G Bronzini, 'The European Social Model and the Constitutional Treaty of the European Union' in Ch Joerges, B Stråth and P Wagner (eds), *The Economy as a Polity: The Political Constitution of Contemporary Capitalism*, (UCL Press, London 2005) 183–201; J Weiler, 'A Constitution for Europe? Some Hard Choices' in G Bermann and K Pistor (eds) *Law and Governance in an Enlarged European Union* (Hart Publishing, Oxford and Portland, Oregon 2004) 39–59.

social' is negotiated and determined in Europe nowadays. Here, if one looks at the actual developments currently affecting the social sphere in Europe, one goes back to Leibfried's concern quoted above, as it turns out exactly to be the developments of the enlarged market and the judges of the ECJ responding to them.

ECJ judgments in the *Laval*[55] and *Viking*[56] cases can serve as a particular illustration of this turn of events. In both those cases, side-effects of the exercising of economic freedom on a post-enlargement scale led to an unprecedented intrusion of the ECJ into national social regulation, which is crucial for the maintenance of the democratic legitimacy of member states.[57] This intrusion, however, remains a purely deconstructive exercise, as 'the Court can only destroy existing national solutions, but it cannot itself create "Social Europe"'.[58] Thus, instead of building a social common, the current situation has resulted in destructive intervention in sensitive national systems, without offering a supranational alternative. Moreover, intervention by the ECJ, due to the specificity of its normative framework, offers no place for an adequate consideration of the national concerns at stake, which leads to a situation where 'the flimsiest impediment to the exercise of the European liberties may override even extremely salient national policy legacies and institutions'.[59] This tendency, if consistently applied, which seems to be the practice of the ECJ, may have detrimental consequences for 'the social' both in Europe and in its member states, and may in the long run call legitimacy at both levels into question.

To conclude, 'the social' in Europe, as uncomfortable and problematic as it may be, keeps popping up in various areas of European intervention, posing questions that will, in the end, require constructive answers. Having moved away from the idea of the economic purity of the integration process, the EU now has to face the consequences of the promise, which it has used as a justification for furthering its expansion. Having made that initial step in Maastricht, the EU provoked a chain reaction, and, with the enlargement, the opportunities for tensions have increased significantly. Thus, Europe must find and define a new balance for the economic and the social. Left to the judges and the market, 'Social Europe' may become a burden too heavy for the EU to carry; and at some stage the socioeconomic consequences of market integration will have to be positively confronted. If the ambition is to re-embed the European market, it will take more than the jurisdiction of the ECJ, declaratory documents, or the OMC.

---

55 C-341/05 *Laval un Partneri Ltd v Svenska Byggnadsarbetareförbundet* [2007] ECR I-11767.

56 C-438/05 *International Transport Workers' Federation and Finnish Seamen's Union v Viking Line ABP and OÜ Viking Line Eesti* [2007] ECR I-10779.

57 See the elaboration in: FW Scharpf, 'Legitimacy in the Multilevel European Polity' (2009) 1 *European Political Science Review* 173–204.

58 Ibid 198.

59 Ibid.

2. Research Question

In this book I present a critical perspective on the current direction of the development of the European food safety regulation. Through a combined analysis of three regulatory mechanisms—mutual recognition, scientific risk regulation and standardisation—and an evolutionary study of the development of food legislation in the EU, I intend to show how the current framework is becoming inadequate, with regard to the new challenges facing the system, among which globalisation and the last two enlargements are the most spectacular and consequential. I argue that in an enlarged and more diversified Europe, the socioeconomic implications of market regulation should no longer be disregarded. If not properly acknowledged and reflected in the regulatory scheme, they can lead to the gradual 'disembedding' of the regulatory framework. Moreover, the current trend towards unification can have serious and irreversible consequences for European diversity, which according to the founding fathers, deserves as much respects as they greatly strived for unity. Thus, I suggest that the existing regulatory approach should be reconsidered, to admit a wider set of relevant socioeconomic implications that might protect diversity more strongly. One possible way of achieving this objective would be by rebalancing the system so that it becomes more open and responsive. A shifting of the use of existing regulatory mechanisms would allow diversification of regulatory intervention, so that it could better respond better to the valid objectives of a given field.

Karl Polanyi's The Great Transformation,[60] although published in 1944 and in a completely different context, still seems strikingly relevant for the current European situation. Polanyi argues that markets will always be socially embedded. In other words, they are not independent of social relations, politics and religion, but are in fact subordinate to them.[61] Inspired by Polanyi's observation, I intend to show that just as the market *itself* cannot be considered separately from its social context, the regulation of the market must also be analysed in connection with its social context, if this regulation is to be efficient and purposive.[62] Disconnecting market regulation from its social basis might be seen as leading to a kind of 'disembedding' of the market. This disembedding, although fictitious and impossible according to Polanyi, may nevertheless have some very concrete and tangible consequences for society. The market itself loses much of its social legitimacy when the two are conceptually separated or

[60] K Polanyi, *The Great Transformation. The Political and Economic Origins of our Time* (Beacon Press, Boston 1957).

[61] See Fred Block's introduction to the 2001 edition, and literature quoted by him in the context of 'embeddedness', xxvi.

[62] Ibid especially 45–70.

disembedded, as the recent financial crisis has shown. Also, and more importantly for the present purpose, market regulation that does not take social concerns and contexts into consideration will ultimately prove detrimental to the market it is supposed to promote and support. In this dissertation, therefore, I follow up on Polanyi's observation by suggesting that various elements of the European regulatory system of today do in fact contribute to a kind of disembedding of the market from society, and that this is contrary to the declared goals of the Social Europe model. After having identified and analysed this paradox, which is at the core of the present European regulatory system, I also make some suggestions about methods that could be considered in Europe for an eventual 'reembedding' of the market and society.

There are few areas under the contemporary EU regulatory framework that more clearly brings out this dual tension—between diversity and unity, on the one hand, and between embedded and disembedded markets, on the other—than the field of food regulation, where universal concerns meet local preferences, and where the issue's economic and social aspects interact in the regulatory process. This is why food regulation has been chosen as the main object of analysis in this thesis.

My theoretical framework for analysis follows three regulatory principles and legal methodologies, all of which have been used in EU product regulation and reflect the dominance of the different sets of objectives that influence the legal structure of the European market. All three regulatory structures—namely, mutual recognition, scientific risk regulation and standardisation—have constituted important phases and developmental steps for the EU legal system in the field of food. Their importance, however, has changed over time as one structure gained preference over the others. My hypothesis is that this evolution was neither accidental nor driven solely by legal considerations. Rather, it was an outcome of the particular settings of different factors that affect legal developments. In the case of EU food safety regulation, those factors can be organised in three basic categories: internal factors (such as the common market project or the BSE crisis), external factors (such as the influence of the WTO and Europe's participation in the global market), and external/internal factors (such as enlargement, which has gradually moved from being external to internal). It is not my intention to study the WTO as an alternative regulator of transnational trade or the related issues of risk and safety, but only to review briefly the influence that participation in the WTO has on EU law, European legislative choices and regulatory policies. The problems to which I give special attention are the balance of factors that influence regulatory developments, and the question of whether Europe, by blindly following one set of objectives, is not missing some vital values, which not only seem important objectively but are also at the roots of the European project. I do not suggest a precise value balance to be adopted, but rather identify those values which seem to be neglected, and discuss regulatory mechanisms that could help to determine the weight to be given to each one, as well as to increase the transparency of their social and economic implications. I ask whether we are departing too far from the primary ideals of the common market and the logic of *Cassis*. Are we giving up on quality and diversity, in the search for profitability and safety?

Those concerns will be the starting point for my analysis of the development of the European legal and regulatory architecture in the field of food, from the foundation of the common market until today. I look not only at the development of laws and institutions, but also at the objectives behind certain changes and their influence on the law-development process. I trace food regulation back to its agricultural roots. I then analyse the separation of food from its agricultural legal scheme, and its individualisation as a product during the common market building phase. Subsequently, I discuss the regulatory shift towards consumer protection and safety, and I examine the reform of food law and institutional architecture propelled by the BSE crisis. Finally, I look at the external and internal pressures directing current developments in food legislation, namely those stemming from enlargement, from participation in international trade and from developments in other areas of EU law.

My hypothesis in this analysis is that European regulation seems, under current circumstances, to be heading more and more towards homogeneity. My focus, therefore, is the possibility of rebalancing the legislative objectives and instruments towards a 'cognitive opening of law' as advocated by Luhmann,[63] and towards wider and more organised inclusion of non-legal factors in regulatory development. Thus, my research questions concern the ability of the current European legal structure of risk regulation to accommodate a wide range of socioeconomic concerns within its regulatory procedures and legal instruments. A number of important non-legal factors—such as safety, environment or consumer protection—already play an important role in the European legislative framework. Some of them, however, although present in the regulatory process, are not generally given due recognition. Firstly, then, I ask whether a rebalancing is legally possible under existing conditions. I attempt to discern whether legal means exist within the current legal paradigm that would enable the system to respond to a wider selection of socioeconomic concerns, or whether, on the contrary, certain reforms are necessary in order to achieve that goal. Secondly, assuming the latter is the case, I ask how we might rebalance the system and create space for such considerations—for example, through a modification of legal instruments or the modes of their application.

---

[63] N Luhmann, *Law as a Social System* (Oxford University Press, Oxford 2004) 106 (translated by KA Ziegert, original title: *Das Recht der Gesellschaft*, Suhrkamp Verlag, Frankfurt am Main 1993).

My methodology follows an evolutionary approach and studies the law in context. I trace the development of the European regulatory structure in the food sector, not only with regard to its regulatory objectives and legal instruments, but also to its application of those instruments, their effectiveness in tackling regulatory goals, and the way in which they have affected regulatory choices. I attempt to show that the development of a legal framework for food in Europe has not been accidental but rather the outcome of various sets of regulatory objectives. Hence, shifts of balance among those objectives have been reflected in legal and regulatory changes. In other words, legal systems tend to prioritise certain sets of objectives at certain periods of time, and the prevalence of certain settings leads to the development of different forms of legal instruments. In my analysis, I do not concentrate on particular examples of food legislation or on specific sectors of regulation. Instead, I focus upon the development of the food safety legal system as a whole, examining the waves of reform of the regulatory instruments. By looking at the evolution of the legal framework over a certain period of time and under certain sets of influences, I intend to show that the timing of regulatory developments has not always simply been coincidental. By studying legal sources and policy documents, I show the causal connection between those developments and the influencing factors and feedback mechanisms.

This evolutionary analysis makes it possible to study the ways in which socioeconomic concerns do matter. Although they may not always be clearly visible, these concerns are present and relevant. In terms of regulatory adjustments, they are often accepted by default. It is important to emphasise again that socioeconomic factors are not new to the European legal system, but that they are often simply not explicit.

Being aware of their existence and their influence on both regulatory process and legislative developments, the major concern of mine, as a lawyer, is to find the available legal means of integrating them with procedures in an organised and transparent way, which would allow a balancing of these factors and of their influence on legislation. I do not attempt to analyse why certain socioeconomic factors are prioritised over others, and whether such prioritisation is appropriate; this is a task for social scientists. Rather, I argue that, as lawyers, we have to be aware of the socioeconomic concerns that affect legislative and regulatory developments, and that we need to consider legal methods for integrating a wide variety of them in a transparent and balanced way.

What are these factors? A cursory overview shows not only the width of the nexus between socioeconomic concerns and legal regulation but also its political influences: on economic situations within the regulated sector; on the overall condition of a given economy; on the environment and biodiversity; on labour markets and social welfare; on societal acceptance and satisfaction, especially in situations where the regulatory instruments conflict with social expectations as well as with cultural or religious preferences; on regional diversity and specificity; on local patterns of production and consumption; and on trade levels.

This list is not exhaustive; it merely illustrates the variety of regulatory implications that must be considered, and the complexity of regulatory embeddedness. This regulatory embeddedness is manifested whenever one seeks to analyse legal provisions, their application and their significance, without looking at the environment it is intended to regulate and which it affects. The law, in other words, makes little sense without its context. This is the main reason why context plays such an important role in this thesis. Rather detailed descriptions of seemingly insignificant factors—such as geographical conditions or technical aspects of certain production patterns—are necessary for the analysis of this regulatory embeddedness, this nexus between socioeconomic factors and legal regulation. For example, when one speaks of cow-rearing, in one sense one is also speaking of the law. This is because the rearing is conducted according to the law, and European herds are affected by European legislation. In the end, then, it is the European legislation that changes the landscape of European agriculture and food production. Following Polanyi, I argue that it is absolutely essential to establish and understand the law's context in order to evaluate the legislative measures in question and to assess the regulatory impact of their provisions. The analysis of food regulation, therefore, would become a purely theoretical exercise without an acute sensitivity to the role played by economic, political and social interests in the development of legislation.

3. Outline

In Chapter II, I suggest and develop an analytical framework for examining and understanding socioeconomic implications of the legal approaches to the unified regulation of risk. Contemporary research has largely been concerned with analysing the institutional problems of risk regulation, focusing upon the role of science in the policy-making process, the separation of risk assessment and risk management, and the related problems of legitimacy and accountability. Until now, however, very little attention has been given to the economic and social impact of the risk regulatory decisions and distributive concerns involved in the process. In this volume I propose a way of looking at risk regulation that goes beyond traditional patterns and explores hitherto overlooked dimensions. I suggest three independent but interrelated paths of approaching the socioeconomic dilemmas of integrated risk regulation, which not only illustrate the advantages and disadvantages of the current approach, but also emphasise the relevance of the problem, and the relevance of its potentially critical challenges, to European solidarity and social policy, if not given due regard and recognition. The three approaches are built upon the three current regulatory strategies and legal methodologies used by the European Union in the field of product risk regulation. I explore their logic, their functioning and the regulatory objectives which they follow. I also examine their relative openness to inclusion of socioeconomic considerations in regulatory legal procedures.

The first path follows a particular contemporary market-regulating pattern, which is used as a tool for balancing the aim of creating a common market with the challenges of its diversity, namely the mutual recognition principle. I will look at the origins of mutual recognition, the legal basis of its functioning, and the legal as well as practical consequences of its application.

The second path goes back to the foundations of risk analysis and explores the implications of current trends in international risk regulation, which considers science as the universal judge and the basis for the regulation of global trade. I analyse the legal context of the application of this regulatory method and examine the scope of its effectiveness for transnational market regulation, as well as its appropriateness as a basis for legal reasoning and regulatory decisions. I intend to show the advantages and disadvantages of this approach, and to explore alternative methods of legislation in the field, which might encourage more embeddedness of systematic regulatory responses to risk by going beyond the technocratic recourse to science and into the natural social contexts of regulation.

The third path analyses standardisation as a risk regulatory tool and explores its effects on the market. I investigate the legal foundations and specific features of the formation and application of international safety standards, as well as the ways in which they affect different players in the arena of global trade. I also examine their influence on market participants, not only with respect to their individual trade potential but also with respect to their effect on whole separate economic systems. I confront the ideals of private governance with some practical aspects of its application. In this context, I argue that questions need to be asked and choices made about responsibility for the implications of standardisation, and I suggest how the making of those choices might be assisted, in order to allow the inclusion of neglected socioeconomic factors such as solidarity and distribution.

I review these three approaches with the aim of creating a theoretical framework to analyse the evolution of the EU's food safety legislation, which will make it possible to identify the objectives of legislative and regulatory choices and to address the dilemma of the socioeconomic implications of unified risk regulation in Europe. Each of the three approaches will, therefore, be referred to later, in my empirical analysis, in the context of their specific application in the field of European food safety legislation, because, as previously stated, they are not simply theoretical models but also vital regulatory tools, which are widely used in contemporary risk governance in Europe and worldwide.

Chapter III is devoted to the empirical analysis of the development of EU food policy and legislation. I provide a chronological overview of the evolution of food regulation and the paradigm shifts it has gone through. Balancing between agricultural and market regulation, between free trade and consumer-safety concerns, food regulation has always been happening 'amidst' other concerns, in a nexus between competing interests. It has always dealt with confronting and sometimes hardly compatible rationales, which have put food regulation in a unique position within the legal system and have shaped its structure and character. I begin this part of my thesis by tracing food policy back to its roots in agriculture, specifically to the Common Agricultural Policy (CAP). I then study the decoupling of food from agriculture and the move towards regulating food as a commodity, like any other type of product. Thereafter, I address the next paradigm shift: namely, the turn towards the consumer. I review the development of the comitology governance in the food sector, and its greatest failure—the BSE crisis. I then analyse the reforms undertaken in the aftermath of that crisis and plot their general direction. I also develop hypotheses about why the post-BSE 'from farm to fork' reform might be interpreted as being rather selective, emphasising scientifically assessable consumer-safety concerns without raising related questions—about other socioeconomic consequences of regulation, and about distribution. Finally, I conclude this part of the thesis by considering the traces of 'social' factors in other fields of European product regulation. I review the existing legal provisions and current legal developments in EU product law, which might suggest that the significance of wider socioeconomic concerns is slowly gaining recognition in other areas of EU law. This overview aims to prepare the ground for an analysis of EU food safety regulation and possible ways in which to reform it. It should be explained here that I do not try to engage in full-scale comparison of different types of product safety regulation; rather, I look at selected areas, such as the regulation of chemicals, in order to gain an appreciation of other possible approaches.

In Chapter IV, I consider the most significant of the many challenges facing the European market at present: namely, the two latest enlargements of the European Union. Before looking at the new internal challenges, however, I take a step back to look at Europe in a larger context, not only as the governor of an integrated market, but also as a player in a global trade arena. I therefore look at the tensions connected with the EU's double role in front of the WTO, as well as the pressures and conflicts arising from it. I do not attempt to explore the logic and architecture of the WTO as an alternative system of regulating transnational trade and the related issues of risk and safety. Instead, I explore the influence of participation in the WTO on European legislative choices, as well as the pressures resulting from the EU's role as a representative of regulatory choices by its member states, and the responsibility connected with this function. I then analyse how demands previously external to the EU have become internalised by means of the enlargement process. The last two enlargements have exercised significant pressure, inside as well as outside the EU, which has had a great influence on the shaping of the current debate and policy proposals. They have also radically increased the significance of the socioeconomic aspects of unified regulation of risk, and have made distributive questions even more complex and crucial. In particular, I analyse in detail the accession of Poland to the EU. I do so not only because Poland has been and remains an economy and a society which is highly dependent upon agriculture both for internal consumption and for export, but also because of the structure of its market, which in some ways can be seen as typical of the recently acceded states, and in other ways unique.

I discuss the approximation process in the agri-food sector, the enforcement of European measures before and after accession, as well as responses of Polish producers to the requirements of the new regulatory framework. I analyse two particular regulatory measures in detail, which allow member states to retain national divergences from the *acquis*; these are, firstly, instruments for geographical protection of origin, and secondly, treaty possibilities to legislate against harmonised standards with regard to a particular national situation. I study Poland's attempts to make use of these measures, and analyse their effectiveness—both in particular cases as well as in general—in the context of the protection of diversity in the common European food market.

Finally, Chapter V describes a summary of my research, concentrating on the vital questions that have appeared in its course. In this concluding chapter I look again at the three regulatory structures reviewed in Chapter II: namely, mutual recognition, scientific risk regulation and standardisation. In what ways are the current legislative mechanisms and decision-making procedures in the field of food safety tackling contemporary regulatory problems? How has the legal and regulatory architecture evolved, and in which direction is it now headed? Can we imagine rebalancing European legal instruments in a way that would guarantee achievement of the desired levels of safety, but which would at the same time be more responsive to a wide range of various non-legal concerns and capable of accommodating the growing challenges of diversity? In order to tackle those questions, I return to my initial remarks on the specificity of food, on the one hand, and the specificity of Europe and its legal system, on the other. Through this particular lens, I consider the possibility—as well as the desirability—of such a rebalancing of European regulatory structures, to encourage greater openness to non-legal factors and greater sensitivity to the founding values of 'unity in diversity'.

CHAPTER TWO

THREE REGULATORY APPROACHES TO THE DILEMMA OF THE EUROPEANISATION OF RISK REGULATION

1. Introduction: Theoretical Framework for Analysis of Risk Regulation—Regulatory Tools as Analytical Concepts

Contemporary research on the legal aspects of transnational risk regulation has largely been concerned with analysing the institutional problems of risk regulation. It has focused on the role of science in the policy-making process; precaution; the separation of risk assessment and risk management; and the related problems of legitimacy and accountability. Accordingly, most of the regulatory reform effort initiated by the European Commission has concentrated on those aspects while trying to establish a reliable risk assessment system, which could provide a solid basis for regulatory decisions and gain accountability and the trust of the European public. Little attention, however, has been given to the economic and social impact of risk regulatory decisions and the distributive concerns involved in the regulation process. It is not simply that no significant reforms have been carried out in the field of food safety in that respect, but the problem is not even mentioned in the general debate or considered for eventual deliberation. Although the difficulty and gravity of the questions is undeniable, it is clear that general developments in the architecture of Europe and in world trade have enhanced their importance. The economic and social dimensions of European risk regulation might—if not duly recognised, analysed and integrated with the political and legal processes—lead to critical challenges to European solidarity and social policy. Thus, it is interesting to consider methods of approaching the questions and giving them due recognition.

The following paragraphs outline a proposal for a theoretical framework of analysis of risk regulation, which diverges from the current debate, and which points to those aspects of risk regulation that so far have not been given appropriate attention: namely, the socioeconomic implications. As academic research and literature in this area is rather scarce, I borrow ideas and constructions from other legal disciplines, such as environment law, and from other sectors of the common market, such as the free movement of persons and services. I also build analogies with the regulation of international trade under the regime of the WTO, and I refer to research pertaining to similar problems at a different level of governance. Those analogies could, of course, be applicable only to a certain extent, but they nevertheless remain instructive.

My proposal for a theoretical framework of analysis of risk regulation incorporates three approaches to the issue, which are based on three established regulatory structures and legal instruments currently used in European food law and risk regulation. These are mutual recognition, scientific risk regulation, and standardisation; all have become vital tools of European product regulation, although the importance and impact of each has changed over time, in accordance with the changing sets of objectives driving the development of the common market. Those legal tools will primarily be studied from a theoretical point of view, but their application, as well as their consequences, will also be examined. Finally, I trace the objectives behind the changing patterns of regulation and study their individual openness towards inclusion of non-legal concerns in the European legislative and decision-making process in the fields of food safety and, more generally, risk regulation. By these means I build an analytical background for my empirical study of the development of food safety legislation in Europe, which follows in Chapter III. It is my aim that this theoretical framework will help me understand the evolutionary mechanisms transforming the European legal system of food safety, and explain the changes of legal instruments with regard to varying factors that have influenced European legislation and policy-making in general.

The first approach follows the market-regulating pattern of mutual recognition as a means of balancing the aims of the common market with the challenges of its diversity. The second approach explores the established model of risk regulation, which is based on scientific risk analysis. The third analyses standardisation as a risk regulatory tool and explores its effects on the market. It should be emphasised again that all three approaches to market regulation are commonly used in Europe. There is nothing new, foreign or extraordinary about them. It seems, however, that some of their vital aspects escape analysis, and consequently their implications on the market and the societies have remained overlooked.

Finally, it has to be emphasised that separation of the three mechanisms and differentiation made here is of a purely analytical and functional character. I am well aware the interconnections between all three tools, as well as the inevitability of their coexistence and co-application in many regards. I found it useful and helpful, however, to analyse them separately, as it highlights the varying degree of emphasis on regulatory objectives pursued by each of them. It also allows to trace more clearly the changing modes of their application in the European food regulation, which will be done in the following—empirical chapter. Therefore, admitting that the classification may be accused of being artificial and somewhat detached, I find it useful for the overall analysis, as it allows emphasis to be put not only on how the three instruments function, but also on what they represent in terms of regulatory objectives and values.

2. Mutual Recognition in Food Safety Regulation—Preserving Diversity or Comparative Advantage?

> National homelands are rooted in the collective conscience. It is impossible to eradicate them. And yet, why should we? That diversity is at the same time our strength, our richness and our main problem. That is why even the most radical federalists have never thought of doing so and, when nationalists accuse them of trying to so, either they do not know what they are saying or they are demagogic.[1]

2.1. *Unity in Diversity? The Ideological Foundations of the Common Market*

The building of a common market for goods, persons, services and capital through the liberalisation of internal trade has always been at the core of the European integration process. The idea, however, was to unite respective national markets of the member states, without necessarily unifying them. Although formally acknowledged as an official motto only in the Constitutional Treaty signed on 29 October 2004, 'Unity in Diversity' has been at the core of European integration since its very beginning, illustrating its quest to reconcile the interests of 'the common' and 'the individual'. Retaining the 'regional flavour' of goods circulating freely in the European trading area was supposed to be the distinctive feature of the EC, as well as a kind of self-regulating stabilisation mechanism.[2] This was because a 'regional flavour' is not only the result of differences in geographical and climate circumstances, of various national cultures and traditions, but also a consequence of varying market conditions, which influence production processes and the economic state of affairs. The 'regional flavour' reflects the origin of the product, not only with regard to its taste and colour but also to the specific economic and social situation of the place where it was manufactured. 'Regional flavours' bring great diversification to the common market. But such diversification may go further than the eye can see, as it not only creates a richness of different goods available in the same market, but also brings about a situation where products which are seemingly the same are in fact different. The single-market mechanisms were initially

---

[1] H Brugmans, *Europe—Rêve—Aventure—Réalité*, (Elsevier, Brussels 1987) quoted after A Mattera, 'The Principle of Mutual Recognition and Respect for National, Regional and Local Identities and Traditions' in F Kostoris Padoa Schioppa (ed), *The Principle of Mutual Recognition in the European Integration Process* (Palgrave Macmillan, Hampshire 2005) 22.

[2] On EU approaches to diversity, see: E Philippart and M Sie Dhian Ho, 'From Uniformity to Flexibility. The Management of Diversity and its Impact on the EU System of Governance' in G de Burca and J Scott (eds) *Constitutional Change in the EU From Uniformity to Flexibility* (Hart Publishing, Oxford 2000) 299–336.

intended to protect both these visible and invisible differences. And mutual recognition, which will be the object of deliberations in the following paragraphs, is one of those mechanisms.

2.2. *Mutual Recognition*

2.2.1. *Foundations of the Principle of Mutual Recognition*

2.2.1.1. *Recognition of the Right to Diversity*

Globalisation and increased access to information have made us accustomed to living in a diversified society, and value of heterogeneity is now emphasised more than ever. We are, however, also more aware of the various troubles and tensions that this heterogeneity conveys. It will probably take the effort of great minds and generations of activism to battle problems of xenophobia, fundamentalism, religious wars and social exclusions. Lawyers can help in that process by finding regulatory tools that will help to accommodate heterogeneity in contemporary reality. Mutual recognition is a specific such tool that facilitates the management of heterogeneity in a product market. It allows a local product to become a global one by separating rights and obligations from geographical location. It does this by making the law enforced in one state enforceable in another.[3]

The principle of mutual recognition, also referred to as *functional parallelism* or *functional equivalence*, is an intermediate device that helps reconcile tensions stemming from regulatory diversity in an integrated market.[4] Mutual recognition can be defined as a contractual norm between governments that commissions a transfer of regulatory power from the country in which the transaction takes place to the country in which the good was produced.[5] *Recognition*, in this context, means acceptance of the equivalence of a foreign regulatory system, while *mutuality* implies reciprocity of such acceptance. In practical terms, goods complying with the technical requirements of one state can be marketed freely in another, provided that the standards applicable in the first state are functionally parallel to the standards of the recipient state. Briefly speaking, there are two general conditions under which the member state of destination is required to accept products manufactured in accordance

[3] For an excellent historical perspective on mutual recognition, see F Kostoris Padoa Schioppa, 'The Cultural Foundation of Mutual Recognition' in F Kostoris Padoa Schioppa (ed), *The Principle of Mutual Recognition* … (n 1) 224–231.

[4] JHH Weiler, 'Mutual Recognition, Functional Equivalence and Harmonization in the Evolution of the European Common Market and the WTO' in F. Kostoris Padoa Schioppa (ed), *The Principle of Mutual Recognition* … ibid 25–26.

[5] See elaborate definition in K Nikolaidis, 'Globalization with Human Faces: Managed Mutual Recognition and the Free Movement of Professionals' in F Kostoris Padoa Schioppa (ed), *The Principle of Mutual Recognition* … ibid 132–133.

with the rules of the member state of origin. The first condition is that the product guarantees an appropriate level of protection and satisfies a legitimate objective equivalent to that of the member state of destination. The second condition requires that the level of protection is reasonable and satisfactory, with regard to the results of scientific research in the field.[6] There is, however, so much more to the meaning and impact of mutual recognition that it is necessary to go beyond this brief presentation of the general rules, and give it deeper consideration.

Due to its inherent characteristics, mutual recognition is the key to global administrative law. Breaking away from the conceptualisation of global governance in terms of national *contra* international, mutual recognition suggests a third, 'middle' way of transnational economic regulation.[7]

A similar significance enjoyed by the mutual recognition principle in Europe is assigned, in the international (WTO) forum, to the distinction between product regulation and the production process.[8] The product/process distinction, however, and the elaboration of its implications for international trade regulation, have not yet attracted as much academic attention as they deserve. Due to the fact that, initially, the rationale for market integration in Europe provided little ground for process regulation, such a distinction and analytical differentiation has not been applied within the EU context, although it has occurred in some European academic writing.[9] One of the reasons, perhaps, is that the analytical distinction between product-oriented and process-oriented regulation has turned out to be far less clear if the outcomes of European policies are considered.[10] Although this is a slightly different type of regulatory

---

[6] Compare A Mattera, (n 1) 17–18.

[7] Compare K Nikolaidis and G Shaffer, 'Transnational Mutual Recognition Regimes: Governance without Global Government' (2005) 62 *Law and Contemporary Problem* 266–267.

[8] R Howse and D Regan, 'The Product/Process Distinction—An Illusory Basis for Disciplining "Unilateralism" in Trade Policy' (2000) 11 *European Journal of International Law* 249–289; RE Houdec, 'The Product-Process Doctrine in GATT/WTO Jurisprudence' in M Bronckers and R Quick (eds), *New Directions in International Economic Law: Essays in Honour of John H. Jackson* (Kluwer Law International, the Hague 2000) 187; 'Processes and Production Methods (PPMs): Conceptual Framework and Considerations on the Use of PPM-based Trade Measures' (1997) 137 OCDE/GD <http://www.oecd.org> accessed 25 May 2011; SE Gaines, 'Processes and Production Methods: How to Produce Sound Policy for Environmental PPM-Based Trade Measures? (2002) 27 *Columbia Journal of Environmental Law*; JH Jackson, 'Comments on Shrimp/Turtle and the Product/Process Distinction', (2000) 11 *European Journal of International Law*; DA Kysar, 'Preferences for Processes: the Process/Product Distinction and the Regulation of Consumer Choice' (2004) Cornell Law School Legal Studies Research Paper Series, Paper 8.

[9] See, for example, Ch Joerges, 'Integrating Scientific Expertise into Regulatory Decision-Making. Scientific Expertise in Social Regulation and European Court of Justice: Legal Framework for Denationalized Governance Structures' (1996) EUI Working Paper RSC No.96/10; F Scharpf, *Governing in Europe: Effective and Democratic?* (Oxford University Press, Oxford 1999) 91–98.

[10] Ch Joerges, 'Integrating Scientific Expertise …' ibid 5–6. The author gives the following example to support his thesis: 'As the Community's safety at work legislation in particular demonstrates, the "technical" and "political" interdependence of product and process regulation can be such that they are dealt with as one sole package.'

philosophy, it is worth mentioning here as it shows important similarities to mutual recognition in Europe, reflecting analogous theoretical ideas of the rationale of market organisation.

2.2.1.2. *Mutual Recognition and Mutual Trust*

The immense variety of products circulating on the market, which results in a multiplicity of choice for consumers and increases market competitiveness, is a reflection of the expansion and liberalisation of world trade, as well as of the galloping development of new technologies of production and distribution. Such variety, however, can also be a source of great uncertainty and tension, on the part of national administrations and economic operators as well as of consumers. This anxiety is often reflected in the creation of barriers against foreign products and the limitation of market access, which can result in an overall reduction of the benefits of the integrated market.

In contrast, the underlying idea behind the principle of mutual recognition, which seems so natural that it is rarely even mentioned but which is decisive for its effectiveness, is one of mutual trust and mutual confidence. The adoption of and adherence to such a principle signifies the emergence of cohesion and integration between states which, despite differences in national traditions, standards and legislations, have common cultural and scientific roots in a way which gives them a sense of belonging to a particular community. If this community is also linked by a common body of law, jurisdiction and a common institutional setting, a situation arises in which, to paraphrase Mattera, the 'guarantees offered' are such that they justify the need for each state to exhibit confidence in its neighbours and their legislation, administrative structures and control procedures.[11]

If perceived from the perspective of a conflict of laws, as advocated by Ch. Joerges, the mutual recognition rule can be conceived as finding a 'meta norm' that conflicting systems are both ready to accept and according to which regulatory differences between the states can be balanced.[12]

---

[11] Compare A. Mattera (n 1) 11. The idea of mutual confidence can be traced in the jurisprudence of the ECJ; see, for example, its judgement in the case *Bouchara*, the ECJ explicitly said, referring to the principle of acceptance of outcomes of tests, controls and analyses performed by other members states, that 'that rule is a particular application of a more general principle of mutual trust between the authorities of Member States'. See Case 25/88 *Esther Renée Bouchara, née Wurmser, and Norlaine SA* [1989] ECR 1105, par. 18.

[12] Ch Joerges, 'Free Trade with Hazardous Products? The Emergence of Transnational Governance with Eroding State Government' (2005) 10 *European Foreign Affairs Review* 556; Ch Joerges, 'The Idea of Three-Dimensional Conflicts Law as Constitutional Form' [2010] RECON Online Working Paper 2010/5; Ch Joerges and F Rodl, 'Reconceptualising the constitution of Europe's post-national constellation—by dint of conflict of laws' in I Lianos and O Odudu (eds), *Regulating Trade in Services in the EU and the WTO: Trust, Distrust and Economic Integration* (Cambridge University Press, Cambridge 2010).

2.2.1.3. *Application of the Principle of Mutual Recognition*

Even though one might easily be misled by the name and an *a priori* reading of the definition of the concept, it has to be pointed out clearly here that the application of mutual recognition principle is far from automatic. It stems from both the jurisprudence of the ECJ and the Commission's communications that the principle does not *per se* imply automatism. In fact, it is very rare these days that the principle of mutual recognition is applied in its pure form, which would imply an unrestricted right of market access, with a reallocation of control authority from the host to the home state. Instead, mutual recognition systems vary in their regulatory scope and frequently allow the host state to retain some vestigial powers. These may include mutual monitoring and cooperation between regulatory authorities, as well as the introduction of ex-ante or ex-post conditions.[13] The questions therefore arise: to what extent is it really 'recognition', and to what extent is this recognition 'managed'? According to many commentators, mutual recognition, irrespective of its incarnation, is always conditional and involves a political process of the assessment of compatibility between two national regulations.[14] Moreover, the content and the necessary extent of such compatibility are themselves often contested. K. Nikolaidis, to give a good illustration, analyses the phenomenon of managed mutual recognition in the field of services, with regard to the recognition of professional qualifications.[15] Such a regime does not require prior harmonisation, which would be highly problematic in the field of qualifications, but instead builds a system of recognition, in which various degrees and conditions of access are envisaged that aim to compensate for differences between national regulations. Within those systems, mutual recognition, which comprises mutual monitoring and information exchange, should also be viewed as a dynamic process of mutual learning and progressive liberalisation.[16]

Such *managed mutual recognition* systems vary in intensity along the lines of four criteria: prior conditions, automaticity, scope of access and ex-post guarantees, all of which can imply different types of compensatory requirements.[17] Nikolaidis argues correctly that such managed mutual recognition regimes, both in the European and in the transatlantic contexts, are probably the most desirable mode of governing regulated professions, as they encourage regulatory convergence and increase professional mobility.[18] One can imagine, analogically, that in the field of products, where the imported foreign 'element'

---

[13] K Nicolaidis, 'Mutual Recognition of Regulatory Regimes: Some Lessons and Prospects' (1997) Jean Monnet Working Paper, No. 7/97, par. 6.

[14] K Nikolaidis and G Shaffer, 'Transnational Mutual Recognition Regimes ...' (n 7) 264.

[15] K Nikolaidis, 'Globalization with Human Faces ...' (n 5) 129–189.

[16] Ibid 131.

[17] Ibid 142–144 and 152–157.

[18] Ibid 142.

is less invasive, managed mutual recognition would also provide a beneficial solution to transnational trade dilemmas. It can even be assumed that the degree of management that is necessary in the area of services, due to the characteristics of the field and the opening of the national market to the continuous and long-lasting influence of an external factor, could be much reduced with regard to products.

2.2.1.4. *Implications of Mutual Recognition*

2.2.1.4.1. *Economy of Mutual Recognition.* Market integration, especially if combined with an effort to overcome and minimise regulatory failures, should ideally lead to an increase in welfare. It has been pointed out, however, that this may not always be the case when dealing with highly divergent preferences in health and safety or environmental protection.[19] The insensitive application of market integration rules and harmonisation via qualified majority voting legislation may lead to the disregarding of stricter local preferences in some states. Consequently, in those states common regulation will have a welfare-decreasing effect. Hence, the EU regulatory system provides measures that enable it to respond to such regulatory problems. Pelkmans points, firstly, to an escape clause of Article 114(4), which allows member states to retain stricter regulation without mutual recognition. Nevertheless, since this clause has hardly ever been invoked, it has proved to have little practical implication. The second option is to retain stricter regulation over mutual recognition, which in effect pushes the burden of regulatory costs on the suppliers in a given state.[20] It is, therefore, worth examining whether, in such situations, the alternative offered by mutual recognition is able to provide regulatory benefits.

For the sake of economic analysis of mutual recognition, national standards and regulation can be regarded as cost-increasing entry barriers that allow national producers to operate in a somewhat protected market. Adoption of the principle of mutual recognition will then change the competitive exposure of those producers. At the same time, it will maintain the competitive advantage of producers in those states, where the regulatory regime is less strict and production costs are lower. In this simplified but logical perspective, mutual recognition can be seen as a clearly pro-competitive regulatory regime.[21] Nevertheless, it must be borne in mind that the application of the principle of mutual recognition, especially in its 'managed' context, is not cost-free. Mutual

---

[19] See, for example J Pelkmans, 'Mutual Recognition in Goods and Services: An Economic Perspective' in F Kostoris Padoa Schioppa (ed), *The Principle of Mutual Recognition* ... (n 1) 97.

[20] Ibid.

[21] Compare J Pelkmans, ibid 97–102. In his article, the author also suggests an alternative perspective on the economic effects of mutual recognition by looking at national standards as voluntary and treating conformity assessment as quality signalling.

recognition has in fact proved to produce considerable transaction costs in information, compliance and monitoring, both for the states and the business operators. In the EU, several studies performed in the second half of the 1990s revealed a great deal of scepticism, among both producers and states, towards mutual recognition, and suggested that uncertainty costs may often outweigh the benefits of the principle in relation to harmonisation. In reality, however, such costs can be minimised or even eliminated by means of proactive politics by transnational governance bodies, which aim at establishing friendlier circumstances for the functioning of the principle within a system.[22]

Some commentators, such as J. P. Trachtman, point to the possible emergence of more far-reaching and much less 'offsetable' costs of establishing transnational mutual recognition systems; namely, the costs for less-advantaged states.[23] Mutual recognition regimes may result in reduced market access for developing countries. Even if such a regime is formally open and allows developing states to participate, they may lack the material capacity to comply with the requirements of mutual equivalence, which may hinder market access for the products of those states. Thus, mutual recognition regimes should ensure they do not put developing countries in a competitively disadvantaged position, or put excessive pressure on their economies by requiring compliance that goes beyond their resources. Trachtman, however, although very convincing in his argumentation, speaks about mutual recognition regimes that include the establishment of harmonised standards.[24] For the clarity of my approach, I need to point out that I treat such regimes as examples of standardisation rather than mutual recognition. I will, therefore, revisit Trachtman's theory later in this chapter when I discuss standardisation and its implications on transnational trade.[25]

2.2.1.4.2. *The Economic and Social Benefits of Mutual Recognition.* Among the direct and most straightforward benefits of mutual recognition, one should mention not only the reduction of the costs of compliance for international companies, but also the enhancement of regulatory competition. Regulatory

---

[22] In the EU, for example, the Commission takes a proactive approach to facilitating the operation of the mutual recognition principle. In some sectors, such as the recognition of qualifications, it takes a form of legislation that provides a framework for recognition. In others, it can take softer and less invasive means. In the area of the trading of goods, for example, guidelines are communicated by the Commission which aim at creating a mutual recognition culture in the product sector. The latest Commission interpretative communication on facilitating the access of products to the markets of other member states: the practical application of mutual recognition will be discussed later in this chapter.

[23] JP Trachtman, 'Embedding Mutual Recognition at the WTO' (2007) 14 *Journal of European Public Policy* 780–799.

[24] Ibid 794–795.

[25] See Part 4 of this chapter.

competition is a dynamic process of regulatory adjustments of national legislation which is encouraged by the impact of cross-border exchange of goods.[26] With increased international trade under the mutual recognition regime, systems with costly regulation may find themselves under pressure from their national business operators, who, when faced with import competition from less costly states, will plead for a reduction of their regulatory burden. Hence, as fears of a 'race to the bottom' or the creation of a 'regulatory gap' have not proven right in cases of regulatory competition, one can expect that it will be beneficial for the internal market.[27] The market will, one can assume, enforce a degree of regulatory convergence between states, at least with regard to the essential requirements, and will discipline states in their regulatory activities. Moreover, in some cases states may choose to retain stringent regulation in order to satisfy local quality preferences. Higher costs for producers and the economy in general, in those states where there are more stringent regulatory conditions, will be outweighed by the demand for the specific quality they represent, and this, in the long run, will protect local products from import competition. From that perspective, therefore, regulatory competition implies that the maintenance of regulatory differences gains economic justification due to consumers' diverse preferences.[28]

This brings us to the most refined and probably the greatest benefit of mutual recognition: its sensitivity and respect for diverse needs and circumstances. Mutual recognition allows economies that are more developed and financially stronger to accept higher production costs, anticipating their consumers' willingness and ability to pay for the extra quality they gain. But even more importantly, as every coin has two sides, it allows states that are less well-off to retain the regulatory status they can afford. Even more so, it allows less developed states to take advantage of their specific economic circumstances, such as their lower labour costs or cheaper commodities, and to use those extra benefits for the betterment of their economic performance; they are not pushed to invest in technologies they do not have the resources for. In the long run, it seems, such developments work towards the same kind of regulatory convergence, but the path will be smoother and the negative impact on the markets and economies of poorer states will be reduced. Such a situation is also beneficial for consumers, whose safety will be guaranteed by the market-induced essential requirements, which the poorer states will have to comply with anyway, but whose variety of choice is richer and whose specific regional preferences

[26] Just a general clarification: this phenomenon also relates to the cross-border exchange of services and persons, of course, but for the sake of clarity and because in my analysis I limit myself to products, I tend to mention only them.

[27] J Pelkmans, 'Mutual Recognition in Goods and Services ...' (n 19) 114–115.

[28] Ibid 114.

are attended to. On the other hand, this is possible without confronting consumers with the radical price increases that would otherwise result from the cost-passing by producers faced with overburdening and costly harmonised requirements.

2.2.2. *Mutual Recognition as an EU Legal Principle*

Mutual recognition, although mentioned in two articles of the EC Treaty (now TFEU),[29] has never acquired the prestigious status of a Treaty principle, and its definition cannot be found in primary legal sources. The principal of mutual recognition as it relates to the free movement of goods was established by the ECJ in 1979 in its milestone judgement in the *Cassis de Dijon*[30] case. The mutual recognition rule was taken up by the EU institutions and was further developed in case law and Commission communications,[31] eventually becoming the guiding strategy for the common market integration proclaimed in the 1985 White Paper on the Completion of the Internal Market.[32]

The core idea of the principle is the acceptance by each member state of any product that has been lawfully produced and marketed in another member state, even if it has been produced according to different technical standards or quality requirements, insofar as it meets the legitimate objective that the legislation is meant to achieve.[33] Consequently, 'where a product 'suitably and satisfactorily' fulfils the legitimate objective of a member state's own rules (public safety, protection of the consumer or the environment, etc.), the importing country cannot justify prohibiting its sale in its territory by claiming that the way it fulfils the objective is different from that imposed on domestic products'.[34] It can be acknowledged, therefore, that mutual recognition in Europe rests on the assumption that member states have equivalent regulatory objectives for the protection of health, safety, consumers and the environment. All member states are expected to care for their citizens, and their products cannot

[29] Mutual recognition is invoked in the context of freedom of establishment in Article 47 (now Article 53), in relation to recognition of diplomas, certificates and other evidence of formal qualifications, as well as in Article 293 (repealed by the Treaty of Lisbon), with reference to the recognition of companies or firms within the meaning of Article 48 (now Article 54).

[30] Case 120/78 *Rewe-Zentral AG v. Bundesmonopolverwaltung für Branntwein* [1979] ECR 649.

[31] Commission (EC), Communication from the Commission concerning the consequences of the judgment given by the Court of Justice on 20 February 1979 in case 120/78 ('Cassis de Dijon') OJ C 258, 03 November 1980, 2; Commission (EC), Communication to the Council and the European Parliament: Mutual Recognition in the Context of the Follow-up to the Action Plan for the Single Market, COM (99) 90 final, 16 June 1999.

[32] Commission (EC), Completing the Internal Market: White Paper from the Commission to the European Council, COM (85) 310 final, 14 June 1985.

[33] See judgment in Case 120/78 (n 30) par.14, compare comment in A Mattera (n 1) 8.

[34] Commission (EC), Communication from the Commission concerning the consequences of the judgment given by the Court of Justice on 20 February 1979 in case 120/78 (n 31) 3.

be presumed to be unhealthy or unsafe just because the technologies of their manufacturing or technical specifications are different. The other side of the coin, however, is that mutual recognition implies that, when adopting technical regulations likely to influence the free movement of goods, member states are bound to refrain from basing such regulations entirely on national objectives.

The mutual recognition principle in Europe has never been the sole guiding rule of the common market, but rather has always complemented and interacted with market liberalisation and legal approximation. The advantage of the principle is that in areas where the equivalence of the objectives of national legislations can be established, mutual recognition allows to avoid the costly, time-consuming and often controversial exercise of harmonisation. It therefore reduces the regulatory burden for the EU and simultaneously precludes overregulation by the member states. Consequently, the potentiality of costly regulatory failures is greatly diminished. Where mutual recognition is not available due to lack of equivalence, however, approximation becomes necessary, but it can be limited to merely regulating the essential requirements, while leaving specific technical details to standardisation.[35] This logic was followed by the EU and greatly facilitated the development of the 'New Approach', which was based on the idea of minimum harmonisation of the essential objectives by Community legislation, combined with the standardisation of technical requirements by specialised organisations.[36] Approximation, in this context, can be viewed as a 'written agreement on equivalence'.[37]

Analysis of the application of mutual recognition as a judicial and regulatory principle of the European trade in products leaves no doubt about its influence on the functioning and shape of the common market. Not only has it contributed to the removal of a large number of all sorts of technical and quite commonly protectionist trade barriers, but it was also the basis for the development of an entirely new approach to product-safety regulation. By the end of the 1990s, following the Atkins Study for the Single Market Review, almost half of all intra-Community trade in goods was subject to mutual recognition, with the other half being covered by the old and new approaches. Among the 50% covered by the mutual recognition regime, around 20% pertained to unregulated goods, while the other 30% related to nationally regulated goods.[38]

---

[35] Compare J Pelkmans, 'Mutual Recognition in Goods and Services ...' (n 19) 88–97.

[36] New Approach to Harmonization and Standardization will be analysed in more detail in chapter III of the volume.

[37] J Pelkmans, 'Mutual Recognition in Goods and Services ...' (n 19) 93.

[38] WS Atkins, 'Technical Barriers to Trade, Study for the Single Market Review' (1998) Sub-series III.1, Office for Official Publication of the EC, Kogan Page, quoted after J Pelkmans ibid, see also AR Young, 'The Single Market. A New approach to Policy' in H Wallace, W Wallace and MA Pollack (eds), *Policy-Making in the European Union* (Fifth Edition Oxford University Press, Oxford 2005) 102–103.

2.2.3. *Managed Mutual Recognition in the European Product Market*

In its 2002 Report on the Application of the Principle of Mutual Recognition in the Single Market,[39] the Commission stated explicitly that, where overriding requirements to protect public health, consumers or the environment were involved, 'mutual recognition is not automatically applicable: the host member state retains the possibility of requiring that the degree of protection afforded by a product from another member state is equivalent to that provided for in its national regulations'.[40] In its 2003 Interpretative Communication on the Practical Application of Mutual Recognition, the Commission went even more into detail, saying that 'mutual recognition … can be affected by the right of the member state of destination to verify the equivalence of the level of protection provided by the product under scrutiny, compared with the level of protection provided by its own national rules', and that when exercising this right, 'it may use the practical tools proposed by this communication to examine the equivalence of the level of protection. These tools define the conditions applicable to the exercise of this right to balance it correctly with the fundamental right of free movement of products.'[41] Such supervision by the host state, however, has to be based on objective, non-discriminatory criteria, which are known in advance and may not be used arbitrarily.

The Commission goes on, firstly, to describe the nature of the supervision by the member state of destination, and secondly, to present three stages of conformity examination of products subject to mutual recognition by that state. It is a long (four pages) and detailed list of the available means of checking conformity that relate to the state of origin and to the product itself.[42] They are, of course, not be applied unconditionally, but the conditions given are not very specific and are subject to further interpretation. They include general and rather neutral techniques, such as general data collection from the home state, the communication of technical requirements and the purpose of national legislation. However, they also include invasive means, such as sampling and additional testing of products, the requirement to provide information, documents and translation from the economic operator in question, as well as verification of equivalence of levels of protection by different national systems. When one considers that the main purpose of the principle of mutual recognition is to

---

[39] Commission (EC), Report from the Commission to the Council, the European Parliament and the Economic and Social Committee, Second Biennial Report on the Application of the Principle of Mutual Recognition in the Single Market, COM (2002) 419 final, Brussels, 23 July 2002.

[40] Ibid, part 1.1.

[41] Commission (EC), Commission interpretative communication on facilitating the access of products to the markets of other Member States: the practical application of mutual recognition [2003] OJ C 256/2, 1.

[42] Ibid 6–9.

simplify trans-border trade, and that the biggest benefit expected by business operators is the avoidance of costly and time-consuming conformity checking procedures, one wonders whether this is the same mutual recognition as that which is discussed above as a theoretical concept. The degree of 'management', which seemed appropriate and still beneficiary to service-providers in Nikolaidis' analysis of the mutual recognition of professional qualifications, when applied to products seems not to fit equally well. It definitely raises concerns that such managed mutual recognition, in the case of trade in goods, might in fact develop into a quasi-requirement of pre-market approval. One might also wonder to what extent it will tend to influence national systems, which could potentially retain their specificity with regard to their production and processing methods, and force them to adjust to a 'mutual recognition-friendly' regime.[43] In foodstuffs sector, this could definitely have far-reaching consequences and, in effect, reduce not only much regional variety but also a considerable degree of competitive advantage on the side of less-developed member states.

In the foodstuffs sector, however, an even less welcome occurrence can be observed, which has to do with the gradually decreasing significance of mutual recognition. Extensive harmonisation in this area of product regulation has marginalised the significance of mutual recognition and largely deprived the market from the benefits of its application. In the Second Biennial Report on the Application of the Principle of Mutual Recognition in the Single Market, the Commission explicitly mentions various types of food products when referring to sectors where EC harmonisation will continue to be the most suitable solution. In those sectors, according to the Commission, due to existence of considerable differences in the levels of protection afforded by national rules, the principle of mutual recognition cannot play its role properly.[44] This seems to suggest that not even a highly 'managed' form of recognition would be suitable for the food trade. Consequently, with regard to those products that

[43] Compare K Nikolaidis, 'Globalization with Human Faces ...' (n 5) 169–170, where the author argues that one of the implications of adhering to a mutual recognition system is a dynamic process of adjustment of the national system, in order to adapt to an acceptable degree of compatibility with its counterparts. The author refers to it as 'creating national environments that are mutual recognition-friendly'.

[44] The Second Biennial Report on the Application of the Principle of Mutual Recognition in the Single Market (n39) par. 6. This view is also partly supported by some economists, who claim that harmonisation of food regulation has positive effects on intra-community trade, and increases exchange of products, although this effect varies significantly with regard to different sectors. See, in particular, BH de Frahan and M Vancauteren, 'Harmonisation of Food Regulations and Trade in the Single Market: Evidence from Disaggregated Data' (2006) 33 *European Review of Agricultural Economics* 337–360. This analysis, however, is focused on the purely economic effect on trade in the single market, without addressing the effect on national economies of member states.

require the most sensitivity, and where diversity in its traditional sense and its competitiveness-increasing sense is most required, mutual recognition, which is the most 'tolerant' and least invasive method of trade regulation, and which could encompass all those extra values, is not deemed appropriate and is being eradicated.

In opposition, it is argued here that mutual recognition in its modern, managed form could be very beneficial for the common product market. Concentrating on the essential features of products, without unifying requirements for production methods, would allow market integration in food sector to proceed without hindering diversity, and without pressing uniform burdens on a non-uniformly integrating market. It would allow the poorer states to use their competitive advantage for their economic betterment, which is beneficial for the whole EU. And consumers' considerations, which are invoked against this type of diversified approach, would have been taken into account anyway, because the market, the citizens and the overall welfare-protecting function of member states would not have allowed otherwise.

3. Scientific Risk Regulation—Re-Embedding Regulation in its Social Context

3.1. *Risk in Legal Theory and Practice*

3.1.1. *Risk and Regulation—Introductory Remarks*

> While modernity's organizing principle was to conquer the human condition of scarcity, postmodern people confront the risks caused by modern society in the form of its systems and technology. In this sense, human society, rather than nature, has become the source of danger. Reflecting the new obsession with risk, questions of threat and hazard insinuate themselves into all facets of life, through the air we breathe, the water we drink, the food we eat, as well as through procreation and health and through transportation and shelter. As a result, people are continually confronted with new kinds of risk choices and risk tradeoffs, becoming burdened with unprecedented responsibilities for differentiating between what is safe and hazardous in the face of inherent uncertainty. Unlike the general acceptance of risk that characterized modernity, aversion to risk becomes a postmodern preoccupation.[45]

Risk is undeniably one of the most prominent catchphrases of our times. Defined in a modern sense by Ulrich Beck,[46] then numerously redefined in

[45] ME Edelstein, '"Outsiders Just Don't Understand": Personalization of Risk and the Boundary Between Modernity and Postmodernity' in MJ Cohen (ed), *Risk in Modern Age. Social Theory, Science and Environmental Decision-Making* (Palgrave MacMillan, London 2000) 123–124.

[46] U Beck, *Risk Society. Towards a New Modernity* (Sage Publications, London1986, 1992).

postmodern contexts, risk undergone a fully-fledged paradigm shift, in the Kuhnian[47] sense of the concept, and for a considerable period of time it has instituted a dominant discourse in many contemporary humanistic disciplines.[48] Although theories of risk were initially established in response to certain new practical developments, it soon transgressed these and transformed into a point of reference on its own, becoming a reality-making factor. Thus, risk is now used to assess certain existing circumstances, and it is through the lens of risk that we evaluate them and apply solutions. Why, one may wonder, this career of risk? It may perhaps be due to the fact that risk is indeed a very intriguing concept. Perhaps it is because it is situated directly between what we can and what we cannot scientifically establish. It may also be because the turbulent developments of today's reality have served as a fertile ground for theoretical seeds. After all, we are all humans, and our human condition makes us look desperately for explanations to everything. What we cannot explain, we imagine. What we cannot foresee, we fear. But still we have to deal with it somehow. And this is exactly where the concepts of risk and uncertainty become as handy as we could ever wish.

3.1.2. *Risk and the Law*

With regard to its significance for legal theory and practice, risk is often perceived merely as a tool. But even if one accepts such a subordinate approach towards risk, its significance for legal theory cannot be contested. Risk, in modern legal theory, is often thought of as enabling decisions and helping to explain the possibility of responsible action.[49] Why has risk been so readily accepted as a key concept of regulatory decision-making in our times? Have we become more prone to think in those terms, or have risks suddenly become more significant in general? Many social theorists (in particular Beck[50] and Giddens[51]) seek answers to these questions by referring to the distinctive nature of contemporary risk. The globalisation of international relations, trade and conflicts has forced us to measure contemporary risk on a different scale. It has also put risks in a different timeframe, and has given its impact a bigger perspective. The development of new technologies and mass communication

---

[47] TS Kuhn, *The Structure of Scientific Revolution* (Third Edition The University of Chicago Press, Chicago 1996).

[48] For the most coherent, important and interesting approaches to risk theories, see also N Luhmann, *Risk. A Sociological Theory* (Aldine Transaction Publishers, New Brunswick 2005); D Garland, 'The Rise of Risk' in RV Erickson and A Doyle, *Risk and Morality* (University of Toronto Press, Toronto Buffalo London 2003).

[49] J Steele, *Risks and Legal Theory* (Hart Publishing, Oxford 2004) 4, and her subsequent reflections on the current debate on the role of risk in legal theory.

[50] See, for example, U Beck, *Risk Society* ... (n 46).

[51] A Giddens, 'Risk and Responsibility' (1999) 62 *Modern Law Review* 1–10.

has also contributed to the raising of awareness about risks, and to bringing the risks closer to the citizens. This creates a paradoxical situation, in which risks, although so personalised and vital for every individual, are decided further and further away from them, as they are defined, assessed and managed not even regionally or nationally, but to an increasing extent at an international level.

3.2. *Regulating Risk in Transnational Settings*

3.2.1. *Theorising Risk Regulation*

3.2.1.1. *The Foundations of Risk Regulation*

For the purpose of regulatory deliberation, risk is usually defined as a probability of adverse consequences, which is not calculable in practice. The term 'regulation of risk' is consequently used to refer to various attempts to control that risk, mainly by establishing and enforcing safety standards for products or activities. Thus, risk regulation is a method of interfering in market behaviours and social processes which aims to control potential adverse consequences for health or the environment.[52]

The development of the phenomenon of risk regulation, with its various forms and models, and the rise of political and academic debate about it, has been interpreted by many as a reflection of a broader political and cultural transformation within contemporary societies as well as contemporary regulatory patterns. A model describing the coexistence of a technical understanding of risk and a social science perspective of it has emerged over the last two decades, developing an approach to risk as both a potential for harm as well as a social construction of worry.[53] On the one hand, sociologists such as Beck and Giddens have connected this development with the broader debate on the birth of the 'risk society' and the spread of new types of risk associated with 'advanced modernity'.[54] On the other hand, scholars of socio-politics and law have seen links between risk regulation and the rise of the 'regulatory state',[55] which encompasses a new institutional style of policy-making, in which the government's role as a regulator dominates over its previous role as a property-owner, and in which new forms of governance emerge.

Risk regulation has many faces; it's likely that for every risk, 'risk society' and 'regulatory state' we come across, we'd find a different regulatory system. The approaches, methods and intensity of risk regulation vary between states,

[52] For more, see C Hood, H Rothstein and R Baldwin, *The Government of Risk. Understanding Risk Regulation Regimes* (Oxford University Press, Oxford 2001) in particular chapter I: 'What Are Risk Regulation Regimes? Why Do They Matter?' 3–19.

[53] O Renn, CC Jaeger, EA Rosa and T Webler, 'The Rational Actor Paradigm in Risk Theories: Analysis and Critique' in MJ Cohen (ed), *Risk in the Modern Age* ... (n 45) 35.

[54] U Beck, *Risk Society* ... (n 46); A Giddens, 'Risk and Responsibility', (n 51).

[55] G Majone, 'The Rise of the Regulatory State in Europe' (1994) 17 *West European Politics* 77–101.

but—even more importantly—they also vary within them, depending on the nature of hazard they are meant to respond to. The application of a particular risk-regulatory regime has its historical, cultural and political grounds, and reflects the current approaches of a given political entity. It should respond to the fears and concerns of a society, adjusting the level of intervention to a particular degree of risk-aversion for each field. Nevertheless, it will also depend on the organisation of a state and of the legal and political system which gave rise to it; from this perspective, the variety of risk regulation regimes can be analysed along the lines of the three dimensions of the system—the gathering of information, the setting of standards and the modification of behaviour.[56] To use the clear and helpful systematisation of Hood et al., each and every risk regulatory regime is shaped on the one hand by its *context*, and on the other hand by its *content*. A regime's context, in this sense, is determined by three influential elements—the type of risk in question, public preferences and attitudes, and the nature and impact of organised interests. Its content, on the other hand, is determined by its fundamental architectural characteristics, which are its size, structure and style of regulation.[57] The contextual elements and the content characteristics are tightly interrelated; thus, it is interesting to observe the way that the context influences the shape of the risk regulatory regime and its content. On that basis, we can analyse three contextual driving forces of risk regulatory regimes and see how they determine regulatory attitudes and methods. The literature differentiates regimes that (1) are functionally oriented or market-failure-oriented, (2) are responsive to populism or to opinion, and (3) are driven by corporatism or by interest.[58]

3.2.1.2. *Elements of Risk Regulation*

From an operational point of view, risk regulation is a chapeau concept used to refer to a range of activities performed at different levels of governance. In its ideal archetype, it is described as being composed of three basic elements: risk assessment, risk management and risk communication.

The first component, risk assessment, can most simply be defined as a 'systematic approach to organizing and analysing scientific knowledge and information for potentially hazardous activities or for substances that might pose risk under specified conditions'.[59] The European Commission, to give an example of a more 'local' way of approaching it, speaks about classical risk assessment as implying 'recourse to methods and knowledge, no matter how

[56] R Hood *at al.*, *The Government of Risk* ... (n 52) 20.
[57] Ibid 28–29.
[58] Ibid 61–69.
[59] National Research Council, *Science and Judgment on Risk Assessment* (National Academy Press, Washington DC 1994) 4.

uncertain, based on rigorous methods for testing hypothetical explanations of natural or social facts and systems'.[60] Irrespective of the origin of the definition, therefore, risk assessment tends to be perceived as a purely technical phase of analysis, left to be pursued by highly specialised scientific experts who possess the necessary knowledge and skills, which legitimises the public trust vested in them through the regulatory process. The aim of risk assessment is to provide decision-makers, on the basis of the identification of a hazard, its analysis and characterisation, with the underlying factual information that is required in order to make a regulatory determination.[61]

The second phase of the risk regulatory process, risk management, is the phase where values other than scientific expertise come into play, and where decisions are a fruit of political process. Risk management aims to establish, after careful consideration of the scientific risk assessment, and taking into account political, economic and social aspects, the acceptable level of risk, and then aims to design ways of achieving it.

Risk communication, finally, refers to an interactive process of exchange of information and opinions about risk by the involved parties, and their dissemination to a wider public.[62]

This, as previously pointed out, is an ideal model, and it must be borne in mind that, in reality, a strict delineation between the phases of the process is not so clear; the dividing line between the technical (scientific) and the political elements is often vague and difficult to draw. While the role of policy in risk assessment has been acknowledged openly, the functional separation of assessment and management activities reflects a continuous belief in the value of separating the scientific and the political. This is the basis for the contemporarily emphasised desire to de-politicise scientific risk assessment and to hand the ultimate political management decision to democratically accountable entities.[63] This is true especially in transnational situations, where the variety of interests, the multi-level character of governance and the problematic nature of democratic legitimacy pose additional challenges to risk regulation. In this context, it is worth pointing out that the European Commission gave a clear statement on the issue in its White Paper on Food Safety, saying that 'legislation

[60] Commission (EC), Communication from the Commission on the Collection and Use of Expertise by the Commission: Principles and Guidelines 'Improving the knowledge base for better policies' COM (2002) 713 final, 11 December 2002, 3.

[61] C Button, *The Power to Protect. Trade, Health and Uncertainty in the WTO* (Studies in International Trade Law, Hart Publishing, Oxford and Portland Oregon 2004) 96. For a broader review, see E Fisher, *Risk Regulation and Administrative Constitutionalism* (Hart Publishing, Oxford Portland Oregon 2007) 185–200.

[62] Compare C. Button, *The Power to Protect* ... ibid 96–97; M Kritikos, 'Traditional Risk Analysis and Releases of GMO's into the European Union: Space for Non-Scientific Factors?' (2009) 34 *European Law Review* 420–423.

[63] C. Button, *The Power to Protect* ... ibid 100.

implies a political decision and involves judgments not only based on science but on a wider appreciation of the wishes and needs of society. There must be a clear separation between risk management and risk assessment'.[64]

The complexity of decision-making in face of uncertainty has, thus, led to increased proceduralisation and structurisation of both the generation of knowledge and the generation of decisions on risks that are based on that knowledge.[65]

3.2.2. *Risk Regulation through the Lens of Science*

The above analysis of the risk regulatory model clearly illustrates that regulatory problems involving risks have traditionally been resolved by recourse to science. The rise of the role of science in the process of risk regulation is a consequence of the rise of role of science and technology in production methods and product design.[66] Science, perceived as an autonomous and universal arbiter, has been expected to provide uncontroversial grounds for regulatory decisions that go beyond borders of national divides and interests, and that can be accepted by all actors in play. Years of experience, however, have cast doubt on these expectations, revealing that scientific expertise is not always either so autonomous or so universal. Ladeur commented directly on the changing role of science and experts in administrative decision-making: 'In the past, the administration asked experts for explanation of phenomena which it did not understand enough. Nowadays, in processes of decision-making on risk, scientists, engineers and other experts are themselves confronted with problems which they do not completely understand'.[67] Scientific expertise, in fact, has often shown to be more of a weapon in transnational conflicts than the arbiter it was supposed to be. Moreover, and particularly importantly here, the prevalence given to science in risk regulation has tended to suppress all other important values and interests, which should ideally be taken into consideration as well.

Thus, one can speak of the external and internal limits of scientific risk assessment. Its external limitations stem from the fact that science follows its own clear-cut logic and therefore is often blind to other interests and values. This limitation, it has to be emphasised, is mainly perceived as an advantage of science rather than a drawback. Ideally, other values that should be taken

[64] Commission (EC), White Paper on Food Safety, COM (1999) 719 final, par. 32.
[65] K-H Ladeur, 'The Introduction of the Precautionary Principle into the EU Law: a Pyrrhic Victory for Environmental and Public Health Law? Decision-Making under Conditions of Complexity in Multi-Level Political Systems' (2003) 40 *Commmon Market Law Review* 1464.
[66] Ibid 1462.
[67] Ibid 1462–1463.

into account in the decision-making process are included in the risk management phase, where they are represented and deliberated by legitimate entities and where their political significance is weighed. Whether this occurs in reality remains uncertain. Very often, risk managers simply apply the decisions of risk assessors without further, more value-inclusive deliberation, and other interests simply get 'lost in the translation' of scientific expertise into regulatory decision-making.[68]

The internal limitations of scientific risk assessment reflect the limits of the scientific method itself. In contemporary circumstances, science is frequently faced with various uncertainties and gridlocks, which can be of a gravity that precludes the application of proper scientific methods. Even when faced with such situations, scientists are nevertheless expected to provide an answer to an existing problem in order to fulfil their obligations in the risk regulation regime. Hence, they will use various techniques and assumptions in order to circumvent the limitations of the classical scientific method and will fill in the inevitable knowledge gaps. Such assumptions and techniques, referred to as 'science policies', have become a part of the mainstream scientific method.[69] This leads to a situation where different regulatory regimes may apply different science policies; consequently, two assessments of the same risk might produce different results and lead to the adoption of different management decisions. Both decisions will be based on universal science; each one, however, will reflect different science policies, which have employed different sets of assumptions and methodological tricks. Does that mean that one decision is wrong? This does not seem to be the case. In cases of conflict, however, judges will have to validate one. Is this where governance by science reaches its limits? Just to show that this problem is not a purely hypothetical one, two examples of transnational trade conflicts can be quoted, in which invoking science as a universal judge showed its limitations: the WTO disputes between the 'old' and the 'new' worlds, firstly over the use of hormones in beef,[70] and secondly over the acceptance of genetically modified organisms.[71] What should a judge

[68] I borrow the terminology from C. Joerges, 'Integrating Scientific Expertise into Regulatory Decision-Making …' (n 9), for a detailed analysis of such science-dominated risk management practices see M Kritikos, 'Traditional Risk Analysis and the Releases of GMO's …' (n 62) especially 423–225.

[69] Compare C. Button, *The Power to Protect* … (n 61) 97–99. Compare also Joint FAO/WHO Consultation, Risk Management and Food Safety, FAO Food and Nutrition Paper 65, Rome 1997, available at <http://www.fao.org/docrep/W4982E/W4982E00.htm> accessed 25 May 2011, especially part 8.

[70] *European Communities—Measures Concerning Meat and Meat Products (Hormones)*, Report of the Appellate Body, adopted 13 February 1998, WT/DS26/AB/R, WT/DS48/AB/R.

[71] *European Communities—Measures Affecting the Approval and Marketing of Biotech Products*, Panel Report adopted 29 September 2006, United States (WT/DS291/R), Canada (WT/DS292/R) and Argentina (WT/DS293/R).

or a regulator do in such a situation? What other legitimate factors should we turn to when science gives no definite answer?

3.2.3. *Beyond Scientific Recognition*

3.2.3.1. *The Social 'Embeddedness' of Risk Regulation*

Risk regulation, just as any other aspect of the market, has to be embedded in the social structure that gave rise to it and that contextualises its existence and development. Here, I follow Polanyi's embeddedness thesis[72] and apply his ideas to contemporary risk regulation as a vital element of market governance. Borrowing from Polanyi, I intend to show that regulation of the market, like the market itself, must be embedded in its society in such a way that both are interrelated and cannot function properly when disconnected.[73] Disconnecting risk regulation from its social basis causes a gradual disembedding of the market in which it functions, which, in effect, deprives the market of its social legitimacy and is detrimental for its development.

I argue, therefore, that in order to ensure the acceptance and efficiency of risk regulatory decisions, they must be socially embedded. They must relate to the societies which they are directed to, and they must reflect their particular contexts. Commentators have organised the factors that shape risk perception and allow the embeddedness of risk regulation in two main groups: culture and social structure.[74]

Evaluation of information, as well as the decision-making based upon it, are highly constrained by the context in which they take place. Risk perception will always be determined by the cognitive system of norms, values and beliefs that form the culture of a given society, as well as the trust and confidence that the society has in the risk management performance of its institutions.[75] Cultural forces, therefore, always influence the ability to discern risk and the ways of recognising it, by highlighting particular activities as potentially dangerous and by defining the notion of danger to begin with. Cultural mediation not only has great influence on risk perception, but also carries important implications for the legitimacy of the exercise of power in relation to risk, which depends on the extent to which the society trusts its regulators and their ability to protect them by productive risk-decisions.[76]

---

[72] K Polanyi, *The Great Transformation. The Political and Economic Origins of our Time* (Beacon Press, Boston 1957).

[73] Ibid 45–70.

[74] K Purcell, L Clarke and L Renzulli, 'Menus of Choice: the Social Embeddedness of Decisions' in MJ Cohen (ed), *Risk in the Modern Age* ...(n 45) 62–79.

[75] See the analysis of the role of trust in risk perception in P Slovic, 'Perceived Risk, Trust and Democracy' (1993) 13 *Risk Analysis* 675–682.

[76] See K Purcell et al. (n 74) 67–68.

As pointed out above, however, with regard to risk perception and risk choices, societies are also subject to structural mediation. Structural factors divide societies both vertically and horizontally, with regard to knowledge and information imbalances, where a deep understanding of highly technological specificities is reserved for a limited segment of a society, the experts. Knowledge gaps affect people's freedom of choice simply by preventing them from considering alternative possibilities, or from weighing the potential costs and benefits of other options.[77]

3.2.3.2. *Listening to Social Voices in Transnational Risk Regulation*

In an ideal model of risk regulation, scientific risk assessment would only give an informative basis for regulatory decisions to be taken in the management phase. Apart from the scientific results, regulatory decisions should also take into consideration other relevant factors, such as the economic feasibility, the intended level of protection, the social demand for regulation and the impact of the planned regulation on market, trade and production patterns. The important questions that follow, however, are: how far can regulatory decision-making be influenced by consideration of these 'other factors'? Can they justify decisions that would depart from the findings of the scientific assessment?

Despite the fears of diluting and diminishing the consistency of international trade regulations that essentially rely on scientific risk assessment, several commentators now acknowledge the existence of other factors in risk regulation, and the possibility of including these in regulatory systems. It is obvious that the public perception of risk differs significantly from that of experts. To use Beck's words, 'the two sides talk past each other. Social movements raise questions that are not answered by the risk technicians at all, and the technicians answer questions which miss the point of what was really asked and what feeds public anxiety'.[78] Due to their different points of departure, societal contexts, scientific backgrounds and emotional engagements, the two groups tend to assess and rank risks in different ways. Although it is commonly argued that the social perception of risk is often irrational, unfounded and biased by the manipulative use of information by the media or corporate interests, many have countered that recognition of such contextual differences by risk regulators is not only rational but also necessary.[79]

3.2.3.2.1. *Observations de lege lata.* International regulatory bodies have shown far less acceptance of these types of considerations. While EU institutions

[77] Ibid 72–74.

[78] U Beck, *Risk Society* ... (n 46) 30.

[79] CR Sunstein and R Pildes, 'Experts, Economists, and Democrats' in CR Sunstein, *Free Markets and Social Justice* (Oxford University Press, New York 1997) 128–148.

at least declare that risk management should aim to balance scientific risk assessment with consumers' confidence and factors such as societal, economic, ethical, traditional and environmental considerations,[80] the SPS Agreement, within the WTO system,[81] is much more careful and makes very little mention of the extent to which various social values and consumer considerations should be taken into account, imposing a strict requirement of scientific justification.[82] The Codex Alimentarius Commission, on the other hand, allows other legitimate factors to be considered in risk management, but only to the extent that they do not affect the scientific basis of risk analysis and do not create unjustified barriers to trade.[83] Considering the implicit connection of those two systems under the WTO umbrella, and the significance of its jurisprudence for the development of the system, it will be interesting to observe the development of the Appellate Body decisions in that respect. Its decisions so far, even in the two abovementioned transatlantic cases, where science provided no definitive answer, have been rather reserved. According to Button, however, sooner or later the WTO will have to decide to what extent it will allow cultural or societal preferences to shape national regulations, remaining cautious that public fears do not affect them.[84] The same will have to happen to Europe. The tensions of reconciling expert knowledge and non-expert public perspectives are still in the open. As Scott and Vos point out in reference to the Commission's policy on precautionary principle, its 'spoken commitment to science in risk regulation, alongside transparency, participation and social acceptability, may be laudable, but as far as the tensions lurk unacknowledged it remains unconvincing'.[85] They point to the fact that the most troublesome issues in relation to the democratisation of risk regulation are, firstly,

---

[80] See Regulation (EC) 178/2002 of the European Parliament and of the Council of 28 January 2002 laying down the general principles and requirements of food law, establishing the European Food Safety Authority and laying down procedures in matters of food safety [2002] OJ L 31/1, especially Preamble par. 19 as well as Article 6.3.

[81] Agreement on Sanitary and Phytosanitary Measures, 15 April 1994, Marrakesh Agreement Establishing the World Trade Organization, Annex 1A.

[82] See, in particular, Article 5.1, which requires risk-regulatory decisions to be 'based on science', and Article 5.2. For a broader perspective on the character of those provisions, see their interpretation by the Appellate Body in *EC Hormones* case (n 70) 182–191; J Scott, *The WTO Agreement on Sanitary and Phytosanitary Measures. A Commentary* (Oxford University Press, Oxford 2007) 76–137.

[83] See Codex Alimentarius Commission, Criteria for Consideration of the Other Factors Referred to in the Second Statement of Principle, Decision of the 24th Session of the Commission, 2001, ALINORM 01/41, 83. Quoted in C Button, *The Power to Protect* ... (n 61) 106, as well as MD Masson-Matthee, *The Codex Alimentarius Commission and Its Standards* (TMC Asser Press, the Hague 2007).

[84] Compare C Button, *The Power to Protect* ... ibid 108.

[85] See J Scott and E Vos, 'The Juridification of Uncertainty: Observations on the Ambivalence of the Precautionary principle within the EU and the WTO' in Ch Joerges and R Dehousse, *Good Governance in Europe's Integrated Market* (Oxford University Press, Oxford 2002) 284.

the problem of gathering, measuring and evaluating public opinions, and secondly, the possibility of invoking them to justify trade restrictions.[86] In this sense, it is of major importance that appropriate mechanisms are present in a risk regulatory system, which articulate the role and define the limits of public opinion and which allow consideration of public acceptability. Otherwise, any decision apart from scientific finding that gives an ear to public perspectives will be an easy target for accusations of disguised protectionism. The existence of any procedural or institutional framework for the inclusion of public voices will make this element of risk regulation more serious and more legitimate, and will, finally, allow for their genuine incorporation in the decision-making process.

3.2.3.2.2. *Theoretical Reflections.* Among the academics who advocate the inclusion of societal and cultural preferences in risk-regulatory decision-making, some propose ways to reconcile expert opinions with public perception. They look for alternative ways to legitimise social concerns and shape them against allegations of irrationality. Sunstein, for example, departing from the assumption that public perception of risk is always faulty, suggests ways of overcoming that imperfection.[87] He admits that people not only suffer from a shortage of information, but also are psychologically determined to be affected by various misconceptions (misjudgements), such as the availability heuristic, social cascades, the influence of media and one-sided visions, as well as emotions and intuitions. Hence, he suggests a method of improving popular ways of thinking about risks through use of a cost–benefit analysis and democratic deliberation. Sunstein, however, perceives the cost–benefit analysis mainly as a 'natural corrective', which can focus people's attention on the actual effects of regulation or non-regulation, but which does not help them to decide whether or not to regulate. If the public wants to proceed after receiving that accounting, the government cannot refuse to act even if the estimated costs exceed the estimated effects. Cost–benefit analysis, in this sense, becomes a tool that overcomes public ignorance, fortifying democratic goals by ensuring that government decisions are responsive to well-informed public judgements. It also helps to overcome people's tendency to take only part of the problem into account by providing a global perspective on the consequences of seemingly isolated actions.[88] Implicitly, it also enables people to differentiate between cognitive errors and important value-judgements which, despite their

---

[86] J Scott and E Vos, The Juridification of Uncertainty … ibid 284–285.

[87] CR Sunstein, *Risk and Reason. Safety, Law, and the Environment* (Cambridge University Press, Cambridge 2002) 28–52, CR Sunstein, *Laws of Fear. Beyond the Precautionary Principle* (Cambridge University Press, Cambridge 2005) 64–105 and 149–174.

[88] CR Sunstein, *Risk and Reason* … ibid 35.

cost–benefit expensiveness, survive reflection.[89] Cost–benefit analysis shows what the distribution of risk is, and who may win or lose due to regulation. It therefore allows the regulator to find ways to minimise the burdens faced by the most disadvantaged members of society.[90]

There are, however, cases where a cost–benefit analysis does not provide an answer. Regulators, aware of the limits of that method, look for further guidance in democratic deliberation or turn towards 'libertarian paternalism', which preserves freedom of choice while steering people in directions that will promote their own welfare.[91] Sunstein recognises the importance of the inclusion of social concerns and risk perception, but by being aware of its shortcomings, he also suggests means of improving it, which can sometimes be seen as dangerously close to social planning and socio-techniques. Nevertheless, what Sunstein does not deal with extensively is the situation where social fears are already at stake. Should a regulator respond to public concerns, irrespective of whether they are justified or not? Can a regulator reject the findings of a scientific risk assessment if the public demand for regulation is sufficiently strong?[92] Renn and Klinke suggest that the dual nature of risk should be reflected in a dual strategy of its management, where social concerns play the role of driving agents for the identification of topics where risk assessment is needed, while evaluation of the magnitude of risk should be based on technical expertise.[93] What such a model misses, however, are the situations where intervention is necessary because a real risk exists, despite the public's acceptance of it, which brings us back to Sunstein's 'libertarian paternalism'.

3.2.3.2.3. *Suggestions* de lege ferenda? This section brings theoretical reflections back to the field of international trade regulation and speculates about the possibility of including social concerns and public perceptions in risk regulation in the global trade arena. It can be argued that if members of global trade community were free to restrict trade in response to public fears and against rational scientific argument, the whole carefully designed and negotiated system of international trade regulation could be undermined. It would create the possibility to introduce the kind of protectionism that the WTO system was created to avoid. It must, however, be clearly pointed out that there is a whole galaxy of options between reliance only on science and reliance on public fears. And it is this galaxy that needs to be explored, in order to find

[89] Ibid 50.

[90] Ibid 294.

[91] CR Sunstein and R Thaler in CR Sunstein, *Laws of Fear* … (n 87) 175–203.

[92] See the discussion in C Button, *The Power to Protect* … (n 61) 111.

[93] A Klinke and O Renn, 'A New Approach to Risk Evaluation and Management: Risk-Based, Precaution-Based, and Discourse-Based Strategies' (2002) 22 *Risk Analysis* 1076.

the right balance of both rational science and the far less rational, but relevant and legitimising, public perception. Such balance is certainly possible to find, although the barrier against this possibility is still strong.

Some academics share this opinion and advocate such possibility. Howse, for example, imagines ways to combine the goal of international trade liberalisation with the quest for democratisation and global welfare maximisation.[94] He suggests that the WTO might very well remain true to its mission of eliminating trade barriers by acknowledging that social factors are not necessarily irrational; he argues that, although the SPS Agreement is built upon the idea of universal judgement of science in transnational regulation, it should not be taken to forbid any recognition of cultural and social features.[95] If global trade liberalisation is to happen at the cost of democracy, he argues, then its general value and its promise of global and domestic welfare maximisation become questionable. As a consequence, the WTO system as a whole risks losing its 'social legitimacy'.[96]

Promises of democracy are more likely to be fulfilled when citizens are given adequate information about the risks at stake, as well as the costs and benefits of alternative regulatory solutions, and when their popular choices, even if different from those which are the outcome of experts' deliberations, are given due respect, when they were made in awareness of the facts and in a legitimate manner. Their utility would be seriously impeded if citizens who believed that they needed certain regulation were deprived of it and left feeling exposed to a risk that they deemed significant; it must be borne in mind that the utility of regulation comes not only from the reduced likelihood of an undesired event, but also from the psychological security that results from one's belief in the protection received.[97] Sunstein and Pildes, following the same reasoning, argue

[94] R Howse, 'Democracy, Science, and Free Trade: Risk Regulation on Trial at the World Trade Organization' (2000) 98 *Michigan Law Review* 2330, 2333 and 2340.

[95] R Howse, 'Adjudicative Legitimacy and Treaty Interpretation in International Trade Law: The Early Years of WTO Jurisprudence' in JHH Weiler (ed), *The EU, the WTO and the NAFTA: Towards a Common Law of International Trade* (Oxford University Press, Oxford New York 2000) 65–68. Howse sees traces of a tendency towards a more democratic approach to risk regulation that demands more openness to social and cultural outcomes in the deliberations in the AB report in the EC Hormones case. Even though the outcome of the case did not reflect such a tendency, and nor did the following jurisprudence, Howse welcomes the reasoning of the Appellate Body as a signal of the possibility of future development. See R Howse, 'Democracy, Science, and Free Trade …' ibid 2340–2349.

[96] See the concept as used by Joseph Weiler in the European context, which distinguishes between 'social legitimacy' and 'formal legitimacy', where the former is understood as 'a broad, empirically determined societal acceptance of the system … [and] occurs when the government process displays a commitment to, and actively guarantees, values that are part of the general political culture, such as justice, freedom, and general welfare', in JHH Weiler, 'The Transformation of Europe' (1991) 100 *Yale Law Journal* 2468–2474.

[97] R Howse, 'Democracy, Science, and Free Trade …' (n 94) 2330, 2337 and 2350.

that although scientific expertise has an important role to play in appropriately structured deliberative processes of regulation—for example, as a corrector of empirical mistakes and misinformation-based prejudices—many other factors that are not considered in scientific assessment have a legitimate place in risk determination from a democratic perspective.[98]

4. Regulating Risk by the Use of Standards—the Market Implications of Safety Regulations

4.1. *Standardisation as a Regulatory Concept*

4.1.1. *Introduction—Regulation, Self-Regulation and Standardisation*

Although it is an established fact that the concept of regulation plays a central role in the European political economy, it is not always obvious how many faces regulation has. The term *regulation* refers to a wide range of political and legal activities that govern economic behaviour and its consequences. Market governance is, therefore, at the heart of regulation, and it encompasses the creation of rules, methods of their implementation and enforcement, as well as the institutions responsible for their administration and control. Regulation as a 'defining feature of any system of social organisation' is central to the definition of relations between economic actors, social interests and the state.[99]

Traditional forms of regulation have recently gone through a serious crisis, in which their efficiency in new transnational settings has been put under question. However, it was not their existence *per se* that was contested, but rather that a new approach to regulation and a shift of focus in regulatory activities were called for. As the biggest advocate of 'Europe as a regulatory state', Giandomenico Majone describes:

> … the scepticism in the ability of the state to act as entrepreneur, planner and direct provider of services did not lead to demands for a return to laissez-faire as the more radical advocates of deregulation and privatisation seemed to expect. Instead, there was a demand for better focused and more flexible forms of public intervention, and more attention to those areas of social regulation (environment, consumer, civil rights) which had been largely neglected by the welfare policies in the past.[100]

[98] CR Sunstein and R Pildes, 'Experts, Economists, and Democrats' (n 79) 128–148.

[99] MP Egan, *Constructing a European Market: Standards, Regulation and Governance* (Oxford University Press, Oxford 2001) 18.

[100] G Majone, 'Cross-national Sources of Regulatory Policy-Making in Europe and the United States' (1991) 11 *Journal of Public Policy* 82.

The development of new technologies, as well as the growing dynamics of market conditions, have presented traditional forms of regulation with new sets of challenges. The response of the market can be observed in the emergence of a new wave of voluntary self-constraint mechanisms, such as guidelines, codes of conduct and standards, which, as a rule, are meant to provide a minimum level of uniformity and to improve market efficiency. As a result of this development, governments have been forced to look for ways to acknowledge such new methods of regulation and to cover them with the protectionist umbrella of the state. Such new wave of regulatory developments has also occurred in the common European market.

It is a general assumption that self-regulation, as an alternative method of governance, offers a wide range of important advantages. It operates in an environment of advanced expertise and technical knowledge, and can therefore rely on these to a larger extent than a public institution might. On the other hand, by operating closer to stakeholders it can be more responsive to their needs, but also more flexible and adjustable in changing circumstances. Moreover, since the making of rules is privately done, the system is usually less formalised and more efficient, while at the same time the engagement of stakeholders in the rulemaking process increases their readiness to implement and enforce decisions. These features, according to many commentators, explain why in most industrialised countries, technical standardisation has very successfully been delegated to self-regulatory organisations.[101] Private rulemaking, however, is certainly not free from criticism. Not only is its legitimacy questioned, but whether the delegation of responsibility for the safety of citizens to private organisations can be accepted at all is also contested. The latter, however, becomes largely neutralised, as contemporarily technical standardisation is an outcome of a public–private cooperation and consensus, where the involvement of governmental authority makes up for the abovementioned shortcomings. In such public–private settings, standardisation should in principle become a deliberative exercise of a network of interested stakeholders (industry representatives, public officials, scientists), in which the knowledge, concerns and competences of all are represented in the final outcome.

Standardisation provides a response to the growing complexity of life and, consequently, the need for more extensive control. Standards, to quote Sullivan, 'are the documents that carry these controls throughout the social structure'.[102] They are not, however, a novelty. As early as dealings between individuals needed to be controlled, standards were there to facilitate them

[101] G Majone, *Dilemmas of European Integration. The Ambiguities and Pitfalls of Integration by Stealth* (Oxford University Press, Oxford 2005) 102.

[102] CD Sullivan, *Standards and Standardization. Basic Principles and Application* (Marcel Dekker, New York 1983) x.

and to safeguard the honesty of transactions. The earliest written standards date back some 5000 years, when the Egyptians developed a standard of measurement based on the length of pharaoh's forearm.[103] It was according to this standard that the pyramids were build.[104]

Standards may control different aspects of products or services on the market: their quantity, quality, value and methods of their production. Looking at products as consumers, we are often unable to judge them ourselves. We believe, however, that they are safe and of good quality, because we trust in the standards in accordance with which they are produced. Of course, the effectiveness of standards will vary, depending on people's acceptance of the value they serve, as well as their willingness to observe them. This is where the notion of 'voluntary' standards needs to be given some consideration. Although the literal meaning of the notion would indicate that we are dealing with standards that one can choose to observe or to reject, the practical reality is different. When a society places a high value on conformity, and when a considerable part of that society accepts a common standard, the others are almost compelled to follow, and those who insist on diverging sooner or later find themselves in a seriously disadvantaged position. To put it simply, the standard voluntarily adopted by a group of interested parties becomes much less voluntary when it is successfully put into practice.[105] In some cases, especially when actors are highly dependent on relationships with third parties, the standard becomes practically coercive.[106]

Here, another problematic issue of standardisation has to be considered: that of the origin and legitimacy of standards. Who are the people who have voluntarily developed and committed to a standard, and what is their basis for enforcing the standard on all other market participants in a much less voluntary fashion? It has to borne in mind that, in the majority of cases, standards are developed by minorities; hence, those who must respect standards in order to participate in a market on equal grounds often have very little or no influence on their formation. The issue becomes even more obvious when analysed in the context of international standardisation. Here, differences in technical and economic development between advanced countries and less developed states are not reflected in the standardisation process, which as a result may lead to *de facto* discrimination, preventing those who lack the facilities to meet the set standards from competing in the world market.[107] Other important issues are

[103] It was approximately 20.63 inches long and was divided into 6 palm-widths and 24 finger-widths.
[104] After CD Sullivan, *Standards and Standardization* … (n 102) 5.
[105] Compare CD Sullivan, ibid 8–10.
[106] N Brunsson, B Jacobsson *et al.*, *A World of Standards* (Oxford University Press, Oxford 2000) 134.
[107] CD Sullivan, *Standards and Standardization* … (n 102) 11.

the recognition of standards by national or international regulatory institutions, and its consequences. How do they chose which standards deserve recognition? What meaning and legal effect does that give to those standards? What impact does it have on the market? In the following paragraphs, those questions will be approached in more detail, providing a brief and informative background for the world of standards, which is intriguing and yet open to new discoveries.

4.1.2. *The Origins of Standards and the Implications of Their Recognition*

From a practical point of view, standards are hardly ever either completely public or exclusively private. If public authorities develop standards, they must rely to a very large extent on private expertise and cooperation with private organisations or professional bodies. On the other hand, if the private bodies themselves set up standards, the intervention of the public authorities—in the form of influence on their formation or application, with the aim of protecting publicly recognised values—can be almost automatically expected.[108]

The categories of standard-setting bodies, thus, have to be understood rather broadly and with a high degree of flexibility with regard to their forms and procedures. They can also be differently situated in relation to the state and public agencies. Thus, it is often easier to talk about these bodies as networks, without trying to press them into closed categories or strict divides. Suffice it to say standards are a product of compromise, a deliberation between producers, consumers and controllers, between technical experts and state officials, between private and public interests.[109] In principle, then, they ought to be consulted and negotiated with regard to economic, technical, social and political values, in order to create an equilibrium that will be acceptable to all stakeholders.

For the same reasons, the procedures for producing international standards are not uniform and often vary from one field to another, responding to the specificity of a given realm. Some generalisations can be made, however. Standardisation procedures take at least the following steps: (1) deliberation on a draft standard by technical committees representing all stakeholders' interests; (2) reaching consensus on the draft standard; (3) public consultation on the draft standard, collection and review of comments, and subsequent redrafting, if necessary; (4) reaching consensus on the final draft and ratification of the final draft by the standard-setting body; (5) periodical review of the standard.[110]

---

[108] H Schepel, *The Constitution of Private Governance. Product Standards in the Regulation of Integrating Markets* (Hart Publishing, Oxford 2005) 4.

[109] See, for example, N Mohan Reddy, 'Technology, Standards, and Markets: A Market Institutionalization Perspective' in H Landis Gabel (ed), *Product Standardisation and Competitive Strategy* (Elsevier Science Publishers B.V., Amsterdam 1987) 58–63.

[110] See H Schepel, *The Constitution of Private Governance* ... (n 108) 6, and documents from various standards bodies quoted therein.

Even though markets can themselves be effective standard-setters, they can be imperfect and are sometimes prone to failure. It is therefore necessary to establish some form of an institutionalised framework to coordinate the process and conflict resolution. That is why standardisation has gradually become an exercise of negotiation within committees of experts, who represent particular interests and operate according to agreed procedures.

Although standards are, in fact, merely voluntary requirements developed by expert committees with arguable democratic legitimacy, they gain their quasi-legal status because they are used as references in technical regulations, and by those means, they gain recognition of legitimate bodies. This leads into a bigger debate on the 'delegation' of regulatory powers, which concerns the existence of appropriate means of securing the public interest in the process of standardisation, as, in the long run, this process has a public character and should be subordinated to some kind of social control.[111] Especially in post-national constellations, where all the classical divisions of powers and traditional ways of conceptualising democratic values have become blurred, this debate gains a particular momentum. G. Teubner, for example, deliberating on the idea of the social constitutionalisation of law-making that takes place outside the classical sources of international law, and that is created through agreements between global players or multinationals, by private market-regulation or standardisation processes, claims that by acknowledging the rationality of external law-making processes, the law confers on them the quality of legal norms and, consequently, socially upgrades them.[112]

4.1.3. *Types of Standards*

Types of standards, and their degree of 'gravity' and intervention, are numerous, ranging from mere information measures to rigid requirements of prior approval for products. Academics have suggested various systematisations and methods of qualifying standards; here a couple of examples will be invoked, which appear the most suitable in the context of this volume.

Standards can be classified on the basis of their purpose, such as quality, variety-reduction or compatibility. Quality standards assure the criteria of reliability and fitness for the purpose; variety-reduction standards reduce superfluous duplication; and compatibility standards allow different products or components to work together to provide interoperability.[113] Standards can also be

---

[111] For more on the 'delegation' debate in the context of standardisation, see H Schepel, *The Constitution of Private Governance* … ibid 249.

[112] G Teubner, 'Societal Constitutionalism: Alternatives to State-Centred Constitutional Theory' in Ch Joerges, I-J Sand and G Teubner (eds), *Transnational Governance and Constitutionalism* (Hart Publishing, Oxford 2004) 24–25.

[113] MP Egan, *Constructing a European Market* … (n 99) 53.

classified by the function they serve with regard to the product. Here we can distinguish between product standards, which refer to the specific characteristics which a product must possess, and process standards, which refer to the production methods, conditions and procedures under which a product was manufactured.

A. Ogus suggests categorising standards into three subdivisions: target standards, performance standards and specification standards.[114] Target standards, according to this systematisation, prescribe no specific criteria for output or production process but impose liability for any eventual harmful consequences of the product. Performance or output standards impose certain conditions on the product's quality, but leave to the producer the choice of how to achieve that result. Finally, specification or input standards impose on producers established types of technical procedures, production methods or materials; as such, these are the most invasive of all the given types.[115]

4.1.4. *Economy of Standards*

4.1.4.1. *Costs and Benefits of Standards*

Among the costs of regulatory standards, one can distinguish between administrative costs, compliance costs and other indirect costs.[116] In this classification, administrative costs are the costs borne primarily by the public agencies connected with formulating standards and with control of their application, while compliance costs are the costs borne mainly by business operators in connection with their adaptation to standards. Indirect costs are probably the most interesting. They often reflect the unintended consequences of standardisation, such as allocative inefficiency, which leads to resources not being put to their most valuable social use. Estimation of these costs is particularly difficult, as their relevant effects are widespread and detailed data is difficult to acquire.[117]

Standardisation, on the other hand, is also a source of important and numerous benefits, and although these are much more difficult to quantify than the costs, they should be given due consideration. Standardisation may, for example, reduce production costs by allowing greater economic scale, and by saving the costs of knowledge attainment.[118] Standardisation also contributes to the promotion of market information and confidence by signalling a product's quality, and it also facilitates production and marketing management. Last but not least, in

[114] A Ogus, *Regulation. Legal Form and Economic Theory* (Hart Publishing, Oxford 2004) 151.
[115] Ibid 151–152.
[116] Ibid 155.
[117] Ibid.
[118] J Farrell and G Saloner, 'Competition, Compatibility and Standards: The Economics of Horses, Penguins and Lemmings' in H Landis Gabel (ed), *Product Standardisation and Competitive Strategy* (n 109) 6.

the contemporary world of post-national constellations, where the organisation of trade and industry often makes it difficult to point to a clear sovereign source of power, standardisation offers relatively legitimate rules and makes it possible to achieve coordination without a legal centre of authority. Hence, standardisation can be seen as a method of providing necessary regulation in such situations, without resorting to market solutions or state intervention.[119]

4.1.4.2. *Distributional Concerns*

In the cost–benefit analysis of standardisation, one more aspect must be taken into consideration: the question of distributional concerns. Despite the consensual character of the standardisation process, standards pose significant distributional questions, which cannot simply be settled by reference to technical principles.

As standards determine an acceptable level of risk and cost, standardisation necessarily involves deliberation about political and socioeconomic criteria. Hence, even if the maximisation of welfare is clearly defined as the ultimate goal of regulatory reform, exactly which sections of society will incur the costs of a new measure and which will benefit from its introduction must also be considered. As it is a very challenging and values-based exercise, it is commonly assumed that in the cost–benefit analysis of regulatory measures, quantifiable effects will always dominate over qualitative ones, even if the latter are considered more important. Consequently the market rationale commonly prevails. Nevertheless, it is sometimes necessary to provide a more detailed assessment of costs and benefits than a simple statement that benefits clearly outweigh costs, as the policy-makers who must decide whether to approve a proposed measure may require information on its distributional impact. Inevitably, this is a very problematic part of the process, because the evaluation of non-market assets tends to be extremely difficult and often reflects no more than the standard-setter's own interpretation of values. Following this reasoning, one can assume that implementing a qualitative effect through a quantitative judgement will necessarily imply a certain element of subjectivity, which, on the one hand, enables the inclusion of non-economic concerns into the analysis, but, on the other, may also allow public-interest aims to be outweighed by private-interest considerations.[120]

Such private-interest capture may lead to standards having an anti-competitive effect, as it may allow a particular segment of the market to internalise the benefits of standards and, consequently, to impose higher

---

[119] More in N Brunsson and B Jacobsson, 'The Pros and Cons of Standardisation—An Epilogue' in N Brunsson, B Jacobsson *et al.*, *A World of Standards* (n 106) 169–171.

[120] See A Ogus, *Regulation …* (n 114) 159–160.

costs on their competitors. This can be the case especially in situations where the majority of a specific technical expertise necessary for the development of a standard is accumulated in the hands of a group of large producers. It gives them the possibility to affect and even dominate the evaluation process, making the standard-setting body vulnerable to interest-capture. Thus, it is often a question of uneven distribution of resources available for effective participation in the standardisation process that can allow a dominant market group to affect the outcomes and steer the process in a direction where distribution of costs and benefits will favour their own interests. Hence, as a consequence, standards developed in such a manner may have negative impact on competition.[121]

Deliberations on the effect of standardisation on competition can, to a large extent, be transferred to the international arena and applied to competition between companies located in different countries. In this context, the influence of standardisation may be twofold. On the one hand, standards contribute to the spreading of technological information and research and development, allowing producers from regions that could not afford such expertise access to innovation and modern techniques. Frequently, however, due to high adaptation costs, this can be a double-edged sword, as producers from less developed states who did not take part in the standardisation process may simply not be able to afford the implementation of standards, and may consequently be in a disadvantaged position. Standards can also increase the competitiveness of domestic products and economies in general, by improving the quality of goods produced according to an approved standard, as well as by increasing perceptions of the quality of those products both nationally and abroad. Form another perspective, however, standards can have a restrictive effect on trade and competition and can be a competitive handicap for some trade partners against the others. Lastly, standardisation may lead to a reduction of product diversity and, as a consequence, can reduce incentives for international trade.[122]

4.2. *The Role of Standards in Transnational Safety Regulation*

The use of new regulatory strategies that promote coordination of differing national legislative requirements has swiftly gained momentum within the transnational trade governance system. Both Europe's and the WTO's systems have chosen standardisation as a regulatory tool in many areas involving risks to consumers, and in both forums similar problems arise.

---

[121] K Blind, *The Economics of Standards. Theory, Evidence, Policy* (Edward Elgar Publishing, Cheltenham 2004) 43–44.

[122] Ibid 45–49.

4.2.1. *The Origins of International Safety Standards and Their Application*

4.2.1.1. *Standards and the Common Market*

The phenomenon of standardisation is not foreign to the European market. Since the launching in 1985 of the New Approach program, technical standardisation has gradually been introduced in areas formerly regulated by detailed, project-specific directives, in order to replace the previous inefficient system. The New Approach delegated the task of standard-setting to a number of self-regulating organisations. Technical specifications adopted by European standardisation bodies are not legally binding, but create a presumption on the side of the national authorities that products manufactured in accordance with those specifications comply with essential health and safety requirements, in accordance with the relevant New Approach directive.[123] There are, thus, three basic elements of the New Approach philosophy in Europe. Firstly, directives are limited to regulating essential requirements for products. Secondly, they are no longer adopted for each and every type of product, but have a horizontal character and cover entire sectors of products. Thirdly, technical specifications for products are drawn by recognised standardisation bodies such as CEN and CENELEC, and compliance with national standards implementing the harmonised standards developed by those bodies produces a presumption of conformity with the essential requirement of the directive, so that the products in question can circulate freely through the entire common market. Although the application of standards remains voluntary, the producer who chooses other means of securing compliance with essential requirements may face additional tests and certification procedures.[124]

4.2.1.2. *Standards in International Trade*

Similarly, at the international level, in the context of global trade regulation, highly specialised technical issues requiring professional knowledge and expertise are dealt with by means of standardisation. Just to mention a handful of examples, the International Organisation for Standardisation (ISO),[125] founded in 1926 and comprising of more than 100 national members,[126] develops international standards in a large number of highly technical product areas.

---

[123] Compare G Majone, *Dilemmas of European Integration* ... (n 101) 102–106; for a more detailed analysis, see H Schepel, *The Constitution of Private Governance* ... (n 108) 64–66, and MP Egan, *Constructing a European Market* ... (n 99) 133–165.

[124] For a more detailed analysis, see H Schepel, ibid 64–70, 225–258.

[125] It was in fact established under the name of the International Federation of National Standardising Association, and has used its current name since 1946.

[126] They are: 94 full national members, 37 correspondent members and 15 subscriber members. For figures and details on the different types of states, see H Schepel, *The Constitution of Private Governance* ... (n 108) 183, and the documents referred to there.

Under the umbrella of the WTO, the Technical Barriers to Trade Agreement (TBT) and the Agreement on Application of Sanitary and Phyto-sanitary Measures (SPS) aim to lift international trade barriers by relying on international standards. Those standards, however, have to be distinguished from the technical standards as developed by CEN and CENELEC in Europe, and internationally by ISO, due to a number of significant features, which will be discussed in this chapter.

The SPS Agreement, which is the more relevant for my field of research, contains a strict obligation for its members to base their measures on international standards, guidelines and recommendations, and it contains a positive presumption of conformity: namely, measures that conform to international standards are presumed to be necessary to protect human, animal or plant life. All measures ought to be based on scientific principles, and cases that diverge from international standards can only be allowed if the member state in question provides sufficient scientific justification for such a decision.[127]

As for the sources of international standards, the SPS Agreement identifies three intergovernmental standards organisations: the World Organization for Animal Health, previously L'Office International des Epizooties (OIE) for measures related to animal health and zoonoses affecting both animal and human health; the International Plant Protection Convention (IPPC) for measures pertaining to plant health; and the Codex Alimentarius Commission (CAC, the Codex) for measures relating to food safety. The three organisations receive prominence through recognition of standards they set, as a basis for alleged compliance with the SPS.[128] The Codex Alimentarius Commission will receive special attention here, as the most important one for this study.

The Codex Alimentarius Commission was established by the United Nations Food and Agriculture Organisation (FAO) and the World Health Organisation (WHO) in 1962, with the aim of implementing a joint food standards program and developing a set of product-specific standards, guidelines and codes of conduct to protect the health of consumers and guarantee fair trade. As its focus was highly technical, its activity went generally unnoticed by the broader international community until 1994, when, with the establishment of the WTO, the Codex's standards gained a new importance as benchmarks in international food safety disputes, under the provisions of the SPS Agreement.

---

[127] See Article 3 of the SPS Agreement, and, for its interpretation in the *Hormones* case, *European Communities—Measures Concerning Meat and Meat Products (Hormones)*, Report of the Appellate Body, adopted 13 February 1998 (n 70)

[128] For more details on the provision in question and the three organisations, see T Josling, D Roberts, D Orden, *Food Regulation and Trade: Toward a Safe and Open Global System* (Institute for International Economics, Washington DC 2004) 40–44.

Currently, the Codex covers 165 member states, as well as a large number of non-voting international governmental and nongovernmental organisations, and its work is organised around a system of committees that deal with particular thematic areas. Here, the most important feature distinguishing the CAC and its standards from the technical standards setting bodies (CEN, CENELEC, ISO) and their activity, should be emphasised. In contrast to the technical standards setting bodies, which are composed of stakeholders and function as private organisation, the CAC consists of member states, assisted by scientific bodies, which makes it more of a public organisation, governed by a completely different set of rules, and to a large extent political in nature. Consequently, 'products' of the two types of standard-setting bodies differ significantly in their characteristics and impact.[129]

In the context of its role in developing international food safety standards, there are two major sources of criticism about the Codex that are relevant for this study. Firstly, it is often argued that, although it formally serves the dual purpose of protecting the health of consumers and promoting free trade, generally trade interests prevail.[130] Secondly, it is claimed that although Codex standards are deemed international, they are often merely a reflection of the bargaining power of a set of well-known, mostly developed countries.[131] Differences in technical and economic development between the advanced countries and the less-developed states are, thus, not adequately reflected in the standardisation process, which may then lead to *de facto* discrimination and the prevention of those who lack the facilities to meet the set standards from competing in the world market.[132]

Another interesting problem to be discussed in this context is the legitimisation of standards by the WTO; in this case, the legitimisation of the international standards developed by the CAC. It needs to be emphasised that by recognising the Codex as the relevant standard-setting organisation in the area of food safety, the SPS Agreement has performed a form of positive harmonisation, by which Codex standards, guidelines and recommendations are used as points of reference for evaluating the consistency of national regulations with

---

[129] Detailed analysis of the CAC and its activity in MD Masson-Matthee, *The Codex Alimentarius Commission...* (n 83).

[130] For details on the CAC mandate see Statutes of the Codex Alimientarius Commission in Procedural Manual of the Codex Alimentarius Commission, 15th edition, Section I, Article 1, available at: <http://www.codexalimentarius.net>, and for criticism of the practical application of its provisions see for example: DL Post, 'Standards and Regulatory Capitalism: The Diffusion of Food Safety Standards in Developing Countries' (2005) 598 *Annals of the American Academy of Political and Social Science* 170.

[131] DL Post, 'Standards and regulatory Capitalism ...' ibid 171; J Braithwaite, P Drahos, *Global Business Regulation* (Cambridge University Press, Cambridge 2000) 602–603.

[132] CD Sullivan, *Standards and Standardization* ... (n 102) 11.

the WTO. Hence, as the Codex is assigned the task of scientifically evaluating risk, risk management and standards formulation, which in reality means determining internationally acceptable levels of risk, its activity has been given recognition and has become integrated in the governance process under the umbrella of the WTO.[133] Consequently, the SPS Agreement makes it very difficult for a member to depart from the substantial equivalence approach prescribed in the Codex Guidelines. As members can depart from the Codex's standards only when sufficient scientific evidence is provided, the standards are practically binding. Because of the enhanced status of its standards under the SPS Agreement, one might expect the CAC to provide sufficient legitimacy for carrying out such advanced regulatory tasks.[134] It appears, however, as Herwig's interesting analysis shows, that neither substantive nor procedural legitimacy are at a premium in this case. From the substantive point of view, the mandate of the Codex remains rather limited—to factors relevant for health protection and trade impact of SPS measures. This implies that other relevant factors, such as environmental costs, collective preferences or ethical considerations, cannot be considered. It is, thus, evident that the way the Codex integrates the cost–benefit analysis and normative considerations into its governance procedures has relative deficiencies. From a procedural legitimacy perspective, on the other hand, it can be observed that there is significant inequality of participation by non-business organisations of civil society in the CAC regulatory procedures, which puts industry representatives in a much more influential position. The same is true for representation of developing countries, which are often restricted by financial and structural impediments from exercising their participation rights. Existing differences in technical and financial resources between those states and the representatives of the developed world preclude them from representing their interests and concerns in the standardisation procedures on an equal footing, and reduce their influence on the adopted measures.[135] Thus, it seems that the role and importance that have indirectly been assigned to the Codex under the SPS Agreement in determining food safety regulations for the WTO members lack solid legitimacy, and promote international standards, which are more 'private' than a first glance might suggest.

---

[133] A Herwig, 'Taking Pluralism Seriously—How the WTO should Regulate Food Safety and Consumer Choice Aspects of Trade in Genetically Modified Foods', Thesis submitted for the JSD degree at New York University School of Law, September 2005, 87; see also F Veggeland, SO Borgen, 'Negotiating International Food Safety Standards: The World Trade Organization's Impact on the Codex Alimentarius Commission' (2005) 18 *Governance: An International Journal of Policy, Administration, and Institutions* 675–708.

[134] A Herwig, 'Taking Pluralism Seriously ...' ibid 91–92.

[135] Ibid 92–97.

4.2.2. *The Market Implications of International Standardisation, and the Question of Compensation*

As the preceding paragraphs argue, international standards recognised and legitimised by international trade organisations are sometimes developed by a minority of strong states,[136] and enforced on less-developed countries without regard to their socioeconomic situation. Frequently, the less privileged trade partners have little or no influence on the setting of standards and have few resources for their implementation. This can have far-reaching consequences on the economies and societies of those states. If standards are unilaterally imposed on poor states without offering them either some degree of moderation or financial support, the consequences can be twofold. The states may choose to not comply with the standards and so risk trade restrictions, or they implement standards against their national economic rationality at the cost of other sectors of their economy and, in the longer run-citizens. Although the issue is given very little attention in Europe, where scientific and consumer safety discourse have dominated the discussion, it has already been recognised in some academic analyses of the WTO.

Trachtman, for example, raises the problem of market foreclosure for developing countries, which may lack the capacity to participate in the formation of international standards and the resources to comply with them.[137] He argues that international trade arrangements should avoid placing poor states in disadvantaged positions, or requiring excessive expenditure from their own limited resources. He foresees the possibility of technical assistance arrangements that could help to prevent possible damage to their economies, which would otherwise occur as a result of standard-implementation. Howse and Regan go even further in their critique, simply asking who should pay for the internalisation of standards; they envisage the possibility of assistance for poorer states.[138] In Europe, these aspects of standardisation seem to have been disregarded somewhat. There is pre-accession assistance for adjustment, but states that have become members are expected to provide the same level of compliance, regardless of any discrepancies in economic and technical development, which with the last two accessions were greater than ever before.

---

[136] See DL Post, 'Standards and Regulatory Capitalism ...' (n130) 171, where the author discusses the discrepancy between formal membership and practical participation in the development of standards in the Codex Alimentarius Commission.

[137] JP Trachtman, 'Embedding Mutual Recognition ...' (n 23) 794–795; see also JP Trachtman, 'International Trade as a Vector in Domestic Regulatory Reform: Discrimination, Cost-Benefit Analysis, and Negotiations' in K-H Ladeur (ed), *Public Governance in the Age of Globalization* (Ashgate, Aldershot 2004) 289–304; TW Schillhorn van Veen, 'International Trade and Food Safety in Developing Countries' (2005) 16 *Food Control* 491–496.

[138] R Howse and D Regan, 'The Product/Process Distinction—An Illusory Basis for Disciplining "Unilateralism" in Trade Policy' (2002) 11 *European Journal of International Law* 282.

In the European context, a very interesting analysis has been undertaken of Polish EU accession and its harmonisation of standards for the production of pork, which clearly illustrates the potential consequences of the blind imposition of unified standards and the possible 'Trojan' character of this type of approach.[139] Dunn's analysis shows how standards can fail to create the expected harmonisation effect. She examines the way in which international standards are embedded in local social, institutional and historical contexts, and how, by reducing trade barriers which are targeted by standards, new unintended ones can be created. This happens because standards are more than just simple technical rules; they are complex technologies that regulate social and ethical behaviour in capitalist markets, and when they enter specific local circumstances, with a particular context and legacy, they become geographically variable and produce unique regulatory landscapes rather than the intended uniformity.[140] They create different costs for different localities and for different producers within each local setting. They impose unequal burdens and contribute to the creation of entirely new settings, when new barriers to trade appear where they are least expected and new constellations of privilege are created. In Dunn's view, the current rhetoric of standards leads to an overestimation of potential risks to human and animal life and health, while it underestimates the high costs that SPS measures pose for local economies.[141]

5. Conclusions: Balancing Incentives in Regulatory Reform

In the above evaluation of the three regulatory mechanisms, I showed that each mechanism responds to different sets of needs, corresponds to different objectives and follows a different set of values. To put it briefly, one could express the relationships thus: standardisation—unification; mutual recognition—preservation of essential requirements while respecting and promoting diversity; scientific risk regulation—technocratic approach to risk regulatory decision-making in order to arrive at a universal and value-immune judgement. This is a simplification, of course, but it helps to identify the differences mentioned above, and to classify the regulatory mechanisms for the sake of my analysis.

All three approaches are useful and have important roles to play in the regulation of the common market. They are not exclusive, but can be used with

[139] EC Dunn, 'Trojan Pig: Paradoxes of Food Safety Regulation' (2003) 35 *Environment and Planning A* 1493–1511.
[140] EC Dunn, 'Trojan Pig ...' ibid 1494–1495.
[141] Ibid 1501–1502.

various degrees of intensity in different market areas where their objectives are best aligned with the aims of the regulator in that particular field.

The goals of optimal regulation should be to ensure that no single mechanism overshadows the others in the overall regulation of the market, and occupies areas whose sets of perspectives do not correspond to what the mechanism can offer. Europe, throughout the development of the internal market, seems to have been shifting from one regulatory approach to another, rather than distributing their application accordingly. That is a pity, as a multiplicity of tools would allow the system to respond to the multiplicity of challenges posed by the common market, and it would be a great benefit to be able to pick the best-fitting regulatory option for each area. Especially now, when internal and external challenges make the management of the European market particularly difficult, one should be able to consider all the available regulatory solutions.

To summarise the relevant ideas about the values and objectives that the three analysed legal mechanisms represent, I will now recapitulate briefly my findings about each.

First, let us return to mutual recognition. The principle of mutual recognition, also referred to as functional parallelism or functional equivalence, is an intermediate device that helps reconcile tensions stemming from regulatory diversity in an integrated market,[142] as it disciplines states to reciprocally accept the equivalence of protection granted by a foreign legal system. Thus, it trespasses the traditional national–international dichotomy, creating a transnational meta-norm that aims to reconcile differences in the national legislations of various trade partners in the globalised market. In contemporary circumstances, an automatic application of mutual recognition is relatively rare. Instead, various forms of managed mutual recognition apply, under which states retain some degree of their vestigial powers.[143]

The value of mutual recognition, as presented in my analysis above, is that it is the most sensitive and least intrusive mechanism of market regulation. It allows a balance to be retained between the common requirement for protection, on the one hand, and local preferences and the circumstances of diverse societies and states, on the other. Moreover, the sensitivity of mutual recognition also applies to the economic sphere. Here, mutual recognition allows economies that are more developed and financially stronger to accept higher production costs, expecting their willing and able consumers to pay for the extra quality they gain, while allowing states that are less well-off to retain the regulatory stage they can afford. Even more so, it allows less developed states

[142] JHH Weiler, 'Mutual Recognition, Functional Equivalence and Harmonization …' (n 4) 25–26.

[143] K Nikolaidis, 'Globalization with Human Faces …' (n 5) 129–189.

to take advantage of their specific economic circumstances, with lower labour costs or cheaper commodities, for example, and to use those extra benefits for the betterment of their economic performance, instead of pushing them to invest in technologies they do not have the resources for.

Turning to the values represented and the regulatory objectives served, mutual recognition brings flexibility, sensitivity, openness and inclusiveness. In its modern form, it manages to fulfil its regulatory role of coordinating market regulation, but without implying uniform regulatory practices, and consequently it avoids excessive intrusion into the legal and economic systems of states. Thus, it seems to offer a relevant opportunity in terms of the regulatory reform direction, and it is one I would like to be considered more widely.

A different set of values and objectives can be identified in connection with the contemporary use of scientific risk analysis methods in market regulation. Risk regulation has been defined in academic literature as a method of interfering in market behaviours and social processes with the aim of controlling potentially adverse consequences to health or the environment.[144] In its archetypical form, risk analysis for the sake of regulation comprises three basic elements—risk assessment, risk management and risk communication. Risk assessment represents the provision of technical knowledge by scientifically informed specialists; risk management refers to regulatory decisions taken by politically accountable entities on the basis of that assessment and taking into account other valid concerns. As I have systematically emphasised, the practical application of this model is far from the archetype. Not only are the boundaries between assessment and management far from clear, but, more importantly, the management phase does not always fulfil its role of gathering and weighing the various interests and concerns *vis a vis* scientific considerations; instead, it tends to blindly follow the recommendations of scientists. Science, however, has not always been able to reach appropriate levels of objectivity and universality in its analysis of the increasingly complex problems of food safety. On the contrary, both in the European as well as in the international regulatory context, science has occasionally become part of the problem rather than the solution. This tendency has been further exacerbated by the growing importance of scientific technology in food production, which has increased even more the significance of science in regulatory procedures. This development, too, has confronted scientists with questions to which they have not always been able to find unanimous answers.[145]

---

[144] For more, see C Hood, H Rothstein and R Baldwin, *The Government of Risk …* (n 52) 3–19.

[145] K-H Ladeur, 'The Introduction of the Precautionary Principle into the EU Law: a Pyrrhic Victory for Environmental and Public Health Law? Decision-Making under Conditions of Complexity in Multi-Level Political Systems' (2003) 40 *Common Market Law Review* 1462–1463.

My main criticism of the method, which I presented above, pertains to its one-dimensional character, which allows technical science to dominate regulatory decision-making and remain blind to other considerations. Following the logic of science, legislators have put enormous emphasis on improving the quality of the science involved in regulatory decision-making, but also the ways in which this inclusion takes place and the procedural guarantees of transparency, professionalism and impartiality, leaving aside the most consequential of all—the management side of the process. A strong emphasis on reforming the provision of expertise and the conditions of scientific assessment has, naturally, strengthened this aspect of the procedure. Consequently, decision-makers in the management phase tend to blindly follow the decisions of risk assessors, which are based solely on science. This phenomenon leads to a situation where science is the only basis for a regulatory decision, and other values, of economic, social or ethical character, have little chance of being considered. As a consequence, science can now become such a strong foundation that risk managers will find it difficult to provide arguments based on any other values and interests, which should ideally be taken into consideration in a regulatory procedure. In such a situation, deciding against the findings of risk assessment can become very problematic, if not impossible. This, as a consequence, can create a situation where non-scientific arguments—or, perhaps, insufficiently scienticised arguments—are not given due consideration and recognition. Instead, established, traditional science will dominate the decision-making process to such a degree that it becomes its only overriding rationale, despite the fact that decisions might have to be made about problems that have not been exhaustively treated by such traditional science. Basing decisions solely on science is not only contrary to common sense; it is also—and more importantly—against the established and approved rules of risk regulation, according to which the risk management phase should take precedence over the scientific risk assessment phase, and deliver decisions based on all relevant values. Among these relevant values we find societal concerns, the social and economic impact of regulation, and consumer preferences.

This has far-fetched consequences for market regulation, especially in such a science-intensive and yet sensitive area as food safety. Risk regulation, as much as any other aspect of the market, has to be embedded in the social structure that gave rise to it and that contextualises its existence and development. Disconnecting risk regulation from its social basis causes a gradual disembedding of the market in which it is exercised, which in effect deprives it of social legitimacy and is detrimental for the market generally. This, in my opinion, is definitely not the path Europe should follow.

With regard to the values of and objectives it represents, risk regulation through scientific lens tries to offer security, universality and professionalism.

As I have argued, however, contemporary circumstances significantly diminish the capability of this type of regulation to actually achieve those objectives. Instead, we might end up with decision-making based on ambiguous quasi-scientific assumptions, without taking account of any other considerations, be they social, economic or environmental. It seems, therefore, that this type of regulation is no longer able to respond to the wider catalogues of needs of the contemporary European market. In my view, scientific risk regulation still serves as an important and inevitable element of the regulatory framework, but its shape and implementation should be reconsidered in order for it to be compliant with the model it is based on, as well as to be better embedded in the market it serves. One way to achieve this would be through the improvement of the management phase, so that it actually takes into consideration a wider scope of values and interests. Another important improvement would be the introduction of some form of concern-assessment,[146] which has already been advocated in the literature but has still not sufficiently made its way onto the political agenda.

Finally, let me summarise my observations about the values and objectives of regulation by means of standardisation. Standardisation is an important element of the new wave of voluntary self-constraining regulatory mechanisms, which, as a rule, are meant to provide a minimum level of uniformity and contribute to the improvement of market-efficiency, and which emerged as a response to the expansion of new technologies, as well as to the growing dynamics of market conditions. In demanding transnational circumstances, such a coordinative private–public regulatory exercise offers a wide range of advantages.

Firstly, as standardisation operates in an environment of advanced expertise and technical knowledge, it can rely on them to a greater extent than any public institution. Simultaneously, operating closer to the stakeholders, it can be more responsive to their needs, and more flexible and adjustable to changing circumstances. Finally, as private rulemaking, it is less formalised and can therefore be expected to be more efficient. On the other hand, however, standardisation raises a number of important concerns. Firstly, its legitimacy can be questioned, and it can be contested whether the delegation of responsibility for the safety of citizens to private organisations can be accepted whatsoever.

[146] See, for example, the work of the SAFE FOOD group, as well as the work of the International Risk Governance Council, which will be discussed in more detail later in this study; see M Dreyer and O Renn (eds), *Food Safety Governance: Integrating Science, Precautions and Public Involvement* (Springer-Verlag, Berlin Heidelberg 2009) and the International Risk Governance Council (IRGC), 'Policy Brief: Appropriate Risk Governance Strategies for Nanotechnology Applications in Food and Cosmetics', Geneva 2009 <http://www.irgc.org/IMG/pdf/IRGC_Report_FINAL_For_Web.pdf> accessed 25 May 2011.

Contemporarily, however, public involvement in the overall standardisation process diminishes the relevance of these concerns. Another important set of concerns has to do with the notion of the 'voluntariness' of standards, indicating that standards are free to be observed or disregarded. In practice, however, when a society places a high value on conformity, and when a considerable part of it accepts a common standard, the others will almost automatically be expected to follow, and those who neglect it will sooner or later find themselves disadvantaged. Hence, a standard adopted as voluntary by an unforced action of a group of interested parties will become much less voluntary when successfully put into practice.[147]

Therefore, despite the possible first impression, the objective that standardisation pursues is in fact unification. In transnational situation, such common standards are often imposed on less-developed countries without regard to their socioeconomic situation. This can have far-reaching consequences for the markets and economies of those states, which often have no say in standard-setting, and have no resources for their implementation in any case. If standards are unilaterally imposed on poorer states without offering them either some degree of moderation or financial support, the consequences may be twofold. The states may choose to not comply with the standards and then risk trade restrictions, or they can implement standards against their national economic rationality, to the cost of other sectors of the economy and citizens.

International trade organisations such as the WTO and the EU justify their strong regulatory reliance on standards by referring to their duty of ensuring, by reliance on scientific principles, that all competitors are subjected to an equal regulatory burden. Their claim, however, that standards create a level playing field for all competitors must be questioned. The research presented here suggests a contrary observation. Harmonised standards can only lead to the creation of regulatory homogeneity on a limited scale. This is primarily due to the fact that international standards are always embedded in local social, economic and institutional circumstances. Moreover, externally imposed standards can often function as 'Trojan horses', entering specific regulatory environments and local sets of conditions, and then producing unintended side-effects.[148] This is partly because international standards are more than just scientifically developed technical rules of market organisation; they also intervene in particular local societal and economic situations and attempt to regulate ethical market behaviours. Hence, markets created by standards are, in fact, different from place to place, depending on the circumstances under which they are implemented. Thus, they create unique regulatory landscapes

---

147 Compare CD Sullivan, *Standards and Standardization …* (n 102) 8–10.

148 EC Dunn, 'Trojan Pig …' (n 139) 1494.

instead of a uniform regulatory environment. From an economic point of view, the prospect of the creation of a level playing field for all competitors in the standardised market is also an illusion. Standards implemented in different locations impose burdens that are definitely unequal, and create costs that are significantly different for different producers, depending on the specific circumstances in which each operates. The long-term effects of such developments, in both the economic and social spheres, cannot be easily foreseen but should definitely be considered.

Standardisation aims to unify market practices by providing a certain degree of flexibility, but only with regard to technological progress and market development, rather than to the specific circumstances of the local markets where the standards are applied. When applied in translational settings and without any countervailing mechanisms, which would negotiate the side-effects of standards for less-developed trade partners, standards can contribute to the gradual disembeddedness of market regulation, applying common solutions in dramatically different sets of circumstances, which were often not considered when developing the standard in question. It has to be acknowledged that, in many market areas, especially those involving high technical specialisation, standardisation has proven to be relatively successful at achieving its objectives. Nevertheless, its success always comes at a price, and its costs are not spread evenly among market participants; often they are too high for some participants to bear. Moreover, as it has been argued, in areas such as food safety, unification may not always be the optimal regulatory outcome.

Before I move on to examining these three regulatory tools in practice, I would like to make a couple of more general comments.

By analysing the three instruments, which are in fact currently in use in the European common market, one can see how they serve different purposes and follow different sets of objectives. Since they coexist and are not exclusive, one can imagine their selective application in those areas whose regulatory objectives are similar to those represented by each of those mechanisms. By such means, one could more easily achieve an intended result and minimise any unintended side-effects. A multiplicity of needs and values requires the application of a multiplicity of legislative mechanisms. The goal is to develop such mode and degree of their application that the system answers properly to the challenges at stake without having to jump to grand new reform whenever a problem arises. Looking at the three regulatory tools through the perspective of the sets of values they represent can help one to reach a legal situation where a balance of values, as well as the flexibility of the system to respond to challenging developments, can be achieved. It seems, however, that European legislators often apply one-dimensional logic, and prefer reforms that can be 'tagged' and that represent a common solution for a large number of market areas, without account being taken of the specificity of a given field, or of the achievements and risks of the regulatory options at stake.

As all the three forms of regulation discussed have, in various time periods and with differing intensity, been used to regulate EU markets, including the regulation of foodstuffs, it is useful to observe how the development of food legislation progressed, as it shifted between different forms of governance. It is particularly important to analyse the objectives behind each regulatory change, and how the regulatory mechanisms discussed above found their way into and out of the regulatory framework. Those changes, their aims and their consequences will be the object of the next chapter, which provides an analysis of the evolution of food regulation in the EU.

CHAPTER THREE

WAYS AND MEANS OF REGULATING FOOD SAFETY IN EUROPE

1. Introduction

1.1. *An Evolutionary Analysis of Food Safety Legislation in Europe*

In the following paragraphs I present an evolutionary analysis of the development of the legislative and regulatory structures in the field of food safety in Europe. Departing from the assumptions assembled on the basis of the theoretical considerations of the previous chapter, I look at the evolution of legislative attitudes towards the regulation of foodstuffs, studying the changing rationale that motivates it, shifts in the application of various legal instruments, and their implications on the market. Finally, I discuss the driving forces of the regulatory reforms of European food safety legislation. I examine how the European legislative framework responded to existing concerns and tensions, in order to find out how the ideas of market integration and the problematic specificity of diversified food products were weighed up against one another in the process leading towards a final regulatory outcome.

From an evolutionary perspective, European food safety regulation can be perceived as an ideal example of the development of EU policies, being one that illustrates both the quintessence and the meanderings of the 'European project'. Food-safety regulation has followed mainstream thinking about the EU and its role in national legal systems. It mirrored current streams of regulatory approaches and, thus, it was bound to be guided by not only their principles but also by their mistakes. Through decades, it seemed to have functioned quite smoothly, but the number of omitted problems and mistakes was rising, reaching a peak during the BSE crisis of the 1990s, which probably changed ways of thinking about food-safety regulation in Europe forever. A clear dividing line between 'before' and 'after' is commonly observed in the literature and, to a large extent, will be visible in this volume as well. Here, however, the EU food-safety problem is approached at a different level, referring to questions that were not challenged by the BSE crisis and were therefore not discussed and resolved during the post-BSE reforms. Hence, EU food safety regulation will be approached from the perspective not only of regulation of risk, but also of regulation of the market.

The following paragraphs return to the roots of the problem and trace food safety regulation to its agricultural background, more specifically to its regulation under the umbrella of the Common Agricultural Policy. The consequences of legislating food under the agricultural scheme are discussed with regard to the legal instruments used, the regulatory problems tackled, as well as aims and effects of application of field-specific regulatory mechanisms. Furthermore, the consequences of the regulatory separation of food from agriculture, and the transformation towards governing food under the general product harmonisation scheme, are also analysed. The analysis examines, in particular, the functional differentiation of agricultural and non-agricultural food regulations, paying special attention to how it addressed social and economic challenges. It will follow further developments and mal-developments of food legislation through the different phases of market integration and policy proposals before the BSE outbreak. The different legal mechanisms that were used in different phases of the building of the common market are analysed, in order to assess their impact on the area of foodstuffs.

The study then examines the breakdown of the pure product approach to food, which culminated in the outbreak of the BSE pandemic, as well as the reforms propelled by the BSE crisis. By those means, this chapter indicates yet another shift of thinking in European food regulation: from being purely market-oriented, it developed towards a greater reflection of consumer concerns and concentrated on the safety paradigm. The legal and institutional reforms in the aftermath of the BSE crisis are reviewed, with the aim of assessing their ability to respond to the challenges with which the European regulatory framework was presented, as well as their effectiveness in serving a broader set of objectives valid in the contemporary phase of the development of the EU. From that perspective, the analysis discusses problems that were not tackled in the post-BSE reforms, and links them to other challenges and sets of factors that influence the development of the European legal system as a whole.

Finally, the concluding paragraphs review the existing regulatory instruments, which allow for the inclusion of social concerns in other fields of European market regulation. Traces of such an approach can in fact be found in the new chemicals regulation under the REACH system. Channels of including 'the social' in REACH regulation are then analysed in more detail, to establish whether they can be treated as models, and whether a similar mechanism could be applied in the field of the European food regulation.

1.2. *The Background: The Evolution of the Common Market*

Food is a part of our culture. The way we define it and conceptualise it in our everyday lives is shaped by our traditions. Food is linked to the history of our countries, their geographical and climatic conditions and their social circumstances. We care for it and have opinions about it not only because we enjoy it, but also because we cannot do without it, and because what we eat affects our life and health. That is also why we have our ideas about what 'good food' or 'safe food' is, and generally we are not willing to compromise on them easily.

Food, however, although undeniably specific and very important, is just one of many categories of products circulating on the European common market. An analysis of the specificity and importance of food regulation would, thus, be incomplete and out of context if not set against the background of the development of the common market. Therefore, before presenting the evolution of food regulation, this introduction offers a short overview of the history of European market integration, highlighting those milestones which guided the development of food legislation.

The establishment of the freedom of movement of goods required that both tariff and non-tariff barriers to trade between member states be eliminated. The development of a policy to eliminate quantitative restrictions and measures having equivalent effect was twofold, and involved what Craig and de Burca refer to as 'interconnection between judicial and legislative initiatives for attaining the Community's objectives'.[1] Thus, on the one hand, the jurisprudence of the ECJ on Articles 34–36 TFEU (ex Articles 28–30 TEC) cases, following the landmark *Cassis de Dijon*[2] judgement, introduced the concept of mutual recognition, which enabled market integration that respects differences in national regulatory regimes. Simultaneously, legislative action was undertaken at the European level to harmonise those aspects of national legislations which could not be resolved by the mutual recognition exercise, as they involved protection of important public interests, and where the establishment of commonly accepted minimum standards was desirable. The complexity and density of harmonising legislation, however, grew so enormously that, a couple of years later, the Commission had to revise its initial position and come up with a new, more efficient and less engaging strategy for the completion of the common market. The New Approach to Technical Harmonization and Standardization[3] established a sort of bridge between the two logics and developed a new transnational mode of governance, in which the essential safety requirements for products were laid down in harmonising European legislation, while the task of providing technical details was delegated to non-state standardisation bodies at the European and national levels.

---

[1] P Craig and G de Burca, *EU Law. Texts, Cases and Materials* (Third Edition Oxford University Press, Oxford 2003) 614.

[2] Case C 120/78 *Rewe-Zentral AG v. Bundesmonopolverwaltung fur Branntwein* [1979] ECR 649 (Cassis de Dijon). Both the judgement itself and the development of the freedom of movement of products regulations will be analysed in more detail in Section 2 of this chapter.

[3] Commission (EC), The New Approach to Technical Harmonization and Standardization, COM (85) 19 final, 31 January 1985.

The public–private partnership in the development of product-safety regulation was, however, not the only case of such specialised delegation in areas of high technical complexity. The establishment of the committee system, which assists the Commission in performing its delegated legislative duties, constitutes another development that marked the transition of the European regulatory system towards an opening-up of the law to other disciplines and a sophisticated proceduralisation of their relations. The committee system gives structure to the transfer of knowledge into the realm of law, through the organised cooperation and deliberation of field experts appointed by member states in areas such as safety and consumer protection, which additionally facilitates the acceptance and implementation of European measures by giving member states a sense of participation and control over European developments.

Perhaps even more advanced development in the field of technocratic and national involvement in supranational governance is the phenomenon of 'agencification', which is manifested through the participation of specialised bodies in the European regulatory process. Here, European agencies, contrary to their American 'regulatory' archetypes, are not independent law-making entities, but rather auxiliary bodies of the Commission, which provide the necessary expertise in specialised fields, gather and spread information within the network of national counterparts, and sometimes perform minor administrative functions such as licensing.

This brief overview of the major developments within the system of product regulation, as short and as simplified as it can be, serves simply as a background for my specific field of study: the development of food regulation in Europe. All the problems highlighted in the paragraph above are given due attention in the following parts of this chapter, in the particular context of food.

2. The Legacy of an Agricultural Past versus the Implications of the Market-Integration Rationale

A common EU food policy never was an intentional, carefully planned project on the European agenda. On the contrary, food regulation was emerging on the outskirts of other EU undertakings. This is probably one of the reasons why neither a far-reaching program nor real comprehensiveness was ever at a premium. To a large extent, at least at the beginning, it was more a matter of adventure and of *ad hoc* action than of strategy.

The Treaty of Rome did not originally contain any reference to food issues. Some of the Treaty provisions, however, indirectly required the regulation of particular aspects of the foodstuffs field. These were mainly questions of agricultural production and of free trade. On the one hand, the Treaty called for a unified approach to organising the production and marketing of agricultural products, and on the other, the Single Market provisions envisaged the elimination of trade barriers, in order to allow the free circulation of goods from all member states throughout the EU.[4] These two Treaty goals, in combination, demanded some harmonisation of national laws on foodstuffs, and, at the same time, they shaped the initial stages of European food regulation. This particular decoupling, which left food policy issues hanging between two contrasting market-regulation paradigms—namely, interventionist and 'total regulation' agricultural scheme on the one hand, and a free-market rationale on the other—has left a schizophrenic legacy in food regulation and has contributed to its fragmentation along the lines of product and production-process divisions, and separation between the production of primary resources and the final products. Consequently, in order to trace the EU foodstuffs regime back to its roots and to understand its problematic nature, one has to look simultaneously at the development of the two Treaty rationales within food regulation, and to analyse their influences and consequences. The first aspect of the development of the EU food law and policy, its agricultural background, will be the subject of the following paragraphs, while the Single Market aspect will be evaluated later in this chapter.

2.1. *The Early Days of Regulation: Food Regulation as Part of an Agricultural Scheme*

2.1.1. *The Specificity of the Common Agricultural Policy*

2.1.1.1. *The Treaty Foundations of Agricultural Policy*

Agriculture has always been afforded a special status in the EU, which has been justified by the large degree of 'exceptionalism' attached to that sector. Inelasticity in demand, risks connected with production, and, above all, food's fundamental importance to national interests all served to rationalise the shape and scope of European agricultural regulation. Its foundations in the Treaty of Rome reflect a compromise among the six founding states, balancing the need to secure the political and social participation of disadvantaged social groups, highly protective national farming policies, and the aim of creating common market organisations, which were expected to reduce the risks of agricultural production and to systematise income redistribution. The result of this compromise is a complex system of governance that is neither purely intergovernmental nor genuinely supranational, and which provides, to

[4] C Lister, *Regulation of Food Products by the European Community* (Butterworths, London 1992) 7.

paraphrase Rieger, an 'addition to' rather than 'a subtraction from' the powers of the national political systems.[5]

According to Article 38 of the Treaty of Rome (now Article 38 TFEU), trade in agricultural products should be subject to the same provisions that relate to the establishment and operation of the common market which apply to any other type of product. On the other hand, however, Article 39 (now Article 39 TFEU) differentiated the matter seriously, advocating the inclusion of additional considerations of predominantly social nature in the regulatory process. These two provisions constituted a foundation of the complex EU policy in the field of agriculture, which is probably the most ambiguous creature of the EU. The political decision to include non-economic objectives within the framework of an international economic community gave the agricultural policy a specific, separate rationale. Serving economic integration through supranational institutions, but with the inclusion of nationally sensitive social values, has created a mixed mechanism that is not only costly but also, to a large extent, unpredictable, and which additionally causes major problems in international trade relations.[6]

In order to achieve the objectives of the Treaty, the building of a common market for agricultural products was accompanied by the establishment of the Common Agricultural Policy (CAP), which placed agriculture outside the economically strict institutional framework of the common market.[7] As F. Snyder comments in the introduction to his 1985 agricultural law handbook, 'Farm policy ... has sometimes been conceived, formulated and implemented as if the agricultural sector existed in isolation, whereas in fact it is integral to the food chain and society as a whole'.[8]

The Treaty's provisions on agriculture articulated only its general principles and goals, and the process of negotiating detailed rules governing the CAP took another five years to be concluded. The foundations of the CAP can be generalised with reference to six general principles, three of which stem directly from the Treaty, the other three being added by the first wave of agricultural legislation as well as in subsequent interpretations and jurisprudence.[9]

---

[5] E Rieger, 'The Common Agricultural Policy. Politics Against Market' in H Wallace and W Wallace (eds) *Policy-Making in the European Union* (Fourth Edition, Oxford University Press, Oxford 2000) 183.

[6] See the criticism of E Rieger, 'The Common Agricultural Policy ...' ibid 180–181.

[7] Compare E Rieger, 'Protective Shelter or Straitjacket: An Institutional Analysis of the Common Agricultural Policy of the European Union' in S Leibfried and P Pierson (eds), *European Social Policy: Between Fragmentation and Integration* (Brookings, Washington DC 1995) 220; M Cardwell, *The European Model of Agriculture*, (Studies in European Law, Oxford University Press, Oxford 2004) 20–21.

[8] F Snyder, *Law of the Common Agricultural Policy* (Sweet and Maxwell, London 1985) 1.

[9] For a more detailed description of the principles see JA Usher, *EC Agricultural Law* (Oxford EC Law Library, Second Edition Oxford University Press, Oxford 2001) 39–44; F Snyder, ibid 1516.

The Treaty principles provide for (1) the inclusion of agriculture in the common market scheme,[10] (2) exceptions to general Treaty rules with regard to agriculture,[11] and (3) the establishment of a coherent agricultural policy at the EC level.[12] The further three principles, implicit in the Treaty but only explicitly added in secondary regulations and developed by jurisprudence,[13] are (4) the principle of the unity of the market, which was the basis of European pricing regulation, (5) the principle of EC preference,[14] and (6) the principle of financial solidarity.[15]

Although the CAP quickly became 'widely notorious for creating many distortions at both the EU and international level',[16] it must be borne in mind that the CAP did not create interventionist policies in European agricultural economies, but merely transformed mechanism that already existed at the national level. The CAP was implemented through intensive market intervention by means of price supports, infrastructure investments and market-stabilisation mechanisms that assured the continuity of farmers' employment. By the mid-1960s, meat, poultry, eggs and dairy products, as well as rice, grains and many other agricultural goods, were covered by a complex network of 300 EU regulations.[17] Food policy within the CAP, as such, focused on the two most pressing problems: (1) food security, meaning the production of food which is sufficient to satisfy the needs of European consumers, making Europe self-sufficient; and (2) guaranteeing the viability of European agriculture through active market intervention directed towards modernisation and stabilisation.[18] For many years, thus, food safety and health protection were far outside the core objectives; consequently, food policy, if it existed, was dominated by the objectives of the CAP.[19]

The foundations of the CAP have placed agricultural regulation in a values matrix of the common market objectives of Article 38 TFEU and the social ambitions of Article 39 TFEU, which include ensuring a fair standard

---

[10] See Article 38 (1) TFEU.

[11] Article 38 (2) TFEU.

[12] Article 38 (4) TFEU.

[13] See the Commission's interpretation in Commission (EC), *The Agricultural Policy of the European Community*, Third Edition, 1982, 14–15.

[14] See Case 5/67 *Beus v. Hauptzollamt München* [1968] ECR 83, with regard to Article 44 (2).

[15] See Article 2 (2) of Regulation 25/62 on the financing of the common agricultural policy [1962] OJ 30.

[16] B Andreosso-O'Callaghan, *The Economics of European Agriculture* (Palgrave Macmillan, London, New York 2003) 76.

[17] M Carson, 'From Common Market to Social Europe? Paradigm Shift and Institutional Change in European Policy on Food, Asbestos and Chemicals, and Gender Equality' (2004) Acta Universitatis Stockholmiensis, Stockholm Studies in Sociology N.S. 22/2004, 98–99.

[18] M Carson, ibid 98.

[19] T Ugland, F Veggeland, 'Experiments in Food Safety Policy Integration in the European Union' (2006) 44 *Journal of Common Market Studies* 612.

of living for the agricultural community, in particular by increasing the individual earnings of persons engaged in agriculture, on the one hand, and by ensuring that supplies reach consumers at reasonable prices, on the other. Cases of disputes before the ECJ have, from the earliest days, shown that deliberation on and mediation of the conflicting aims of the CAP requires difficult political decisions. In its judgment in *Beus*, the ECJ held that 'these objectives, which are intended to safeguard the interests of both farmers and consumers, may not all be simultaneously and fully attained'.[20] Policy-making in this area, therefore, requires giving temporary priority to certain objectives above certain others, where the choice of current prioritisation is at the discretion of the Commission and the Council. Commentators have pointed out, however, that the choice of a long-term prioritisation has to be relatively consistent with the Treaty's own ranking of objectives. Following such interpretative readings of Article 39 led the ECJ to invoke the priority of the 'social' over the 'economic', as well as the priority of producers' interests over those of consumers.[21]

2.1.1.2. *Decision-Making within the CAP*

The special status of agriculture among EU policies is also reflected in the various advantages it enjoys with regard to the functioning of the legislative process and the bureaucracy.[22] First and foremost, agriculture has its own individual institutional structure. It is equipped with its own Directorate General for Agriculture in the European Commission, and its own Council of Agriculture Ministers, which is handled by its own Special Committee on Agriculture rather than the COREPER. Secondly, agriculture retains a specific relation with the European Parliament. Extension of the EP prerogatives, following the Treaty revisions of Maastricht and Amsterdam, included introduction of the co-decision procedure in many agriculture-related issues, such as environment, public health and consumer protection. Nevertheless, laws passed under Article 43 TFEU (ex Article 37 TEC), which serves as the legal basis for the core of agricultural legislation, remain subject to consultation procedure.[23] Following the same rationale, the role of the ECJ in reviewing those acts is significantly restricted. The ECJ has consistently followed the idea that 'in matters concerning the common agricultural policy, the Community legislator

[20] See C 5/67, *Beus* (n 14) 98.

[21] Compare cases 114/76 *Bela-Mühle Josef Bergmann KG v. Grows-Farm GmbH and Co. KG* [1977] ECR 1211, 1229; 5/73 *Balkan-Import-Export GmbH v. Hauptzollamt Berlin Packhof* [1973] ECR 1091, 1112, as well as comments by F Snyder (n 8) 19–22 and G Druesne, *La Politique Agricole Commune devant la Cour de Justice des Communautés Européennes 1958–1978* (Éditions techniques et économiques, Paris 1980) 13–20.

[22] M Cardwell (n 7) 8–12; JA Usher (n 9) 173–201; and JA McMahon, *Law of the Common Agricultural Policy* (European Law Series, Longman, Harlow 2000) 34–40.

[23] For a more detailed analysis, see M Cardwell, ibid 9.

has a discretionary power which corresponds to the political responsibilities imposed by Articles 40 and 43 (now Articles 40 and 43 TFEU)',[24] and therefore accepts that the ECJ's authority to review such a decision should be limited to 'examining whether it contains a manifest error or constitutes a misuse of power or whether the authority in question did not clearly exceed the bounds of its discretion'.[25]

Both, the institutional structure and the decision-making process illustrate the significance and predominance of national interests in European agricultural regulation. The Council of Agriculture Ministers has retained a strong position, remaining in charge of the most crucial matters. In executing its powers, it has often acted more as an international conference than as an EU institution, giving voice to national interest groups and state agencies.[26] Although after the first transitional phase of the establishment of the CAP, the Council was supposed to start acting by a qualified majority, the empty-chair policy adopted by France led to a continuation of the use of unanimity. Even though this practice has declined since the late 1960s and explicit vetoes are rather rare, the *de facto* requirement of unanimity in decisions on the most pressing agricultural issues, where important national interests are at stake, still shades the picture. The domination of particular interests in the decision-making process of the CAP is additionally strengthened by the activity of the Special Committee on Agriculture, whose role in the preparation and functioning of the Council is crucial, and which is made up of senior agricultural officials from the member states.

Retaining decision-making powers in the most important CAP matters, the Council delegated the implementation of agricultural market rules to the Commission. Within the Commission structures, the protection of national interests is secured by a web of committees, which assist the Commission in executing its functions and play a crucial role in the decision-making process. The committee system of management is analysed in detail later in this chapter; for now, let me point out some field-specific features. Firstly, each agricultural market organisation has its own management committee, composed of representatives of the member states and chaired by an official of the Commission. Secondly, for matters of structural policy, the Commission is assisted by the Committee on Agricultural Structures (STAR), composed according to the same logic. Lastly, the Agricultural Advisory Committee allows the Commission to consult stakeholders, including the most vital, the Comité des Organisations Profesionelles Agricoles (COPA), which is the strongest advocate of

---

[24] Case 265/87 *Schräder* [1989] ECR 2237, 2270.

[25] Case 138/79 *Roquette* [1980] ECR 3333, 3358–3359.

[26] Compare E Rieger, 'Protective Shelter or Straitjacket ...' (n 7) 203.

farming interests in the EU and represents major national agricultural organisations. Overall, the prevalence of national, protectionist thinking and its influence on agricultural regulation have increasingly transformed the CAP into what Rieger refers to as a 'passive instrument of the member states in the highly protective regulation of international agricultural trade'.[27]

The administrative apparatus of agricultural regulation by the EU, however, does not provide for a direct link with farmers. Some commentators have claimed that, before the MacSharry reform,[28] this specific system of regulatory decision-making, despite its intensity and density, maintained a peculiar market illusion among those who were the most affected by it: farmers. As they were rarely in contact with the bureaucracy, they were not aware how intensely regulated the market actually was. The complicated system of price support, which allocated income using market mechanisms, kept many farmers unaware of the fact that they were subject to income transfers from the rest of their society. This, as a result, made them over-confident in the efficiency of their work and managerial skills, and simultaneously made the level of support to farmers vague and non-transparent for consumers and taxpayers, whose own income was subject to the redistribution exercise.[29] It all made the CAP much easier to rationalise, which for a considerable time prevented the mobilisation of a political opposition that would press for reform.[30]

All things considered, agriculture developed into the most closely and intensely regulated sector in the EU; indeed, the scale of its political governance can be compared to that of a federal government. The volume of legislation and case law on agricultural issues amounts to a highly significant proportion of the overall EU production. At the same time, the costs of sustaining the

---

[27] Ibid 194.

[28] In essence, the major goals of the MacSharry reform of 1992 were to decouple the income problem from pricing policy, and to orient the pricing policy more towards the efficient functioning of the market. It introduced a three-year reduction in the level of prices in the main production sectors (arable crops and beef) to bring them closer to the world market prices and, by those means, increased the competitiveness of the Community products. Farmers' loss of income caused by this development was mitigated by the introduction of various compensatory payments, direct income payment to farmers and a mandatory set-aside scheme. It also introduced a range of compensatory payments and aid schemes for environmentally friendly farming and the protection of landscape and natural resources. For a more detailed description and impact analysis M Cardwell (n 7) 40–53.

[29] C Daugbjerg, 'Policy Feedback and Paradigm Shift in EU Agricultural Policy: The Effects of the MacSharry Reform on Future Reform' (2003) 10 *Journal of European Public Policy* 429. To support his thesis, Daugbjerg quotes statements by the Comité des Organisations Profesionelles Agricoles (COPA), which is the strongest representative of farming interests in the EU, responding to the MacSherry reform proposals, which claim either that 'the agricultural policy should not be changed into a social policy' or that 'the price policy must be maintained. It cannot be replaced by social benefits'.

[30] Ibid; also E Rieger, 'The Common Agricultural Policy …' (n 5) 198.

CAP capture a considerable portion of EU budget expenditure. Hence, with the systematic reduction of the economic significance of agriculture, it is getting increasingly more difficult to explain and justify.

2.1.1.3. *The CAP and Its Social Aspects*

Rieger suggests that a good way to understand the CAP is to look at it as an integral part of the western European welfare state, with its particular 'moral' economy, and to acknowledge its political rationale. Contrarily to other welfare-state institutions, though, an agricultural policy connects production with income-related aims, which makes it difficult to separate the distributive and the regulatory dimensions. Following this underlying principle, the EU agricultural policy uses political power to offset or modify market operations, in order to achieve goals which the market would not achieve on its own. As a consequence, the major aim of market regulation becomes absolutely contrary to the market function and is only concentrated on distribution of income.[31]

The CAP regulations created a comprehensive system of income redistribution among European farmers. Naturally, certain features of the CAP propagated a perception of it as an example of a redistributive social policy. According to Rieger, it led to a situation where 'the institutions of the Union—not the market economy—are the central mechanism for the allocation of resources and the principle source of conflicts and tensions', which has led some to refer to the 'welfare dimension' of the CAP.[32] The system has been heavily criticised, not least for functioning in relative isolation from the economic rationale and without reference to actual needs of its beneficiaries, which allowed some of its aspects to be led astray and to contribute to disproportionate advances and an even greater discrepancy in the market.[33] On the other hand, the CAP has been regarded as a forerunner of more extensive integration and the most successful example of institutional and political federalisation of an area of European governance. The CAP, in that sense, developed into 'something that could be called a welfare state for farmers', which explains the dominant role of the agricultural interest in its making and functioning.[34]

Food-related aspects of the CAP have been connected primarily with securing supply by means of increasing productivity and efficiency, and in this respect the CAP has been perceived as very successful. Perhaps it was even a

---

[31] Ibid 182–186.

[32] E Rieger, 'Protective Shelter or Straitjacket ...' (n 7) 195.

[33] M. Carson (n 17) 99.

[34] Compare E Rieger, 'The Common Agricultural Policy: External and Internal Dimensions' in H Wallace and W Wallace (eds), *Policy-making in the European Union* (Oxford University Press, Oxford 1996) 104.

bit too successful, as within ten years of the introduction of these policy objectives, EU food production was already in surplus.[35]

2.1.2. *How Much Food in Agriculture? How Much Agriculture in Food?*

One last issue to be considered is the particular linkage between agriculture and food production, and its reflection in the regulations. It is practically impossible to assess to what degree food production is an agricultural activity and thus should fall under the agricultural regulatory scheme. It is, however, of crucial importance to be aware of the existence of this interrelation, and of the legacy that the influence of agricultural regulations has left in the food sector.

Much as people have moved away from the source of the food they consume, the specialised production of processed food has, over time, moved away from the land. As the distance between the 'farm' and the 'fork' was getting larger, the chain of intermediaries between them was becoming more and more complex. Gradually, thus, the farming of primary agricultural materials, on the one hand, and production of finished processed foodstuffs, on the other, have become two completely separate endeavours. Accordingly, and following the same dividing lines, they have become subjugated to two different regulatory regimes, one following the 'farming' track, and the other relating to the production and free movement of goods.

Even though this regulatory separation has gradually become more apparent and obvious, the natural link between food and commodities remains strong and important, and the mutual influences between the two are immense and cannot be eradicated by a severance of regulatory regimes. This natural link, however, seems to be completely lost in the legislative sphere, which applies an either/or rationale. Either you are a farmer and you fall under the laws of the CAP, or you are a producer of goods and you are treated just as any other entity enjoying the freedom of the common market.

In the longer perspective, the absence of this specific link has, in the case of foodstuffs, translated into a detachment of the market and the social features of regulation. Although this separation is a general problem in the context of the entire European project (as discussed in the prologue, above), in the case of foodstuffs it seems particularly consequential. Having moved food regulation away from a socially engaged agricultural system and towards a market-driven product-regulation scheme, Europe seems to have given up a lot of its potential capacity to negotiate the specificity, social impact and vulnerability of the food sector. The market logic of product regulation has simply not been given the appropriate tools to accommodate such considerations, be they

[35] M Carson (n 17); see also N Nugent, *The Government and Politics of the European Union* (Fifth Edition Palgrave Macmillan, Basingstoke 2003) 399.

social, ethical or simply redistributive. The consequences of this decoupling have not been compensated in any other regulatory way, and thus the tensions that have resulted have not been given adequate recognition. In my opinion, the chaotic nature of the phase of market-building, when the decoupling took place, allowed these shortcomings to remain practically unnoticed for a relatively long time, especially since the initial phase of product regulation showed a lot more flexibility and openness to socioeconomic concerns than its mature form. With the growing stringency of product regulation and the overall development of food and agricultural trade, however, those concerns have become more visible, as well as more difficult to deal with.

2.2. *Food As Product: Market Regulation and the Free Movement of Goods*

2.2.1. *Harmonisation, Ex Article 28 Case Law, and Their Impact on Food Law*

2.2.1.1. *An Initial Approach to the Harmonisation of Foodstuffs Regulation*

In the formative era, the primary method of achieving the European Single Market was the harmonisation of national laws. Foodstuffs regulation was no different in that respect. Naturally, the greatest concern was the reconciliation of national rules. Foodstuffs regulation, probably more than any other type of regulation, has deeply rooted traditions at the national level. Food, so nationally or even regionally entrenched, is not only close to human stomachs, but also to human hearts. Societies, big or small, have their own powerful cultures of food-making and their own strong ideas about what 'good food' means. This inevitably has led to difficulties that are always connected with the internationalisation of matters which, in essence, remain heavily local. It is a question of preferences, of long-lasting traditions, of historical developments and of national pride. Those are not easy to overcome.

In Europe, member states have for decades treated food issues as their private, national domain. This is probably why the attitude taken by Europe towards food safety regulation was initially marked by a degree of hesitancy. This was partly due to the lack of a strong legal basis for any EU action in the field, but also to the awareness of the great importance attached to food issues at the national level. As a consequence, most EU rules in this area were created on an *ad hoc* basis or were developed through the jurisprudence of the ECJ, and they were generally of a harmonising and trade-facilitating character. Until the outbreak of the food crises of the 1990s, the EU had not developed a comprehensive food safety policy, but rather had a complex maze of isolated sectoral rules.

The harmonised EU rules for foodstuffs have been based on various sources. Initially, they were mostly influenced by the food policies of Germany, France and the Netherlands, which are all significantly different in their approaches and administrative traditions. Secondly, there were issues which only a few member states had regulated before, and in those cases EU rules were rather created than approximated. Finally, national laws were not the sole source of the harmonised EU legislation. It had been highly influenced by the works of the Council of Europe, as well as the Codex Alimentarius Commission, and to a certain extent by the legislation of third countries, especially important trade partners such as the USA. This phenomenon resulted from the fact that already by the 1960s food issues had become increasingly internationalised and interdependent, and it was not possible for the European legislator to disregard the developments and create rules irrespective of them.[36]

Until the mid-1980s, EU activity in foodstuffs regulation, as in other areas of the common market, followed a retail approach.[37] According to this technique, the EU developed a set of detailed and comprehensive standards and requirements for each category of regulated products, which included the definition, the content, the authorised ingredients and unauthorised residues, as well as rules for preparation, presentation, marketing and labelling. The rationale for this harmonisation technique was probably encompassed in a strong belief—dominant at that time—that this was the most effective method of abolishing the existing barriers to trade and of achieving free circulation of European products. This method was supposed to serve a twofold objective. It was, on the one hand, meant to reconcile differing national regulations, and, on the other, to prevent a situation where the lowest common denominator would be accepted as a general EU standard, which could lead towards low-level homogenisation of product quality.[38] The retail approach, however, eventually turned out to be highly inefficient and surprisingly unsuccessful. Burdensome research, lengthy procedures and numerous battles for national exceptions clogged the EU legislative pipeline, which consequently obstructed the adoption of new legislation, let alone its application or enforcement. At the beginning of the 1980s, the inevitability of the development of new legislative policy became evident not only in the area of foodstuffs regulation, but in the whole realm of the product market. The need for a new approach towards harmonisation was also widely advocated by the ECJ in a series of milestone

[36] See C Lister, *Regulation of Food Products by the European Community* (n 4) 16–18; and MP Broberg, 'Transforming the European Community's Regulation of Food Safety', (2008) SIEPS Report 2008: 5, 17–47.

[37] The retail approach was described and strongly criticised in: Commission (EC), 'White Paper on the Completion of the Internal Market' COM (85) 310 final, 14 June 1985, and in an accompanying document: Commission (EC), 'Completion of the Internal Market: Community Legislation on Foodstuffs' COM (85) 603 final, which will be evaluated below.

[38] H-Ch von Heydebrand u.d. Lasa, 'Free Movement of Foodstuffs, Consumer Protection and Food Standards in the European Community: Has the Court of Justice Got it Wrong?' (1991) 16 *European Law Review* 391; and C Lister, *Regulation of Food Products ...* (n 4) 24–25.

judgements on the free movement of goods. A need to redefine EU policy on the free movement of goods became apparent, requiring a careful look back at its Treaty foundations to find an alternative way of managing European trade.

2.2.1.2. *Ex Article 28, Cassis Case Law, and Its Implications*

EC Treaty provisions on free movement of goods were designed to guarantee the removal of duties, quotas and quantitative restrictions to trade in products within the Community. The overarching aim of those provisions was to warrant that competition between goods originating in different member states was not distorted by national regulations that either limit the quantity of import of foreign goods or increase their price by tariff measures (duties, taxes). While the elimination of tariff barriers turned out to be relatively easy and was dealt with quickly and efficiently, the quantitative restrictions and measures having equivalent effect have been present on the political agenda and in the academic debate ever since.

Article 28 of the TEC started the debate. The Article 28 (now Article 34 TFEU) is one of the foundations of the right of free movement of goods.[39] It prohibits the use of measures having equivalent effect to quantitative restrictions in trade between the member states. This general principle is not absolute, however. There are instances when individual member states are allowed to apply import restrictions when they serve to protect certain elementary values. The initial catalogue of exemptions is to be found in former Article 30 TEC (now Article 36 TFEU) which legitimises prohibitions or restrictions justified on grounds of public morality, public policy or public security; the protection of health and life of humans, animals or plants; the protection of national treasures possessing artistic, historic or archaeological value; or the protection of industrial and commercial property. Such prohibitions or restrictions cannot, however, constitute a means of arbitrary discrimination or a disguised restriction on trade between member states. Interestingly, most of the landmark Article 28 TEC jurisprudence resulted from cases that had to do with food. It was also in a food-related case that Article 30 TEC was found to be too narrow for the needs of the modern, ever-closer common market.[40]

[39] The free movement of goods Treaty regime includes provisions on the customs union, abolishing, in trade between member states, customs duties and measures having equivalent effect, a ban on quantitative restrictions and measures having equivalent effect, and some provisions on internal taxation.

[40] There is extensive literature on former Article 28 and 30 TEC, and on the ECJ jurisprudence. See, for example, P Craig and G de Burca, *EU Law. Texts, Cases and Materials* (n 1) 613–679; P Oliver, 'Some Further Reflections on the Scope of Articles 28–30 (ex 30–36)' (1999) 36 *Common Market Law Review* 738; WPJ Wils, 'The Search for the Rule in Article 30 EEC: Much Ado About Nothing' (1993) 18 *European Law Review* 475; J Steiner, 'Drawing the Line: Uses and Abuses of Article 30 EEC' (1992) 29 *Common Market Law Review* 749; E White, 'In Search of the Limits of Article 30 of the EEC Treaty' (1989) 26 *Common Market Law Review* 235.

Cassis de Dijon[41] was the first of the series of judgements of the ECJ that developed the interpretation of the main mechanisms governing the free movement of goods.[42] It was undoubtedly a judgement of pivotal importance and consequence. The case and the Court's decision have been thoroughly described and researched in the literature,[43] but a brief summary of at least some aspects of the decision will be useful here. The applicant in the case intended to import a liqueur called 'Cassis de Dijon' from France to Germany, but was refused an authorisation to do so because of the product's insufficient alcoholic strength. Under German legislation, this type of alcoholic beverage ought to have an alcohol content of 25%, while the French liqueur typically had only 15% to 20%. The German authorities justified their decision by reference to the 'protection of public health' and the 'protection of consumers against unfair commercial practices'. The ECJ, however, decided in response that:

> … the requirements relating to the minimum alcohol content of alcoholic beverages do not serve the purpose which is in the general interest and such as to take precedence over the requirement of the free movement of goods … There is therefore no valid reason why, provided that they have been lawfully produced and marketed in one of the member states, alcoholic beverages should not be introduced into any other member state; the sale of such products may not be subject to a legal prohibition on the marketing of beverages with an alcohol content lower than the limit set by the national rules.[44]

This fragment of the Court's judgement, as discussed in the previous chapter, served as a basis for the 'principle of mutual recognition' in the law of the EU internal market. It provides that goods, once they have been lawfully produced and marketed in one member state, should be admitted into any other member state without restrictions, unless the state of import can successfully invoke one of the mandatory requirements.

Following that logic, the long-term effect of *Cassis* was, in a sense, deregulatory, as it rendered inapplicable the rules that prevented goods lawfully marketed in

---

[41] C 120/78 *Rewe-Zentral AG v. Bundesmonopolverwaltung für Branntwein* [1979] ECR 649.

[42] The development of this part of the free market jurisdiction, put simply, started with the *Dassonville* judgement: C 8/74 *Procureur du Roi v. Dassonville* [1974] ECR 837, which laid down a foundation for the broad understanding of the notion of 'measures having equivalent effect to quantitative restrictions' and the 'rule of reason', which were later developed in *Cassis de Dijon*, and slightly revised in *Keck* C-267 and 268/91, *Criminal Proceedings against Keck and Mithouard* [1993] ECR I-6097. For more, see P Craig and G de Burca, *EU Law* … (n 1) 615–668.

[43] See, for example, KJ Alter and S Meunier-Altsahalia, 'Judicial Politics in the European Community: European Integration and the Pathbreaking Cassis de Dijon Decision' (1994) 26 *Comparative Political Studies* 535; LW Gormley, 'Cassis de Dijon and the Communication from the Commission' (1981) 6 *European Law Review* 454.

[44] See judgement in case C 120/78, *Rewe-Zentral* … (n 41) par. 14.

one member state from being imported into another.[45] Mutual recognition was expected to lead to some sort of competition among states and rules, and to create a situation where producers only have to comply with the national legislation of one state and would be able to choose the one they deem the most suitable, while consumers can choose between products that conform to those rules. The consequence this leads to is, as Maduro points out, 'a competitive process among the different national rules: the choice of producers of where to produce and of consumers of what to buy will determine "the best rules" '.[46] The mutual-recognition rule, regarded as a great, new, effective and to a large extent self-executing strategy, remained for many years the core of the ECJ's and the Commission's policy.[47]

It was not without problems, however. Interestingly, it was the food-standards regulation that was used in literature as an example of the traps of mutual recognition and as an illustration of its limited effectiveness.[48] Lasa, for example, contested the approach of the ECJ, which negates national food standards on the grounds that they are not saved by mandatory requirements and that the same protective effect can be achieved by use of less restrictive labelling policy. He argues, contrary to the ECJ's assumption, that food standards perform functions that cannot be substituted by labelling. First, food standards preclude economic adulteration of products by preventing the manufacturer from substituting inferior ingredients. Secondly, food standards serve as yardsticks against which superior and inferior quality can be measured.[49] Labelling, on the other hand, is unable to perform either function and thus is unable to effectively protect consumers' interests. Lasa also pointed out that mutual-recognition regime can often lead to reverse discrimination of national food producers, but also, even more importantly, that the member state of export can, by way of the economic damage caused by inverse discrimination, impose its food standards or standard-free food law on the member

---

[45] For further analysis P Craig and G de Burca, *EU Law* … (n 1) 639; see also the analysis of the political implications and consequences in D Chalmers, 'Deliberative Supranationalism and the Reterritorialization of Authority' in Ch Joerges, 'Rethinking European Law's Supremacy' (2005) EUI Working Paper Law No. 12/2005, 29–44.

[46] MP Maduro, *We the Court. The European Court of Justice and the European Economic Constitution* (Hart Publishing, Oxford 1998) 132.

[47] The mutual recognition rule was further developed in the Commission Communication to the European Parliament and the Council: Mutual Recognition in the Context of the Follow-up to the Action Plan for the Single Market, 16 June 1999.

[48] See: H-Ch von Heydebrand u.d. Lasa, 'Free Movement of Foodstuffs …' (n 38); O Brouwers, 'Free Movement of Foodstuffs and Quality Requirements: Has the Commission Got it Wrong?' (1998) 25 *Common Market Law Review* 237.

[49] H-Ch von Heydebrand u.d. Lasa, ibid 401–403.

state of import.[50] Last but not least, the big common market concern caused by mutual recognition was that it promotes free trade, but leaves uncertainty about its conditions. Specifically, it eliminates the national barriers that hinder trade, but leaves that space without positive action by the EU. This negative harmonisation phenomenon started raising serious concerns about the future shape of the internal market.[51]

2.2.1.3. *A New Approach to Harmonisation*

An important prerequisite to the change of this regulatory approach was the Treaty amendment, which reduced one great obstacle to harmonisation: the requirement of unanimity. In December 1985, the Single European Act (SEA)[52] added a new Article 100a (now Article 114 TFEU), which permitted qualified majority voting in the Council to approve harmonising directives that aim to establish and improve the functioning of the internal market. In this respect, the SEA was an essential step towards further and faster progress of market integration. It also opened the door for a delegation by the Council of subsidiary and technical measures to the Commission and the committees, which encouraged the wider use of the simplified committee procedures to approve harmonising regulations. Last but definitely not least, the internal-market project was strengthened by the adoption of the new Article 7a, which obliged the EC to attain, by 31 December 1992, an internal market that, in accordance with paragraph 2 of the Article (now Article 26 TFEU), 'shall comprise an area without frontiers, in which the free movement of goods, persons, services and capital is ensured in accordance with the provisions of the Treaty'.[53] By providing such a strong new legislative procedure to facilitate the adoption of internal-market measures, the EC took a big step towards a new and more efficient approach to harmonisation, although the traditional method, even in its reformed version, was still imperfect and weakened by various deficiencies. Specifically, it was slow, it often led to excessive uniformity, and it had not managed to find ways to develop links between harmonisation and standardisation.[54] These various shortcomings were summarised and analysed in the Commission White Paper, where a proposal of a New Approach to

[50] Ibid 408–413; This line of criticism was later developed, especially in relation to the EU policy on trade description of food products, in C MacMaolain, 'Free movement of foodstuffs, quality requirements and consumer protection: have the Court and the Commission both got it wrong?' (2001) 26 *European Law Review* 413.

[51] Compare S Weatherill and P Beaumont, *EU Law* (Third Edition Penguin Books, London 1999) 599.

[52] The Single European Act [1987] OJ L 169/ 1.

[53] More in C Lister, (n 4) 29–31; P Craig and G de Burca, *EU Law* ... (n 1) 1179–1189.

[54] J Pelkmans, 'The New Approach to Technical Harmonization and Standardization' (1987) 25 *Journal of Common Market Studies* 249, 252–253.

Technical Harmonization and Standardization was forwarded to the Council and the European Parliament.[55]

The Commission admitted the necessity of reconsidering its previous harmonisation policy, and in 1985 launched its famous 'Completion of the Internal Market' program. The White Paper[56] envisaged a concentration of the harmonisation effort on those national measures that created obstacles to free trade. The Commission acknowledged that the previous approach was much too detailed, slow and inflexible, and as a consequence ineffective. It was also far too cumbersome to allow fast responses to technological progress and innovation. The Commission therefore tried to find a method that would be more flexible than the total (recipe-type) vertical regulation, but which would provide more uniformity than mutual recognition of varying national standards. The result was the establishment of the New Approach Towards Harmonization, under which EU law would only establish the essential requirements for the free movement of goods, by means of framework directives.[57] For the establishment of further regulatory details, the Commission expected to rely on technical standardisation bodies, such as the European Committee for Standardization (CEN) or the European Committee for Technical Standardization (CENLEC), with a long-term aim of replacing national standards with the European ones in all areas. Those European standards, however, would not take the form of EU laws but instead would be evaluated by the abovementioned specialised standard-setting bodies, with the broad participation of stakeholders.[58] Other sector-specific bodies would act in various parts of economy, where they were expected to ensure that the standardisation process took place in parallel with the harmonisation measures adopted by the Council, and that it was based on the 'essential requirements'.[59]

In the field of foodstuffs, the Commission decided to focus on two priorities. Firstly, it concentrated on measures designed to protect human life and health, and secondly, on rules concerned with fair trade and consumer protection. The

---

[55] Commission (EC) White Paper on Completion ... (n 37) par 64.

[56] Ibid.

[57] Ibid par. 65–72.

[58] For more analytical literature on the New Approach and Standardization, see C Joerges, H Schepel and E Vos, 'The Law's Problems with the Involvement of Non-governmental Actors in Europe's Legislative Process: The Case of Standardisation under the "New Approach"' (1999) EUI Working Paper LAW No. 99/9; J Falke, 'Achievements and Unresolved Problems of European Standardization: The Ingenuity of Practice and the Queries of Lawyers' in C Joerges, K-H Ladeur and E Vos, *Integrating Scientific Expertise into Regulatory Decision-Making. National Traditions and European Innovations* (Nomos, Baden-Baden 1997); Ch Joerges, J Falke, HW Micklitz and G Brüggemeier, 'European Product Safety, Internal Market Policy and the New Approach to Technical Harmonisation and Standards' (1991) EUI Working Papers LAW Nos.91/10–14; H Schepel, *The Constitution of Private Governance: Product Standards in the Regulation of Integrating Markets* (Hart Publishing, Oxford 2005).

[59] J Pelkmans, 'The New Approach ...' (n 54) 256.

first priority gave rise to legislation on manufacturing and treatment processes, food additives, materials and articles in contact with food, food contaminants, as well as dietary foodstuffs. Following the second priority, measures were taken regarding the labelling, presentation and advertising of foodstuffs, and on the official checks and inspections.[60] When in 1989 the Commission issued a comprehensive Communication on the Free Movement of Goods within the Community,[61] it presented its concise position on the question of the free movement of foodstuffs in relation to the *Cassis de Dijon* judgement through a more recent *Commission v. Germany*, commonly referred to as the 'German beer' or 'Rheinheitsgebot' case.[62] In the Communication, the Commission interpreted the judgement as providing the foundation for rendering two most pressing problems of the free movement of foodstuffs: namely, the question of trade description (the name under which the imported food product is sold) and the presence of additives in the imported food. It evaluated on those two aspects of food trade, concluding that European foodstuffs regulation must ensure a high level of public-health protection by providing adequate information to consumers' about the nature, content, characteristics and, where appropriate, the origin of the product.[63] All in all, a pressing need for horizontal legislation was pronounced.

2.3. *Between Farm and Fork: Integrating Decoupled Food Regulation*

As a result of the variety of problems and approaches in the foodstuffs sector, Europe has built a complex and often inconsistent legal pattern, characterised as an outcome of 'the uneasy marriage between the Community's food and agricultural policies'[64] and probably an even more uneasy separation of those two. Assigned to different Commission segments, with different goals and separate constituencies, the components of EU food regulation tend to overlap and collide. In that complicated structure, however, three main forms of approach can be identified. The first group of legislative instruments are vertical regulations, which focus on a particular product or category of products; these are often referred to as 'recipe laws'. Despite the announcement and enactment of the new approach, this type of regulation still remained in force, and even continued to be introduced to the European body of law in the foodstuffs area.

---

[60] See White Paper: Completion of the Single Market of Foodstuffs (n 37) 6–11, as well as C Lister (n 4) 28–29.

[61] Commission (EC), 'Commission interpretative communication concerning the free circulation of foodstuffs within the Community' COM (89) 256 final, 24 October 1989, 3.

[62] C 178/84 *Commission v. Germany* [1987] ECR 1227.

[63] For more R O'Rourke, *European Food Law* (Palladian, Bembridge 1998) 20–21; C MacMaolain, *EU Food Law. Protecting Consumers and Health in a Common Market* (Modern Studies in European Law, Hart Publishing, Oxford, Portland Oregon 2007) 413–428.

[64] C Lister, (n 4) 32.

The second type are regulations on a wholesale basis, which address certain issues horizontally and establish requirements applicable to a broader category of dissimilar products, mainly by setting up minimum standards for the free movement of goods. Finally, the third category is the sectoral type of directives, which identify groups of similar products and create requirements for the whole division.[65] Nevertheless, no matter how we approach the European regulations of that time—whether we take a chronological approach, a functional diversification or any other form of classification—the general conclusion must be that their overarching principle and goal was market integration. Neither consumer protection and environmental considerations nor any form of social or redistributive concerns were even mentioned at that time.

The initial subordination to the agricultural scheme, where the inclusion of social and economic concerns is inherent in the Treaty, was later followed by the separation and subjection of food regulation to pure market mechanisms, creating a lacuna in the system, which has been uncomfortable to admit and difficult to fill in. During all the time when 'food' was no more than a 'good', free-movement considerations constituted a primary inspiration of regulatory interventions.

Similarly to all types of product regulation, however, food regulation that establishes certain common denominators in order to sustain a required level of safety intrinsically leads to socioeconomic consequences for the market. Joerges points to three categories of such consequences: administrative costs; costs to manufacturers, retailers and consumers; and implications on industrial or economic policy for a member state or a segment of its economy.[66] In the first phase of development of the European food safety policy, this fact seems to have been completely overlooked.

In my opinion, reasons why socioeconomic implications of food regulation and the distributive concerns connected with it were not 'on the menu' at that time are connected with the particular stage of European integration process, and with the complicated regulatory setting described above. Firstly, to mention some of the reasons from the first group, the EU was then still a relatively homogenous structure, and discrepancies in the level of technological and economic development of various member states were not so relevant. Secondly, the overarching aim of market integration was still strong and hardly questionable, especially given that the initial benefits of obstacle-free European exchange had started to become visible and were encouraging. Thirdly, at that point European integration was still only about the market, and the

---

[65] C Lister, ibid 32–34.

[66] Ch Joerges, '"Good Governance" Through Comitology?' in Ch Joerges and E Vos, *EU Committees: Social Regulation, Law and Politics* (Hart Publishing, Oxford 1999) 324.

promise of deeper involvement pronounced in the Maastricht Treaty revision was not yet vital or even much contemplated.

From a regulatory point of view, the main reason why those socioeconomic aspects could be missed was the multiplicity and variety of regulatory tools, which not only made it difficult to navigate in the European market organisation, but also veiled the consequences and impact of adopted instruments and mechanisms on member states' markets and societies. The mix of mutual recognition, total regulation, and minimum harmonisation was probably not only difficult to apply, but its effectiveness and implications were also complicated to analyse. Additionally, under the minimum-harmonisation approach, many member states were tempted 'to maintain and often to introduce more stringent regulatory standards than those prescribed by EC legislation, for the purpose of advancing a particular social or welfare interest',[67] which led to further divergences. Concentrating product policy and legislation on free trade for providers seems to have occupied this phase of market integration to an extent that put the receiving side in much less highlighted position. This, however, was soon to transform, and this transformation towards a new stage of development of EU food regulation is the object of the following paragraphs.

3. The Turn Towards Consumers: Developing the Safety Paradigm

It is commonly known that the Treaty of Rome makes no mention of the consumer. Following the guiding principles of market integration, the common market in its early years developed smoothly without being seriously distorted by consumers' claims. The consumers, as well as the concern for their safety, remained national, although the first attempts to create a European consumers' representation had taken place already in the 1970s.[68] During the next decade, consumer rights were modestly making their way into European legislation, but it was only in the middle of the 1990s that we see a real breakthrough and a structured trend towards integration of consumer protection in the regulation of the EU market.

The introduction of consumers' interests into the *acquis* had three major components. The first was of a legal character and provided for an introduction of 'the consumer' into the Treaty. As a point of departure, the Treaty of Maastricht was equipped with the first provision containing an explicit reference to consumer protection. Later, Article 153 (added by the Amsterdam

[67] M Doogan, 'Minimum Harmonization and the Internal Market' (2000) 37 *Common Market Law Review* 853.

[68] G Trumbull, *Consumer Capitalism. Politics, Product Markets, and Firm Strategy in France and Germany* (Cornell University Press, Ithaca and London 2006) 173.

Treaty) contained a requirement for consumer protection to be incorporated into new EC policies. Currently, after changes introduced by the Treaty of Lisbon, Article 12 TFEU entails that consumer protection requirements shall be taken into account in defining and implementing other EU policies and activities.

The second component was of an institutional character and envisaged the creation of a number of institutions, which had as their goal the promotion of consumers' interests in the EU. The most important one was the Directorate General for Health and Consumer Protection. Interestingly, however, consumer protection, in its EU-defined form, was left to be implemented and enforced by the member states in accordance with their national regimes.

Finally, the third component was of a financial character, under which the EU started to assign funds for the support of national consumer groups. The overarching aims of the exercise were to create a new context for policy discussion among consumers in the EU and to install consumer protection as a European basic right, which could potentially reinforce the legitimacy of EU activities on the market.[69]

The European regulator was soon to discover, however, that consumer protection matters tend to be incredibly complex, and, once pronounced, require constant systematic engagement. Regulatory solutions in the field of consumer protection often necessitate the involvement of highly technical scientific knowledge, which must be weighed against the expectations of market forces and the diffuse interests of consumers. This task is anything but simple. Hence, bringing 'safety' into the regulatory forum has far-reaching consequences. To name only a few crucial examples, it requires a reform of procedures to accommodate scientific expertise, the means for funding such expertise, the establishment of appropriate forums in which consumers' voices can be properly included in the regulatory decision-making, as well as the development of criteria for the selection of experts and stakeholders' representatives.

In the food sector, the road to recognition of consumers' interest had a particular twist. The food scares of the 1990s, which propelled the pro-consumer changes in EU law and administration, had shaken the core of food regulation and forced a complete rethinking of food, consumers and the administrative links between the two. After an era of regulating food issues without paying much attention to consumers, the new regulatory wave was concerned almost entirely with their protection. 'Safety' suddenly became a very prominent concept, and it swiftly penetrated political debates and legislative negotiations.

---

[69] G Trumbull, ibid 176; MP Broberg, 'Transforming the European Community's Regulation ...' (n 36) 62–80.

3.1. *Comitologising the Regulation of Foodstuffs*

Progressive development, as well as technological advancement in the field of food production, forced the European regulators to further reform legislation and procedures for decision-making. Specific scientific expertise was gradually making its way into the regulatory process. Hence, a need became apparent for the establishment of a type of consultative platform, where scientific expertise could meet stakeholders' concerns and political interests. In the case of the EU regulatory architecture, and in the face of the expectations of interested parties, this need for a deliberative institutional setting gave rise to the phenomenon of comitology. In the field of foodstuffs regulation, where a need for modern science, a magnitude of consumer concerns and the enormity of financial interest involved tend to create a rather explosive cocktail, comitology was seen as a means for the resolution of conflicts, for the creation of coherent and balanced legislation, and for the institutionalisation of deliberative ways of decision-making.

3.1.1. *The Phenomenon of Comitology*

3.1.1.1. *The Rise of Comitology*

The origin of committees in the European regulatory structure can be traced back to the 1960s, when the first management committees were established in the agricultural sector. They were, initially, formed to answer two combined interests: the need for specific knowledge and the demand of member states to control the execution of discretionary powers delegated by the Council to the Commission. All in all, the rise of comitology as a regulatory concept in Europe should be seen as a policy implementation technique driven by necessity rather than as an institutionalisation of a presupposed, constitutional-type regulatory model.

In the 1970s the committees were found to provide a useful mechanism to respond to yet another problem: of the democratic legitimisation of procedures in cases where some regulatory powers were delegated to the Commission. The broad formula for the participation of stakeholders representing different categories of interests, as well as for the provision of technical and scientific knowledge in specific policy fields, contributed to the shaping of the committee structure as a popular and massive regulatory tool in the EU.[70] Particularly in politically sensitive fields, such as health and safety regulation, comitology has had an increasingly important role to play. In such areas, where the legal

[70] See E Vos, 'The Rise of Committees' (1997) 3 *European Law Journal* 211–212; C Bertram, 'Decision-making in the EEC: the management committee procedure' (1997) 68 *Common Market Law Review* 246–265.

and institutional bases for European activity were rather problematic and where the need for highly specialised knowledge created additional obstacles to effective decision-making, it was hoped that comitology would provide a key mechanism to handle mutual distrust between member states.

These expectations were based on two specific features of comitology. Firstly, comitology systematises the transfer of knowledge into the realm of law through the organised cooperation and deliberation of field experts. Secondly, those experts are appointed by member states; this facilitates the acceptance and implementation of European measures by giving member states a sense of participation and control over European developments.

The Commission has, thus, gradually found itself more and more entangled in a web of different types of committees in an increasing number of fields of its activity. The first type is the scientific committees, which gather experts in a given area and which serve the Commission with highly specialised knowledge. The second type is the advisory and consultative committees, which are meant to reflect the variety of interests in each specific field. Finally, the third type is the management and regulatory committees, which are comprised of representatives of national administrations and participate in the framing of implementing measures. It is important to note, however, that although all those bodies form a part of the complex committee structure adherent to the Commission, only the committees whose consultation is compulsory for the Commission can formally be qualified as comitology committees.[71]

The phenomenon of comitology remains a source of controversy and criticism, but it is also hailed as an example of a successful and efficient regulatory strategy in the field of social regulation, where many—often conflicting—interests must be taken into consideration.[72]

---

[71] This division is clearly illustrated in the General Budget of the European Union; see, for example, the General Budget of the European Union for the European Union for the Financial Year 2000, Annex I, Part A [2000] OJ L 40/1. For a review of the historical development of different types of committees, see CF Bergström, *Comitology—Delegation of Powers in the European Union and the Committee System* (Oxford University Press, Oxford 2005) chapters 1–4.

[72] The phenomenon of comitology has interested many academics, resulting in an impressively prolific literature. For example, Ch Joerges and E Vos, *EU Committees: Social Regulation* ... (n 66); Ch Joerges, K-H Ladeur and E Vos (eds), *Integrating Scientific Expertise...* (n 58); Ch Joerges and J Neyer, 'From Intergovernmental Bargaining to Deliberative Political Process: The Constitutionalisation of Comitology' (1997) 3 *European Law Journal* 273; RH Pedler and GF Schaefer (eds), *Shaping European Law and Policy: The Role of Committees and Comitology in the Political Process* (European Institute of Public Administration, Maastricht 1996); M Andenaes and A Türk (eds), *Delegated Legislation and the Role of Committees in the EC* (Kluwer Law International, the Hague 2000); K Bradley, 'Comitology and the Law: Through a Glass Darkly' (1992) 29 *Common Market Law Review* 693; K Lenaerts and A Verhoeven, 'Towards a Legal Framework for Executive Rule-making in the EU? The Contribution of the New Comitology Decision' (2000) 37 *Common Market Law Review* 645–686; CF Bergström, *Comitology* ... ibid, and other work referred to in this chapter.

There exists a vast literature on various aspects of comitology, however the study undertaken in this volume is limited to only those aspects that are of major importance for the research question. Thus, I concentrate on the ability of comitology to provide a means of inclusion of wider social considerations in the regulatory process. My study begins, however, with a short presentation of the main features of the comitology system and the most important aspects of its functioning.

3.1.1.2. *Legal Basis and Structure*

Article 202 third indent of the EC Treaty, as reformed by the Single European Act, initially served as legal basis for the transference of implementing rights on the Commission, and provided the conditions for such conferral.[73] According to this provision, implementing powers may be delegated only if this is foreseen in the basic act and in line with the requirements set forth by the Council, by means of a decision adopted in advance.[74] Such a delegation by the Council of implementing powers to the Commission had become necessary mainly due to an increase of situations where scientific and technical uncertainty as well as unexpected circumstances had to be dealt with quickly and efficiently. In such situations, the Council procedures turned out to be inadequate. Since, however, the member states were eager to retain some influence over the ways policy was implemented by the Commission, the Council obliged it to consult a framework of committees, under the umbrella of the First Comitology Decision of 1987.[75] The First Comitology Decision was repealed and replaced in 1999[76] in order to respond to criticism after the BSE scandal, as well as to recognise the strengthened position of the European Parliament after Maastricht and Amsterdam. It was further amended in 2006,[77] yet again after renewed claims from the European Parliament for inclusion and according to

[73] Article 202 third indent EC reads: 'To insure that the objectives set out in this Treaty are attained the Council shall, in accordance with the provisions of this Treaty .. confer on the Commission, in the acts which the Council adopts, powers for the implementation of the rules which the Council lays down. The Council may impose certain requirements in respect of the exercise of these powers. The Council may also reserve the right, in specific cases, to exercise directly implementing powers itself. The procedures referred to above must be consonant with principles and rules to be laid down in advance by the Council, acting unanimously on a proposal from the Commission and after obtaining the opinion of the European Parliament'.

[74] Article 202 was repealed by the Treaty of Lisbon, and replaced in substance by provisions of Article 16 (1) TEU and Articles 290 and 291 TFEU.

[75] Council Decision (EEC) 87/373 of 13 July 1987 laying down the procedures for the exercise of implementing powers conferred on the Commission [1987] OJ L 197/33.

[76] Council Decision (EC) 1999/468 of 28 July 1999 laying down the procedures for exercise of implementing powers conferred on the Commission [1999] OJ L 184/23.

[77] Council Decision (EC) 2006/512 of 17 July 2006 amending Decision (EC) 1999/468 laying down the procedures for the exercise of implementing powers conferred on the Commission [2006] OJ L 200/11.

some commentators, in the spirit of emergence of bits and pieces of reforms adopted by the failed Constitutional Treaty.[78]

The Second Comitology Decision, provided for three implementing procedures, which are distinguished according to the varying powers of the committees. Within the first—the advisory procedure[79]—the committee delivers an opinion on the draft, which the Commission should take 'the utmost account of', but which is not legally binding. The advisory procedure shall be used in cases in which it is considered the most appropriate, provided that it does not enter the realms reserved for the two other types of procedures.

The second—the management procedure[80]—obliges the Commission to consult the committee, which then reaches a decision on the basis of qualified majority voting. In the case of a negative opinion, the Commission must refer the matter to the Council, which, acting by a qualified majority, may take a different decision. Management procedure is used with regard to management measures, in particular when the proposed instruments relate to the application of common agricultural and fisheries policies or programs with substantial budgetary implications.[81]

Under the third—the regulatory procedure[82]—the Commission adopts the proposed measures only if the committee approves them by a qualified majority. In the case of a lack of approval or a lack of opinion, the Commission shall submit to the Council a proposal relating to the measures in question, and it shall inform the European Parliament. If the Council opposes that proposal with a qualified majority, the Commission has to re-examine it and either resubmit the amended proposal to the Council or submit a legislative proposal. If, however, the Council has neither adopted nor opposed the proposal within the given time period, the proposed implementing act shall be adopted by the Commission. Regulatory procedure should be used for the adoption of measures of general scope, designed to apply essential provisions of basic instruments, including measures concerning protection of the health and safety of humans, animals or plants. The use of this procedure is also foreseen with regard to the adoption or updating of certain non-essential provisions of the basic instrument, if the basic instrument itself stipulates the possibility of their adoption by way of implementing procedures.[83]

The 2006 amendment of the Comitology Decision added a fourth type of procedure called 'regulatory procedure with scrutiny'.[84] Its use is restricted to

---

[78] See Editorial Comment (2006) 43 *Common Market Law Review* 1243–1250.
[79] See Article 3 of Council Decision (EC) 1999/468 (n 76).
[80] Article 4 of Council Decision (EC) 1999/468, ibid.
[81] Ibid, Article 2 (b).
[82] Ibid, Article 5.
[83] Ibid, Article 2 (c).
[84] Article 1 (7) of Council Decision (EC) 2006/512 (n 77).

measures of general scope designed to amend a non-essential element of the basic instrument, *inter alia* by deleting or adding some of those elements, but only with regard to acts subject to the co-decision procedure. The specificity of this procedure lies in the extended power of the European Parliament to intervene and oppose the adoption of measures in three types of situations: (1) where the proposed measure exceeds the implementing powers provided for in the basic instrument; (2) where the draft measure does not comply with the aim or the content of the basic instrument; or, finally, (3) where the draft does not respect the principles of subsidiarity or proportionality. All in all, the grounds for intervention by the European Parliament are restricted to a review of the legality of the proposed measure and not their advisability or suitability. Another change instituted by the 2006 amendment in comparison with the classical regulatory procedure, is the altered way of proceeding the proposal in the case of opposition or the lack of a decision by the committee, which involves the European Parliament in the adoption and eliminates the possibility of adoption by the Commission in the case of the lack of a decision by the Council within the given time limitation.

Following the adoption of the Lisbon Treaty, which reshaped the EU legal architecture as well as the institutional balance between the institutions in the legislative process, the Comitology Decision was replaced.[85] The new Regulation 182/2011 adapts the rules to the new typology of acts introduced in the Lisbon Treaty, where legislative, delegated and implementing acts are distinguished, and it implements new Article 291(3), which empowers the EP and the Council to lay down rules for control by member states of the exercise of the Commission's implementing activities.

The new Regulation foresees two comitology procedures—the advisory procedure and the examination procedure. The advisory procedure is basically the same as in the old Comitology Decision, while the examination procedure replaces the management and regulatory procedures. The examination committee can approve or reject the implementing measure with qualified majority. In case no decision is taken, depending on the subject matter of the implementing measure, the Commission can either adopt the measure or submit it to an appeal committee, where new, final voting takes place. The important novelty is, thus, the abolishment of the Council's role as an appeal body in cases when the comitology committee rejects the Commission draft or fails to issue an opinion. Moreover, the Commission has been granted restricted flexibility as to adoption of draft measures which

[85] Regulation (EU) No 182/2011 of the European Parliament and of the Council of 16 February 2011 laying down the rules and general principles concerning mechanisms for control by Member States of the Commission's exercise of implementing powers [2011] OJ L 55/13.

have received no opinion in the Committee. Contrary to the previous situation, the Commission will no longer be obliged to force adoption of such measures, but can reconsider and modify the proposal, although its flexibility is restricted in certain areas and situations.[86] The impact of the new rules remains to be seen, and initial attempts to evaluate it present mixed conclusions.[87] On the one hand the reform is expected to open comitology up to more transparency, accessibility and influence. On the other, opinions are mixed if this will slow down or speed up the process. Finally, replacing the Council by a committee in the appeal process is by some seen as turn towards more technocracy and de-politicisation, and by others, as merely an ornamental change of a name.

3.1.1.3. *Promises of Comitology*

The rise of comitology in the field of social regulation created high hopes for better decision-making and more effective governance in the areas of greatest technological complexity and socioeconomic sensitivity. It has to be pointed out, however, that those hopes for comitology as a problem-solving regulatory mechanism were accompanied by concerns about its democratic legitimacy and accountability. Hopes were also tainted by a fear of technocratic governance that takes place behind closed doors, far away from citizens and their democratic representatives, and which does not provide sufficient attention to the rights of interest groups to participate.[88] Leaving aside these drawbacks for the moment, I will concentrate on the promises of comitology and its undeniable fortes.

The first expected benefit of comitology is derived from the direct participation of national representatives in regulatory decision-making. The original reason for such involvement, as pointed out above, was the demand of the member states to take part in delegated implementation by the Commission, in order to retain similar control over its activity, which they would normally enjoy via their representatives in the Council. Thereby, however, comitology has created a linkage between the EU and national administrations, which in itself became its second *raison d'être*.[89] Thus, comitology has been seen as creating 'a supranational process by which political considerations are balanced against

[86] See Artcile 5 (4) of the Regulation 182/2011, ibid.

[87] See M Weimer, 'What Price Flexibility?—The Recent Commission Proposal to Allow for National "Opt-Outs" on GMO Cultivation under the Deliberate Release Directive and the Comitology Reform Post-Lisbon' (2010) 4 *European Journal of Risk Regulation* 347–354, as well as A Hardacre and M Keading, 'Delegated and Implementing Acts. The New Comitology. EIPA Essential Guide' (European Institute of Public Administration, 2011).

[88] See, for example, HCH Hoffmann and AH Türk, 'Policy Implementation' in HCH Hoffmann and AH Türk (eds), *EU Administrative Governance* (Edward Elgar Publishing, Cheltenham 2006) 78.

[89] Compare HCH Hoffmann and A. H Türk, 'Policy Implementation', ibid 82.

expert (rationalising) advice'.[90] It has thus become a platform for deliberation and mutual learning towards the inclusion of national values and concerns, which, in effect, promises more eager enforcement and better effectiveness of commonly negotiated and achieved supranational decisions. It often also leads to the creation of complex formal and informal networks, which facilitate information exchange, cooperation and, consequently, the smooth functioning of the system. The most prominent theoretical approach towards the comitology governance advocated by Joerges and Neyer—the theory of 'deliberative supranationalism'—assumes that such a continuous practice of cooperation and mutual information exchange will, in effect, lead to the strengthening of links and understanding between national representatives and will guarantee that this cooperation is conducted through good-faith deliberation rather than interest bargaining.[91]

Another important benefit of comitology is its ability to address questions of the socioeconomic implications of the regulatory mechanisms it considers. The economic consequences and distributive effects of Europeanised risk-regulatory decisions will always differ from one state to another. Although comitology itself may have very little power to actually answer and remedy such distributive problems, it can at least offer an opportunity to raise them. It provides a platform for a discussion of outcomes and an opportunity to work towards the inclusion of the economic concerns of poorer states in agenda-setting. The problem gets more difficult when the implementing legislation deliberated on by the comitology committees gives no leeway for the actual inclusion of distributive concerns and some states end up disadvantaged, despite having raised legitimate concerns. As Joerges points out, EU product regulation gives a normative basis for the rejection of regional or sectoral economic arguments. Consequently, the advantages or drawbacks of product regulation for a particular economy can be treated as legally irrelevant, and financial transfers compensating for the economic disadvantage are not foreseen.[92] There is, however, one example where the losses of one particular state, which carried a large part of the financial burden in securing the food safety of the whole EU, were compensated. Although this took place in connection with the BSE crisis and the circumstances were exceptional, it shows that there are ways and means, and that the existence of mechanisms such as comitology, even

[90] M Everson, 'The Constitutionalization of European Administrative Law' in Ch Joerges and E Vos (eds), *EU Committees …* (n 66) 303.

[91] Ch Joerges and J Neyer, 'From Intergovernmental Bargaining to Deliberative Political Process …' (n 72) 273–299, and further discussion on the theory in Ch Joerges, '"Deliberative Supranationalism"—A Defence' (2001) 5 *European Integration online Papers*; Ch Joerges, '"Deliberative Supranationalism"—Two Defences' (2002) 8 *European Law Journal* 133–151; Ch Joerges and J Neyer, '"Deliberative Supranationalism" Revisited' (2006) EUI Working Papers, Law No. 2006/20.

[92] Ch Joerges, '"Good Governance" Through Comitology?' (n 66) 325.

though it has drawbacks and limits, does matter.[93] It is not a perfect answer and it failed the efficiency test during the most challenging regulatory crisis in Europe. Nevertheless, although its effectiveness in situations of high and unequally distributed economic consequences can be questioned,[94] it remains a functioning system of the everyday management of the European market.

3.1.2. *Comitology System of Governance in the Food Sector*

In the initial stage, three major committees were established in the foodstuffs sector. The gradual delegation of an ever-wider variety of food issues to the Commission necessarily needed to be followed by the creation of adequate institutional guarantees for the member states' interests in this sensitive sector. Already in 1969 the Council had created a Standing Committee for Foodstuffs, consisting of representatives from all member states.[95] Its main objectives were to facilitate cooperation between the Commission and the states, and to provide the Commission with easier access to national governments' expertise with regard to food issues. Practically, it was given the authority to act as a substitute of the Council, with the powers to approve new regulatory policies and evaluate national derogations.[96]

Faced with the complexity of delegated matters and a growing need for scientific assistance in food management, the Commission created a Scientific Committee for Food. The Committee should function as a point of systematic contact with independent scientists and experts on various aspects of the field, such as health and safety, processing and composition of food, and food additives or contaminations.[97] Many of the scientists sitting on this Committee were also members of national consulting committees, which again built a link between EU and national policies. The Scientific Committee, since the beginning of its functioning, has enjoyed a great deal of importance in the field of risk assessment, developing methods of analysis and sampling, and deciding on various technical issues.[98]

One year later, with an aim of widening the range of interests represented in the European political process, a third important committee was established

---

[93] The case of EC compensation during the BSE crisis is discussed further in Chapter 3.2.

[94] S Krapohl and K Żurek, 'The Perils of Committee Governance: Intergovernmental Bargaining During the BSE Scandal in the European Union' (2006) 10 *European Integration online Papers.*

[95] Council Decision (EEC) 69/414 of 13 November 1969 setting up a Standing Committee for Foodstuffs [1969] OJ L 291/ 9.

[96] C Lister, *Regulation of Food Products …* (n 4) 12; for more on the Standing Committee for Foodstuffs, see M Hasselgard, 'Playing Games with Values of Higher Importance? Dealing with 'Risk Issues' in the Standing Committee on Foodstuffs' (2003) ARENA Report No.2003/01.

[97] Commission Decision (EEC) 74/234 of 16 April 1974 relating to the institution of a Scientific Committee for Food [1974] OJ L 136/1.

[98] C Lister, (n 4) 12–13.

by the Commission in the food sector. The Advisory Committee on Foodstuffs allows consultations with representatives of the industry, trade, agriculture and different consumers groups, which provides the Commission with stakeholders' views regarding specific implications of draft regulatory measures.[99]

In addition to those three major foodstuffs committees, the Council has created a number of specialised advisory committees that deal with technical questions in specific regulatory fields, such as feedstuffs, plant health or pesticides. They consist of national regulators, who assist in formulation of European food policies with regard to those particular technical aspects. The provisions of several directives, however, have empowered them with review responsibilities as well, and in that sense, they can be perceived as 'specialised alternatives to the Standing Committee, which itself is a surrogate for the Council'.[100]

3.2. *The BSE Scandal and Its Regulatory Impact*

3.2.1. *The BSE Crisis: A Search for Responsibility*

First detected in the United Kingdom in 1986, BSE (Bovine Spongiform Encephalopathy) is one of the transmissible spongiform encephalopathies that affect various animal species: in this case, cattle. The first measures to combat this disease were undertaken by the British authorities in 1988, and were later supplemented by EU action, starting from 1990. Following the discovery of a possible link between BSE and a new variant of Creutzfeldt-Jacob disease (vCJD), which affects humans, the Commission adopted a series of individual measures to combat the problem, starting with the imposition of a ban on British beef and beef products. There was, however, no political will, either on the side of the EU institutions or on the side of the member states, to undertake and invest in common, comprehensive anti-BSE measures. Eventually, in 2000, after a long period of being treated as an entirely British difficulty, it was officially acknowledged that BSE had become a European problem. The Scientific Steering Committee opinion on the geographical scope of BSE risk[101] stated that in almost all member states (except Austria, Finland and Sweden), the risk of internal BSE infections was high, due to previous imports of British cattle and feedstuffs. Only a few weeks later, this prediction proved right. This gave European countries an incentive to take comprehensive and coordinated action, which previously they had tried to avoid.

---

[99] Commission Decision (EEC) 75/420 of 26 June 1975 setting up an Advisory Committee on Foodstuffs [1975] OJ L 182/35.

[100] C Lister, (n 4) 14.

[101] Final Opinion of the Scientific Steering Committee on the Geographical Risk of Bovine Spongiform Encephalopathy (GBR) of 6 July 2000.

The Commission started to act swiftly by taking a set of the most pressing measures. The epidemio-surveillance programme was reinforced, with the introduction of rapid post-mortem testing in BSE monitoring.[102] Moreover, the Commission finally managed to successfully regulate the problem of specified risk materials, introducing a prohibition of their use and regulating a procedure for their safe destruction.[103] The use of meat and bone meal was temporarily prohibited in feedstuffs for all farm animals.[104] The introduction of new regulatory measures was followed by EU financial support for member states, which reduced the economic impact of the new provisions and facilitated their enforcement.[105]

This set of actions undertaken by the Commission, however, turned out to be too late to avoid the high economic, social and political costs of the crisis. It raised serious doubts about the EU's ability to govern. A search for a gap in the system that might be held responsible for the failure shed light on the complexity of the European decision-making process, the secrecy of the committees' actions and the ambiguity of their rules of procedure, revealing the important and far-reaching shortcomings of this governance mechanism.[106]

In July 1996, the Temporary Committee of Inquiry into BSE was set up by the European Parliament to investigate the affair and gather necessary evidence.[107] The first 'Report on alleged contraventions or maladministration in

[102] Commission Decision (EC) 2000/374 of 5 June 2000 amending Decision 98/272/EC on epidemio-surveillance for transmissible spongiform encephalopathies [2000] OJ L 135/27.

[103] Commission Decision (EC) 2000/418 of 29 June 2000 regulating the use of material presenting risks as regards transmissible spongiform encephalopathies and amending Decision 94/474/EC [2000] OJ L 158/76.

[104] Council Decision (EC) 2000/766 of 4 December 2000 concerning certain protection measures with regard to transmissible spongiform encephalopathies and the feeding of animal protein [2000] OJ L 306/32.

[105] Commission Decision (EC) 2000/639 of 13 October 2000 on the list of programmes for the monitoring of BSE qualifying for a financial contribution from the Community in 2001 [2000] OJ L 269/54; and Commission Decision (EC) 2000/773 of 30 November 2000 approving the programmes for the monitoring of BSE presented for 2001 by the Member States and fixing the level of the Community's financial contribution [2000] OJ L 308/35.

[106] For details as well as British experiences of dealing with BSE on the national level and methods applied, see G Chambers, 'The BSE Crisis and the European Parliament' in Ch Joerges and E Vos (eds), *EU Committees: Social Regulation ...* (n 66); L Frewer and B Salter, 'Public Attitudes, Scientific Advice and the Politics of Regulatory Policy: The Case of BSE' (2002) 29 *Science and Public Policy*; S Krapohl, 'Risk Regulation in the EU between Interests and Expertise—The Case of BSE' (2003) 10 *Journal of European Public Policy*; G Little, 'Reports. BSE and the Regulation of Risk' (2001) 64 *Modern Law Review*; E Millstone and P van Zwanenberg, 'Politics of Expert Advice: Lessons from the Early History of the BSE Saga' (2001) 28 *Science and Public Policy* 99; J Neyer, 'The Regulation of Risk and the Power of the People: Lessons from the BSE Crisis' (2000) 4 *European Integration online Papers*; K Vincent, '"Mad Cows" and Eurocrats—Community Responses to the BSE Crisis' (2004) 10 *European Law Journal* 499–517.

[107] Established by: Decision setting up a temporary committee of inquiry [1996] OJ C 261/231.

the implementation of Community law in relation to BSE'[108] by the European Parliament identified a series of problems at different levels of the regulatory structure, the effects of which were cumulative. It pointed out the main sources of difficulties, some of which are worth mentioning here. The first concerned the policy of disinformation applied by the Commission, not only with regard to the public, but also towards the other European institutions and national authorities. The second concerned the way in which national and industrial interests managed to prevail over the interest of Europe. The so called 'British thinking' phenomenon, which had a great deal of influence on the Commission's decisions, occurred as a result of a dominating influence by a number of British officials sitting on two committees operating in the field: the Veterinary Scientific Committee, composed of highly regarded scientists, and the Standing Veterinary Committee, composed of national representatives. It transpired that their activities at that time were subject to intense political pressure and, as a result, neither independence nor transparency was at a premium. The third important factor concerned the working methods of the Committees and the Commission, and the ambiguity of their relations that is to say, the lack of supervision and control, the lack of coordination, as well as the already mentioned predominance of national and industrial interests in the decision-making processes.[109]

The Temporary Committee's investigation gave rise to practical proposals for improvements to ensure that a similar situation would not occur in the future. The Committee recommendations dealt with five aspects of EU activity, but only the most important of them will be quoted here. Firstly, the committee called for greater transparency in the action to combat BSE. This was to be achieved through the widest possible dissemination of relevant research data and findings. Secondly, it emphasised the necessity for procedures to monitor measures designed to combat BSE, as well as to protect public and animal health. Finally, it recommended the adoption of a whole set of relevant measures necessary for the protection of public health and of measures necessary to restore the smooth operation of the market.[110]

3.2.2 *The White Paper and the New Approach to Food Regulation*

There is no doubt that the BSE crisis forced the EU and all member states to face the problem of policy shortcomings and to take firm action to reform

[108] European Parliament, Report on alleged contraventions or maladministartion in the implementation of Community law in relation to BSE, without prejudice to the jurisdiction of the Community and national courts, 7 January 1997, A4-0020/97.

[109] Compare Report on alleged contraventions … ibid, Part A.I.4, as well as E Vos, 'EU Food Safety Regulation in the Aftermath of the BSE Crisis' (2000) 23 *Journal of Consumer Policy* 231–233.

[110] See Report on alleged contraventions … ibid, Part A.II.

the European food-safety system. One of the first steps to be taken was the immediate creation of a strong legal basis for EU actions in the field. This was embodied in the Amsterdam Treaty Amendment, which introduced the requirement for all EU policies and actions to ensure a high level of human health protection. Article 95 TEC (now Article 114 TFEU)—a special 'harmonisation provision' introduced by the Single European Act, which committed the Commission to base harmonisation proposals on a high level of protection of public health, safety, as well as environmental and consumer protection—was extended by requiring it to 'take account in particular of any new development based on scientific facts'. Furthermore, Article 152(1) TEC (now Article 168(1) TFEU) was radically strengthened, stating that 'a high level of human health protection *shall be ensured* in the definition and implementation of all Community policies and activities'.[111] Finally, Article 153(1) TEC (now Article 169(1) TFEU) on consumer protection was developed by adding a phrase: '. . . the Community shall contribute to protecting the health, safety and economic interest of consumers . . . '[112] This was taken, as Lafond has correctly pointed out, to mean that the aim of European food regulation would no longer simply be to mitigate the side-effects of implementing the single market, but also to protect public health and consumers as fully acknowledged objectives of the European integration process.[113]

Simultaneously with the reform of the legal basis, initial institutional adjustments were undertaken. Faced with the critique of the EP Report, the Commission declared it would immediately initiate relevant actions, as recommended by the Report, starting with reforming its own organisation. In order to avoid dangerous conflicts between industrial and consumer interests, all relevant committees dealing with public-health measures were placed under the authority of DG XXIV,[114] which was renamed the Directorate-General on Consumer Policy and Health Protection (DG SANCO).

The next step towards the improvement of foodstuffs regulation and the fulfilment of the Report recommendations was the announcement by the

[111] The original version only required it to '*contribute to*' high level of human-health protection. Emphasis added in both cases.

[112] For more analysis, see E Vos, 'EU Food Safety Regulation ...' (n 109) 235–236; and B van der Meulen, *Food Safety Law in the European Union: An Introduction* (Wageningen Academic Publishers, Wageningen 2004) 130.

[113] See FD Lafond, 'The Creation of the European Food Authority. Institutional Implications of Risk Regulation' (2001) 10 *European Issues* 6.

[114] Commission (EC), Decision (EC) 97/579 of 23 July 1997 setting up Scientific Committees in the field of consumer health and food safety [1997] OJ L 237/18. On the basis on this Decision, there were eight scientific committees of that kind, dealing with the following issues: food; animal nutrition; animal health and welfare; veterinary measures relating to public health, plants, cosmetics and other non-food products intended for consumers; medicinal products and medicinal devices; toxicity; ecotoxicity; and the environment.

Commission of a radical change in the approach to food-safety regulation in Europe. The reform proposal was proclaimed in the Commission Green Paper on General Principles of Food Law in the EU,[115] later followed by the White Paper on Food Safety of 12 January 2000.[116] The new policy aimed to cover the whole food chain and all stages of the decision-making process. Three pillars of risk regulation in the field of food safety were identified: risk assessment, risk management and risk communication. The creation of a European Food Authority was also proposed.[117] Since one of the main aims of the White Paper was the restoration and maintenance of consumer confidence, it presented a very ambitious political and legislative programme. After reviewing the European food legislation, the White Paper made 84 law and policy proposals,[118] which were intended to make European food law more coherent and comprehensive, but also to strengthen its enforcement.[119]

3.3. *New Food-Safety Policy: Between BSE Trauma and Enlargement Anxiety*

3.3.1. *The 'From Farm to Fork' Strategy and the Establishment of the New Food Safety Authority*

3.3.1.1. *New Ideas of Comprehensive Regulation*

The new policy ideas presented in the Green and the White Papers, announcing a comprehensive reform of the EU foodstuffs regime, resulted in the adoption of a new Regulation on the general principles and requirements of food law,[120] which provided for a coherent conceptual approach to the issue. The Regulation treats food production as a continuum, running from the primary production of animal feed to the supply of food for the end consumer ('from the farm to the fork', as the propaganda announced). The Regulation expressly introduces the principles of food law, including the precautionary principle, and establishes the European Food Safety Authority as an independent source of scientific advice, information and risk-communication. According to the provisions of the Regulation, the Authority is expected—as a new scientific body—to provide

[115] Commission (EC), Commission Green Paper on The General Principles of Food Law in the European Union, COM (1997) 176 final.

[116] Commission (EC), White Paper on Food Safety COM (1999) 719 final.

[117] A detailed analysis of the proposed provisions concerning the new Food Safety Authority included in the White Paper will be provided in the following paragraphs of this thesis.

[118] They were enumerated in the Annex to the White Paper, under the heading "Action Plan".

[119] See B van der Meulen, (n 112) 142–145.

[120] Regulation (EC) 178/2002 of the European Parliament and of the Council of 28 January 2002 laying down the general principles and requirements of food law, establishing the European Food Safety Authority and laying down procedures in matters of food safety [2002] OJ L 31/1.

the Commission with scientific advice in an independent, objective and transparent manner. It is also meant to be at the centre of a network of national scientific institutions. In this way, the EFSA should enable member states to become more closely involved in scientific matters, and to establish and coordinate close cooperation between the Authority and the national scientific institutions. Finally, the Regulation indicates the division of responsibilities among food and feed business operators, the member states and the EU institutions.[121]

Regulation 178/2002[122] consists of five chapters, preceded by a lengthy preamble, which emphasises the importance of the regulated issues. Declaring the new open and inclusive approach, it begins with the following statement:

> The free movement of safe and wholesome food is an essential aspect of the internal market and contributes to the health and well-being of citizens, and to their social and economic interests.

This sentence in fact contains the essence of the problem: the problematic relationship between free trade in the internal market, on the one side, and the health, well-being and social needs of European citizens on the other. It implies that the Regulation was meant to be a major step towards comprehending the problem and finding the best solutions. Whether it has lived up to these expectations and answered all the dilemmas is questionable. It would be impossible, and probably also unnecessary, to analyse the whole Regulation in great detail here. Accordingly, this section just provides a brief overview and explores only those points which seem to be of major relevance for the discussion. Before turning to the analysis of this body of law, a brief look at its legal basis is in order. It is interesting that, contrary to almost all previous acts establishing European agencies, whose only legal basis was Article 308 TEC (now

[121] For further analysis of the influence of the BSE crisis on the development of the European food-regulation, see FD Lafond, (n 113); M Hagenmeyer, 'Modern Food Safety Requirements—According to EC Regulation No 178/2002' (2002) 4 *Zeitschrift für das gesamte Lebensmittelrecht*; E Millstone, 'Recent Developments in EU Food Policy: Institutional Adjustments or Fundamental Reforms?' (2000) 6 *ZLR*; D Chalmers, '"Food for Thought": Reconciling European Risks and Traditional Ways of Life' (2003) 66 *Modern Law Review*; S Krapohl, 'Risk Regulation in the EU between Interests and Expertise …' (n 106); and L Buonanno, S Zablotney and R Keefer, 'Politics versus Science in the Making of a New Regulatory Regime for Food in Europe' (2001) 5 *European Integration online Papers*.

[122] Ibid, very detailed analysis of the whole Regulation as well as its separate parts can be found in D Holland and H Pope, *EU Food Law and Policy* (Kluwer Law International, the Hague 2004); B van der Meulen and M van der Velde, (n 112); and Instituto di dritto agrario internazionale e comparato (IDAIC), 'La sicurezza alimentare nell'Unione Europea' (2003) 1–2 *Le Nuove Leggi Civili Comentate*.

Article 352 TFEU),[123] Regulation 178/2002 is much more solidly based. Specifically, it has been based on Articles 37, 95, 133 and 152(4)(b) of the Treaty (now respectively Articles 43, 114, 207 and 168(4)(b) TFEU).[124] This undoubtedly offers much more than just the 'last resort' clause of Article 308 (now Article 352 TFEU). Surprisingly, however, among these widely sketched legal foundations, Article 153 TEC (now Article 169 and 12 TFEU) on consumer protection was not included. This might have been done to reduce the ability of member states to introduce higher standards of protection and thus depart from the commonly established system, which is much more difficult under Article 95 (now 114 TFEU) than it would be under the consumer-protection clause. Nevertheless, is appears to be somewhat paradoxical.

The first chapter defines the aim and scope of the Regulation, as well as the most important terms used in it. Article 1 declares that the Regulation provides the basis for the assurance of a high level of protection of human health and consumers' interest in relation to food, taking into particular account the diversity in supply of food, including traditional products, whilst ensuring the effective functioning of the internal market. It is interesting to note that, in contrast to the first sentence of the preamble, as cited in the preceding paragraph, the first article puts consumers' health and interest in the first place, and only later does it refer to internal market efficiency.

The principal idea of the new food safety policy—the idea of treating food issues as a continuum 'from the farm to the fork'—is envisaged in the definition of 'food law' in Article 3.[125] It says that 'food law' means the laws, regulations and administrative provisions governing food in general and food safety in particular, whether at EC or national level; it covers every stage of the

[123] Former Article 308 of the Treaty (now Article 352 TFEU) is a provision of a very general and open nature; it reads: 'If action by the Community should prove necessary to attain, in the course of the operation of the common market, one of the objectives of the Community, and this Treaty has not provided the necessary powers, the Council shall, acting unanimously on a proposal from the Commission and after consulting the European Parliament, take the appropriate measures'.

[124] This compound legal basis gives the Regulation the ground in and the linkage to the provisions on common agricultural policy, internal market-building and harmonisation, as well as the common commercial policy and the protection of public health.

[125] It is worth noting that Article 2 of the Regulation 178/2002 provides a new definition of the term 'food'. Since this word is one of the most commonly used in this book, it seems necessary to provide the proper, if somewhat simplified, definition. According to the Regulation, 'food' (or 'foodstuff') means any substance or product, whether processed, partially processed or unprocessed, intended to be, or reasonably expected to be ingested by humans. 'Food' includes drinks, chewing gum and any substance, including water, intentionally incorporated into the food during its manufacture, preparation or treatment. 'Food' shall not include feed, live animals (unless they are prepared for placing on the market for human consumption), plants prior to harvesting, medicinal products, cosmetics, tobacco and tobacco products, narcotic or psychotropic substances, residues and contaminants.

production, processing and distribution of food, and also of feed produced for, or fed to, food-producing animals.

The second chapter of the Regulation lays down the general principles and requirements of food law, and the general obligations of food trade. They apply, in accordance with Article 4.1, to all stages of the production, processing and distribution of food, and also of feed produced for, or fed to, food-producing animals. In Article 5, which amplifies the general objectives of food law, referred to above, reference is made to the international standards established in the field. According to this provision, where such standards exist or their completion is imminent, they shall be taken into consideration in the development or adaptation of food law. This should not be the case, however, when such standards or relevant parts would be an ineffective or inappropriate means for the fulfilment of the legitimate objectives of food law, or where there is a scientific justification, or where they would result in a different level of protection from the one determined as appropriate in the EU. The next provision develops the notion of 'risk analysis', emphasising its clear division into risk-assessment and risk-management. Further articles introduce the precautionary principle and the principle of traceability, as well as the general obligations of the food trade.

Particularly worth noting in this context is that in Article 14, the legislator gives a kind of negative definition of food safety. First of all, it is stated that food shall not be placed on the market if it is unsafe. Secondly, an explanation is provided, according to which food shall be deemed to be unsafe if it is considered to be injurious to health or unfit for human consumption. Lastly, detailed instructions are given in order to make a determination of the above-mentioned factors. The second chapter ends with a series of provisions regarding the responsibilities of food and feed business operators.[126]

Chapter three of the Regulation—on the organisation and operation of the European Food Safety Authority—will be discussed in detail in the next section of this volume.

Chapter four lays down rules for the establishment and operation of a rapid-alert system for food and feed (RASFF), as well as provisions on emergency measures and crisis-management. The RASFF is a notification network that is concerned with direct and indirect risks to human health deriving from food and feed, with the aim of the immediate implementation of emergency measures.

The fifth chapter of the Regulation consists of rules on committee and mediation procedures, as well as some final provisions. One important innovation is a conflict-resolution mechanism, which is to be used whenever a divergence of scientific opinion arises. According to Article 30, the EFSA should exercise

[126] Regulation 178/2002, (n 120) Articles 19–21.

vigilance in order to identify at an early stage any potential source of divergence between its scientific opinions and the scientific opinions issued by other bodies carrying out similar tasks. Where such substantive divergence over scientific issues has been identified and the body in question is of a member state, the EFSA and the national body are obliged to cooperate with the aim of either resolving the divergence or preparing a joint document that clarifies the contentious scientific issues and identifying the relevant uncertainties in the data, which will then be made public. The inclusion of this provision in the Regulation indicates that the regulators have acknowledged that the problem of varying scientific opinions requires a solution. In this sense, it can certainly be seen as a step forward. Nevertheless, it places the EFSA in the position of a watchdog, rather than giving it any supremacy over conflicting national opinions. That is, it obliges the EFSA to seek and encourage compromise without entitling it to have the final word. On the one hand, such a solution can be considered very appropriate, as it would be difficult to find grounds for legitimising scientific supremacy of a European institution over national ones. On the other hand, though, one might question how relevant such a solution would be in practice, and what role the EFSA would serve. Hence, I will now offer an analysis of the Authority itself.

3.3.1.2. *The Establishment of the European Food Safety Authority*

The core of food-regulation reform in the aftermath of the BSE crisis was the development of a new institutional architecture, which would prevent similar crises in the future and provide an operative framework for further development of a consumer-friendly food-safety organisation. On the basis of the analysis of experienced shortcomings and expected challenges connected with the enlargement of the EU, four different options for the new food-safety architecture were considered. These were: a directorate within a current or new Directorate General, an independent Commission service, an inter-institutional office, and an independent agency.[127] Why was the agency model chosen? The answer to this question is complex. It might be useful, therefore, to begin with a short theoretical consideration of the agency structure of governance. Following a brief overview of existing agency models, their applicability to the food sector will be analysed.

3.3.1.2.1. *'Agencification' of the European Union?*. 'Agency' may, at a first glance, seem to be a rather straightforward concept. It is, however, a concept which holds many meanings. A lot has been written about the agency system of governance, and several types of agency models have been differentiated

---

[127] P James, F Kemper and G Pascal, 'A European Food and Public Health Authority. The Future of Scientific Advice in the EU' (European Commission, December 1999) 6.

and described in the legal literature.[128] Agency has gained popularity in Europe largely due to the development of a discourse contrasting it with committees and highlighting features which distinguish it from the latter. Crucial among those features are the following: agencies possess legal personality, they are supported by their own administrative structure, and they enjoy a considerable degree of administrative independence. The agency model of governance advocated in Europe firstly and mainly by Giandomenico Majone[129] is based on deliberative rather than majoritarian thinking, and prioritises administrative market integration, to be carried out by fully independent agencies that should bring together technical and economic expertise. This agency model, referring to agencies which have the power to translate broad legislative guidelines into concrete instruments, has not been achieved in Europe, due to the very narrow and strict interpretation of the Treaty taken by the ECJ in the Meroni[130] judgement, such agencies cannot be created in the EU. The creation of true 'regulatory' agencies in Europe would require either a revision of the Meroni doctrine or an amendment of the Treaty.

The phenomenon of 'agencification' may be considered, on the one hand, as a variant of a 'decentralized integration' model of administration, and, on the other, as a next step in the direction of deliberative supranationalism. Justification for this consideration lies within the characteristics of the agency structure of governance. Firstly, administrative tasks are assigned to a wide number of bodies at different levels of administration, which act interdependently and are disciplined by procedural rules. Secondly, a multiplicity of subjects is involved in the exercise of their functions, which provides for broad

[128] E.g., E Chiti, 'The Emergence of a Community Administration: The Case of European Agencies' (2003) 37 *Common Market Law Review*; M Everson, 'Independent Agencies: Hierarchy Beaters?' (1995) 2 *European Law Journal*; D Geradin and N Petit, 'The Development of Agencies at EU and National Levels: Conceptual Analysis and Proposals for Reform' (2004) Jean Monnet Working Paper 01/04; A Kreher, 'Agencies in the European Community—a Step Towards Administrative Integration in Europe' (1997) 2 *Journal of European Public Policy*; G Majone and M Everson, 'Institutional Reform: Independent Agencies, Oversight, Coordination and Procedural Control' in O de Schutter, N Lebesis and J Patterson, *Governance in the European Union* (European Commission, Luxembourg 2001); E Vos, 'Agencies and the European Union' in T Zwart and L Verhey (eds), *Agencies in European and Comparative Law* (Intersentia, Antwerp 2003); D Geradin, R Muñoz and N Petit (eds), *Regulation through Agencies in the EU. A New Paradigm of European Governance* (Edward Elgar Publishing, Cheltenham 2005).

[129] G Majone, *Regulating Europe* (Routledge, London 1996); G Majone, 'The New European Agencies: Regulation by Information' (1997) 4 *Journal of European Public Policy* 262; G Majone, 'European Regulatory Agencies: The Dilemma of Delegation of Powers in the European Union' in G Majone (eds), *Risk Regulation in the European Union: Between Enlargement and Internationalization* (RSCAS, Florence 2003).

[130] The Meroni doctrine was developed by the ECJ in its judgement in case C 9/56 *Meroni v. High Authority* (1957–1958) ECR 133. It provides an extremely narrow interpretation of the possibility to delegate competences by the European Commission, meaning basically that only clearly defined executive powers may be delegated to institutions other than the Commission itself.

participation by stakeholders, as well as the consideration and inclusion of their differing interests.

The emergence of the agency concept led to the formation of sixteen European Agencies by 2003.[131] By 2009 a further eight had been established.[132] Due to the lack of a unified recipe for agency formation, all differ significantly in their functions, their modes of operation and their roles in the decision-making process. In 2003, the Council established a uniform legal basis for the creation of executive agencies, which are meant to be entrusted with certain tasks relating to the management of one or more EU programmes.[133] On the basis of that Regulation, six executive agencies have already been established.[134]

Nowadays, the official classification of European agencies, proposed by the Commission, categorises EU agencies into three groups. The first group consists of 'regulatory agencies and bodies.' They embrace three subcategories: 'policy agencies', which are set up by an act of secondary legislation in order to

---

[131] They are: the European Environment Agency (EEA), Regulation 1210/90 [1990] OJ L 139/1; the European Training Foundation (ETF), Regulation 1360/90 [1990] OJ L 131/1; the European Monitoring Centre of Drugs and Drug Addiction (EMCDDA), Regulation 302/93 [1993] OJ L 036/1; the European Agency for the Evaluation of Medicinal Products (EMEA), Regulation 2309/93 [1993] OJ L 036/1, recently refurbished and renamed as the European Medicines Agency under Regulation 726/2004 [2004] OJ L 136; the Office for Harmonization in the Internal Market (Trade Marks and Designs) (OHIM), Regulation 40/94 [1994] OJ L 011/1; the European Agency for Safety and Health at Work (EASHW), Regulation 2062/94 [1994] OJ L 216/1; the Translation Centre for Bodies of the European Union (CdT), Regulation 2965/94 [1994] OJ L 314; the Community Plant Variety Office (CPVO), Regulation 2100/94 [1994] OJ L 227/1; the European Foundation for the Improvement of Living and Working Conditions (EUROFOUND), Regulation 1365/75 [1975] OJ L 139/1; the European Centre for the Development of Vocational Training (CEDEFOP), Regulation 337/75 [1975] OJ L 039/1; the European Monitoring Centre on Racism and Xenophobia (EUMC), Regulation 1035/97 [1997] OJ L 151/1, recently replaced by European Fundamental Rights Agency (EFRA), Regulation 168/2007 [2007] OJ L 53/2; the European Agency for Reconstruction (EAR), which terminated its activity on 31 December 2008, Regulation 2667/00 [2000] OJ L 306/7; the European Food Safety Authority (EFSA), Regulation 178/2002 [2002] OJ L 031/1; the European Maritime Safety Agency (EMSA), Regulation 1406/2002 [2002] OJ L 208/1; and the European Aviation Safety Agency (EASA), Regulation 1592/2002 [2002] OJ L 240/1.

[132] The European Network and Information Security Agency (ENISA), Regulation 460/2004 [2004] OJ L 77/1; European Centre for Disease Prevention and Control (ECDC), Regulation 851/2004 [2004] OJ L 142; the European Railway Agency (ERA), Regulation 881/2004 [2004] OJ L 164/1; the European Agency for the Management of Operational Coordination at the External Borders (FRONTEX), Regulation 2007/2004 [2004] OJ L 349; the European Fisheries Control Agency (CFCA), Regulation 768/2005 [2005] OJ L 128; the European GNSS Supervisory Authority (EGSA), Regulation 1321/2004 [2004] OJ L 264/1; and the European Chemicals Agency (ECHA), Regulation 1907/2006 [2006] OJ L 396/1; The European Institute for Gender Equality, Regulation 1922/2006 [2006] OJ L 403/9.

[133] Council Regulation (EC) 58/2003 of 19 December 2002 laying down the statute for executive agencies to be entrusted with certain tasks in the management of Community programmes [2003] OJ L 11/1.

[134] They are: the Education, Audiovisual, and Culture Executive Agency (EACEA); the European Research Council Executive Agency (ERC); the Executive Agency for Competitiveness and Innovation (EACI); the Executive Agency for Health and Consumers (EAHC); the Research Executive Agency (REA); and the Trans-European Transport Network Executive Agency (TEN-TEA).

accomplish a very specific technical, scientific or managerial task; 'Common Security and Defence Policy agencies' and 'Police and judicial cooperation in criminal matters agencies.' The second group refers to the 'EURATOM agencies and bodies'. Finally, the third group are the 'executive agencies', which are established in accordance with Council Regulation 58/2003 mentioned above.[135]

The main question here concerns the general appropriateness of the agency structure to the food sector and the modes of its applicability in that field. Before this is done, however, it seems appropriate to examine briefly all options which were taken into account when these crucial legal and policy choices were being made.

3.3.1.2.2. *Proposed Concepts of the European Food Authority.* Numerous preparatory reports and documents were presented and various visions of the architecture of the new food-safety institution were offered to the Commission. In the following paragraphs, two most influential proposals will be reviewed in more detail. They are, namely, the James/Kemper/Pascal Report[136] and the Commission White Paper on Food Safety.[137]

3.3.1.2.2.1. The 'European Food and Public Health Authority' Proposed by the James/Kemper/Pascal Report. In October 1999, P. James, F. Kemper and G. Pascal were requested by the Director General of DG XXIV, Mr H. Reichenbach, to undertake a reanalysis of the organisation of scientific advice in the light of the previous two years' experience with the new system, which was established in the first set of reforms instituted in April 1997. In their report they analysed four possible institutional solutions previously proposed by the Commission. These were: (i) a directorate within a current or new DG; (ii) an independent Commission service; (iii) an inter-institutional office; and (iv) an independent agency. Having considered the pros and cons of all four options in the light of the demands of the existing situation, they reached the conclusion that the best choice for the EU administration in this field would be the creation of a European Food and Public Health Authority, which, in their opinion, was closer to the third option (inter-institutional office) than to an agency model. It seems, however, having compared descriptions of these two options, that this was more a question of terminology than anything else.

The point of departure for the Report was the necessity for an operative system to provide scientific advice which would be independent, transparent,

---

[135] See < http://europa.eu/agencies/> accessed 25 May 2011.
[136] See James/Kemper/Pascal Report, (n 127).
[137] White Paper on Food Safety (n 116).

of excellent scientific quality and capable of being readily understood by non-experts, the European Parliament, the member states, the industry and the Commission. Hence, the Report proposed creation of a new institution to deal with all public health, environmental and food issues, with the exception of the assessment of drugs, which should continue to be dealt with by the European Agency for the Evaluation of Medicinal Products (EMEA). The authors believed that such an institution should be based in Brussels, which would facilitate rapid interaction with the Commission and other EU institutions. It should also cooperate closely with member states and international organisations. In order to signify its unique character, they claimed, it should be named an 'authority' rather than an 'agency'. It would have some features in common with the US Food and Drug Administration but remain more independent of political and industrial interests and be linked closely with the Commission. The Authority would develop mechanisms for ensuring appropriate governance in six particular areas:

- an effective system for the monitoring of European public health, including a proper audit of national surveillance and control processes;
- policy analysis and options for policy developments that would ensure public health in all member states;
- evaluation of the implications of scientific opinions relating to legislative and regulatory proposals;
- a research analysis and research policy group, with a coherent research programme relevant to public health and food safety;
- a communications unit; and
- mechanisms and procedures for crisis management.[138]

It was suggested, therefore, that all the fields covered by the existing nine scientific committees established within the DG SANCO in 1997[139] be retained under the control of the Authority, since experience had shown that they were deeply interconnected and often required complex multidimensional analysis. Hence, there was a need to consider the food chain, public health and a wide range of environmental issues as a whole, and consequently to approach them in a coherent manner, which the Authority would guarantee.

---

[138] See James/Kemper/Pascal Report, (n 127) 6–20.

[139] These are: the Scientific Committee on Food, the Scientific Committee on Animal Nutrition, the Scientific Committee on Animal Health and Animal Welfare, the Sub-committee on Animal Welfare, the Scientific Committee on Veterinary Measures relating to Public Health, the Scientific Committee on Plants, the Scientific Committee for Cosmetic Products and Non-food Products intended for Consumers, the Scientific Committee on Medicinal Products and Medicinal Devices, the Scientific Committee for Toxicity, Ecotoxicity and the Environment Field of Competence, and also the Overall Scientific Steering Committee, which deals with multidisciplinary issues such as the BSE crisis.

From an organisational point of view, the authors of the Report presented some interesting suggestions. They suggest, for example, that the Authority should be assisted by an appropriately sized secretariat in order to be able to cope with the complexity and range of issues submitted for scientific analysis. They strongly emphasise this particular need, criticising the EU for having underestimated it so far. Each major committee acting within the Authority would need at least three highly qualified scientists working on an ongoing basis, and a full-time administrator with appropriate secretarial assistance. This 'secretarial assistance' is perceived by the authors as the key to good communication and coordination between the risk assessors (in the Authority) and the risk managers (in the Commission), in order to achieve a close working relationship from the beginning of the process, when scientific questions are formulated, to the phase when political decisions are adopted. To achieve optimal efficiency, members of the secretariat should be able to understand both the science and the implications of the advice for legislators and policy-makers. Another important proposal is that the secretariat be accessible to the other stakeholders, including the representatives of the administration of the member states, petitioners and representatives of various interest groups.

The authors of the report place great emphasis on the issue of the involvement of stakeholders in the functioning of the Authority. Interestingly enough, the authors not only claim that a theoretical possibility of involvement is necessary, but they also underline the necessity of financial support for certain groups, to make it practically possible for them to become involved. These are, naturally, consumer, environmental and other public-interest groups, which would otherwise be disadvantaged in comparison with the representatives of industry. A system of observers is proposed as one potential option of making the authors' vision a reality.

3.3.1.2.2.2. The Concept of the 'European Food Authority' in the Commission White Paper on Food Safety. The Commission White Paper on Food Safety,[140] adopted in 2000, recommended a series of legal and institutional improvements in the field of food safety, which the Commission deemed necessary to make up for previous failures and to avoid such situations in the future. The key priority, as declared by the Commission, was to take effective measures to ensure a high level of consumer protection, through which consumer confidence could not only be restored but also maintained. Therefore, the system to be implemented had to be durable and have the appropriate flexibility. According to the Commission, a series of major structural changes was required, among which the most crucial was the establishment of a new Authority, whose role was to be defined in the context of the process of risk analysis.

[140] White Paper on Food Safety, (n 116) par. 29.

For the clarity of further deliberation, it seems to be appropriate here to make a few comments on the process of risk analysis, as interpreted by the Commission. The crucial elements of risk analysis, namely risk assessment, risk management and risk communication were assigned the following meanings:

- *Risk assessment* means the provision of scientific advice, the gathering and processing of information, as well as monitoring and surveillance of a given field.
- *Risk management* comprises legislation and control. Legislation refers to primary and implementing legislation and involves decision-making based not only on available scientific data, but also on political choices and an appreciation of public needs and concerns. Due to the above-mentioned factors, the Commission opts for clear and strict separation of the risk assessment and risk management functions.
- *Risk communication* aims at ensuring that the public is kept properly informed, and thus at reducing the risk of unwarranted food safety concerns arising. Proper risk communication requires that scientific data be made widely and promptly accessible. It also involves consumer education and information on wider issues of health protection and control.[141]

The main advantage of an Authority in this context, according to the Commission, is that it facilitates broader acceptance of scientific risk assessment, which is an essential prerequisite for the effectiveness, appropriateness and rapidity of every action undertaken in the field. The responsibilities of the Authority primarily include the preparation and provision of scientific advice, the collection and analysis of the necessary information, as well as the monitoring and surveillance of developments concerning food safety issues and the communication of its findings to all interested stakeholders. In performing its functions, the Authority shall demonstrate the highest level of independence, scientific excellence and transparency of its operations.

In the view of the Commission, such an Authority would be an ideal institution to develop flexible and rapid responses to challenges arising in the food sector. It would not only act as a point of scientific reference for European and national institutions, but would also be available to consumers and provide them with necessary advice and guidance. Furthermore, it would constitute the centre of a network of the national scientific agencies of member states

[141] Ibid, par. 30–34. For further academic debate on risk regulation and risk issues in general, see the analysis in the previous Part and the literature referred to therein; for example, U Beck, *Risk Society. Towards a New Modernity* (Sage Publications, London 1986, 1992); C Hood, H Rothstein and R Baldwin (eds), *The Government of Risk. Understanding Risk Regulation Regimes* (Oxford University Press, Oxford 2001); and S Lash, B Szerszynski and B Wynne (eds), *Risk, Environment and Modernity: Towards a New Ecology* (Sage Publications, London 1996).

and would work in close cooperation with these agencies. In order to fulfil its objectives in the best possible fashion, the Authority must, in all its actions, demonstrate a high level of accountability to the European institutions and the general public. It must, therefore, be guided exclusively by the best science, and be independent of industrial and political interests. It must also be scientifically authoritative and open to rigorous public scrutiny. Hence, it should have a legal existence and personality separate from the current institutions, which will enable it to carry out its tasks of risk assessment and risk communication in a fully independent and accountable manner.[142]

Naturally, the Commission's vision of the Authority prevailed and the new Food Safety Agency was, in the end, constructed according to its model. This is not at all surprising. Nevertheless, one may still wonder why all those reform ideas were so narrowly targeted from the beginning. Why, having faced a food scandal that shook the core of the whole organisation of the product market, did the reform only concentrate on securing the provision of appropriate scientific risk assessment, while other parts of the process were not even deliberated? Was it a question of time? Or was it rather a question of the nature of the crisis and its challenges? Before those questions are approached, a more detailed analysis of the European Food Safety Authority is provided.[143]

3.3.1.2.3. *The European Food Safety Authority*[144]

3.3.1.2.3.1. Mission and Tasks

> The Authority shall provide scientific advice and scientific and technical support for the Community's legislation and policies in all fields which have direct or indirect impact on food and food safety. It shall provide independent information on all matters within these fields and communicate on risks. The Authority shall contribute to a high level of protection of human life and health, and in this respect take account of animal health and welfare, plant health and environment, in the context of the operation of the internal market.[145]

This general statement of the mission of the EFSA is developed further in Article 22 of Regulation 178/2002, where it is stated that the Authority shall collect and analyse data to allow the characterisation and monitoring of risks

---

[142] White Paper on Food Safety, (n 116) par. 35–43.

[143] For a general overview, see L Buonanno, 'The Creation of the European Food Safety Authority' in C Ansell and D Vogel (eds), *What's the Beef? The Contested Governance of European Food Safety* (The MIT Press, Cambridge MA 2006) 259–278; B Rudolf and J Simons, 'European Governance of Food Safety' in CH Hofmann and AH Türk (eds), *EU Administrative Governance* (n 88) 153–174.

[144] It is interesting to point out the transformation of the name of the agency from the *'European Food Authority'* envisaged in the White Paper, to the *'European Food Safety Authority'* laid down in the Regulation 178/2002. The *'Safety'* component of the official name was in fact introduced upon insistence of the European Parliament.

[145] Regulation 178/2002 (n 120) Article 22, par. 2, 3.

that have a direct or indirect impact on food and feed safety. It is elaborated in the following paragraphs, with an exemplification of the main components of EFSA's mission. The mission includes the provision of:

a) scientific advice and scientific and technical support on human nutrition in relation to EU legislation and, at the request of the Commission, assistance concerning communication on nutritional issues within the framework of the Community health programme;
b) scientific opinions on other matters relating to animal health and welfare and plant health; and
c) scientific opinions on products other than food and feed relating to genetically modified organisms as defined by Directive 2001/18/EC[146] and without prejudice to the procedures established therein.

The scientific opinions of the Authority are meant to serve as the scientific basis for the drafting and adoption of EU measures in the field falling within its mission.

Apart from enumerating components of EFSA's mission, Article 22 gives guidance on methods of its accomplishment. It is emphasised there that the Authority shall carry out its tasks in conditions which enable it to serve as a point of reference, by virtue of its independence, the scientific and technical quality of the opinions it issues and the information it disseminates, the transparency of its procedures and methods of operation, and its diligence in performing the tasks assigned to it. Moreover, it shall act in close cooperation with competent bodies in the member states that carry out similar tasks at the national level.

Article 23 of the Regulation consists of a list of twelve tasks of the EFSA. It is appropriate to quote all twelve of them here, in order to be able to get the complete picture and proper basis for the further analysis. The tasks of the Authority, as defined by law, are the following:

a) to provide EC institutions and the member states with the best possible scientific opinions in all cases provided for by EC legislation and on any question within its mission;
b) to promote and coordinate the development of uniform risk assessment methodologies in the fields falling within its mission;
c) to provide scientific and technical support to the Commission in the areas within its mission and, when so requested, in the interpretation and consideration of risk assessment opinions;

[146] Directive (EC) 2001/18 of the European Parliament and of the Council of 12 March 2001 on the deliberate release into the environment of genetically modified organisms, and repealing Council Directive 90/220/EEC [2001] OJ L 106.

d) to commission scientific studies necessary for the accomplishment of its mission;
e) to search for, collect, collate, analyse and summarise scientific and technical data in the fields within its mission;
f) to undertake action to identify and characterise emerging risks in the fields within its mission;
g) to establish a system of networks of organisations operating in the fields within its mission and be responsible for their operation;
h) to provide scientific and technical assistance, when requested to do so by the Commission, in the crisis-management procedures implemented by the Commission with regard to the safety of food and feed;
i) to provide scientific and technical assistance, when requested to do so by the Commission, with a view to improving cooperation between the EC, applicant countries, international organisations and third countries, in the fields within its mission;
j) to ensure that the public and interested parties receive rapid, reliable, objective and comprehensible information in the fields within its mission;
k) to express independently its own conclusions and orientations on matters within its mission; and
l) to undertake any other task assigned to it by the Commission within its mission.

Having read the task-list it is interesting to observe how much the legislator expects of the Authority. On the other hand, it is a common strategy to draft a range of tasks rather broadly in order to create a multiplicity of options, and so not end up in a situation where the means and resources are in place but there is no legal basis to act.

3.3.1.2.3.2. Organisational Structure. The Authority is composed of four bodies: the Management Board, the Executive Director, the Advisory Forum, and the Scientific Committee with permanent Scientific Panels.[147]

The Management Board. The Management Board is the organ responsible for the general functioning of the Authority. It is to ensure that the EFSA carries out its mission and performs its tasks in accordance with the law.

In order to guarantee the effectiveness of the EFSA's activities, the Management Board adopts multi-annual and annual programmes of work, which are to be consistent with the overall framework of EU legislative and policy priorities in the area. In order to monitor compliance, it reports on the

[147] For detailed rules concerning the composition and tasks of all EFSA counterparts, see Articles 24–28 of the Regulation 178/2002 (n 120).

Authority's activities every year. The Management Board adopts the Authority's internal rules of procedure and takes some strategic internal decisions, such as the appointment (and dismissal) of the Executive Director and the appointment of members of the Scientific Committee and Scientific Panels. Due to the multiplicity of its functions and their relevance for the EFSA's independence, it is of crucial importance to guarantee adequate organisation and functioning of the Board.

The Board is composed of fourteen members appointed by the Council in consultation with the European Parliament from a list drawn up by the Commission, and a representative of the Commission. Four of the fourteen members should represent consumer and interest groups, and the rest shall be appointed in a way that guarantees the highest standard of competence, a broad range of relevant expertise, and the broadest possible geographical distribution within the EU.

A few interesting observations can be made on the basis of the above presented provisions of Article 25 of the Regulation establishing the EFSA. First and foremost, the composition and the mode of appointment of the members of the Authority vary considerably from that of the other EU agencies. Perhaps the most significant difference is that the members of the Board do not represent member states. In all other contemporary European agencies, members of the Management Board are directly or indirectly appointed by the member states.[148] Similarly, in the case of the other agencies, member states have a 'guaranteed' number of representatives (one or two per state), whereas the total number of the EFSA's Management Board is fifteen, far fewer than the current twenty-seven member states of the enlarged EU. The second interesting provision in the appointment rules is the requirement that the Board represent 'the broadest possible geographic distribution within the Union'. This, in accordance with the Preamble, presupposes a rotation of the different countries of origin of the members of the Management Board, without any post being reserved for nationals of any specific member state.[149] The idea of rotation members is, on the one hand, a method that guarantees broad geographical representation by allowing representatives of different countries and regions to meet in different configurations and have their say in the Board of fifteen members. On the other hand, however, it also seems to be a mechanism that seeks to avoid the monopolisation of the Board by representatives of just one member state. In this context, it may be perceived

[148] For details, see the relevant Regulations establishing European agencies, or E Vos, 'Agencies …' (n 128) Table 2: Organizational Structure of the Existing Agencies, 144–147.

[149] See the Preamble to Regulation 178/2002 (n 120) rec. 41.

as a device to prevent anomalies such as the one that took place in the case of the BSE crisis.

The Executive Director. The Executive Director is appointed by the Management Board after an open competition procedure, on the basis of a list proposed by the Commission, and can also be removed by the Board by a simple majority of its members. This inevitably leads to close interconnection and a certain degree of dependence by the Director on the Board. The Director's main responsibility is to be the legal representative of the Authority. The Director is also accountable for its day-to-day administration, drawing up proposals for the Authority's work program, as well as for its implementation. Moreover, the Director is responsible for developing and maintaining appropriate contacts with the European Parliament, and for ensuring a regular dialogue with its relevant committees. In addition, the Director exercises important functions relating to reporting, as well as with regard to financial and budgetary affairs.

The Advisory Forum. The most interesting feature of the Advisory Forum is its composition, as it seems to reflect the recurrent urge to preserve some sort of 'representativeness' within European institutions. Since it was disregarded in the Management Board, the composition of the Forum seems to have taken over the idea of representativeness, to reflect the current configuration of the EU or to compensate for the loss of it in the structure of the Board.[150] On the other hand, it can be assumed that the particularity of its function requires this sort of design. The Advisory Forum is composed of representatives of competent bodies of the member states that undertake tasks similar to those of the Authority, where each state designates one candidate. It is chaired by the Executive Director of the Authority.

The main formal task of the Forum is to advise the Executive Director in the performance of his/her duties, in particular by drawing up a proposal for the Authority's work program. The Forum may also be asked to advise on the prioritisation of requests for scientific opinions. Moreover, the Forum is meant to act as a mechanism for the exchange of information on potential risks and for the pooling of knowledge, and this second function seems to be far more important than the first one. It is charged with guaranteeing close cooperation between the Authority and the competent bodies of the member states in the following areas:

- Avoiding duplication of scientific studies.
- Cooperation in a situation of scientific divergence.

[150] See also similar comments in E Vos, 'Agencies ...' (n 128) 122–124.

- Promoting the European networking of organisations operating in the field, as required by the Regulation.
- Action in the case of the identification of an emerging risk by the Authority or a member state.

Considering its composition and range of tasks, the Advisory Forum has a very important role to play in the network-building and the integration-strengthening mission of the Authority. It also reinforces the coordinative and deliberative aspects that the previous system was lacking, and which were not inherent in the national structures.[151] In implementation of its functions, the Forum is supported by two bodies. The first one, the Working Group on Communications, focuses on enhancing the coherence of food safety messages across the EU. Its job is to foster collaboration on risk communication between all those involved in communications in the member states' national food agencies and administrations.[152] The second, the Steering Group on Cooperation, acts as the interface between the Advisory Forum and the Scientific Committee in providing strategic oversight and steering the implementation of the strategy on scientific cooperation and networking.[153]

The Scientific Committee with Permanent Scientific Panels. The scientists, whose activity is supposed to constitute the essence of the Authority's functioning and the purpose of its existence, are organised in the Scientific Committee and permanent Scientific Panels. Each of the Panels acts within its own range of competences, while the Scientific Committee is responsible for general coordination and ensuring the consistency of the delivery procedure of scientific opinion. It provides opinions on multisectoral issues that fall within the competence of more than one Panel, or that fall outside the scope of competence of any of them. In such a case, or in the case of necessity, the Committee may set up working groups. The Scientific Committee and Expert Panels are supported by the EFSA's own scientific staff. In addition, the Authority expects to reinforce its own Science department by creating a series of expert service 'teams', each dedicated to a specific area of risk assessment.

---

151 The question of the absence of initial functioning network of national food safety agencies, which was simply caused by the fact that not all member states traditionally had one and some decided not to establish one even encouraged by Community reform, differentiated the EFSA from some other European agencies, such as the EMEA, which built its potential and success on the national network it could rely on. For details on the potential consequences of such situation and the path-dependency of those two types of network building and market organisation see S Krapohl, 'Thalidomide, BSE and the Single Market: An Historical-Institutionalist Approach to Regulatory Regimes in the European Union' (2007) 46 *European Journal of Political Research* 25–46.

152 See for details <http://www.efsa.europa.eu/en/af/afwgs.htm> accessed 25 May 2011.

153 For details, see <http://www.efsa.europa.eu/en/af/sgc.htm> accessed 25 May 2011.

In accordance with Article 28 of the Regulation, the following nine Scientific Panels were initially established:

a) the Panel on food additives, flavourings, processing aids and materials in contact with food (AFC);
b) the Panel on additives and products or substances used in animal feed (FEEDAP);
c) the Panel on plant health, plant protection products and their residues (PPR);
d) the Panel on genetically modified organisms (GMO);
e) the Panel on plant health (PLH);
f) the Panel on dietetic products, nutrition and allergies (NDA);
g) the Panel on biological hazards (BIOHAZ);
h) the Panel on contaminants in the food chain (CONTAM); and
i) the Panel on animal health and welfare (AHAW).

It is possible, however, for the Commission, at the request of the Authority, to adapt the number of Panels in the light of technical and scientific developments. In executing this possibility, the Commission's Committee on Food Chain and Animal Health requested in December 2007 to modify the founding Regulation and replace the AFC Panel by two units: the Panel on Food Additives and Nutrient Sources Added to Food (ANS) and the Panel on Food Contact Materials, Enzymes, Flavourings and Processing Aids (CEF), which both became active on 10 July 2008. All Scientific Panels receive direct secretariat support from the Risk assessment directorate. Additionally, by 2009 six more supportive scientific units had been established:

- the Pesticide Risk Assessment Peer Review Unit (PRAPeR);
- the Animal Diseases Transmissible to Humans (Zoonoses) Unit;
- the Scientific Cooperation Unit;
- the Data Collection and Exposure Unit (DATEX);
- the Emerging Risks Unit (EMRISK); and
- the Assessment Methodology Unit (AMU).

An important issue, in the context of the excellence and independence of the scientific advice offered by the Authority, is the mode of appointment of its scientists. The members of scientific bodies of the EFSA are appointed by the Management Board, acting upon a proposal by the Executive Director following an open competition. There is, therefore, no national representation factor in the selection procedure. Neither the member states nor the Commission have any formal influence on the selection process.

In the course of 2011, the EFSA is meant to undergo yet another restructuration, in order to improve its efficiency in response to its growth since 2002, as well as to the growing demand for its engagement. According to the new structure, the EFSA is organised in five directorates overseen by EFSA's Executive Director: three science directorates: Risk Assessment and Scientific Assistance, Scientific Evaluation of Regulated Products and Science Strategy and Coordination; the Communications Directorate; and finally the Resources & Support Directorate. The scientific directorates are meant to support the work of EFSA's Scientific Committee and Panels. The first phase of the reform was completed in May 2011, but the new structure shall be fully operational by January 2012.[154]

3.3.1.2.3.3. Rules Governing the Functioning of the Authority. In accordance with Article 29 of Regulation 178/2002, the Authority is in charge of issuing scientific opinions on matters falling within its mission, at the request of the Commission or on its own initiative. The European Parliament and member states have the right to request an opinion on a matter falling within the EFSA's mission, but the EU interest has to be proven in the accompanying documents.

Scientific opinions shall be delivered within the time limit specified by law, or, if there is none, within the time limit specified in the request. Exceptions can only occur in duly justified circumstances. In case of requests concerning the same issue, or concerning an issue on which the EFSA has already delivered a scientific opinion, the Authority may refuse the request, provided that there is no new data justifying re-examination.

Over 120 questions were received by the EFSA in the first year of its existence. After that first year, it was expected to deliver between 100 and 200 expert opinions per year. In these circumstances, meeting deadlines has turned out to be problematic. At its first meeting—held in Parma, the Authority's permanent location, in April 2004—the EFSA Management Board confirmed its commitment to delivering independent, high-quality scientific advice within reasonable timeframes. They emphasised, however, that deadlines cannot be met at the expense of scientific excellence. This seems to be a very reasonable and proper attitude, but the European Commission does not appear to share it. A few legislative proposals by the Commission included provisions which allowed the Commission to review or overturn EFSA decisions.[155] This seemed like an attempt to introduce some sort of administrative review of EFSA opinions. Members of the Board expressed their greatest concern and authorised

[154] See details at < http://www.efsa.europa.eu/en/efsawho/efsastructure.htm?wtrl=01>.

[155] The Management Board document gives two examples of such proposals, where the words 'review' and 'withdraw' are used in this context. They are: Proposal for a Regulation of the European Parliament and of the Council on maximum residue levels of pesticides in products of plant and animal origin (Council document no. 7737/04), and Proposal for a Regulation of the European Parliament and of the Council on materials and articles intended to come into contact with food (Council document no. 7781/04).

the chairman to write to the appropriate legislative bodies, underlining the concerns of the Authority. It seems that the Commission managed to tolerate the scientific 'hegemony' of the Authority for only two years before it started to claim back its superiority.

Another very interesting issue concerns the provision of Article 33 of the Regulation, concerning the collection of data by the Authority. According to this provision, the Authority shall search for, collect, collate, analyse and summarise relevant scientific and technical data in the field of its mission, which shall be done in close cooperation with all organisations operating in the field of data-collection in the member states, applicant countries, third countries and international bodies. Particular attention is given to information of the highest importance—that is, data that aids with the identification of emerging risks. This shall involve the establishment of monitoring procedures and a systematic search and exchange of information. This is the key to two very important functional achievements of this Regulation: the establishment of the rapid alert system, and the networking of organisations operating in the field of food safety.

The organisational aspect of the Regulation contains a series of provisions on independence, transparency, confidentiality, communication and access to documents. These are all fairly obvious and need no special attention. It is worth pointing out, however, that the mere fact that they are included in Regulation 178/2002 is a legislative achievement in itself.

The last, but definitely not the least, issue that needs to be addressed in this section is the provision in Article 30 of the Regulation that concerns diverging scientific opinions. The primary assumption is that the Authority should exercise vigilance in order to identify at an early stage any potential source of divergence between its scientific opinions and the scientific opinions issued by other bodies carrying out similar tasks. When it identifies such a potential source of divergence, it shall contact the body in question to ensure that all relevant scientific information is shared and in order to identify any potentially contentious scientific issues. The general idea, therefore, seems to be that avoiding divergence is a priority, and that all possible steps should be undertaken in order to avoid conflicts. When a substantive divergence over scientific issues has been identified, however, the Authority and the body concerned are obliged to cooperate, with a view to either resolving the divergence or preparing a joint document that clarifies the contentious scientific issues and identifies the relevant uncertainties in the data. Interestingly, the only scientific bodies other than the Authority mentioned in this provision are other EU agencies, one of the Commission's Scientific Committees and a member state body. This Article, then, only covers those conflicts which arise within the EU and are either of a horizontal character (between different EU bodies) or a vertical character (between an EU body and a member state body). This provision may become very important in the process of building 'European science', serving, on the one hand, as a conflict-resolution clause, and, on the other, as a basis for thorough consultations of scientific data processed and interpreted by different bodies at different levels of European governance. As regards its effectiveness in the achievement of those objectives, a lot will depend on the factual application of that clause and on the attitudes of the Authority and the other bodies mentioned.

3.3.2. *Further Changes—Similar Rationale*

The establishment of the general food law was followed by a series of other legislative reform undertakings. Although they concerned many different areas of foodstuffs legislation and amended various aspects of regulations, the overarching rationale of all those endeavours was similar to that of the general food law reform. The point was not only to avoid food pandemics such as BSE in the future, but also to avoid the conflicting situations which indirectly gave rise to it, and the regulatory and structural problems that it revealed.

One of the elements of that reformative movement was to further diminish the regulatory differences between member states by limiting the flexibility of EU laws. It served as a means to reduce the member states' ability to implement European laws their own way and in accordance with their national particularities. The most evident illustration of this tendency is the increasing number of regulations in EU food matters, as well as the growing trend to replace directives, which previously regulated a certain area, with regulations. By those means, the European legislator covers those areas in more and more detail and eliminates situations where implementing national legislation could deviate from the common standard and create potential sources of tensions and management problems.

The most obvious example is the legislation pertaining to food hygiene. This area had initially been covered by a general directive[156] and a series of product-specific directives, which left some room for the member states to manoeuvre. Following a 2006 reform, food and feed hygiene is now covered with detailed and directly effective regulations, a so-called 'hygiene package'.[157]

[156] Council Directive (EEC) 93/43 of 14 June 1993 on the hygiene of foodstuffs [1993] OJ L 175/1.

[157] The 'Hygiene Package' consists of the following: Regulation (EC) 852/2004 of the European Parliament and of the Council of 29 April 2004 on the hygiene of foodstuffs [2004] OJ L 226/3; Regulation (EC) 853/2004 of the European Parliament and of the Council of 29 April 2004 laying down specific hygiene rules for food of animal origin [2004] OJ L 226/22; Regulation (EC) 854/2004 of the European Parliament and of the Council of 29 April 2004 laying down specific rules of official controls on products of animal origin intended for human consumption [2004] OJ L 226/83; Regulation (EC) 882/2004 of the European Parliament and of the Council of 29 April 2004 on official controls performed to ensure the verification of compliance with

Other examples, to mention just a few, include food labelling,[158] materials coming into contact with food,[159] pesticide residue levels,[160] as well as feedstuffs labelling and marketing regulation.[161] Recent legislative initiatives show that this trend is continuing.

The idea behind the regulatory development is understandable. Moving away from harmonisation towards a unification of conditions aims to avoid problems stemming from a lack of implementation, as well as from wrong or partial implementation by member states, and to avoid conflicts that could arise out of differences that are acceptable under the harmonised rules. The aim of such regulatory strengthening is probably also to make sure that consumers are protected equally throughout the EU, which was especially important in face of the last two enlargements, which introduced a dozen states which had been commonly perceived as backward, less developed and less secure. The side costs of such developments were probably not considered at the time of the reform. Unification is not always a remedy for diverse levels of development or, in this case, of consumer protection. Consequently, it may not always be the best answer to the fears of consumers from the old member states as well as the managers of the food market. Unification can, in fact, often turn out to be a double-edged sword, which eliminates problems at one end but at the same time causes them in another area. It tends to be one-dimensional and, concentrating on the one particular element that it is directed to highlight,

feed and food law, animal health and animal welfare rules [2004] OJ L 191/1; and Regulation (EC) 183/2005 of the European Parliament and of the Council of 12 January 2005 laying down requirements for feed hygiene [2005] OJ L 35/1.

[158] Proposal for a Regulation of the European Parliament and of the Council on the provisions of food information to consumers COM (2008) 40 final, 30 January 2008. The proposal combines the provisions of Directive (EC) 2000/13 of the European Parliament and of the Council on the labelling, presentation and advertising of foodstuffs and of Council Directive (EEC) 90/496 on nutrition labelling for foodstuffs.

[159] Regulation (EC) 1935/2004 of the European Parliament and of the Council of 27 October 2004 on material and articles intended to come into contact with food and repealing Directives 80/590/EEC and 89/109/EEC [2004] OJ L 338/4.

[160] Regulation (EC) 396/2005 of the European Parliament and of the Council of 23 February 2005 on maximum residue levels of pesticides in or on food and feed of plant and animal origin and amending Council Directive 91/414/EEC [2005] OJ L 70/1. Prior to this Regulation, each member state applied its own maximum residue levels for pesticides. Previous European legislation set different levels for different kinds of product: some fruit and vegetables (Directive 76/895/EEC), cereals (Directive 86/362/EEC), foodstuffs of animal origin (Directive 86/363/EEC), and plant products, including fruit and vegetables (Directive 90/642/EEC). The new Regulation repealed all these directives, proposing harmonised maximum levels for all foodstuffs instead. It includes the same level of protection for animal feedingstuffs.

[161] Regulation (EC) 767/2009 of the European Parliament and of the Council of 13 July 2009 on the placing on the market and use of feed, amending European Parliament and Council Regulation (EC) No 1831/2003 and repealing Council Directive 79/373/EEC, Commission Directive 80/511/EEC, Council Directives 82/471/EEC, 83/228/EEC, 93/74/EEC, 93/113/EC and 96/25/EC and Commission Decision 2004/217/EC.

remains blind to other aspects of the problem it is aiming to tackle. It has to be emphasised that the problems we are dealing with here, in the case of food regulation, are everything but one-dimensional. The negative consequences of such a development can, thus, be ample, and some of them will be discussed in the following paragraphs.

3.3.3. *Can 'Scientific' Be 'Comprehensive'? The Omitted Elements of the Post-BSE Reforms*

The food-regulatory reform after the BSE crisis must be analysed as a result of a specific setting. The failure of the EU legal and administrative mechanisms not only to prevent the crisis, but also to deal with it once it occurred, shaped the reform in a very particular way. Firstly, reform had to be made quickly and in a well-organised manner, in order to make up for the criticisms of inefficiency, mismanagement, obstruction and institutional confusions. Secondly, reform had to be spectacular and cater for consumers, in order to try and regain consumers' confidence in European regulation after the failure, but also to bring positive reviews back in the press. Finally, it had to be based on an unquestionable and indisputable foundation, which in this case was science. As a consequence, the reform was dominated by scientific and consumer-protection thinking, which resulted in its partiality and a sense of lost opportunity. Hanging between the BSE trauma and the fear of potential consequences from the approaching enlargements, the reform reflected the kind of anxiety that dictates radical and short-sighted solutions to ever-developing and complex problems.

One-dimensional regulation resulting from such partial reform, which only takes into consideration one selected aspect of a regulatory area, can affect the market in many problematic ways. Partial regulation, regulation that emphasises only some features of a problem, or regulation that creates an imbalanced approach to a matter can be imagined as exemplary possible scenarios. In the case of European food law, we are dealing with a situation where, firstly, market rationale was the driving force of the harmonising legislation, and secondly, a consumer-protection rationale took over and became the dominant dimension of the reform. As a consequence, the post-BSE reform could not be anything but partial. It definitely deals with some aspects of the problem. First and foremost, it includes consumer protection as a valid aspect of regulatory activity. Secondly, it settles a lot of institutional and procedural issues, which has resulted in increased inclusiveness and transparency of European decision-making, and which has provided better mechanisms for the prevention and settlement of conflict. Hence, most probably, if a new BSE-type crisis was to occur in Europe now, the EU would be better prepared to deal with it. The reform, however, leaves a whole range of issues overlooked, which may have detrimental effects on future developments.

The paradoxical result of this partiality in the post-BSE reform is that while we might now be better prepared for the *unexpected*, it is doubtful whether we are any better prepared for the *expected*. What if the risks connected with a potential outbreak of some sort of crisis are, in fact, by far outweighed by the risks connected with our legal and potentially safe everyday practices? What I am trying to point to here is a problem of food quality. *Quality* in the longer and less direct way translates to *safety*, but the risks connected with poor quality food are not as spectacular or explosive as those of disease outbreak. They are, however, much more common, as the deterioration of the quality of the food we consume every day, as well as the poor nutritional habits our societies have developed, have become part of our 'room-temperature reality'. This is not to say that science-based regulation is to blame for this development, but rather that this type or regulation is not able to properly address the problem, or to intervene in the situation at hand.

The mono-dimensional emphasis of European food regulation after the BSE crisis has concentrated upon potential 'outbreaks', 'scandals' and 'scares', while our existing food-related problems—specifically those connected with nutrition, such as obesity, which in its turn contributes to other devastating health consequences (heart diseases, blood pressure diseases, cancers and strokes)—which in practice affect a much wider population, escape any EU regulatory control. Moreover, the nature of the EU regulations on free movement makes it impossible for member states to intervene and counteract these negative developments by means of national legislation. As a consequence, no significant action can be undertaken against nutritional problems or obesity at any level of European governance. Hence, European regulation has omitted important aspects of the total field of food safety by overemphasising the exceptional 'crises' and overlooking the mundane threats to the health of consumers.[162] While the cause for this imbalance may seem obvious and natural enough—that a spectacular crisis takes precedence over acceptable risks—it is argued here that the regulatory system itself allows for this imbalance to be reproduced indefinitely, and contributes to its demonstrated inability to tackle the totality of food-safety concerns, which it has nonetheless been politically tasked to fulfil.

Furthermore, the reformers have put enormous emphasis on improving the quality of the science involved in regulatory decision-making, as well

[162] Compare C Macmaolain, *EU Food Law. Protecting Consumers and Health in a Common Market* (Modern Studies in European Law, Hart Publishing, Oxford, Portland Oregon 2007) 12, 14–15, 221–239.

as the ways in which this inclusion takes place and the procedural guarantees of transparency, professionalism and impartiality. This approach made the reformers concentrate upon the risk assessment phase of the decision-making process, leaving aside the most consequential: the risk management aspect. A strong emphasis on reforming the provision of expertise and the scientific assessment conditions naturally strengthened this part of the procedure, which inevitably had consequences on the functioning of those new rules in the market. Very often in the risk-regulatory process decision-makers in the management phase tend to follow blindly the decisions of risk-assessors, which are based solely on science. This phenomenon leads to a situation where science is the only basis for a regulatory decision, and other values—of economic, social or ethical character—have little chance of being considered. Any further strengthening of the science-based risk assessment aggravates the risk that such a tendency will dominate. Science can now become such a strong foundation that risk managers will find it difficult to provide arguments based on other values and interests, which should ideally be taken into consideration in a regulatory procedure. In such a situation, deciding against the findings of risk assessment can become very problematic, if not impossible.

This, as a consequence, can create a situation in which non-scientific arguments—or perhaps insufficiently scientific arguments—may not be given due consideration and recognition. Instead, established, traditional science will dominate the decision-making process to such a high degree that it becomes the only overriding rationale of decisions, despite the fact that they might often have to be made about problems which have not been exhaustively treated by science. Basing decisions solely on science is not only contrary to common sense. It is also—and more importantly—against the established and approved rules of risk regulation, according to which the risk management phase should gain precedence over the scientific risk assessment phase, and should take a comprehensive stance in making a decision, having included *all* relevant values in the deliberation. Among these relevant values are societal concerns, the social and economic impact of regulation, and consumer preferences.

Although this problem is rarely discussed in the literature, there have been voices advocating inclusion of 'concern assessment' in the risk-regulatory procedure.[163] According to this view, risk regulatory decisions should take

---

[163] M Dreyer and O Renn (eds), Food Safety Governance: Integrating Science, Precautions and Public Involvement (Springer-Verlag, Berlin Heidelberg 2009) and the International Risk Governance Council (IRGC), 'Policy Brief: Appropriate Risk Governance Strategies for Nanotechnology Applications in Food and Cosmetics', Geneva 2009 < http://www.irgc.org/IMG/pdf/IRGC_Report_FINAL_For_Web.pdf>; similar messages expressed also in M Dreyer and O Renn, 'Some

account of relevant societal concerns through an assessment of 'socio-political ambiguity', taking into consideration any divergences in individual perceptions of risk, any amplification effects in the media, as well as any social or ethical concerns. Hence, it seems that under contemporary conditions the problem should be given more attention, as new regulatory challenges—such as the increased diversity of the EU following its enlargement, the growing influence of global trade rules on European legislation, as well as the growing sensitivity of consumption issues—have made the impact-assessment stage of regulatory decision-making even more problematic, and the traditional natural-science-based regulatory approach may find itself incapable of addressing all necessary regulatory aspects.

The last problem to be raised in concluding this evaluation of the development of food regulation in Europe concerns economics. It is interesting to observe that, since redistributive questions were not directly and immediately raised by the BSE crisis, the post-BSE reforms never addressed them. Additionally, the sensitivity of debating financial issues within the CAP probably made it even more complicated and undesirable in that context. Consequently, as there were no direct questions, the regulator avoided mentioning economic concerns in the reform debates and addressing them in the final reform package, concentrating instead on consumer safety and the credibility of institutions.[164] Moreover, a financial-assistance scheme for farmers who were directly affected managed to respond to the most urgent redistributive problems caused by the crisis, providing compensation for industry losses. Consequently, it diminished the economic and social impact of the post-BSE policy and superficially solved the issue at the time. This might be why no more redistributive claims were made and no discussion of the socioeconomic impact was initiated when working on the general food-law reforms. The domination of the safety discourse managed to protract for longer, and even when the existence of economic concerns became evident as the EU anticipated its latest enlargements, the problem remained unchallenged. Paradoxically, economic concerns became even more concealed when a series of pre-accession measures were taken under the slogan of consumer safety, while in fact they were economically driven.

One final remark to be made, before I look at the European case from the outside, is that the neglect of socioeconomic and redistributive concerns is not

---

Suggestions for a Structured Approach to Participation In Food Risk Governance with a Special Emphasis on the Assessment Management Interface' in E Vos (ed), *European Risk Governance—Its Science, its Inclusiveness and its Effectiveness* (2008) CONNEX Report Series No. 6, 89–121.

[164] E Vos and F Wendler, 'Food Safety Regulation at the EU Level' in E Vos and F Wendler, *Food Safety Regulation in Europe. A Comparative Institutional Analysis* (Intersentia, Antwerp 2006) 65–138.

a new phenomenon in the EU. If a generalised observation can be made on the basis of the available examples, it is interesting to see that redistributive and social problems have rarely been treated seriously enough, especially when in the context of common market activities. Looking back at the history of the food market, one comes across the famous Spanish strawberries case, where France was taken to the ECJ for its lack of disciplinary action, which would have prevented French farmers from destroying shipments of Spanish strawberries intended for French consumers.[165] The case, if one looks at the core of the problem, clearly concerned the social impact of food market regulation. It was treated by the ECJ, however, merely as a pretext to proclaim and promote the principle of loyalty, whereas the other side of loyalty—solidarity—was not even considered.

4. Conclusions: Traces of the 'Social' in the European Legal Framework

These concluding thoughts begin with a summary of the evolutionary analysis of the EU food regulations presented in this chapter, highlighting some of the most important developments. The point of departure for this analysis is that a common EU food policy was never an intentional, carefully planned project on the European agenda. In fact, food regulation seems to have emerged as a side-effect of other EU undertakings, be it common-market regulation, agricultural legislation or consumer-protection laws. The Treaty called for a unified approach to the organisation of the production and marketing of agricultural products, while the single market provisions foresaw the elimination of trade barriers to allow free circulation of goods. From this decoupling, between two contrasting market-regulation paradigms—the interventionist agricultural scheme on the one hand, and the free-market rationale on the other—food regulation inherited its specific dualism and its highly consequential fragmentation.

From the middle of the 1980s, the sector followed the development of many other areas of market regulation: from detailed product-regulation, through the New Approach harmonisation and towards standardisation. This was accompanied by development of procedural mechanisms and institutional structures. The establishment of the committee system, which marked a transition of the European regulatory system towards its cognitive opening, was the first attempt to include a wider set of interests in regulatory decision-making. The misconception of the interest involvement, however, led to the

[165] Case C-265/95 *Commission v. France* [1997] ECR I-6959.

most spectacular failure of the system, the BSE crisis, which provoked further reforms. The reform following the crisis could be seen as another opportunity to look at food regulation in its wider context and open it up for a wider set of considerations.

This opportunity was, regrettably, not adequately taken. The reformatory activities concentrated on the safety paradigm, leading to a new wave of development of legislation and institutional structures that aimed to strengthen consumer-protection and to retrieve consumers' trust in the system. It culminated with the establishment of the European Food Safety Authority, which was responsible for independent and professional scientific risk assessment. A number of important issues, however, which were not directly challenged by the BSE crisis, remained overlooked. In particular, there was a problem of looking at EU food-safety regulations from the perspective not only of the regulation of risks but also of the regulation of the market. The market, which since 2004 has become bigger and more diverse, at the same time, has become more and more contingent on developments at the international level.

Those two factors—the increased diversity within the EU and the growing interdependence on the global arena—are what, in my mind, may force European food regulations to become more flexible and to include a wider set of concerns in policy- and law-making. Nevertheless, up till now, developments in that direction have been limited and theoretical, and their impact on factual decision-making and legislation has been minimal. There are areas of EU regulation, however, where a tendency towards more openness is already being developed. It is, thus, unfortunate that in the food area, the latest big reform projects and legal developments after the enlargement have not taken these ideas into consideration. The evolution of the EU food law presented above seems to be encouraging more openness in the system, so it is surprising and slightly disappointing that non-scientific concerns, which are present in the EU regulation already in the CAP legislation, have been lost in the transformation of the system. In my view, the overall developments will require reconsideration.

One gets the impression that much new European legislation and policymaking has been done in the heat of the moment, following a certain trend, flashily named and promoted by the European Commission. The trends and their fancy names have changed over time, giving rise to waves of regulatory reform undertaken under their headline, such as 'single market completion', 'new governance', 'consumer protection' or 'better regulation'. The main problem with such tagged reform waves is that they can often lead to a situation where one trend forgets the previous one and is blind to other values. It is my opinion that many problems of European food regulation are partly a consequence of the historical lack of an overarching philosophy of food safety.

Instead, it was always subsumed under such tagged reforms, and it was always promised that a new reform will tackle all the problems of the previous system, while in fact the new reform only dealt with what it was tagged for, leaving all other problems overlooked. I also believe that if European food safety regulation is taken out of this gridlock and is considered for what it is and what it should be, it could achieve far better results. The irony of the matter is that the post-BSE reform seems to have fallen back on the instruments that contributed to it. In an attempt to respond to the failures of industrialisation, it introduced measures that created a new deficit, while no sustainable cure for the disembedding process is provided.

I am far from advocating revolutionising European food regulations once again, this time under the 're-embeddedness' and 'flexibility' tag, and forgetting all the previous lessons learnt. I am convinced, however, that if they are not duly recognised, the socioeconomic implications of food regulation will prove that the system is inefficient and may have detrimental consequences for the functioning of European food production and trade, as well as negative long-term consequences for European consumers. I am instead trying to show that reform is possible without a revolution, and that by means of small steps the system might be opened up to a wider set of considerations and could then be able to respond better to the development of the EU and its new requirements.

In order to support my claim for greater openness towards a wider set of concerns in European regulation, and to show that there are possible EU-compliant ways of doing it, I will next examine examples of particular sectors where socioeconomic considerations have been given explicit recognition and have, to some extent, been included in the regulatory process. Traces of openness towards socioeconomic concerns can be found, to some extent, in GMO regulations[166] and in the pharmaceutical sector. The most spectacular example and the most mature form of such inclusion, however, is the regulation on chemicals under the new REACH programme. The limited scope of this volume will not allow a detailed analysis of these regulations, yet such an examination does not even seem necessary. The point is merely to look at it as a functioning example of a possible method of accommodating diverse factors within

---

[166] In the GMO regulation, the new reform proposal by the Commission to allow member states flexibility to decide on restricting or banning GM cultivation on their territory constitutes an interesting example of acknowledging the socio-economic implications of regulatory decision on GMOs, by handing them back to the member states. The example will be discussed in more detail in the following chapter. For details on the proposal see: Proposal for a Regulation of the European Parliament and of the Council amending Directive 2001/18/EC as regards the possibility for the Member States to restrict or prohibit the cultivation of GMOs in their territory, COM (2010) 375 final, 13.7.2010; and its evaluation in M Weimer, 'What Price Flexibility?—The Recent Commission Proposal to Allow for National "Opt-Outs" on GMO Cultivation under the Deliberate Release Directive and the Comitology Reform Post-Lisbon'(2010) 4 *European Journal of Risk Regulation*, 347–354.

the framework of the European legal system. It will be interesting to consider whether solutions similar to those developed for chemicals might also be applied in the foodstuffs sector. I believe that building analogies between those two regulatory areas may be credible, as both refer to products of a specific type where the safety of consumers is paramount and the economic interests involved are vast, but where the governance approaches developed by the EU are slightly different.

The new European system of registration, evaluation, authorisation and restriction of chemicals was one of the more mature European projects. It was a complex regulatory reform that replaced an outdated system, taking lessons from its deficiencies and applying modern regulatory techniques, including a wide consultation process and a comprehensive regulatory impact assessment. The outcome of the reform, embodied in the REACH Regulation,[167] encompassed the achievements of both the old and the new in the search for a balance between safety and economic viability. Contrary to the foodstuffs situation from the time of the post-BSE amendments, the existence and significance of the socioeconomic implications of regulatory decisions in the field of chemicals was openly acknowledged and reflected in legislation.

There are many reflections of this phenomenon in the Regulation, and I will now refer to the most significant of them and present them briefly as examples of how to include a wider scope of considerations within European regulatory instruments. First and foremost, the mere inclusion of the socioeconomic assessment as a part of an overall assessment process of chemical substances was a significant step. It means that the European legislator noticed and acknowledged their relevance in the decision-making process, and so allowed the inclusion of non-scientific considerations in regulatory procedures. This is done mainly through two mechanisms foreseen by the REACH Regulation. Additionally, there are smaller references to socioeconomic impacts in various other provisions of the Regulation. This analysis will concentrate on the two major channels through which socioeconomic concerns are considered in the regulatory process.

The first was created through an establishment within the European Chemicals Agency created by the Regulation of the Committee for Socio-Economic Analysis.[168] According to the Regulation, the Committee should be responsible for preparing opinions of the Agency on applications for authorisation,

[167] Regulation (EC) 1907/2006 of the European Parliament and of the Council of 18 December 2006 concerning the Registration, Evaluation, Authorisation and Restriction of Chemicals (REACH), establishing a European Chemicals Agency, amending Directive 1999/45/EC and repealing Council Regulation (EEC) 793/93 and Commission Regulation (EC) 1488/94, as well as Council Directive 76/769/EEC and Commission Directives 91/155/EEC. 93/67/EEC, 93/105/EC and 2000/21/EC [2006] OJ L 396.

[168] Ibid, Article 76.1 (d).

proposals for restrictions, and any other questions that might arise from the operation of the Regulation relating to the socioeconomic impact of possible legislative action on substances. Thus, it can be seen as a platform for non-scientific considerations in the assessment and authorisation processes. Alongside the Committee for Risk Assessment, the Committee for Socio-Economic Analysis issues draft opinions on every application for authorisation.[169] It is interesting to note, however, that the scope of the socioeconomic analysis seems narrower than that of the risk assessment. Whereas the latter should relate to risks to human health and/or the environment arising from the use of certain substances—including the appropriateness and effectiveness of the risk management measures described in the application and, if relevant, an assessment of the risks arising from possible alternatives—the socioeconomic analysis only assesses the socioeconomic factors of the availability, suitability and technical feasibility of alternatives associated with the use of the substances described in the application. Nevertheless, at least the analysis of alternatives takes account not only of risks but also of the technical and economic feasibility, which significantly widens the scope of considerations made during the assessment and the authorisation process.

The second method of including non-scientific considerations is through giving the applicant the possibility to include a socioeconomic analysis in the application dossier.[170] Thus, from the very initial stage of the procedure, this allows for a wider consideration of the implications of issuing or rejecting authorisation. The information that may be addressed in such socioeconomic analysis is listed in Annex XVI to the Regulation. According to the Annex, a socioeconomic analysis may include the following elements: (1) impacts on the industry, e.g. manufacturers, importers, downstream users; (2) impacts on associated businesses, e.g. investment, research and development, innovation, operating costs; (3) impacts on consumers, e.g. product prices, availability, choice, quality, as well as effects on health and the environment affecting consumers; (4) social implications, such as job security or employment; (5) the availability and technical and economic feasibility of alternative substances or technologies, as well as the social and economic impacts of using them; (6) wider implications for trade, competition and economic development, and so on. With regard to the restriction procedure, recommendations for socioeconomic analysis are further developed separately in the Guidelines issued by the European Chemicals Agency.[171] It is, however, interesting to note that the regulation puts a strong emphasis on the impact of any eventual refusal

[169] Ibid, Article 64.

[170] Ibid, Article 62 (5).

[171] European Chemicals Agency, 'Guidance on Socio-Economic Analysis—Restrictions', Guidance for the Implementation of REACH, May 2008.

on industry, employment, trade and competitiveness, which in a way guides the interpretation of those provisions in a strongly industrial and economic direction.

The main objective of this brief presentation of the instruments that allow non-scientific concerns to be included under the REACH regulation has been to show that there are legal options already developed under EU law which allow for such processes to take place. This means that my concerns and claims for food regulation to be more inclusive are neither impossible to consider nor unfeasible to regulate technically. There are already legal instruments in force that could indicate the beginning of a certain new wave of developments in European legislation, which should respond to the new challenges that the EU is facing. The practical significance and impact of the REACH provisions in question is still difficult to assess, as the regulation is in fact still in the prolonged implementation process. Comments in the literature express different views and develop various perspectives of this regulatory innovation.[172] One wonders, first and foremost, how the opportunities given by the regulatory framework will in fact be used in its application, and to what extent the wider realm of concerns will be reflected in the actual decision-making. Heyvaert, for example, correctly raises doubts about what the extent to which applicants will be willing to use the opportunity to include in their applications non-scientific information that would strengthen their case for risk control,[173] which may in fact occur very often. Nevertheless, the most important point for my analysis is that in a heavily scientific sector such as chemicals regulation, a window of opportunity for non-scientific concerns was indeed opened, showing not only that they are relevant, but also that they can successfully be considered in the regulatory process through available legislative means.

Bearing all this in mind, several important questions can be posed: would it not be possible to apply a similar solution in food regulation and thus open it up to a wider spectrum of concerns? Is it the legal framework that does not allow this, or is it more a question of lack of political will? If the latter is the case, is the political will absent because the socioeconomic implications in case of food are not considered relevant, or is it rather because they are considered too problematic? There is no doubt that the openness of the current legal framework for foodstuffs regulation to non-scientific factors is rather limited. If we were to try to follow the path set by the chemicals regulation, it would be necessary to increase the sector's ability to accommodate a wider range of

---

[172] Compare, for example, P Kjaer, 'Rationality within REACH? On Functional Differentiation as the Structural Foundation of Legitimacy in European Chemical Regulation' (2007) EUI Working Papers LAW No.2007/18; and V Heyvaert, 'The EU Chemicals Policy: Towards Inclusive Governance?' in E Vos (ed), *European Risk Governance* ... (n 163) 185–221.

[173] V Heyvaert, 'The EU Chemicals Policy ...' ibid 211.

socioeconomic concerns in the regulatory process, and to look for ways to rebalance the system. I would like to see the chemicals regulation used as an example of the concept of embedding a regulatory framework in a complex setting of social and economic conditions, which both affect and are affected by the regulatory decision-making.

I believe, firstly, that in the case of foodstuffs the interdependency of this whole range of implications is rather obvious. In case of agricultural production, it has even openly been admitted, which can be read in the framing of the Treaty provisions. Even if a sceptical approach were taken, there are many voices—both of academics and policy-makers, referred to above in this volume—which advocate the consideration of a wider set of concerns in regulatory decision-making for food. In my opinion, they have made a strong case for a more inclusive approach.

Secondly, the chemicals regulation has proved that the technical possibility of introducing such an approach in European regulation exists. Irrespective of the varying characteristics of the legal framework in the case of chemicals and in the case of foodstuffs, the transplantation of some regulatory mechanisms could be considered, at least with regard to foodstuffs that require pre-market approval, such as novel foods. Moreover, the chemicals regulation can serve as an inspiration for the continuous reform of food legislation and can set an example that will work, that conforms to common market rules and that does not jeopardise the impartiality of the science-based regulatory approach.

Thirdly, as foodstuffs regulation is more varied and complex than chemicals regulation, due to its wider and more differentiated nature and usage of products, such a cognitive opening-up of the system probably raises more concerns and doubts, as it requires a systematic reform of a large volume of legislation. If one thinks about it from this perspective, however, the REACH programme was also an enormous systematic legal reform, which encompassed a vast number of legislative instruments, but it nevertheless was undertaken and has so far been considered a success. Moreover, such change does not have to entail a revolutionary undertaking. It can very well be taken step by step, as many previous EU law developments have been. Novel food would probably be the best place to start, not only because the mechanisms used in the chemicals regulation could most easily be imitated, due to the nature of the pre-market approval procedures, but also because it is one of the areas where sensitivity to social and economic implications is most obvious; as is becoming increasingly acknowledged, it will sooner or later require some sort of consideration. This is especially so now, when the growing demands of the larger and increasingly diversified European market are becoming more explicit and can no longer be disregarded.

The growing diversity of Europe, which then requires more flexibility and greater openness of the regulatory system, is discussed and illustrated in the following chapter, in order to bring in a wider perspective. The chapter revisits the analysis of the legal framework with a view of the bigger European market and its new participants; I shall return to the idea of re-embedding EU food regulation in the concluding chapter.

CHAPTER FOUR

THE ENLARGEMENT OF THE EUROPEAN MARKET AND ITS IMPLICATIONS: THE EXAMPLE OF POLAND

Probably the biggest challenge facing Europe at the turn of the millennium, and probably the most substantial approximation process since the creation of the common market, has been the European enlargements of 2004 and 2007, which added twelve new members to the EU. An additional complicating factor is provided by the fact that the twelve new states constitute a very specific group, and differ significantly from what the EU had been accustomed to. Not only do they differ from the old members, but there is also significant diversity among them.

Before their accession, most of the new member states had only enjoyed real statehood for slightly more than a decade. Consequently, they have only practised democracy and used a free-market economy for a short time period. The enlargements of 2004 and 2007 were thus not only politically significant; they were also economically challenging and required far-reaching legal adaptations. Hence, both the EU and the new states themselves were presented with an enormous adjustment task, and had to make a large transition effort. At the same time, the accession disturbed the fragile balance of relative European homogeneity, and brought some important and difficult issues back onto the political and legal agenda. It is no wonder, therefore, that this important (r) evolution highlighted a need for legislative reform, as well as for a re-evaluation of the objectives that drove the development of the European legal system.

The significant differences between the old and new members—not only in their legislative traditions but also in their economic, social and political development—necessitated a tremendous legislative effort from both sides. On the one hand, a long and difficult process of legal approximation began, as well as the formal and factual harmonisation of the systems of all the new states. On the other hand, the EU was forced to adapt in order to accommodate the new members without disturbing the operation of its legal and institutional architecture, and without obstructing the relatively smooth functioning of the common market. Those two separate yet interrelated processes have led to a rebalancing of the European regulatory structure, and have provided a vital incentive for the adoption of new legal instruments. This incentive, which was initially purely external but slowly became internalised, seems to have affected both the substance and the form of the European legal instruments, as well as those of the new states. More interestingly, however, it also seems to have significantly altered the direction of regulatory choices and the prioritisation of legislative efforts.

Before taking a closer look at the legal developments pertaining to the building of the bigger Europe in the global conditions of the twenty-first century, this section confronts the internal pressures affecting Europe with the external demands of the global market. The main objectives will be to take a broader perspective on these matters, and look at the problems of a growing Europe in a shrinking world. The analysis will, thus, pertain on the one hand to the ways in which European regulation responds to the external challenges of the growing constraints of international trade regimes, which mainly stem out of its participation in the WTO system. It is not my intention to analyse the WTO system of regulating international trade but rather to look at the way it influences European regulation, and the challenges it poses, as seen from the EU perspective. On the other hand, I examine the way Europe has confronted its internal regulatory constraints, and the means with which it answered the challenging needs of its growing internal market following the 2004 and 2007 enlargements.

In particular, I look at the case of Poland's accession to the EU, which was the most difficult and controversial of all the acceding states in 2004. I analyse the reform of Polish food-safety regulations, which was driven by the prospect of accession, and assess the first outcomes of the process. I have chosen Poland as my case study partly because it is my homeland, and so it is the most familiar to me and I have had practical experience working on its transition. But my choice was also affected by the fact that, from the point of view of the significance of the agricultural and food sectors, Poland can be seen as an exemplary case, being the biggest agricultural and food producer among all new states, but also having the largest consumers' market of the nations that joined the EU in 2004.

The chapter studies the evolution of legal instruments in the EU and in Poland propelled by the prospect of accession, as well as their application and functioning in the first years after accession. It analyses the objectives that drove those legal developments and examines the significance of socioeconomic concerns both in the process of making those regulatory choices and in the wake of their application. It is my intention that this analysis shows how the law has changed in response to the challenges of enlargement, but also how enlargement has changed the conditions of the European market, and has consequently altered the grounds for further legal development and the shifting objectives of it. The study also highlights the growing relevance of rebalancing European legislative efforts to make them more sensitive to increasing socioeconomic concerns.

1. A Bigger Europe in a Smaller World

Over the last decades, the acceleration of globalisation has led to an immense increase in the international flow of goods and services, capital and people. Interdependencies among global trade partners as well as a regulatory system of international trade relations have contributed to a gradual reduction of prices, an increase in consumer choice, and a removal of unnecessary barriers. The regulatory system should, thus, work towards greater prosperity and employment in Europe as well as globally.

As a result of those global developments, the EU economy is entangled not only in a web of multilateral and bilateral trade agreements, but also in a complex system of international market rules and standards, which govern various aspects of trade relations and cooperation. Over the last fifty years the EU has become one of the key players in the global economic system, accounting for about 30% of global GDP and 20% of global trade flows. This important performance standing and the strong position that follows from it puts pressure on the EU to conduct its trade policy in a coherent and responsible manner, in order to promote development, economic prosperity and stability in the global village. Hence, the EU, being the largest and the most comprehensive member of the global market, plays a key role in the operations of the World Trade Organisation. The EU's ambitions to lead and be a driving force in the WTO are visible in its activity in the development of negotiations of the current Doha Round, which, broadly and simply speaking, aims at further opening of markets and at the integration of developing countries into the world trading system, specifically by strengthening assistance to capacity-building and poverty-reduction.

The following section presents some observations about the international food trade regulation, not just for the sake of comparison but also to show the interconnections and interdependencies between the European and the global rules. Now that the EU rules are, to a very large extent, shaped by the global rules, a discussion of the origins and structure of the international trade regulation is necessary for a coherent analysis and understanding of the European system.

1.1. *Food Regulation in the Global Market*

Due to its economic potential, as well as its particular sensitivity with regard to consumer safety, the food market is among the most heavily regulated both in Europe and internationally. The current complex and multi-level governance system is a result of interplay between the global WTO rules, the array of bilateral and multilateral agreements, the rules set by regional trade organisations, and finally national legislations.

The augmentation of the global food trade regulation can be traced back to the Uruguay Round of negotiations of the GATT, which concluded in 1994. The declaration launching the negotiations[1] recognised that the minimisation of the adverse effects of sanitary and phyto-sanitary regulations and barriers on the agriculture trade was a main objective. The Uruguay Round was concluded with a new Agreement on the Application of Sanitary and Phyto-sanitary Measures (the SPS Agreement), which laid down rules for measures to target selected risks to animal, plant and human life and health. At the same time, the code of standards was revised, resulting in the WTO Technical Barriers to Trade Agreement (the TBT Agreement). The package was completed by the Agreement on Trade-Related Aspects of Intellectual Property Rights (the TRIPS Agreement), which included rules on the protection of geographical indications of origin of certain agricultural and food products.[2] The adoption of these new trade measures was strengthened by the establishment of a new dispute settlement mechanism, which was meant to ensure the effectiveness of the new rules.

The GATT/WTO core regulatory framework is surrounded by a constellation of multilateral agreements, which include provisions affecting agricultural food production and trade.[3] Even more importantly, however, the system also relies on various technical agreements, as well as on the international organisations that develop technical standards to facilitate the implementation of these agreements. Among those institutions, three bodies functioning under the auspices of the SPS Agreement require special mention, as they have a particular relevance for the food sector. They are: (1) the World Organization for Animal Health, previously L'Office International des Epizooties (OIE), which is in charge of measures relating to animal and human health, (2) the International Plant Protection Convention (IPPC), which is in charge of plant health measures, and finally (3) the Codex Alimentarius Commission (CAC), in charge of food safety standards. The standards developed by these three organisations are given special recognition in the WTO system. Compliance with those standards creates the presumption of compliance with the provisions of the Agreement. Hence, all three institutions, as well as the rules and standards

---

[1] The Punta del Este Ministerial Declaration of 1986.

[2] For a useful summary, see T Josling, D Roberts and D Orden, *Food Regulation and Trade: Toward a Safe and Open Global System* (Institute for International Economics, Washington DC 2004) 35–63.

[3] For example, the Convention on International Trade in Endangered Species of Wild Fauna and Flora (CITES) and the Convention on Biological Diversity (CBD).

developed by them, should be viewed as part of the multinational governance framework for food.[4]

The most important aspect of this setting, however, is that all the regulatory components discussed here are interlinked. All the regulatory levels—regional, national, European and global—as well as rules produced by private professional standard setters must coexist, and all can, in their different ways, affect a foodstuff produced in a small town somewhere in a European member state. Being part of such global undertaking can sometimes be rather challenging. Particularly when important interests are at stake and different approaches collide, finding a way out of a conflict is an important part of the process. Hence, the role of national, EU and WTO judicial and dispute settlement organs is tremendously important. In the business world, however, conflicts are better resolved before they occur, in order to avoid a potential loss of profit. Therefore, negotiating and creating transnational binding rules and standards should be treated with the utmost care and consideration. In sensitive areas, as the food sector is, where economic interests have to be juxtaposed with health considerations, the social significance of production and consumption, as well as cultural, religious and traditional influences, the role of standard-setters is crucial. If all these aspects are not properly reflected in regulation, participation in this global undertaking can become more of a curse than the blessing it was meant to be.

In case of the EU, the role of the European regulator is twofold. On the one hand, it represents its members in the process of negotiating global standards, and it guarantees their implementation and enforcement by the member states. Thus, it ensures the observance of global rules in Europe and, in the case of non-compliance, it acts as an executor. On the other hand, however, the EU should also protect the interests of its member states ahead of global institutions and see to it that their particular preferences and reservations are given due consideration. In the following paragraph, the EU's dual role in global regulation is examined in more detail, with particular reference to any potential consequences of the diversity of the growing European market.

1.2. *Europe as a Global Player*

The EU conducts its external trade policy through the instruments of the 'Common Commercial Policy' on the basis of Article 207 TFEU (ex Article 133 TEC). According to that provision, in matters of international trade, including

[4] Compare T Josling et al, (n 2) 39–61; KA van der Heijden and S Miller, *International Food Safety Handbook: Science, International Regulation, and Control* (Marcel Dekker Inc, New York 1999) 597–661, 739–767; and C Macmaolain, *EU Food Law. Protecting Consumers and Health in a Common Market* (Modern Studies in European Law, Hart Publishing, Oxford, Portland, Oregon 2007) 133–173.

WTO issues, the EU acts as a single entity. The Commission represents all twenty-seven member states at the global level, and acts on their behalf in negotiations and decision-making, as well as in the conclusion of international agreements. In this role, the Commission is supported by a special committee, which is composed of representatives of all member states and of the Commission. Its main function is to coordinate activities under the EU's trade policy and their implementation.

Formally speaking, the mechanism is straightforward: uniform common external policy, one representation, and common obligations. Its implementation, however, can be (and has been) far less predictable. As explained in the preceding paragraph, the framing of the common commercial policy, read in conjunction with the other Treaty provisions, puts the European Commission in a specifically dual position. On the one hand, the Commission represents the EU and its member states in front of WTO bodies. On the other hand, the Commission, not always having taken into consideration the positions of all member states on a given instrument, takes responsibility for the implementation and enforcement in all twenty-seven states of commonly agreed WTO rules. This specific setting can, in case of highly sensitive issues, prove to be rather uncomfortable. One example of this can currently be seen in the intensely debated issue of the use of genetically modified organisms (GMOs).

To summarise briefly, the conflict between the old world (the EU) and the new world (the US, Canada and Argentina) over the use of GMOs goes back some years. Since 1998 a *de facto* moratorium on the use of GMOs led to the suspension of the approvals of new GMOs in Europe. In 2003, the USA, together with Canada and Argentina, initiated a WTO procedure against the EU, arguing that the EU policy on GMOs created illegal trade restrictions, in particular by: (1) implementing a *de facto* moratorium on the approval of new biotech crop varieties; (2) failing to approve some particular GM crops for which American firms were seeking approval; (3) maintaining a situation in which some member states had unilaterally banned the importing and marketing of GM crops that had been approved at the EU level. In September 2006 the WTO Dispute Settlement Panel ruled in favour of the plaintiffs and requested the EU to bring its GMO approval process in line with WTO regulations.[5] The end result of the conflict is still not certain, however. The Commission did in fact reform its approval procedure, but the main problem lies with the resistance of the member states and their failure to implement the EU rules in that respect. Hence, the lifting of the unilateral bans introduced by many member states, which is necessary to comply with the WTO ruling,

[5] *European Communities—Measures Affecting the Approval and Marketing of Biotech Products*, the Panel Report WT/DS291/R, WT/DS292/R, and WT/DS293/R, issued on 29 September 2006.

is still in the process with uncertain results. The EU is constantly struggling to implement its own GMO regulations and, at the same time, the WTO rules reflected in them. The current reform of the deliberate release regime propose by the Commission, which will be evaluated later in this volume, is just another attempt to settle the problem of three-level legal conflict on GMOs. Thus, the end of this WTO procedure may just be the end of the battle, but not the end of the transatlantic conflict.[6]

One of the main reasons for this kind of scepticism can be found in the roots of the whole argument between the WTO and the EU: a mismatch of the logics of regulation applied by the two organisations. It is not just about a more or less precautionary approach to regulation, which was often debated in the context of both the GMO and hormone cases, but it goes deeper, to the philosophy on which the regulatory instruments are based. To take one example, the WTO relies strongly on the product/process distinction, while Europe mixes the process into the product under the mutual-recognition governance. Consequently, the distinction applied by the WTO, which is the basis of various regulatory solutions, gets lost in European implementation process and is not reflected further in the EU case. As the rationale gets blurred, a mismatch of regulatory solutions is created, which inevitably leads to conflicts in application.

There are many more such problematic differences in the regulatory logics of Europe and the WTO[7] that affect global cooperation and coexistence. Majone goes as far as to accuse the European Commission of misunderstanding and disregarding international standardisation and neglecting the importance of coexistence. According to Majone, the Commission is missing the bigger point of what is really important in standardisation, and is trying to stress the formality of the voluntary/mandatory divide instead of focusing on efficiency and potential economic benefits.[8] The consequence of this is, on the one hand, transatlantic conflicts such as the ones we have seen over the last two decades. On the other hand, however, it has important consequences for the internal market and its participants, as well as for the position of the EU as a global player.

---

[6] For a more detailed description of the case and an interesting analysis of the situation, see: T Bernauer and P Aerni, 'Trade Conflict over Genetically Modified Organisms' in K Gallagher (ed), *Handbook on Trade and the Environment* (Edward Elgar Publishing, Cheltenham 2008) 183–193; RL Howse and H Horn, 'European Communities—Measures Affecting the Approval and Marketing of Biotech Products' (2009) 8 *World Trade Review* 49–83.

[7] P Holmes, 'Trade and "Domestic" Policies: the European Mix' (2006) 13 *Journal of European Public Policy* 815–831.

[8] G Majone, *Dilemmas of European Integration. The Ambiguities and Pitfalls of Integration by Stealth* (Oxford University Press, Oxford 2005) 104.

The transatlantic GMO conflict also illustrates very well the problematic nature of the dual role of the European Commission, and the EU as such, in its participation in the WTO global regulatory system. On the one hand, Europe is becoming larger and more diversified, and the regulation does not seem to respond well to those new challenges; on the other, Europe is a part of a global trade community and has to play by international rules. The first important problem in this context is the one already mentioned before: Europe stands in front of the WTO in its own name but also in the name of its member states, but it still does not always respond to the concerns of its member states. There are situations when the EU implements and obeys the international rules but then some states refuse to do so. In such cases, the EU must use methods of disciplining them. Suitable methods are in theory available, but experience has revealed a lot of resistance and a significant inability of European institutions to guarantee member states' compliance.

Another interesting problem is that the WTO, as a global player, in fact faces similar problems but on an even bigger scale. If the EU has problems with challenges of diversity, what kind of mechanisms would have to be available to organise international trade, but yet respect the diversity of its various participants? Many parallels can be found here in the way the less-advantaged counties are treated by the 'club', be it the EU or the WTO. In both those forums the less-advantaged states have to obey transnational standards, although their particular concerns are systematically overlooked. Naturally, such settings lead to various forms of resistance or non-compliance. If the EU, with its comparatively stronger institutions and wider legitimacy, cannot always find effective methods of responding to non-compliance, can we expect the WTO to find means of combating non-compliance before it becomes systematic?

Continuing the parallels, it has to be emphasised that the WTO and the position of the EU in it have a significant influence on European regulations, their rationale and the legislative instruments they use.[9] Such mutual influence should be beneficial for both the EU and the WTO, but it has to be considered that the WTO is the stronger and more influential partner, so it will

[9] A Battaglia, 'Food Safety: Between European and Global Administration' (2006) 6 *Global Jurist Advances* 1–14; J Wouters and S Verhoeven, 'Regulation and Globalization: Interactions between International Standards-setting Agencies and the European Union' in D Geradin, R Muñoz and N Petit (eds), *Regulation through Agencies in the EU. A New Paradigm of European Governance* (Edward Elgar Publishing, Cheltenham 2005) 246–273; Ch Joerges, 'Constitutionalism in Postnational Constellations: Contrasting Social Regulation in the EU and in the WTO' in Ch Joerges and E-U Petersmann, *Constitutionalism, Multilevel Trade Governance and Social Regulation* (Hart Publishing, Oxford 2006) 491–527; Ch Noiville, 'Compatibility or Clash? EU Food Safety and the WTO' in C Ansell and D Vogel (eds), *What's the Beef? The Contested Governance of European Food Safety* (The MIT Press, Cambridge MA 2006) 307–325; and AR Young and P Holmes, 'Protection or Protectionism? EU Food Safety and the WTO' in C Ansell and D Vogel (eds), *What's the Beef?* … ibid 281–305.

be Europe that will have to adjust. Thus, evolution towards more flexible and inclusive market regulation in Europe will be important, especially for the contemporary—bigger—Europe, which, although stronger and more influential, needs at the same time to deal with a whole range of new challenges stemming from its last two enlargements.

1.3. *The Internal Challenges of the Bigger Europe*

The fall of the Berlin Wall created, metaphorically and indeed literally, a new European landscape. Nevertheless, it was only with the spectacular 2004 enlargement that a real reunification took place. For the first time in the history of the EU, an impressive number of ten new states joined in. This was an enlargement like no other also in kind. A big group of post-communist states, with their specific historical legacies and problems, was to be reintegrated with European structures. Differences between the 'old' and 'new' European states were enormous and concerned basically all aspects of the functioning of the society and the state. It was clear that the final decision to give the green light to the accession of the central and eastern European states was, in the end, political, as economic and organisational conditions had not been entirely met. It was, however, the great value of reunification which was at stake, and which prevailed in the decision.

The problem of reintegrating diverse states is, however, not the sole problem of the 'big Europe' of the twenty-first century. Contemporary Europe, as much as any other continent, is tormented by the troubles of our millennium, such as global warming, international terrorism and the extreme fragility of global financial markets, where problems at one end of the globe affect interest rates across oceans. Europe needs its size and strength in order to compete on the global market, and to effectively influence progress at an international level or counteract dangerous or unfavourable developments that could affect its integrity or interest. Additionally, Europe has to deal with its own old troubles, which date back many years, such as the progressive ageing of its society, the instability of its labour markets and the mismanagement of immigration issues and policies, troubles which were mostly aggravated by the enlargement.

All in all, the new, bigger Europe is a Europe of contrasts, of variable geometries, systemic incoherence, multiplicity of official languages, and an army of bureaucrats. Moreover, it is a project with a lot of mixed feelings about the meaning of it all, where the enthusiasm and joy of togetherness blend with questions about inequality, social differences and expensive policies with one-sided cash-flows. Why bother? Maybe partly because being a European contains an inherent need for reunification and reconciliation. In order to face its rivals in the global market, Europe needs to be bigger and to become a stronger power, too. But also because that is what European Union has always been about. The last two enlargements altered nothing more than the dimension of it all, and highlighted problems that before may have been easier to disregard.

1.4. *Food Trade in the Enlarged Europe*

The 2004 and 2007 accessions marked a new era in the development of the EU. The number of its member states had almost doubled (from fifteen to twenty-seven) in a short time. Bearing in mind that agriculture and food production are among the most important components of the national markets of the new states, it could be expected that the impact would indeed be fundamental.

It is probably still too soon to draw general long-term conclusions, especially since the accessions of Bulgaria and Romania happened only a couple of years ago, but the mere statistics can illustrate the tremendous impact that these two accessions had on the volume of food traded in the EU. At the beginning of the 2009, the food and drink industry of the EU of twenty-seven states generated a turnover of €913 billion, purchasing and processing 70% of the EU's agricultural production. The sector employed over 4 million people and provided for almost 500 million European consumers.[10]

It is not only the volume, however, but also the variety of food production and consumption traditions, as well as the economic conditions surrounding the processes, that have risen significantly. Thus, the accessions changed not only the size of the market but also its pattern of operation. It should, therefore, be taken into consideration that the new, bigger and more diversified food market may require some modification of regulatory approaches.

In the following paragraphs, a closer look will be taken at a particular participant of the new European post-enlargement food market: Poland. The analysis of the Polish example aims to provide an illustration and arguments to support the claim for increased flexibility of regulation as a means of supporting the richness and diversity of the EU-27 common market.

2. The Accession of the Polish Food Industry to the EU

2.1. *The Evolution of Polish Food Law: Towards Meeting the Terms of Accession*

2.1.1. *Historical Implications, Economic and Social Determinants*

Under the communist regime in Poland, agriculture remained among the last bastions of private ownership. Attempts of forced collectivisation introduced

[10] Confederation of the Food and Drink industries of the EU, CIIA Annual Report 2008, 8.04.2009, 4 <http://www.ciaa.be/documents/brochures/CIAA%20RA_17.03.pdf> last accessed 25 May 2011.

in the 1950s were not successful in the majority of cases, which considerably reduced the scale of problems that have to be dealt with now. The collapse of the PGRs (the state-owned farming establishments) in the 1990s was only a taste of what could have had happened, had full collectivisation been successful. The traditional picture of Polish agriculture, which emphasises small-scale, dirty and old-fashioned farms with low income and poor productivity, is a cruel stereotype. There is a grain of truth in it, though. Polish agriculture has been extremely disadvantaged in relation to its counterparts in old EU member states, not only because of the heritage of the previous system of state planned economy, but also because of the lack of subsidy schemes and possibilities to engage in independent and civilised international trade.

As much as 80% of the food industry, on the other hand, was until the 1980s controlled by the state. Only at the beginning of the 1990s, with a radical increase of private investment, including foreign investment, did a structure of ownership start to develop. Towards the end of the decade the figure of state ownership in the sector had dropped to 15%.[11]

During the pre-accession negotiations, attempts to draw comparisons between the Polish and the EU attitudes towards agriculture gave rise to fears rather than comfort.[12] Not surprisingly, considering their different backgrounds and political implications, there were major differences between the Polish agricultural policy and that of the EU. At the beginning of the accession discussions these seemed so impossible to reconcile that they were expected to jeopardise the whole integration process. The most significant differences were, naturally, macroeconomic and structural. Among the macroeconomic dissimilarities, which were analysed in the literature during the 1990s, four require special attention and emphasis. Firstly, Poland's level of economic development, judged on the basis of national income *per capita*, was much lower than in any old member state. Secondly, the percentage of the population employed in agriculture was far higher. Thirdly, Poland was more heavily reliant economically on its agriculture and food production sector than on other sectors; this, however, was not a result of its higher development and efficiency, but rather of the comparatively lower level of development of the other branches of the economy. Fourthly and finally, the Polish economy, as a whole, still had to be considered as an economy 'in transition', while the EU could be treated as a fully developed market economy.

The effects of these differences were numerous. Let me first point out that Poland's lower level of development contributed to the situation, where its

---

[11] Data available at: <http://www.poland.gov.pl> accessed 25 May 2011.

[12] For a comparison of the situation of Polish agriculture with that of the European member states, see: J Bański, 'Selected Aspects of Present-Day Changes in Polish Rural Space' (2003) 76 *Geographia Polonica* 87–89.

economy produced very little surplus that could be transferred to agriculture via budgetary spending such as subventions, or via the market through higher prices. On the other hand, due to high level of employment in agricultural production, this small surplus had to be distributed to a substantial number of recipients. This, in effect, left very scarce budgetary resources for investment and modernisation. Additionally, the low income levels of the population employed outside the agri-food sector did not allow much room for redistribution via market mechanisms, and consequently, all intervention activities that aimed at regulating market prices had to take account of consumers' financial restraints. This particular aspect of the problem was, by the way, one of great fears during the pre-accession period in Poland. Concerns were raised that the development of market prices of goods under the influence of the common market could create a significant imbalance between the part of the population employed in agriculture and the rest of the society. Furthermore, an increase in prices of food products would have put pressure on the market to increase wages, which could in effect have decreased the competitiveness of the whole economy.[13]

Due to all those considerations, Poland could not, before accession, have an agricultural policy that would resemble that of the EU. It also has to be pointed out that, due to its transformation from being a centrally planned economy organisation, the Polish agricultural and foodstuff policy had to deal with plenty of additional problems, unknown to its EU counterparts (e.g. the privatisation of state farming and production units, as well as of food-trade mechanisms), which were often accompanied by serious social tensions, such as a rapid growth in unemployment in agricultural areas. This may help to explain why, in those circumstances, it was so difficult to conduct any forms of production-stabilisation or even a production-reduction policy. In the 1990s, when the EU was stabilising production of all its major agricultural markets under the pressure of the GATT, Poland was merely attempting to control its production of sugar.[14]

In this context, the relevant transformation and approximation processes in the institutional realm had already been initiatedat the beginning of the 1990s.

---

[13] J Rowiński, 'Integracja Polski z Unia Europejska—Niezbędne Procesy Dostosowawcze Polskiej Gospodarki Żywnościowej' in M Moroz (ed), *Sprawy Rolnictwa i Gospodarki Żywnościowej w Umowach Polski ze Wspólnotami Europejskimi* (Fundacja im. Mikołaja Rataja, Warszawa 1992) 38–40.

[14] J Rowiński, 'Integracja …' ibid 40; see also A Jurcewicz, 'Legal problems Resulting from the Assignment of New Tasks to the Agricultural Sector in Poland' in P-Ch Müller-Graff and A Stępniak (eds), *Poland and the European Union—Between Association and Membership* (European Community Studies Association Series, Nomos, Baden-Baden 1997) 31–35; A Czyżewski, 'Macroeconomic Interdependencies in the Process of Transformation of Agriculture' in P-Ch Müller-Graff and A Stępniak (eds), ibid 265–274.

In view of Poland's preparation for accession, as well as its transformation into a market economy system, two governmental agencies were established: the Agency for the Agricultural Market *(Agencja Rynku Rolnego*—ARR*)* and the Agency for the Restructuring and Modernisation of Agriculture *(Agencja Restrukuryzacji i Modernizacji Rolnictwa*—ARiMR*)*. Even though their initial aims and scopes of activity, which corresponded to Poland's current needs, differed significantly from their respective European counterparts, they were planned to be able to be easily transformed and adjusted to perform functions required by the CAP. The ARR was expected to take over the functions connected with intervention in agricultural markets, and the ARiMR was planned to coordinate the EU's structural policy at the national level and to administer EU funds and direct payments.[15]

2.1.2. *European Influences on Polish Agri-Food Sector before the Accession*

It has to be emphasised here that European influence on Polish regulation started well before the prospect of accession became at all realistic. In fact, the initial post-transition reforms had been modelled, to a certain extent, on the EU member states' legislation. In the field of agriculture and food production, the influence was also apparent. The liberalisation of the market for agri-food products had already begun after the transition, but it was only with the signing of the Association Agreement[16] that the really thorough changes started taking place. This Agreement, signed on 16 December 1991, brought about a reduction of trade barriers between Poland and the EU, and established certain trade preferences. The considerable initial asymmetry in the reduction of trade barriers was gradually reduced. Nevertheless, although the Europe Agreement foresaw preferential treatment and other liberalising instruments in trade policy, it did not affect the intervention mechanisms applied by the CAP. Consequently, this unequal application of the new rules, strengthened by competitiveness problems, significantly impeded the use of available trade preferences. This was one of the reasons for the conclusion of a so called 'double zero' agreement on 1 January 2001, the objective of which was to eliminate tariffs and export subsidies for a wide range of raw agricultural products. In 2002 it was followed by a 'double profit' agreement, which covered sensitive goods excluded from the first agreement, and enhanced and furthered its

[15] J Rowiński, 'Integracja …' ibid 42–43. A detailed description (including statistical figures) of the structure, production patterns and development of Polish agriculture, can be found in H Mertens, 'Poland' in S Goetz, T Jaksch and R Siebert (eds), *Agricultural Transformation and Land Use in Central and Eastern Europe* (Ashgate, Aldershot 2001) 223–268.

[16] Europe Agreement establishing an association between the European Communities and their Member States, of the one part, and the Republic of Poland, of the other part, of 16th December 1991 [1993] OJ L 348/2.

application. Those two instruments allowed two-way trade in pork, poultry, meat products, fruit and vegetables. Subsequently, duties and restrictions on products vulnerable to competition from imports were selectively cancelled.[17]

The factual impact of the Association Agreement on trade in agricultural goods, however, was far less significant than had initially been expected. In fact, during the first years after the Agreement was in force, the total value of Polish exports of goods included in the Agreement to EU countries declined. According to commentators, the situation was caused by a matrix of factors, including a very complicated system of procedures of access to the quota system, which forced potential importers to comply with a number of formal requirements, including registration, a proven record of economic activity for at least twelve months, as well as lodging relatively high guarantee deposits. This made the use of the preferential contingents rather costly and time-consuming. Additionally, many contingents were not used, due to the functioning of minimum price systems for some goods. In these systems, when prices in the EU market dropped below a certain minimum level, preferential duties would become meaningless for the importers. As a consequence, evaluations after the first years of the functioning of the scheme established by the Agreement have shown that benefits for the EU countries were two and a half times greater than those for Poland, which clearly contradicted the concessions assumed in the Agreement.[18]

Another important factor in evaluating the impact of the Europe Agreement, which proves that its factual influence on trade was not significant, is the volume of pre-existing trade links between Poland and the EU. In fact, Polish exporting of agricultural products to the EU was reaching 50% to 60% of the total export value during the whole post-war period.[19] It has to be stated, however, that a large part of Polish exporting of agricultural products before the accession was generated by a handful of big companies (often national branches of big multinational corporations), for whom operating in the European market had been regular practice for decades. Consequently, for those companies, transition and adjustment were not problematic, as they had already achieved conformity with the stringent EU standards long before the

---

[17] For more, see A Rytko, 'Analysis of Trade Relations between Poland and the European Union and their Impact on Volume and Structure of Agro-Food Articles Trade' (2005) 8 *Electronic Journal of Polish Agricultural Universities* < http://www.ejpau.media.pl/volume8/issue4/art-06.html> accessed 25 May 2011; S Senior Nello, 'Food and Agriculture in an Enlarged EU' (2002) EUI Working Paper RSC No.2002/58, 15.

[18] A Czyżewski, L Pawelczak, 'The Association Agreement between Poland and the European Union in the agribusiness sector—experience and first evaluations' in P-C Müller-Graff, A Stępniak (eds), *Poland and the European Union* ... (n 14) 235–237; J Rowiński, 'Adjustments of the Polish Agro-food Sector in the Course of the Association Process' in P-C Müller-Graff, A Stępniak (eds), ibid, 239–253.

[19] J Rowiński, 'Adjustments of the Polish Agro-food Sector ...', ibid 240.

legal obligation was established. The problem was, however, that although they made up the bigger share of the market, they constituted a meagre minority of producers, as traditionally Polish agricultural and food production was dominated by small, often family-operated establishments. It was those small-scale production units that were the most affected by the obligation to implement EU standards and had to face the risk of terminating their activities, as practical adjustment was often beyond their individual reach. Consequently, the percentage of trade affected by potential non-compliance was far smaller than the percentage of the population engaged in this type of production, who would suffer from the effects of any loss of market access in the case of a lack of implementation of the EU norms. Consequently, it has to be emphasised, the market perspective differed significantly from the social one.

2.1.3. *The Harmonisation of the Polish Legal System with the Acquis: General Issues*

The first steps towards Polish association with the EU were taken already during the second half of the 1980s. On 16 December 1991 the Polish government signed the Europe Agreement,[20] which established an associate relationship between the EC and the Republic of Poland and initiated the process of European integration.[21] The Copenhagen Summit in June 1993 opened the way for associated countries of central and eastern Europe to gain future membership in the EU, but only after they had demonstrated their ability to meet all the accession conditions, which were identified there and later referred to as 'the Copenhagen criteria'.[22]

On 8 of April 1994 Poland formally applied for membership of the EU. With the commencement of negotiations and screening processes, a necessity arose to reform the rules of the legislative procedure, so as to provide for mechanisms that would control the conformity of Polish draft laws with the *acquis*

---

[20] Europe Agreement, ibid 2.

[21] For an evaluation of the general provisions of the Europe Agreement, see, for example, R Stawarska, 'EU Enlargement form the Polish Perspective' (1999) 6 *Journal of European Public Policy* 824–826; PC Müller-Graff, 'East Central Europe and the European Union: From Europe Agreements to a Member Status' in PC Müller-Graff (ed), *East Central Europe and the European Union: From Europe Agreements to a Member Status* (Nomos, Baden-Baden 1997) 9; K Inglis, 'The Europe Agreements Compared in the Light of their Pre-accession Reorientation' (2000) 37 *Common Market Law Review* 1173.

[22] For more on the Copenhagen criteria and conditionality, see, for example, KE Smith, 'The Evolution and Application of EU Membership Conditionality' in M Cremona (ed), *The Enlargement of the European Union* (The Collected Courses of the Academy of European Law, Oxford University Press, Oxford 2003) 105–139; and M Cremona, 'Accession to the European Union: Membership Conditionality and Accession Criteria' (2001) 25 *Polish Yearbook of International Law* 220.

communautaire and to coordinate efforts that aimed to prepare the country for accession.

The negotiations began on 31 March 1998, and were followed by a series of screening sessions with the purpose of determining the extent to which the Polish legal system needed to be changed in order to achieve conformity with EU law. The outcomes of these screening sessions served as the basis for the development of Polish and European negotiation positions and the National Program of Preparation for Membership in the EU (*Narodowy Plan Przygotowania do Członkostwa w Unii Europejskiej*), which mapped the legal and institutional amendments necessary for Poland to adjust to the EU system before accession.[23] On 1 September that year, Poland had already presented to the Austrian Presidency its first negotiation positions in the first seven (out of twenty-nine) fields. The last, in the area of agriculture, was delivered to the Finnish Presidency on 16 December 1999.

An approximation of the Polish legal system was a great challenge and required intervention at all levels of the national legislation. It started more on a symbolic note, as even the new Constitution of 2 April 1997[24] reflected the accession aspirations of Poland. In Article 90, it gave explicit permission for the delegation to an international organisation or institution of the competences of the organs of state authority in relation to certain matters. This declaration, made in the highest national source of law, was a clear signal of the seriousness of Poland's aims and ambitions both for the EU and for the national administration.

The first practical step taken by the Polish authorities to prepare for approximation was the signing of the tripartite agreement by the Prime Minister and the speakers of both chambers of the Polish Parliament (the *Sejm* and the *Senat*)[25] on 10 July 2000, which aimed to facilitate and accelerate the process of adjusting the Polish legal system to EU law. According to this agreement, the Council of Ministers and the two chambers of Parliament agreed to introduce a special procedure for the adoption of laws that would adjust the Polish system to the *acquis* (so-called 'European laws'). In light of this agreement, some major legal and institutional changes were introduced.

[23] The National Program of Preparation for Membership in the EU was adopted by the Council of Ministers as a governmental document on 23 June 1996. The initial document was amended and updated every year, according to the current state of achievements and their evaluation in the Commission's progress report.

[24] The Constitution of the Republic of Poland of 2nd April 1997, *Journal of Laws*, No. 78, Item 483, 1997.

[25] The *Sejm* and the *Senat* are the two chambers of the Polish Parliament in which the Constitution vests legislative power.

In 1996 the Committee for European Integration (*Komitet Integracji Europejskiej—KIE*)[26] was created. It was meant to be the main governmental body responsible for the coordination of accession negotiations and adjustment processes. The *KIE* initiated the first major change in the Rules of Procedure of the Council of Ministers, which provided for a special procedure to adopt 'European laws'. The procedure involved additional interdepartmental consultations, greater participation of stakeholders, and, above all, an obligation to consider an opinion issued on behalf of the Committee for European Integration by the Office of the Committee for European Integration (*Urząd Komitetu Integracji Europejskiej—UKIE*)[27] on the conformity of drafts with EU law. Such opinions were to be issued at every stage of the procedure and after the introduction of any amendments to the previously accepted text.[28]

An analogous special procedure was created for the 'European laws' in the Parliament. By way of an amendment to the rules of procedure of both chambers, in July 2000 special 'European Law Committees' were established in the *Sejm* and the *Senat* to proceed on the *acquis*-approximating drafts. At the same time, these committees were meant to serve as consultative forums for the representatives of the ministries, the *UKIE* and social partners.[29]

The *UKIE* had a very important and difficult role to play in the integration process. On the one hand, being a governmental body, it served as a link between the Council of Ministers and the Parliament. On the other hand, it was responsible for consultations with the European Commission on various controversial questions. A representative of the *UKIE* Legal Department who was responsible for a particular draft took part in its creation from the first stages (consultation within a ministry on a first draft), through every governmental and parliamentary stage, right up to its final adoption.

On behalf of the Committee for European Integration, the *UKIE* also had the task of coordinating and planning all the necessary adjustment activities in the field of European policy. It was, thus, responsible for planning the

---

[26] Law of 8 August 1996 on the Committee for European Integration, *Journal of Laws*, 30 August 1996.

[27] The Office of the Committee for European Integration (the UKIE) was established on the basis of Article 8 of the Law on Committee for European Integration, in order to 'assist the Committee in the performance of its duties' by a Regulation of the Chairman of the Council of Ministers of 2 October 1996 on the assignment of status to the Office of the Committee for European Integration, *Journal of Laws*, 3 October 1996.

[28] In order to facilitate adjustments in the legal system, in July 2000 the Committee for European Integration adopted two additional regulatory acts: on detailed rules of proceeding governmental drafts of laws adjusting Polish law to the law of the EU, and on the coordination and verification of translations of legal documents of the EU. For more on the procedure within the Council of Ministers, see A Łazowski, 'Adaptation of the Polish Legal System to European Union Law: Selected Aspects' (2001) Sussex European Institute Working Paper No. 45, 14–17.

[29] A Łazowski, ibid 17–19; J Jaskiernia, 'Badanie zgodności projektów ustaw z prawem Unii Europejskiej w sejmowym postępowaniu ustawodawczym' (1999) 7 *Państwo i Prawo* 19–33.

timetables of legislative and administrative work as well as for keeping track of their implementation. Therefore, it not only programmed the major tasks of the administrative authorities at all levels, but it also played the part of a guard, checking the adjustment progress, reporting to the European Commission, and, if necessary, forcing improvements or requiring the acceleration of some processes by responsible national bodies.

Apart from the core Committee for European Integration, a special department for European policy was created in every line ministry. This was intended to facilitate communication and the mutual exchange of information between the *UKIE* and the ministries. It is clear that the efficiency of their relationships was a determinant of good coordination, as well as the correct reporting to the European Commission and other European institutions.

2.1.4. *Enlargement Preparations in the Agri- and Food Sector*

2.1.4.1. *Polish Food Safety Strategy*

Polish food safety legislation dates back to the interwar period. Poland's first comprehensive food safety law was passed in 1929, and revised in November 1970. Poland has been a member of the Codex Alimentarius Commission since its establishment, and the Polish Agricultural and Food Quality Inspection (earlier the Central Inspectorate of Standardisation) has participated in the work of international safety standard-setting bodies. Thus, basic food regulations, passed under the communist regime, did not deviate significantly from international standards. What was different, however, was the way in which food safety laws were implemented, and specifically the communist state's heavy reliance on administrative and penal sanctions.

The economic transformations already underway in the late 1980s called for changes in food regulations mostly because of the changed socioeconomic context in which they applied. Nevertheless, it was not until the late 1990s and the beginning of negotiations for Poland's accession to the EU that these changes began to take place. Under pressure from the European Commission and the threat of the closure of a significant share of Polish milk- and meat-production facilities, the question of food safety started to receive high priority in the Polish government.

Problems with the implementation of the European food safety law and the organisation of the food safety administration before accession were, to a large extent, conditioned by the previous mode of regulation and division of the powers of legislation and administration of the area. Traditionally, food safety has not been the domain of one single ministry, but least two had a particular interest. These were the Ministry of Agriculture and Rural Development (for food products of animal origin) and the Ministry of Health (for other types of foodstuffs). Both wanted to play a leading role in the field. Thus, Poland's first major task was to establish smooth and effective cooperation between them and their respective subordinate agencies, control bodies and laboratories.

The first general initiative taken by the government, in that respect, was to launch a large project that would help all the interested actors to cooperate in developing the National Food Safety Strategy. In order to prepare a coherent strategy that would be acceptable for all and that would guarantee enforcement, the government needed to ensure the participation and consensus of all the actors in play. Therefore, a special working group was established, containing representatives of the Ministries involved, the *UKIE*, the scientific institutes, the sanitary and veterinary inspections, as well as the food and feed business operators and consumer organisations. The task of the group was to prepare a document identifying the necessary improvements to be made, to plan the division of powers and responsibilities at all levels of governance, and to lay down a timetable for the adoption of the necessary legal and administrative adjustments. The National Food Safety Strategy, defining the priorities and methodology of the preparation, introduction and maintenance of food safety at the minimum level of risk, was meant to serve as a solid basis for the implementation of a comprehensive, multi-sectoral system for the protection of public health in the area of foodstuffs. Moreover, its development and implementation constituted one of the requirements of successful preparation for the EU membership.

The Polish Food Safety Strategy[30] developed by this inter-ministerial working group was meant to incorporate all the guidelines and policy proposals laid down by the European Commission in its recommendation of 16 February 2001, 'Guidelines to prepare the Food Safety Strategy', which set out the main elements to be included in all national programs.[31] The Strategy followed the recommendations of the Commission White Paper on Food Safety,[32] the OECD 'Compendium of National Food Safety Systems and Activities',[33] as well as the guidelines of the Codex Alimentarius Commission and the WHO.

The Polish Food Safety Strategy was adopted by the government in February 2002 and was submitted to the European Commission for approval. It consists of two sections. The first concerns various legal and organisational matters of the official food-control system, while the second sets out the progress status of preparatory activities.

---

[30] Food Safety Strategy in Poland, Warsaw, 11 February 2002.

[31] Commission (EC), Guidelines to prepare the Food Safety Strategy of 16 February 2001.

[32] Commission (EC), White Paper on Food Safety COM (1999) 719 final.

[33] OECD, 'Compendium of National Food Safety Systems and Activities', 15 May 2000, SG/ADHOC/FS(2000)5/ANN/FINAL.

Among the Strategy's main objectives, the document lists: (1) guaranteeing food safety throughout the entire food chain, starting with primary production and ending with food distribution to the consumer's table; (2) ensuring, *inter alia*, through border control, that imported food meets the same or equivalent health-quality norms and requirements as those applicable to domestically produced food; (3) the harmonisation of the Polish food laws with the EU law, and its effective practical implementation; (4) the efficient control of the food chain; and (5) the continuous provision of reliable food safety information to the government and the public. The last objective, which I would like to emphasise as being particularly interesting and definitely not originating from the Commission guidelines, was: (6) to build and strengthen the trust of domestic and foreign consumers in Polish food safety, and so to establish favourable conditions for Polish economic interests.[34] This objective, although formulated rather clumsily, illustrates well the government's awareness of the necessity to safeguard Polish economic interests by well-guided and comprehensive national action, instead of by relying solely on EU assistance and the opening-up of the common market.

The text of the Strategy begins with a description of the current national regulatory and institutional situation. Firstly, it gives an overview of the applicable Polish legislation in the field of foodstuffs. Secondly, it identifies the competent national authorities and the most important supervisory procedures. It describes, sequentially, the internal organisation and functioning of the Sanitary Inspectorate, the Veterinary Inspectorate, the Trade Inspection and the Crop Protection Inspection, which together form Poland's complex system of official food control.[35] Finally, the descriptive section ends with a brief presentation of the national advisory bodies and entities that provide scientific expertise in the field of food. Last but not least, it presents the national system of hazardous products information.[36]

The second section of the Strategy is devoted to the activities planned in preparation for accession. The point of departure for the institutional reform was the assumption that the required efficiency of the official food-control system could be guaranteed through the building or strengthening of links between the existing bodies, without revolutionalising the system by creating costly new institutions. Along these lines, the Strategy envisaged a detailed evaluation of current resources—in order to identify shortages, find possible solutions for supplementing those shortages, and develop procedures for the integrated intervention of official food-control bodies.

---

[34] See Food Safety Strategy ... (n 30) 5.
[35] Ibid, Part 1.2, 1/3–1/5.
[36] Ibid, Part1.3-1.5, 1/25–1/30.

The necessary strengthening of control mechanisms was supposed to be undertaken at all levels where effective control is to be performed. At the basic, production level, emphasis was given to a clear identification of the liability of food and feed producers, and on defining comprehensive safety-assurance conditions and internal-control mechanisms, such as the HACCP system. At the level of local official control, the most important challenges were the necessity to strengthen the national network, preparing it to cooperate with the existing European arrangements, as well as the development of a uniform set of methods and standards with respect to the tasks performed by these authorities. With regard to laboratory control, the major task identified was the establishment and accreditation of laboratories that would be able to perform all the types of examinations required by the EU law on a large scale, and to function as reference laboratories for the purposes envisaged in the European legislation. At the national level, finally, emphasis was given to the defining of rules for full and substantive cooperation between the government administration and official food-control bodies.[37]

Apart from the review of the situation with regard to different stages of control, a large number of cross-level problems were emphasised. They generally pointed to Poland's lack of technical capacity, its shortage of trained human resources, and its financial deficiencies. The Strategy, therefore, developed a detailed plan to train and build capacity, starting with concrete legislative proposals, through sketching comprehensive institutional adjustments with regard to all institutions involved, and ending with budgetary provisions, which included the EU's forecast financial assistance.[38] The plan was accompanied by an implementation schedule, with a detailed timetable for all the envisaged activities.[39]

All in all, the Strategy turned out to be a very relevant element of the integration process in the foodstuffs sector, providing a comprehensive action plan for the reform agenda, and obliging both the Polish government and the European institutions to perform their respective commitments undertaken therein.

2.1.4.2. *Legal Approximation in the Food Sector*

Similarly to the accession negotiations in the fields of agriculture, food and fisheries, the process of legal approximation in those areas was complex,

---

[37] Ibid, Part 2.1, 2/1–2/4.
[38] Ibid, Parts 2.2–2.4, 2/5–2/49.
[39] Ibid, Part 3, 3/1–3/3.

time-consuming and accompanied by enormous social and political tensions. The most intensive years—those directly prior to the planned date of accession—were tainted by particular difficulties. Firstly, consecutive Polish governments, aware of the socioeconomic context of the necessary reforms in the agri-food sector, delayed the most critical modifications, which led to them amassing in the last few years preceding accession. Secondly, the complicated political landscape during those years—especially the strong presence of radical anti-European parties, which often represented peasant electorates—frequently impeded or even blocked the necessary legal reforms in the name of the protection of Polish agriculture, the Polish economy and Polish society, and in response to social fears surrounding the accession. Thirdly, the demanding developments of European legislation, combined with the intensified scrutiny of the European Commission, contributed additional pressure, imposing a timetable for approximation that was not always in line with Poland's plans, needs and capacity. Fourthly, the financial burden of the reforms cumulated over the last years before accession and was very difficult to explain and justify nationally, as it went far beyond the potential of the Polish budget. In that situation, laws were sometimes passed in order to comply with the Commission's timetable, although they were already in advance known to be temporarily 'unimplementable' due to Poland's financial shortcomings. Finally, the results of the final round of agricultural negotiations turned out to be well below the people's expectations and the government's promises, and the government tried to compensate for some of the shortcomings by means of legislation. This, inevitably, met with the criticism of the European Commission and so added an extra burden to the already overloaded national administration.

Thus, the legal approximation process in those critical years was a rather taxing exercise. Numerous amendments of the core legal instruments in the food sector filled the legislative agenda, and the strict timetable that had to be observed created an unfavourable environment for efficient lawmaking. Nevertheless, Poland's progress in approximation was considerable, and before the date of accession the system was more or less ready, coherent and functional. In the following paragraphs, I will review the core elements of food legislation in Poland, and describe the building of the system of food safety regulation in Poland.[40]

---

[40] For detailed analysis, see A Surdej and K Żurek, 'The Polish Regulatory System on Food' in E Vos and M Everson (eds), *Uncertain Risks Regulated: Facing the Unknown in National, EU and International Law* (Law, Science and Society Series, Routledge-Cavendish Publishing, Abingdon 2009) 111–126.

2.1.4.2.1. *Law on Health Conditions of Food and Nutrition*
On 11 May 2001 Poland made a major attempt to bring its general food legislation in line with the *acquis* by passing the Law on Health Conditions of Food and Nutrition (hereafter: the Food Law).[41]

The Food Law significantly altered the entire system of food safety regulations in Poland.[42] It started by defining the notion of 'food safety' as 'a set of complex conditions which must be met, and activities which must be undertaken, at all stages of food production and food distribution in order to ensure safety for people's health and life'. These conditions and activities were translated into product and process standards. These specific product and process standards, however, were not part of the basic law. Instead, their formulation was delegated to the Ministry of Health. The Ministry of Health was also assigned the task of supervising the work of the State Sanitary Inspection, which carried out field controls with regard to all foods except foods of animal origin, the control of which was delegated to the State Veterinary Inspection, under the supervision of the Ministry of Agriculture.

The law emphasised the role of science in the setting of rules and standards, as well as in the regulatory decision-making. It also introduced the precautionary principle, which reads: 'official inspection authorities can undertake preventive actions that are anticipatory and proportional to the threat, in order to protect human life and health (*the precautionary principle*)' in cases where 'there is no scientific proof confirming the non-harmful characteristics of food items'.[43] The precautionary principle in its modern European form was a novelty in the Polish food safety regulations introduced under EU influence. The negotiation commitment of faithful legal harmonisation left no room for discussion of its particular shape and scope in the Polish law during the pre-accession adjustment process,

---

[41] Law of 11 May 2001 on Health Conditions of Food and Nutrition, unified text in *Journal of Laws*, No. 31, Item 265, 2005. Even earlier than this, the Law of 24 April 1997 on the control of infectious diseases of animals, examinations of slaughter animals and meat, and on the Veterinary Inspection, (*Journal of Laws*, No. 66, Item 752, 1999 as amended) was passed, which contained provisions concerning food of animal origin. With regard to non-health related food quality, the most important piece of legislation is the Law of 21 December 2000 on Commercial Quality of Agricultural and Food Products (*Journal of Laws*, No. 5, Item 44, 2001, as amended). Important modifications to the Polish Food Law were passed (before accession) on 14 February 2003 and later on 30 October 2003. The state of development for 2006–2007 was analysed against the background of EC legislation and commented on by M Grochowska, *Bezpieczeństwo Żywności i Żywienia. Komentarz do Ustawy oraz Przepisów Wspólnotowych* (ODDK, Gdańsk 2007).

[42] This law served to transpose more than eighty EU directives in the field of food safety. In general, the EU food safety standards had been more stringent than the Polish ones. Nevertheless, in some cases, such as the regulation of additives and preservatives, Polish food safety requirements were more restrictive than EU standards; see __, 'Links to the West' *Warsaw Business Journal* (Warsaw 23 January 2003).

[43] Ibid Article 45, point 2.

and it was, in effect, based thoroughly on the European prototype. Furthermore, the Food Law defined procedures regarding scientific expertise, recommending reference laboratories and national standard-setting bodies that would draw on the best knowledge and experiences of the EU reference laboratories.

In anticipation of regulatory problems relating to biotechnological products, the law laid down a definition of 'novel food' as 'substances or their mixtures, which earlier have not been applied for human consumption'.[44] Genetically modified food was considered a subcategory of novel food, and its production or sale in Poland was placed under the decision of the General Sanitary Inspector. The Inspector was expected to check whether it was properly labelled, and, after seeking and reviewing the opinions of experts and scientific centres, was to issue a decision either allowing or forbidding its production or sale. The law also dealt with problems of the production of food from animals treated with hormones by setting a direct ban on such practices.

The law conformed to the transparency principle by requiring that the State Sanitary Inspector make publicly available a register of decisions, with all documentation of the admissibility procedures, thus allowing for public control of the impartiality of decisions. The law also responded to the recommendations of contemporary regulatory science that regulators should assist consumers to make choices by disclosing scientific information. According to this rationale, the law required that the packaging of all food and nutritional products should contain all the information essential for the protection of human health and life. In particular, packaging should display the composition of the food product; its nutritional value; the presence of permitted additional substances or food additives; its expiry date; instructions for use; as well as data necessary to identify the producer or the company that had placed it on the market. Furthermore, the law required that the information on the food 'should not mislead a consumer with texts or graphic signs' and 'should not attribute to the product nutritional values which it does not possess'.[45]

One of most important changes in the regulatory approach to food safety in Poland was the transition from a reliance on direct penal and administrative law-enforcement to an increasing reliance on producers' own responsibility and self-control. Thus, on the one hand, the system of administrative decisions to enable trade in food (the so-called 'pre-market approval') was eliminated. On the other hand, the law imposed on companies producing and selling food an obligation to safeguard the effectiveness of food safety standards by carrying out internal inspections. The Hazard Analysis and Critical Control Points (HACCP) became the basis for the internal-control system, and the Food Law

---

[44] Ibid Article 3, point 26.
[45] Ibid, Article 24, point 2.

put the obligation to implement and document the proper functioning of the HACCP control system as of the date of accession to the EU on all large companies.[46] Under that system and in accordance with the principle of traceability, if a safety problem is identified, the food must immediately be withdrawn from the market by the producer. The state of the food produced or treated in a given company could, however, also be verified *ex post*, since all food companies were required to store records and samples of their food products for a certain period of time and to allow food inspectors to examine them on request. Operators who produced foodstuffs or sold them in violation of food safety rules were confronted with financial penalties or imprisonment.

The Article 40 (c) of the Food Law made the Minister of Health responsible for cooperation with the European Food Safety Agency. In particular, the Ministry of Health was empowered to send a representative to the EFSA Advisory Forum. It was also given the authority to send requests for scientific opinions, and to lodge the requisite scientific data on Polish food safety with the EFSA. This set of provisions was meant to guarantee an appropriate level of cooperation of the Polish food safety authorities with the EFSA.

When Poland actually acceded to the EU, the law had to be amended. Sections with substantial provisions had to be repealed and replaced by the directly applicable European Regulations, leaving to national legislator only national procedural and institutional issues. Hence, following the accession, legislative efforts were undertaken in order to replace the 2001 Food Law with a new framework regulation. The Law on the Safety of Food and Feed of 25 August 2006[47] marks the end of the adjustment and transition phases, and conforms with the EU's New Approach to Food Safety Regulation. In line with the EU Treaty provisions and policy,[48] the new law limits itself to providing a national framework for the direct application of European regulations. As a consequence, it makes very few substantive adjustments, dealing mostly with procedural matters and the enforcement of the directly applicable *acquis*. Nevertheless, despite some expectations and previous stipulations, the law makes no mention of the creation of a national food safety agency.

[46] Gazeta Wyborcza, 'Pierwsza piekarnia z certyfikatem HACCP nie straszy' *Gazeta Wyborcza* (Warszawa 12 August 2003).

[47] *Journal of Laws*, No. 171, Item 1225, 2006.

[48] The adoption of a general food law in the form of Regulation 178/2002 heralded a change in the EU regulatory regime from a directive-based regime to a far more intrusive, regulation-based regime. For the latest examples of such intense direct regulation, see the two milestone regulations regarding hygiene: Regulation (EC) 852/2004 of the European Parliament and of the Council of 29 April 2004 on the hygiene of foodstuffs; and Regulation (EC) 853/2004 of the European Parliament and of the Council of 29 April 2004 laying down specific hygiene rules for food of animal origin.

2.1.4.2.2. *Other Elements of the Food Law*

The realm of Polish food safety law is complemented by the so called 'veterinary legislation'. The European veterinary legislation was transposed to the Polish legal system by means of five major framework laws and dozens of executive regulations, which together cover the massive veterinary *acquis*. The core of Polish veterinary law consists of the following acts:

- Law of 10 December 2003 on veterinary control of trade;[49]
- Law of 27 August 2003 on border veterinary control;[50]
- Law of 16 December 2005 on products of animal origin;[51]
- Law of 11 March 2004 on the protection of animal health and the eradication of contagious animal diseases;[52] and
- Law of 29 January 2004 on the Veterinary Inspection.[53]

In addition, there are three other pieces of legislation that contain important veterinary provisions: the law of 21 August 1997 on animal welfare,[54] the law of 23 August 2001 on animal feedstuffs,[55] and the law of 2 April 2004 on the system of identification and registration of animals.[56] This enormous body of law has provided a basis for the factual implementation of European veterinary standards, with the aim of achieving the full 'from farm to fork' safety and control of foodstuffs. It has to be noted, however, that most of the abovementioned acts were later thoroughly amended in connection with the 2005 EU food-hygiene law reform. Here, again, the introduction of the 'hygiene package'[57] in 2006, made a large part of this legislation superfluous, giving priority to directly effective EU regulations in that area.

---

[49] *Journal of Laws*, No. 16, Item 145, 2004.

[50] *Journal of Laws*, No. 165, Item 1500, 2003.

[51] *Journal of Laws*, No. 17, Item 127, 2006.

[52] *Journal of Laws*, No. 69, Item 625, 2004.

[53] *Journal of Laws*, No. 33, Item 287, 2004.

[54] *Journal of Laws*, No. 111, Item 724, 1997; unified text in *Journal of Laws*, No. 106, Item 1002, 2003.

[55] *Journal of Laws*, No. 123, Item 1350, 2001.

[56] *Journal of Laws*, No. 91, Item 872, 2004.

[57] The 'Hygiene Package' consists of the following: Regulation (EC) 852/2004 of the European Parliament and of the Council of 29 April 2004 on the hygiene of foodstuffs [2004] OJ L 226/3; Regulation (EC) 853/2004 of the European Parliament and of the Council of 29 April 2004 laying down specific hygiene rules for food of animal origin [2004] OJ L 226/22; Regulation (EC) 854/2004 of the European Parliament and of the Council of 29 April 2004 laying down specific rules of official controls on products of animal origin intended for human consumption [2004] OJ L 226/83; Regulation (EC) 882/2004 of the European Parliament and of the Council of 29 April 2004 on official controls performed to ensure the verification of compliance with feed and food law, animal health and animal welfare rules [2004] OJ L 191/1; Regulation (EC) 183/2005 of the European Parliament and of the Council of 12 January 2005 laying down requirements for feed hygiene [2005] OJ L 35/1.

Secondly, food safety legislation in Poland is complemented by a range of phyto-sanitary regulations, as well as provisions on phyto-sanitary supervision and control. The most important of these are:

- Law of 18 December 2003 on plant protection;[58]and
- Law of 25 June 2003 on seed material.[59]

Finally, two pieces of legislation on cross-cutting issues have to be mentioned in order to give a complete and comprehensive picture:

- Law of 20 April 2004 on organic farming;[60] and
- Law of 22 June 2001 on genetically modified organisms.[61]

In sum, it might be argued that, by the day of accession, Polish food law had been promptly modified to include EU food safety requirements and so contained provisions on the most important contemporary food safety issues. What may be referred to as the nominal harmonisation of Polish food law to EU standards was achieved before accession, mainly in response to EU requirements but also due to the country's commercial interests—that is, in order to avoid the suspension of its food exports.[62]

2.1.4.3. *Building the Administrative Capacity*

In spite of a great deal of criticism from producers' organisations,[63] as well as from some major scientific and analytical institutions, the idea of building Poland's national administrative capacity by relying on its existing institutions—instead of building new ones, which was envisaged in the Food Safety Strategy—was upheld during the reformatory period. Efforts were concentrated on strengthening the links between the existing administrative entities and improving their internal organisation. As a consequence, however, the institutional structure of the Polish food safety system constitutes a complex maze of numerous institutions concentrated on separate aspects of an issue, seemingly lacking strong overarching coordination. The main institutions to be mentioned in the context of the official control of food are the Ministry of Health, the Ministry of Agriculture and Rural Development, the Office for the Protection of Competition and Consumers, the State Sanitary Inspection, the Veterinary Inspection,

[58] Unified text in *Journal of Laws*, No. 133, Item 849, 2008.
[59] Unified text in *Journal of Laws*, No. 41, Item 27, 2007.
[60] *Journal of Laws*, No. 93, Item 898, 2004.
[61] Unified text in *Journal of Laws*, No. 36, Item 233, 2007.
[62] DL Post, 'Diffusion of International Food Safety Standards: Developing Country Experiences' (2004) Working Papers of the Centre on Regulation and Competition No. 58.
[63] See A Gronowska-Senger, H Izdebski, G Trochimczuk and J Czarnecki, *Prawo żywnościowe i strategia bezpieczeństwa żywności*, Stanowisko Polskiej Federacji Producentów Żywności (Warszawa 2002) 30–38.

the Inspection of Commercial Quality of Agri-Food Products, the Trade Inspection, and the Inspection of Plants and Seeds Protection. This section briefly describes these institutions and analyses their roles in the food safety system, the scope of their activity, as well as their affiliations and interconnections.[64]

Traditionally, duties and competences in the field of food have been shared mainly by two central administrative authorities: the Ministry of Health and the Ministry of Agriculture and Rural Development. Generally, the Ministry of Agriculture and its subordinate inspection bodies have been responsible for the supervision of foodstuffs of animal origin, while Ministry of Health kept control of all other types of foodstuffs. This division remained in force during the pre-accession period and was in place on the day of enlargement. The third institution of the central administration involved in food safety has been the Office for the Protection of Competition and Consumers, whose tasks cover the trade- and consumer-related aspects of food regulation. Since a single central body responsible for supervision and steering of a food safety policy was absent, the Minister of Health was put in charge of coordinating all activities in the field on the basis of a regulation of the Prime Minister of 28 June 2002.[65] In performing this function, he is supported by an advisory body called the Inter-Ministerial Group on Food Safety, which is chaired by the Chief Sanitary Inspector and is composed of representatives of the central administrative institutions whose fields of responsibilities are connected with food policy (the Ministry of Health, the Ministry of Agriculture and Rural Development, the Ministry of Environment, the Ministry of Finance, the Office for the Protection of Competition and Consumers, the Committee for European Integration and the Committee for Scientific Research).[66] Such a diffuse management structure was claimed by many to be a potential source of incoherence and conflicts of competences. Nevertheless, although the centralisation of the food safety administration was widely advocated and frequently put forth in political discussions, no concrete proposals were made in the first years after Poland's accession to the EU. Moreover, the dispersed administrative configuration is maintained at the level of control, where there are even more actors in play. There are at least five

[64] For more on Polish institutions that facilitate the functioning of agricultural markets, see P Czechowski, *Proces Dostosowania Polskiego Prawa Rolnego i Żywnościowego do Prawa Unii Europejskiej* (Twigger, Warszawa 2001) 169–199.

[65] Regulation of the Chairman of the Council of Ministers of 28 June 2002 on the specific range of tasks of the Minister of Health, *Journal of Laws*, No. 93, Item 833, 2002.

[66] Established by an ordinance of the Minister of Health of 9 September 2002 on the establishment of a Group on Food Safety, *Official Journal of the Ministry of Health*, No. 9, Item 49, 2002.

supervisory bodies that have to be mentioned in the context of official food safety control:

- the State Sanitary Inspection (SSI);[67]
- the Veterinary Inspection (VI);[68]
- the Agriculture and Food Quality Inspection (AFQI);[69]
- the Plant Health and Seed Inspection (PHSI);[70] and
- the Trade Inspection (TI).[71]

The following paragraphs provide a brief description of each of the official control bodies and describe their organisation and functioning, in order to give at least a schematic picture of the supervisory architecture and clarify the division of responsibilities in this complex system.

The State Sanitary Inspection (SSI) is a control body subordinate to the Minister of Health, and it remains under his supervision. It is headed by the Chief Sanitary Inspector, who performs his duties with the assistance of the Chief Sanitary Inspectorate. At the local levels of public administration, control functions are performed by *Voivod* and *Poviat*[72] sanitary inspectors who, within their respective administrative units, supervise the functioning of the local sanitary and epidemiological stations. The major tasks of the State Sanitary Inspection are to protect public health, in particular by supervising the health quality of food and nutrition, as well as the safety of articles of daily use, and to exercise an on-going and preventive sanitary supervision. In its daily operations, the SSI controls compliance with the regulatory standards that define hygiene and health requirements during the whole 'from farm to fork' chain, including the conditions of the production, transportation, storage and sale of food products, as well as the conditions for the importing of foodstuffs. The material scope of SSI's supervision includes foodstuffs for special dietary purposes, dietary supplements, additives, and materials that come into contact with food. It also performs a number of research, education and consultative functions. It

[67] Established by the Law of 14 March 1985 on State Sanitary Inspection, *Journal of Laws*, No. 90, Item 575, 1998, with later amendments and the Ordinance of the Minister of Health modifying the competences of the General Sanitary Inspectorate of 30 December 1999, *Journal of Laws*, No. 111, Item 1315, 1999.

[68] Established by the Law of 29 January 2004 on the Veterinary Inspection, *Journal of Laws*, No. 33, Item 287, 2004.

[69] Established by the Law of 21 December 2000 on Commercial Quality of Agricultural and Food Products, *Journal of Laws*, No. 5, Item 44, 2001.

[70] Established by the Law of 18 December 2003 on Plan Protection, *Journal of Laws*, No. 11, Item 94, 2003.

[71] Established by the Law of 15 December 2000 on the Protection of Competition and Consumer, *Journal of Law*, No. 86, Item 804, 2003.

[72] The administrative structure of Poland provides for a territorial division of the country into sixteen *voivodes*, while the *poviat* is a lower, local administrative unit with mixed central and local governance tasks.

is supported by a system of laboratories, which perform the microbiological and chemical tests on which the control activities of the SSI are based.

The Veterinary Inspection was established to protect public health by supervising animal health and the safety of foodstuffs of animal origin. The Veterinary Inspection controls all stages of food production, starting from the control of animal health and welfare, through the control of feed production, slaughtering procedures, and ending with the storage and processing of meat. It also, together with the Pharmaceutical Inspectorate and the Inspectorate for Commercial Quality of Agricultural and Food Products, controls the production of pharmaceuticals for animals.

The Law on the Veterinary Inspection provides for the vertical organisation of the Inspection, with direct subordination of the lower levels to the higher ones, independently of the organs of the general public administration.[73] The Inspection is headed by the Chief Veterinary Doctor (CVD), who is subordinate to the Minister of Agriculture and Rural Development. Down the inspection ladder, the *Voivod* Veterinary Inspector, who takes responsibility and heads the Inspection within the territory of his administrative unit, is directly subordinate to the CVD. At the level of the basic administrative unit, the *Poviat* Veterinary Inspector, is responsible for routine inspections of abattoirs, meat-producing plants, etc., within his region. The Veterinary Inspection is supported by a system of laboratories, including the National Reference Laboratories, accredited by the CVD.

Both veterinary and sanitary inspectors can decide to withdraw foodstuffs from the market, suspend food production or even close a production plant, which are decisions that clearly influence the market position of an enterprise.

The Agriculture and Food Quality Inspection, which was established by merging the Central Standardisation Inspectorate and the Inspection of Purchase and Processing of Agricultural Products, is chaired by the Head Inspector, who is directly subordinate to the Minister of Agriculture and Rural Development. He is supported by the Main Inspectorate and the local tasks are performed by the *voivod* inspectors. The main task of the Inspection is to control the trade quality of agricultural and food products during all stages of production, from farming through to the processing, transport and storage of food before it gets to the consumer, as well as imported products of that kind. It also stores and processes information on different agricultural product markets. Reference to the trade quality of the products in question suggests

[73] The previous system of the State Veterinary Inspection, in which organs of the Inspection at different levels of governance were subordinate to the organs of general public administration, was heavily criticised by the EU during the pre-accession process as ineffective and vulnerable to political pressure and fraudulent misconduct. Organisational reform of the Inspection was, therefore, one of the important conditions of accession.

that the Inspection is concerned with the presentation, labelling and correctness and appropriateness of the information that is given to consumers, rather than with the food's health and nutritional characteristics.

The Plant Health and Seed Inspection was formed by merging the Plant Protection Inspection and the Seed Inspection, and its main task is the phytosanitary control of plants, planting areas, stored plants and plant products, with the aim of avoiding the presence and spread of pests. It is also meant to supervise trade in plant-protection products and their use.

The Trade Inspection performs broad tasks that protect the interests of consumers and the economic interests of the state. In the field of food, its main prerogative is the control of foodstuffs present on the market, especially with regard to their labelling and protection against falsification. Similarly to the previous control authorities, it performs its functions via a Main Inspector and regional *voivod* inspectors.[74]

Even a brief look at this organisation pattern of official food control gives an idea about the complexity of the system. Not only are there different inspections looking at different products, but there are often different inspections looking at the same products from different perspectives. The consequences of applying such a strategy are multiple. On the one hand, one can expect that specialised inspections will perform their functions better, as they are more competent within their particular field of expertise. On the other hand, though, the coordination of their activities is very difficult and there is the potential for overlapping as well as for negative institutional competition. Such risks could, of course, be reduced by the establishment of a strong coordinating body that would apply a strict and coherent coordination strategy, and by adopting legislation that clearly delineates the responsibilities of different inspections, leaving no doubts about who is in charge of what. Whether this is the case is Poland will be reviewed by practice. The problem, however, is that the tightness of the system is extremely important, because every leakage can have terrible consequences for consumers and for the market. Additionally, testing of the system 'in practice', which had to be undertaken in the Polish case, increased that risk. Therefore, heavy criticism was raised both in Poland as well as in the EU, and the political decision of the Polish government to follow such multi-institutional path raised great anxieties.

A final institutional remark to be made concerns the establishment of the national food safety agency. As mentioned above, Poland has taken the rather

---

[74] A thorough evaluation of the development of the institutional structure of the food safety system in Poland can be found in L Szponar, H Turlejska, I Traczyk and I Gielcinska, 'Rola urzędowej kontroli żywności w Polsce w realizacji strategii bezpieczeństwa żywności' in L Szponar, I Traczyk, K Stoś (eds), *System Bezpieczeństwa Żywności w Polsce—Wybrane Zagadnienia* (Prace IŻŻ 104, Warszawa 2003).

controversial step to not establish any integrated institution to provide scientific advice in risk assessment. Instead, the ministers in charge of food safety remain embedded in a network of various scientific institutes and laboratories, which fall under their respective supervision. They are reduced to using those scattered resources for their gathering of scientific advice. This rather extraordinary solution has been strongly criticised, but although a number of regulatory and political efforts have been made towards the establishment of a single, well-integrated institution for scientific risk assessment, all have failed at different stages of the decision-making process. This is all the more problematic as it has left Poland without a strong and unified representation of its 'national' scientific opinion, which other states often do have. This, naturally, puts Poland in a disadvantaged position in cases of conflict.

This concern was confirmed by the way in which the Russian embargo on certain Polish food products, introduced following the Polish accession to the EU, was handled. It would probably be easier to argue in favour of the safety of Polish products if those arguments could be supported by solid analytical background information provided by an internationally recognised scientific institution that represents the national scientific standpoint. It will be interesting, then, to observe how this case will affect the Polish approach towards the institutionalisation of scientific risk assessment in food safety. Will Poland be forced, by circumstance and need, to *adapt* to the common solution, or will it rather attempt to answer the need for scientific argument through a more independent *adoption* of institutionalisation? Admittedly, the eventual response to this dilemma will probably depend more upon situational constellations of political needs and scientific resources, as well as infighting between these factors—nationally and internationally—than upon any legal considerations. Yet it is exactly through cases such as this that we can see why the political–scientific nexus should be considered as central to the legal analysis of food safety and its risk assessment, in Europe and elsewhere.

2.1.4.4. *From Legal Adjustment to Practical Enforcement*

As if Poland's formal legal approximations and preparations for reform of its institutional capacity were not sufficiently difficult, the real struggle began with the process of putting the new regulations into practice. Restructuring the whole food sector, from producers to controllers, in order to apply those legal provisions required an enormous effort and the mobilisation of vast amounts of money, time and expertise. The way from formal approximation to practical compliance is always long. In the Polish case, the realisation of its legislative aims and institutional capacity-building was no different.

One of most important changes in regulatory approaches to food safety in Poland was its passage from reliance on direct penal and administrative enforcement to its increasing reliance on producers' responsibility. The system of administrative pre-market approval was eliminated, and new legal provisions imposed on companies that produced and sold food the obligation to safeguard the effectiveness of their food safety standards internally. From the point of view of the food operators, this change was revolutionary. Although it facilitated the placing of products on the market by eliminating the complicated and lengthy administrative approval procedure, it also put the burden of guaranteeing the safety of products on the producers themselves. It forced them to reform their production processes in order to include appropriate procedures of internal control. In order to satisfy European requirements, those procedures, as provided for in the law, were expected to be based on the Hazard Analysis and Critical Control Points (HACCP) system, as well as on the Good Hygiene Practice (GHP) and Good Manufacture Practice (GMP) systems.[75] Food law explicitly made HACCP the basis of the internal-inspection system, requiring that all companies implement and document the proper functioning of the HACCP control system as of the date of accession.

Producers' representatives strongly opposed the introduction of this obligation to implement HACCP until the last moment before accession. This was mainly due to their fear of the high costs of implementing the system, which were estimated to go beyond the capacity of a vast percentage of small- and medium-size establishments. Producers' reticence also illustrated their struggle to accept the whole new philosophy of regulating food safety, where they had to take full responsibility for their products, and where, within an establishment, every person had to personally guarantee safety and quality. The psychological barrier of 'taking over' the responsibility and control tasks was probably as strong as the fear of high costs and the need for technological innovation and training. Additionally, according to the authors of survey on the implementation of HACCP, GMP and GHP conducted in 2001, many of these anxieties were caused by a lack of proper information, and consequently could have been reduced with relevant information campaign and training.[76]

On the other side of the coin, the reform necessitated the restructuring and refocusing of the official control bodies, whose role under the new system was significantly modified. Inspectors needed training in the new control procedures, as well as the new requirements for producers and products in order to be able to enforce them. Constant effort for better qualifications and equipment by the

[75] On the introduction of HACCP, GMP and GHP into the Polish legal system and the rules governing those systems, see H Turlejska, U Pelzner and E Konecka-Matyjek, 'System Kontroli Wewnętrznej w zakładach produkcji, przetwórstwa i obrotu żywnością ze szczególnym uwzględnieniem sytemu HACCP' in L Szponar et al, *System Bezpieczeństwa* … ibid.

[76] E Konecka-Matyjek, H Turlejska, U Pelzner and L Szponar, 'Actual situation of implementing quality assurance systems GMP, GHP and HACCP in Polish food production and processing plants' (2005) 16 *Food Control* 1–9.

inspectorates had to be accompanied by constant affirmation of their vital role in controlling and guaranteeing compliance with the new system.

Another important and interesting issue of the practical implementation of new rules, also very much grounded in the sphere of emotions and sentiment, was the peculiar phenomenon of resistance towards the creation of producers' organisations and towards other types of collective initiatives, which are promoted by the EU's agrarian market structures. The creation of producers' organisations in areas of CAP regulation was one of the prerequisites for participation in the market mechanisms. Although forming such organisations has nothing to do with the transfer of property rights or any other land-use rights, the memory of the attempts of forced collectivisation was still so vivid among Polish farmers that they systematically refused to participate in the organisations which was necessary if they were to profit from the CAP mechanisms. Similar obstacles appeared during the preparation of a dossier for the registration of some regional products, where the cooperation and collective agreement of local farmers was necessary in order to apply for and enjoy the privileges available under the EU system. These examples show that historical experience was, in the Polish case, very influential in the approximation process, and even more so in the implementation of the new system. Despite numerous government initiatives and PR campaigns, even after the date of accession, the EU system was perceived by many as 'foreign' and 'dictated', and any similarities with the communist regime—even far-fetched ones—were met with resistance and hostility.

2.1.4.5. *Financial Assistance*

Pre-accession financial-support mechanisms are an embodiment of both the idealistic and the more concrete sentiments of the EU. In a way, they come as a type of counterpart to the pre-accession conditionality requirements, supporting or sometimes even enabling the attainment of adjustment goals, and enhancing the ability of a state to meet the accession standards in accordance with its set timetable of implementation. They could, thus, be thought of as the manifestation of a specific form of solidarity between the current member states and the prospective member states in their efforts to prepare for joining the community. They also give acceding countries an opportunity to exercise the functioning of the EU's financial programs, which require a vast range of capabilities from both the national and regional administrations, as well as from the potential recipients of financial assistance. Hence, their significance should not be measured only in financial terms. Instead, it is important to emphasise their role as an encouraging and mobilising factor in promoting progress in the adjustment process, by requiring the setting of clear objectives, manifesting performance and meeting set deadlines.

Together with other central and eastern European acceding countries, Poland had been the recipient of a number of different forms of European pre-accession assistance. The aim of this assistance was, *inter alia*, to facilitate the preparation of acceding countries for EU membership, to enable the transition and implementation of European standards, as well as to work towards a reduction of staggering economic and social differences between the regions. The three major aid programs applied in Poland were: PHARE,[77] SAPARD[78] and ISPA.[79]

During the decade between 1990 and 1999, PHARE alone brought to Poland over €2 billion. The assistance programs concentrated primarily on the least-developed regions, and infrastructural development was chosen as the most important target. In the period directly preceding the accession, 30% of PHARE resources were allocated to strengthening the nations' institutions, while 70% went to help develop infrastructure to meet the requirements of the *acquis*.

Support projects under ISPA concentrated mainly on environmental protection and transport improvements, and in 2000 they amounted to over €350 million.

SAPARD, the program of the greatest importance for the sector under study, concentrated mainly on assisting farmers. The introduction of SAPARD in Poland was planned for the year 2000. Unfortunately, however, administrative and consultative procedures, as well as the training of staff, the verification and auditing of procedures, and the services in charge of implementation took much longer than initially foreseen, and SAPARD only began to operate in 2002. In accordance with the analysis of the situation in rural areas and the agri-food sector, the SAPARD Operational Programme for Poland was structured along two priority axes: Improvement of Agri-food Sector Efficiency, Improvement of Business Conditions and Job Creation, and Complementary axis. The strategic objectives which were meant to be achieved by the planned measures were:

- to improve the competitiveness of the Polish agri-food sector both domestically and internationally;
- to adjust the agri-food sector to safety, hygiene, food quality and environmental standards in line with the *acquis communutaire*; and
- to stimulate the multifunctional development of rural areas by supporting the development of technical infrastructure and boosting business activities outside of traditional agriculture.

[77] Poland and Hungary Assistance for the Reconstruction of Economies.
[78] Support for Pre-Accession Measures for Agriculture and Rural Development.
[79] Instrument for Structural Policies for Pre-Accession.

In order to achieve these objectives, seven measures were envisaged.[80] Measure 1: 'Improvement in Processing and Marketing of Food and Fishery Products' consisted of support schemes for the food-processing industry, covering products of animal, fruit and vegetable origin, including support for producer groups. Measure 2: 'Investment in Agricultural Holdings' concentrated on modernisation of milk and meat production facilities on agricultural holdings, as well as environmental protection against the harmful effects of farming. Measure 3: 'Development of Rural Infrastructure' provided support for the development of basic technical infrastructure in rural areas. Measure 4: 'Diversification of Economic Activities in Rural Areas Providing for Multiple Activities and Alternative Income' covered assistance for individual business projects outside conventional farming, as well as marketing initiatives. Measure 6: 'Vocational training' promoted structural, agricultural and rural development by enhancing the human capital in rural areas. Finally, Measure 7: provided technical assistance.[81]

Despite the delay in its operation, SAPARD, with the annual allocation of €170 million, provided significant help to Poland's rural communities. Due to its mode of operation, however, which required a considerable contribution from the recipients, it was absorbed mainly by bigger entities, which even initially were relatively better off and could, thus, afford the necessary investment.[82]

The latter type of assistance, the rural-development aid, was continued after the accession in the framework of the implementation of the Rural Development Plan (RDP).[83] The RDP, following the objectives of the so-called second pillar of the CAP, aims at sustainable and multifunctional support for agriculture, with the overarching aim of establishing a European model of agriculture. It embraces programs such as support for less-favoured areas, agri-environmental

---

[80] It has to be noted that only six of the seven planned measures were in fact implemented. Measure 5: 'Agri-environmental Measures and Afforestation (pilot projects)' was omitted following a decision of the Monitoring Committee in December 2003 due to an insufficient timeframe, with the approaching date of Polish accession to the EU.

[81] SAPARD Operational Programme, proposal as of 12 September 2000, Ministry of Agriculture and Rural Development, available at < http://ec.europa.eu/agriculture/external/enlarge/countries/poland/plan/plan_en.pdf> accessed 25 May 2011.

[82] See J Bański, 'Selected Aspects of Present-Day Changes in Polish Rural Space' (n 12) 90–92.

[83] The legal framework of the RDP is based on the Council Regulation (EC) 1257/1999 of 17 May 1999 on support for rural development from the European Agricultural Guidance and Guarantee Fund (EAGGF) and amending and repealing certain Regulations [1999] OJ L 160/80, and Commission Regulation (EC) 445/2002 of 26 February 2002 laying down detailed rules for the application of Council Regulation 1257/1999 on support for rural development from the European Agricultural Guidance and Guarantee Fund (EAGGF) [2002] OJ L 74/1, which was later repealed by Commission Regulation (EC) 817/2004 of 29 April 2004 laying down detailed rules for the application of Council Regulation 1257/1999 on support for rural development from the European Agricultural Guidance and Guarantee Fund (EAGGF) [2004] OJ L 153/30.

programs, early-retirement schemes, and forestation of agricultural areas. There is, however, another component of the RDP, which is an outcome of the accession negotiations and which was incorporated in the Accession Treaty. This component is temporary and foresees 25% co-financing by the Polish government. Part of those resources was to be reallocated during the first years after accession in order to raise the direct payment rates. Nevertheless, the budget for these programs after the reallocation amounted to over €3 billion in 2004–2006, out of which 75% was to be financed by EAGGF and 25% by the national budget. Financial assistance under this scheme was to be directed to support to bare-subsistence farms, the attainment of EU standards, and support for producer groups that did not fall under the regulation of markets.[84]

Following the accession, Polish agriculture and rural areas benefitted also from structural funds. The Sectoral Operational Programme (SOP), which aimed at 'restructuring and modernisation of the foodstuffs sector and development of rural areas', which constituted a part of the National Plan for Development for 2004–2006, laid down an assistance strategy and listed specific actions to be taken under two main objectives. The first—'Enhancing the competitiveness of the agricultural and foodstuffs economy'—encompassed the following activities: investment in farms; easier starts for young farmers; professional training; support for agricultural consultancy; consolidation of agricultural areas; rural water-resources planning; and improvement of agricultural processing and agricultural product marketing. The second strategic objective—'Sustainable development of rural areas'—covered the following actions: restoration of rural areas and protection of cultural heritage; diversification of agricultural activities and activities related to agriculture in order to ensure alternative sources of income in agriculture; development and improvement of technical infrastructure relating to agriculture; and remedying damage in forests. Actions within the SOP were co-financed by the EAGGF funds; the resources assigned for it for 2004–2006 reached €2 billion. The SOP, in its first strategic objective, has been often referred to as a continuation of SAPARD. However, as B. Smoter has pointed out, SAPARD, which constitutes an instrument of pre-accession assistance, was much more limited with regard to both the number and kind of the measures implemented, as well as in financial terms.[85]

2.1.5. *Transition Periods*

It had been clear from the start that a commitment to complete implementation and compliance with the agri-food *acquis* before the day of accession

[84] B Smoter, 'Polish Agriculture within the Common Agricultural Policy' (2004) 3 *The Polish Foreign Affairs Digest* 102.
[85] B Smoter, ibid 103.

was impossible to achieve. The first step, the legal adjustment, was already a big challenge, considering the amount of reform necessary, the frequent lack of a common denominator to rely on in approximation, as well as the unfavourable political conditions during the critical period of reformatory works, with radical peasant parties obstructing the progress of both negotiations as well as legislation. The second step, however, the factual implementation, was even more taxing. Both the administrative adjustment and the enforcement of standards in each and every farm and production unit were cumbersome and costly undertakings.

Probably the greatest adjustment challenge was faced by the food-processing industry, in particular the meat and dairy sectors, where the European standards, reviewed and strengthened after the BSE crisis, were particularly stringent, and where the European controls were distinctively sensitive. This problem was aggravated by the difficult situation of entrepreneurs in that sector. The specific structure of Polish agriculture and food production, with small, often family-operated enterprises with meagre capital and outdated production facilities and methods, presented a difficult challenge, given the increased need for adjustment and the enormous investment necessary. The importance of this problem was emphasised by the significance of these particular sectors for the Polish food market and its external trade. The original situation, a couple of years before the planned accession, was rather frightening. In 1999, when initial estimations were done, only twenty-four of the over 5000 Polish meat-processing establishments conformed to EU standards.[86] Hence, pre-accession assistance as well as a successful negotiation of the transitory periods were crucial to facilitate the necessary adjustment.

Getting accepted as a new member state requires total implementation and full compliance with the *acquis communautaire* in the food sector, as well as the establishment of an appropriate administrative and scientific capacity, which has the relevant control and inspection facilities as well as appropriate consumer-protection mechanisms. Practically speaking, three of those components—the formal transposition of regulation, the achievement of an adequate administrative capacity, and the installation of sufficient control mechanisms and inspection units—seemed to be within the reach of the government. Their importance was emphasised by the fact that those components had to be accomplished in order for Poland to participate in the common-market organisation and in the CAP instruments. The second phase of adjustment—the factual implementation and compliance by all entrepreneurs with applicable European standards—was clearly out of reach and had to

[86] Gazeta Wyborcza, 'Rzeźnie i Mleczarnie jak Laboratoria' *Gazeta Wyborcza* (Warszawa 4 May 2009).

be negotiated. The most important tools facilitating these types of adjustments are the pre-accession assistance, discussed above, and the possibility of including transitory provisions in the accession treaty.

The Commission Monitoring Report of 2003[87] made explicit the fact that in its preparation for accession Poland was in a difficult situation. It pointed out the need to undertake enhanced efforts in the areas of agricultural and fisheries *acquis* transposition, preparation of national paying agencies for agricultural trade mechanisms, transposition of foodstuffs, veterinary and phyto-sanitary *acquis*, as well as improvement of administrative capacity for application and enforcement in the abovementioned fields. In particular, the need for '*enhanced effort*' was noted in the following areas: trade mechanisms, common market organisations for beef, poultry and eggs, trade in live animals and animal products, animal welfare, animal nutrition, common measures, as well as rural development. At the same time, areas of '*serious concern*' were also mapped, which involved: setting up of paying agencies, implementation of an integrated administration and control system, securing the compliance of establishments operating in the food sector with EU public-health requirements, as well as implementation of the TSE regulations, rules on animal by-products, control of movement of animals, potato diseases and fisheries market organisation. All in all, hardly any area could be 'ticked off' as dealt with, and the majority was affected by serious delays or even negligence.

To make matters worse, in the field of food hygiene, for example, the Commission was already preparing a new and improved legislative package, which would put more stringent obligations on member states and establishments operating on the common market, while Poland had not even transposed, let alone implemented, the hygiene requirements in force at that time. In that situation, there was little doubt that the aim of 'smooth transition' would require recourse to transitory arrangements. Although no pre-determined transitional arrangements were agreed with regard to the free movement of foodstuffs, a number of derogations from the veterinary and phyto-sanitary rules had to be installed.[88]

In the Polish case, 485 food-production establishments were granted temporary derogations for the gradual achievement of compliance with EU requirements by the end of the transitory period. Derogations from the veterinary legislation were established in relation to a number of meat and meat-processing establishments, and it was agreed that they would run until the end

[87] Comprehensive Monitoring Report of the European Commission on the State of Preparedness for EU Membership of the Czech Republic, Estonia, Cyprus, Latvia, Lithuania, Hungary, Malta Poland, Slovenia and Slovakia COM (2003) 675 final—C5-0532/2003.

[88] Compare K Inglis, 'Implications of Enlargement for EC Agri-Food Law: The Accession Treaty, its Transitional Arrangements, and Safeguard Clauses' (2003) 10 *European Law Journal* 601–605.

of 2007. Derogations for establishments dealing with fishery products, as well as milk and milk products, were granted until the end of 2006. Those reservations were applied exclusively to structural requirements and did not affect food-hygiene requirements.

For the duration of the transitory period, products provided by the listed establishments were not to be marketed in any other EU country, but only in Poland alone, and specific marketing and labelling requirements applied in order to guarantee observance of the restriction. Additional transitional periods in the veterinary field concerned laying-hen establishments, where forty-four Polish companies would enjoy derogations until the end of 2009. In the phyto-sanitary sphere, derogations were allowed in the field of potato-disease control, and in the field of plant protection with regard to certain pesticides.[89] Finally, Poland would be excluded from the full financial benefits of the CAP for the first ten years after its accession, during which time the gradual upgrade would take place.[90]

With regard to the Common Agricultural Policy, additional transitional measures were foreseen that were meant to facilitate the transition from the new member states' existing regimes to their new schemes resulting from the application of the *acquis*. Under Article 41 of the Act of Accession,[91] such transitional measures could be introduced for the common organisation of agricultural markets during a period of three years following the date of accession, and their application would be limited to that period. The provision of Article 41 was meant to enable a continuation of the CAP reforms beyond the accession date when implementation by the new states would be achievable.[92]

---

[89] Act of Accession, Annex XII: List referred to in Article 24 of the Act of Accession: Poland [2003] OJ L 236/875.

[90] In the first year after accession, new members would receive 25% of the amount of direct payments applicable to old member states, and only after ten years will the amount due reach 10% of what applies to farmers in the old member states. See Article 1a of the Council Regulation (EC) 1259/1999 of 17 May 1999, establishing the common rules for direct-support schemes under the common agricultural policy [1999] OJ L 160/113, as amended by the Act of Accession. During the Copenhagen summit, the Polish government managed to negotiate a possibility of supplying the EU direct payments from the money guaranteed for the rural-development support scheme, as well as from the national budget during the first three years after the date of the accession, in order to reach 55% of full European direct payment amount in 2004, 65% in 2005, and 65% in 2006. See Article 33 h of the Council Regulation (EC) 1257/1999 of 17 May 1999 on support for rural development from the European Agricultural Guidance and Guarantee Fund (EAGGF) and amending and repealing certain Regulations [1999] OJ L 160/80, as amended by the Act of Accession.

[91] Act concerning the conditions of accession of the Czech Republic, the Republic of Estonia, the Republic of Cyprus, the Republic of Latvia, the Republic of Lithuania, the Republic of Hungary, the Republic of Malta, the Republic of Poland, the Republic of Slovenia and the Slovak Republic, and the adjustments to the Treaties on which the European Union is founded [2003] OJ L 236/46.

[92] Compare K Inglis, 'Implications of Enlargement ...' (n 88) 603.

Another such measure, contained in Article 42 of the Act of Accession, allowed the adoption of transitional measures in the field of veterinary and phyto-sanitary legislation, and again a three-year limit applied to both the adoption and duration of such measures.

These transitional measures were juxtaposed by the possibility of a response from other members of the EU in the case of serious difficulties arising. There was, thus, a possibility of introducing certain safeguard clauses. Article 37 of the Act of Accession granted the ability to introduce measures designed to protect against serious problems within a given sector of the economy. It could be invoked in the case of difficulties arising within the three-year period, and which are serious and liable to persist, or which could bring about a serious deterioration in the economic situation of the given area. The emergency procedures and the granting of protective measures were to be administered by the European Commission, which enjoyed broad discretion in the process. Any such protective measure, however, would have to be proven necessary and aim to rectify the situation, as well as to adjust the sector to the conditions of the economy of the common market. According to the Commission's declaration on safeguard measures,[93] it contemplated introducing such economic safeguards in Poland's agricultural sector, including measures aiming to monitor trade flows between Poland and other member states.

In addition, Poland's Accession Treaty provided for specific measures particular to that enlargement, to be applied by the Commission, as well as the internal market safeguard measures.[94] The internal market safeguard clause empowers the EU to take unspecified measures against a new member state when it fails to fulfil the commitments it undertook during negotiations. This clause provides an additional means of guaranteeing compliance by new states with the *acquis*, apart from the one already existing in the Treaty, namely Article 258 TFEU (ex Article 226 TEC). One also has to remember that the safeguard clauses contained in all secondary legislation applied in this case.

The system of accepting new member states, as described above, constitutes a source of rather unequal treatment in at least two important respects. Firstly, in committing to the fulfilment of the accession criteria, the future member state agrees to harmonise its legal systems with the ever-changing EU legislation, which evolves during the approximation process after the commitment was made. However, as the state is not yet a member of the EU, it does not have equal rights in formulating new legislation and shaping its final form. The case of the 2004 accession and the food safety regulations are a case in point. The BSE scandal and other food scares of the 1990s had led to reforms that had

[93] Declaration 43, Final Act to the Accession Treaty.
[94] See Article 38 and 39 of the Act of Accession (n 91).

made safety standards particularly stringent, and which had been developed precisely as the ten candidates for EU membership were striving to adjust. The new rules on food hygiene and safety, which came as a new improved package, were particularly stringent and demanding, and required additional structural improvement of facilities.[95] For establishments already struggling to comply with the previous requirements, this could easily become too much to bear.

The second example of unequal treatment, which has far-reaching consequences before as well as after accession, is the varied degree of compliance-control applied to the new and the old member states. Due to the fact that only the acceding states are bound by the pre-accession conditionality, only they are carefully scrutinised, while the old states, which often seriously lag behind in implementing and enforcing the new *acquis*, get away with it much easier. An illustration of the double-standards and limited-trust approach stems from a comparison, suggested by K. Inglis, between Article 258 TFEU (ex Article 226 TEC) which applies in cases of non-compliance by member states, and Article 38 of the Act of Accession, which applies only to new states in non-compliance situations.[96] Juxtaposing of these two provisions shows that Article 38 of the Act of Accession has a much more preventive character. Not only does it anticipate failures, but also it gives much greater discretion to the Commission. Unlike Article 258 TFEU (ex Article 226 TEC), it does not grant the new states, which are not directly affected by the measure, a legally established right to submit observations or be heard upon the Commission proposal. Even more importantly, the safeguard clause gives the Commission the right to take action immediately, while the procedure under Article 258 TFEU (ex Article 226 TEC) takes years between the issuing of the reasoned opinion and the actual ECJ case. Irrespective of the actual application of the safeguard clause, it has constituted an important disciplining factor against new member states, especially given that numerous threats to use the clause, at least in the case of Poland, were made. Such disciplining mechanisms are lacking with regard to the old states, which have often had very serious problems with compliance, while the new member states have been forced to accept transitional arrangements and trade restrictions.[97]

One other important problem with the transitional measures is their potential double-edged effect. They provide new member states with additional time for adjustment, but that adjustment takes place under completely different circumstances, for which the new members are often not prepared. Firstly, during the period of time when favourable circumstances apply, the sales market is limited

[95] K Inglis, 'Implications of Enlargement ...' (n 88) 598.
[96] Ibid 608–611.
[97] Commission (EC), Eighteenth Annual Report on Monitoring the application of Community Law, COM (2001) 309, 16 July2001, Annex V, quoted after K Inglis, ibid 610.

by the safeguard provision accompanying the transitional measure, which limits the options of economic operators and affects their marketing and production strategies. Secondly, the situation of economic operators after the date of accession changes significantly in a number of aspects. Not only does pre-accession assistance no longer apply, but the economic situation also transforms entirely, which affects the prices of commodities and production conditions, and can in fact have a derogatory long-term effect on the particular economic sector. Thus, while supporting the adjustment of a limited number of establishments, the measure can have negative economic effects on the sector as a whole. This may happen particularly if the adjustment of those enterprises has not proceeded according to plan and additional safeguard measures are applied. Finally, the industry can fall into the trap of temporality, treating the transitional period as just an excuse for delaying adjustment; consequently, neither the enterprises in question nor the given economic sector will benefit from the measures.

According to the summary balance after the end of the transition periods, and contrary to the fears and pessimistic visions of many, the pre-accession transformation of the Polish food sector can be viewed as a success. During the eight-year adjustment period, with the industry's own resources and the help of the EU, as well as the national preferential loans, total investment in the meat sector alone amounted to €2.5 billion. Together with the compliance pressure from the European Commission and the Polish government, the processing establishments, which were at the biggest risk, were gradually able to achieve compliance in accordance with a predetermined plan and timetable. As a consequence, many in fact managed to make good use of the transitory period. While sustaining production for the local market, they continued their modernisation and adjustment processes; in the end, most of those that were granted transitional arrangements managed to comply by the end of the period. In the milk-processing sector, for example, out of the 148 establishments granted a transitory period,[98] eighty-eight managed to adjust and were approved for common market trade, twenty-seven terminated their activities, and the status of the remainder is undecided.[99]

Finally, an important aspect of the adjustment process was the promotion of consolidation of businesses. Both before and after the date of accession, consolidation progressed, and in fact only a small percentage of small-scale enterprises had to close down; the majority of activities terminated were effects of

[98] Out of the 148, 113 were granted transitory arrangements on the basis of the Accession Treaty and thirty-five on the basis of the Commission Decision 458/2004.

[99] The status of twenty-eight establishments was marked as unknown, three were reclassified and four were suspended until the termination of their modernisation processes. Source: Assessment tables of the Main Veterinary Inspectorate as of January 2007, which was the deadline for transition in the milk and dairy sector, courtesy of Mrs Iwona Zawinowska of the Main Veterinary Inspectorate.

the mergers of companies. As a result, today in Poland only 2500 establishments are active in the meat sector, which is around half the initial number. This does not signify a reduction of overall production capacity, however. On the contrary, the volume of people employed by the sector remained at the same level, reaching 100,000, exactly the same as it was eight years before. Moreover, turnover has reached 30 billion zlotys, in comparison to 22 billion eight years before.[100]

2.1.6. *The Functioning of the System after Accession*

2.1.6.1. *The Influence of EU Food Safety Regulations and Standards on the Polish Food Industry and Polish Trade Relations in the Agri-Food Sector*

The accession had from early on been expected to have important influence on the Polish economy as well as on the regulatory environment in agricultural and food. The reality, however, managed even to outgrow expectations and brought about accelerated and meaningful changes in almost every sector of the Polish economy. In the first two years after accession, Poland experienced a steady economic growth of average 4.2%, to reach 5.8% in 2006.[101] In terms of its convergence with old member states, Polish GDP per capita increased from 40% of the EU average in 1997 to 46% in 2005. Although it is an important move in a good direction, Poland still lags behind, not only with regard to the old but also to most of the new member states. In years 2005–2006 the trade balance with the EU countries became positive, while exports to third countries arrived at record figures. This was, to a large extent, an effect of the liberalisation of trade in foodstuffs, as well as the influence of export subsidies, which after 2004 applied to Poland as well.

In the year of accession, Poland was a net beneficiary in the EU budget, with net transfers amounting to €1.7 billion, which accounts for 0.75% of the state's gross national income. After accession, in 2007 and 2008, the value of the EU funds received by Poland was expected to reach 2.5% and 3.25% of gross national income respectively. Among those new financial instruments, funds for agriculture and rural development amounted to 27%, while funds for structural development constituted 23% of the total, constituting the largest proportions of all financial transfers coming to Poland after accession. Absorption of these funds by the recipients, however, had initially been rather difficult and slow. With the questionable quality of the relevant legal basis, inadequate

[100] Gazeta Wyborcza,'Rzeźnie i Mleczarnie jak Laboratoria' *Gazeta Wyborcza* (Warszawa 4 May 2009).

[101] Facts and figures in this paragraph are taken from the sources of the Main Statistical Office, <http://www.stat.gov.pl/cps/rde/xchg/gus> accessed 25 May 2011, as well as E Balcerowicz, 'The Impact of EU Accession on Poland's Economy' (2007) CASE E-brief 2007/5.

administrative mechanisms and insufficient state resources for co-financing, the absorption was far from satisfactory, but since 2006 the situation has gradually started to improve.

Looking in particular at the agri-food sector, the year of accession had already presented a significant increase of the export value and a positive balance in agricultural trade. After eleven years of a negative trade balance with the EU, Poland made a considerable surplus, and a similar tendency could be observed in agricultural trade with all other countries as well. Hence, in 2004 Polish agri-food trade gained a surplus of US$1.25 billion with the EU and US$1.061 billion with the rest of the world. The main reasons for this change were the (almost) full liberalisation of trade with other member states, as well as considerably lower prices of good quality products in Poland in comparison to the rest of the EU market.[102] It is also interesting to note in this context that, in accordance with the results of research undertaken by the Polish Agency for Enterprise Development in 2004, Polish food products were among the most recognisable and the most respected Polish products, in the opinion of other EU citizens, who pointed out two aspects of their attractiveness: lower prices and good quality.[103]

To sum up the consequences of the first years of Polish membership in the EU with regard to the agricultural and food sectors, analysts have made a number of interesting observations.[104] Firstly, they observe that while, during the first three years after accession, the economic advance in agriculture was mainly due to financial transfers from the EU and the state budget, which resulted from Poland's participation in the CAP mechanisms, in the fourth year an important additional factor influenced the situation: new developments in global economy. The combined impact of three main factors—an increase of the world population, causing greater demand of food products in the developing countries (mainly China and India), speculations in the commodities markets, as well as increased production of biofuels—led to a sudden boost of food prices, which significantly influenced the conditions of the functioning of the EU agricultural sector, including the Polish agricultural market.

Such a beneficial situation led to a considerable increase in agricultural income. Consequently, people employed in agriculture enjoyed the most

[102] M Adamowicz and A Rytko, 'Polish Agro-Food Trade with European Countries Before and After Joining EU', paper prepared for presentation at the 98th EAAE Seminar 'Marketing Dynamics within the Global Trading System: New Perspectives', Crete, Greece, 29 June–2 July 2006, 6–7.

[103] K Jasiecki, *Postrzeganie Polskiej Marki w Krajach Unii Europejskiej. Raport z Badań* (Polska Agencja Rozwoju Przedsiębiorczości, Warszawa 2004) 87–89.

[104] Urząd Komitetu Integracji Europejskiej, *4 lata Członkostwa Polski w UE. Bilans Kosztów i Korzyści Społeczno-Gospodarczych* (UKIE, Warszawa 2008) in particular 54–70 pertaining to agriculture and food production.

spectacular rise in earnings of all social groups. In fact, their average income four years after accession has doubled with regard to the situation in 2000. It has to be borne in mind, however, that due to the same developments, during the first four years of Polish EU membership the costs of agricultural production have also altered significantly. Until 2007, the prices of commodities and the means of production were in fact growing much faster and in larger proportions than those of the final products. Thus, it is important to acknowledge that financial transfers for agriculture have mainly been consumed by the producers of basic commodities, fertilisers, pesticides, agricultural machinery, and so on, which is counterproductive for the modernisation and restructuring, and negatively influences the achievement of the goals of the CAP in Poland.[105]

2.1.6.2. *Unexpected Short-Term Experiences? Discovery by Practice*

The black scenarios painted by Euro-sceptics before accession—which prophesied a radical increase of prices, the total collapse of Polish agriculture, and a literal occupation of Polish territory by wealthy citizens of the old member states buying their second houses in Poland—have, to a large extent, remained unfounded. Although a limited, but noticeable, price increase took place shortly after the enlargement, monetary policy managed to secure stability over the following years. Moreover, not only were the pessimistic expectations not realised, but a series of unexpected positive developments also surprised the society and the state. Hence, contrary to the predictions, the growth rate of exports outpaced that of imports, with the export rate of foodstuffs booming far beyond expectations. Statistics leave no room for hesitation in this case. Between 1 May 2004 and 1 May 2009, Poland's export volume doubled: it amounted to €47.5 billion in 2003, €59.7 billion in 2004 and €114.5 billion in 2008.[106] Not even the biggest optimists had foreseen such an increase.

Equally importantly, Polish producers have become competitive not only because they could offer lower prices but increasingly also because they could offer better quality. In the analysis undertaken four years after the Polish accession to the EU, it became apparent that, despite some negative impacts, the Polish agri-food sector had used its comparative advantage to the best of its ability. At the same time, despite the promoted consolidation pressure, Polish agriculture kept its traditional organisational patterns, with small production units, out of which only 46% are specialised, while the rest still keeps both animal and plant production.[107]

[105] Ibid 58.
[106] Gazeta Wyborcza, 'Jak podbiliśmy unijny rynek' *Gazeta Wyborcza* (Warszawa 2–3 May 2009).
[107] UKIE, *4 lata Członkostwa* … (n 104) 54–55.

Quality, and especially some specific features of it, has become a newly discovered strength of Polish food products. Poland's accession happened to coincide with a gradual development in consumer patterns towards natural, traditional and organic food. Interestingly, this was exactly what Poland could offer. This was mainly due to the backwardness of Polish agriculture and the minimal investment capacity of farmers, but also due to the structure of Polish agricultural space, where small-scale farming had been standard for centuries, and not merely a development in response to current market trends. Those small, often family-operated farms and production units, on which high-tech approaches were not economically viable and which still used natural fertilisers and animal-feeding techniques, were able to offer exactly what was demanded without requiring investment or reorganisation. By those means, and to the surprise of many, Polish backwardness and technological underdevelopment in the field of agriculture and food production has shifted from being a liability to becoming its real advantage. The daunting and discouraging snapshot of Polish agriculture portrayed in the media during the accession years, with a dirty cow and a farmer with horse and carriage, has in fact become the best advertisement for what western consumers were craving: the natural production of healthy and hearty food, and the countryside as it once was.

2.1.6.3. *Trying to Salvage 'the Polish Way'*

Faced with problems of approximation and compliance, as well as social discontent about some developments connected with accession requirements that went against deeply rooted traditions or particularly strong social beliefs and interests, the Polish government had to look for ways to preserve what the nation valued. Having found problems that should have been taken care of during the negotiations, but which had not been properly resolved or had simply been forgotten, the government made several attempts to save the day by means of legislations. Such legislative measures, however, often turned out to be contrary to the *acquis*. Thus, they did not escape the scrutiny of the Commission and had to be repealed by the day of accession, or shortly after. In the face of common market rules, it was important to seek ways for a member state to preserve local values, while still respecting the standards set by EU law. The following paragraphs address two examples of Polish attempts to salvage 'the Polish way' through the use of available legal mechanisms that allow member states to retain a certain degree of divergence from the harmonised measure, under strict pre-established conditions and with the aim of protecting an important good.

The first legal mechanism aims to protect the provenience of specific types of regional products, which, due to their particular characteristics, have received special recognition of their geographical origin, traditional components or production methods, which often could otherwise not be approved by the European authorities. The second mechanism is the procedure under Article 114(5) and (6) TFEU (ex Article 95(5) and (6) TEC), which allows member states to introduce, after the adoption of a harmonisation measure by the Council or by the Commission, a national provision based on new scientific evidence relating to the protection of the environment or the working environment because of a problem specific to that member state that has arisen after the adoption of the harmonisation measure. In that case, the member state shall notify the Commission of the envisaged provisions, as well as the grounds for introducing them, and the Commission shall, within a period of six months, approve or reject the national provisions involved, having first verified whether or not they are a means of arbitrary discrimination or a disguised restriction on trade between member states, and whether or not they constitute an obstacle to the functioning of the internal market.

2.1.6.3.1. *Retaining Regional Flavour Through Geographical Protection of Origin*

2.1.6.3.1.1. On Poland and Regionalisms. 'Offering good fertile agricultural land in exchange for a better geopolitical position—undersigned: Poland.' This witty inscription on a wall in the Jagiellonian University building in Krakow pretty much pinpoints the troubled fate of the big country in the middle of Europe. It also highlights some important aspects of Polish geography and history, which should be mentioned here as a background for the paragraphs to follow. Poland is a relatively big country, geographically very diversified (from mountains in the south, through hills and plains, all the way to the sea up north), enjoys plenty of specific climatic twists, and has, as so few countries in Europe still do these days, four seasons of the year. This diversity has natural consequences for the conditions of farming and food production in the different regions of the country, with their varied topography, climate and biodiversity. Thus, although good fertile agricultural land is to be found in all corners of Poland, its characteristics differ considerably, along the lines of the diverse features described above.

As for the geopolitical situation, although at first it may sound unbelievable, this has also had a significant influence on Polish agriculture and food production in many different ways. Poland's troubled history—with continuous wars, territorial changes and shifting of external frontiers, partitions and migration waves—have created a situation that is rather unusual in Europe. From the point of view of cultural identity, probably only a few of Polish regions could be found to be unproblematic. Nevertheless, experiences teach that the most interesting and wonderful things are created through the meetings of cultures, traditions, customs and nations, and as a consequence of their diffusion. For example, the partitions of Poland in the second half of the eighteenth century had consequences for agriculture and food production that are highly relevant and visible even today. Most superficially, the tables and menus of Joseph II, Frederick II of Prussia and Catherine the Great differed greatly, and influenced culinary traditions in the subordinate regions. More importantly, the structural solutions applied by Prussia, Russia and Austria were implemented on the partitioned Polish territory and effectively changed the agricultural landscape and productions patterns right to the present day. Hence, for example, even today in southern Poland—historically a part of Austro-Hungarian Empire known as Galicia—you will only find very small farming units, due to the fragmentation of the agrarian land policy connected with the abolishment of serfdom by Austria at the end of the eighteenth century.

This rich and diversified heritage has two faces. Due to its variety, Poland has enormous potential to supply specific regional and traditional products. This position is strengthened by the preponderance of traditional and family farming, the availability and relatively low price of a workforce in the countryside, as well as the traditionally rooted environmental considerations of the farming practices. This regional wealth and cultural diversity present a fabulous base for developing a specialisation in traditional and regional products.

On the other hand, however, Poland's historical legacies have contributed to a series of obstacles in the process. Probably the most vital problem in this context is the forced breach of the traditions of local processing of primary agricultural materials by their producers and of direct sales of processed products. Legal obstacles created by the communist system forced producers to sell their basic agricultural materials to the state-owned purchasing centres, without having the right to process them and sell the final products. The state-planned economy shifted the production of certain foodstuffs from one region to the other, and economically consequential decisions were often taken without much forethought and on the basis of non-economic and often irrational considerations. This situation often led to the destruction of regional continuity in production processes, and at the time of accession this was problematic for Poland's claims for regional protection of certain products. It also prevented a situation which is so natural in other European countries, such as Italy or France, where family farms producing milk often produce different types of cheese and sell it on the local market. Thus, such traditions, which were rich and strong before the First World War and even in the interwar era, were eradicated and only survived in limited or even rudimentary forms, often in breach of the law or on the fringe of the regulations. The process of rebuilding these traditions after the transition has been rather slow, and for a long time after the fall of the Berlin Wall legal obstacles still existed.[108] The process of restoration of those old traditions is not easy and requires a lot of effort. Thanks to the people and their memories, however, what was so thoughtlessly destroyed is now being rebuilt and strengthened.

It has to be admitted that the perspective of European integration and the accession to the EU have, in the end, strengthened and supported this process immensely. Not only has it given an extra incentive and new knowledge to local Polish producers, but it has also made available financial support for development and an expectation of the opening-up of a serious consumer market. In Poland alone, interest in traditional and regional products has started to rebuild. As a consequence, grandsons dusted off the formulas and trade secrets of their grandfathers and took up the production that their fathers had been forced to abandon.

2.1.6.3.1.2. On European Instruments of Protection of Origin. 'United in diversity', Europe has had to devote particular attention and care to its regional particularities as well as to the variety of cultures represented in its member states. Specific features of regional and traditional production represent Europe's values, and involve, at the same time, a considerable economic interest. It seems understandable, therefore, that the EU should establish regulatory mechanisms for the protection and promotion of such forms of production. The contemporary turn towards quality thinking only makes the phenomenon of guaranteeing traditional or regional features seem more relevant and better founded, as it constitutes an important element of quality regulation.

The most relevant distinguishing factor of traditional and regional products is their specific quality, which emanates from their production process, which in turn is determined by the cultural heritage of the place of origin, as well as its special climatic conditions, the features of the soil, the local species of plants or animals, and finally the human factor involved. It can also be related to the observation of high environmental or animal-welfare standards. It is due to all those characteristics that the quality and reputation of those products, guaranteed by the protection and cultivation of local customs, become a common good, which can be used by all those connected with a given geographical territory and tradition and who commit to the customary methods and procedures.

---

[108] To give just one (rather extreme) example: until recently, on the basis of the law on the production of wines of 1948, all wineries that dealt with the production and sale of wines had to be equipped with, among other things, a specialised laboratory and a customs house. Naturally, the establishment and maintenance of highly specialised laboratories could only be afforded by large-scale, state-owned production facilities. In these circumstances, no family-operated wineries had a chance of surviving, and it practically destroyed Polish winemaking, which is only now, and on a very small scale, being restored by a number of passionate enthusiasts.

Traditional and regional products in EU member states enjoy the mark of a special guaranteed quality and are celebrated as being a common societal good at local or regional levels, in sense that everybody who adheres to the rules set by the producers themselves can claim a right to that common good. One can speak of such societal ownership of the right, because the product is based on the historical roots, the traditions and the specificity of the place, which is a local value and cannot be transferred. Thus, the European system of the protection of regional and traditional products constitutes a distinct form of intellectual property, which is different from patents and trademarks protections.

The nature of regional and traditional products and specialties forces local producers to self-organise in order to define and initiate the production, promotion and sales of a regional product, as well as to cooperate with various social partners towards the common goal and interest. In the contemporary world—with its overarching industrialisation, wide use of chemicals, processing as well as genetic modification of food—regional and traditional products present consumers with an important alternative. Food production that uses traditional methods is primarily related to regions with a majority of unindustrialised and extensive farming. Often these happen to be the poorest regions, which are at the heart of the European regional policy. Due to their need for large workforces in production processes, traditional products generate new employment opportunities. Moreover, as they constitute an important element that promotes the place where they are manufactured, they add to a region's attractiveness to tourists and so boost local economies in that way. Consequently, they considerably increase the economic profitability of agricultural production in those regions. This, however, is only possible when consumers are able to differentiate regional products from mass-produced articles. Hence, the objective of building of an appropriate market for traditional products is vital. It implies a continuity of a sufficient level of production, sales and promotion of traditional products, in their pure form as well as in their use in further processing and preparation of foods.

European instruments for the geographical protection of origin enable producers to increase the market value of their production, and to protect their high-quality agricultural products from imitation. Consequentially, they encourage high-quality production and diversification of farming and food-manufacturing. At the same time, they help consumers by giving them information concerning the specific character of the protected regional products. The protection system requires self-organisation by producers and their collective action towards a common goal in the name of communal interest. It requires them to think in regional and territorial categories. This presents local business organisations with a particular challenge. They have an important role to play in raising awareness about the products and the protection mechanisms in the local communities, among both producers and consumers, as well as among the local administrative and control authorities.

The EU protection categories date back to 1992 and include Protected Designation of Origin (PDO) and Protected Geographical Indication (PGI) under Regulation 510/2006,[109] as well as a Traditional Speciality Guaranteed (TSG) under Regulation 509/2006.[110] All three categories have specific aims and status, and all require the fulfilment of different sets of conditions. In short and simplified terms, the Protected Designation of Origin refers to foodstuffs that are produced, processed and prepared in a given geographical area using special knowledge, while in the case of the Protected Geographical Indication the geographical link must occur in at least one of the stages of production, processing or preparation. A Traditional Speciality Guaranteed, on the other hand, does not refer to a product's origin but highlights its traditional character, either in its composition or the means of its production.[111]

In order to obtain the European protected status, producers must apply for it, certifying their fulfilment of the prescribed conditions. The registration procedure currently takes about two to five years and may be held up by any possible conflicts with commercial trademarks that have already been registered. Protection status has a second face as well: in order to continue to meet the requirements of the products dossier, any change in quality requirements has to be approved in Brussels, which makes their production less flexible. Currently, over 1000 European products are registered as PDO, PGI or TSG, most of which are cheeses, vegetables or fruit. The member states with the most registered products are Italy, France and Spain.[112]

---

[109] Council Regulation (EC) 510/2006 of 20 March 2006 on the protection of geographical indications and designations of origin for agricultural products and foodstuffs [2006] OJ L 93/12.

[110] Council Regulation (EC) 509/2006 of 20 March 2006 on agricultural products and foodstuffs as traditional specialities guaranteed [2006] OJ L 93/1.

[111] It needs to be pointed out that changes to all three elements of the system were proposed by the European Commission in its Quality Package adopted in December 2010, aiming *inter alia* at consolidation of the three schemes, and better consumer information about the system and products covered. The most extensive reform proposals pertain to the TSG scheme. Details available at <http://ec.europa.eu/agriculture/quality/policy/quality-package-2010/index_en.htm> accessed 25 May 2011.

[112] See Background note: 1000th quality food name registered, MEMO/11/84, Brussels, 15 February 2011, available at <http://ec.europa.eu/agriculture/quality/schemes/index_en.htm> accessed 25 May 2011.

In order to give a broader view of the three instruments of protection under the EU law, a more detailed description of each of them is now presented, analysing their rationale, requirements, status and the protection they offer.[113]

In the context of the PDO, 'designation of origin' refers to the name of a region, a specific place or, in exceptional circumstances, a country, and describes an agricultural product or a foodstuff that bears three cumulative characteristics: (1) it originates in that place; (2) its quality or characteristics are essentially or exclusively due to a particular geographical environment with its inherent natural and human factors; and (3) its production, processing and preparation take place in the defined geographical area.[114] Hence, products bearing the PDO logo posses proven characteristics that result exclusively from the terrain and the abilities of producers of the region with which they are associated. Therefore, they require all stages of food production to take place within that territory. The link between the specific characteristics of the product and its geographical origin must be objective and close.

In the PGI, 'geographical indication' means the name of a region, a specific place or, in exceptional cases, a country, and describes an agricultural product or a foodstuff that fulfils three cumulative conditions: (1) it originates in that region, specific place or country; (2) it possesses a specific quality, reputation or other characteristics attributable to that geographical origin; and (3) its production and/or processing and/or preparation takes place in that defined geographical area.[115] Products bearing a PGI mark, therefore, must have special characteristics or reputation that associate them with a given area, and at least one stage of the production process must take place in that territory, while the raw materials used in the production may come from another region. It is clear, therefore, that the geographical link is far deeper in the case of PDOs than for of PGIs.

Finally, the TGI—'traditional speciality guaranteed'—refers to a traditional agricultural product or foodstuff recognised by the EU for its specific character. For the purpose of this definition, two expressions are additionally explained in the Regulation. Firstly, 'traditional' requires proven usage on the EU market for a time period showing transmission between generations, where the time period should be that generally ascribed to one human generation: at least twenty-five years. Secondly, 'specific character' refers to the characteristic or set of characteristics that distinguish the agricultural product or foodstuff

[113] For more details, see European Commission, Fact Sheet: European Policy for Quality Agricultural Products, KF-76-06-383-EN-C, January 2007 <http://ec.europa.eu/agriculture/publi/fact/quality/2007_en.pdf> accessed 25 May 2011, 4.

[114] Article 2.1 (a) of Council Regulation (EC) 510/2006 (n 109).

[115] Ibid Article 2.1 (b).

clearly from other similar products or foodstuffs of the same category.[116] It has to be understood, therefore, that products bearing the TGI logo posses distinctive features that they owe either to the use of traditional ingredients or the use of traditional production methods.

The crucial advantage of the European system of geographical designation is that the right to use a product name is reserved for the region and not the producer. It is, thus, granted to producers who apply for the registration as well as to all other producers who meet the requirements of the specification. The exclusive right to the name gives the producers in question a specific added value for their product, which distinguishes them for consumers, and which compensates for the extra costs stemming from the specific requirements of the product, which can often include high-quality raw materials, longer and more labour-intensive processing methods, or a prevention of the use of modern technological improvements in the production process.

The scope of protection offered to the designation-holders precludes other producers from taking unjustified advantage of the specific reputation built up by the protected product. It forbids, for example, the direct or indirect commercial use of the registered name for products not covered by the specification, the misuse, imitation or evocation of the name on a non-registered product (for example, through the use of terms such as 'style', 'type' and 'method' that suggest equivalence to the protected product), as well as any false or misleading information about the origin, nature and qualities of the product.[117]

Enforcement and control of the functioning of the European quality system obliges the member states to implement mechanisms of compliance-checking and to establish appropriate control authorities. The marketing of products in competition with the EU registered product without fulfilling the prescribed requirements will result in their removal from the market.[118] An additional improvement was made in 2005, when a WTO ruling required that the EU quality-designation system be brought into conformity with multilateral trade regulations.[119] One of the requirements was to allow third country producers to submit applications and objections to the Commission, so that the system is factually open to third country producers.

---

[116] Article 2.1 (c), (b), and (a) of Council Regulation (EC) 509/2006 (n 110).

[117] Article 13 of Regulation (EC) 510/2006 (n 109).

[118] In certain cases, when the product has been on the market for a period of time prescribed by the Regulation, transitory limited periods may be granted, where the product will be allowed to remain on the market under certain labelling conditions.

[119] Panel Report, *European Communities—Protection of Trademarks and Geographical Indications for Agricultural Products and Foodstuffs*, Complaint by Australia, adopted 20 April 2005, WT/DS290/R, and Panel Report, *European Communities—Protection of Trademarks and Geographical Indications for Agricultural Products and Foodstuffs*, Complaint by the United States, adopted 15 March 2005, WT/DS174/R.

2.1.6.3.1.3. Polish Regional Flavours Protected. In the last years before the planned date of accession, awareness of the need to attain reservations for Polish traditional products in order to save them from vanishing under the common market standards grew considerably. This awareness, however, was met by insufficient consciousness of the available legal means of such protection, and by a lack of readiness by Polish producers to meet the challenges ahead.

There were many problems at stake, which should be mentioned in this context, and which require more in-depth explanation. The first obstacle, which was important not only for the issue of geographical protection, but also regarding the creation of agricultural producers' organisations, was Poland's reluctance to move towards collectivism. The problem was already explained here with reference to historical experiences, where collectivisation and communal organisation were not only forced upon farmers and food producers, but also had consecutively proved ineffective and economically unsound. The second obstacle was the above-mentioned problem of the breaching of the traditions of local production and sales. Finally, neither the producers nor the authorities were properly prepared for the undertaking. Insufficient information about the nature of the protection offered by the European regulations, as well as about the conditions that had to be fulfilled in order to successfully apply for it, raised concerns among local producers. Their concerns were fuelled by fearful reports in the media and statements from anti-European peasant party activists that made references to collectivisation and the return of communist methods.

Arguments raised in the debate about the application of the method of regional protection rightly pointed out that it would offer not only protection for products but also, in the long run, protection for producers. Many traditional production methods used in Poland would not be acceptable under the EU food safety requirements. Consequently, a large number of facilities would have to be closed upon accession, and their regional products would no longer be produced. Hence, regional protection, and the derogation of common standards that would stem from it, was seen as a way to save certain products from disappearing and their production units from closing down. Application for regional protection was, therefore, also perceived as a way of escaping the stringent EU standards in food production. Shortly before accession, when the prospect of non-compliance became apparent in many sectors of agricultural and food production, and when the fear of losing a number of Polish specialties became pressing, efforts were intensified to promote the idea of geographical/regional/traditional protection as a means of preserving endangered products and production units, and the argument gained increasing relevance.

The national campaign was launched with the example of *oscypek*, a traditional smoked sheep's cheese produced by shepherds in primitive mountain cottages in the highlands in the south of Poland. Everybody agreed that *oscypek* was a traditional regional product that deserved the protection offered by the European regulation. It was far more difficult, however, to agree on what *oscypek* really was: how it should be defined and described, how to delimit the geographical region of its production, and how to formulate its recipe, ingredients and production methods. The traditional opposition towards collective action, which is particularly strong among the mountain people, constituted a serious obstacle in the process. Finally, as often in Polish history, an external threat facilitated and accelerated the procedure. The external influence came in a form of conflicting claims to the protection of an '*oscypek*-type' cheese by neighbouring Slovak mountain communities.

With considerable help from the central government and local authorities, the regional Polish cheese producers managed to reach an understanding on the controversial issues and agree on the definition and the formula. Applications for the registration of *oscypek* and *bryndza podhalańska*—another traditional cheese from the region—were prepared and filed in the break of 2005 and 2006.[120] The procedure for *bryndza* went quite smoothly and, with the Regulation of 11 June 2007, it was added to the register of PDOs, with the regulation entering into force twenty days following its publication.[121] *Oscypek* had a slightly bumpier road, with the proceedings suspended by an objection from the Slovak dairy producers. In the end, however, the conflicting parties managed to reach a conclusion, and the Polish right to protection was recognised and entered into the EU register by a Regulation of 13 February 2008.[122]

Towards the end of 2010, Poland has had twenty three agri-food products registered as PDOs, PGIs, or TSG's and thirteen pending applications under

[120] Publication of an application in accordance with Article 6(2) of Council Regulation (EC) 510/2006 on the protection of geographical indications and designations of origin for agricultural products and foodstuffs (2006/C 180/09); Application for registration in accordance with Articles 5 and 17(2), "OSCYPEK", EC: PL/0451/21.02.2005 [2006] OJ C 180/94; and Publication of an application pursuant to Article 6(2) of Council Regulation (EC) 510/2006 on the protection of geographical indications and designations of origin for agricultural products and foodstuffs (2006/C 230/02); Application for registration pursuant to articles 5 and 17(2), "BRYNDZA PODHALAŃSKA", EC: PL/PDO/005/0450/18.02.2005 [2006] OJ C 230/2.

[121] Commission Regulation (EC) 642/2007 of 11 June 2007 registering a name in the Register of protected designations of origin and protected geographical indications Bryndza Podhalańska (PDO) [2007] OJ L 150/4.

[122] Commission Regulation (EC) 127/2008 of 13 February 2008 entering in the register of protected designations of origin and protected geographical indications Oscypek (PDO) [2008] OJ L 40/5.

those three protection schemes.[123] This may seem rather few for such a large country with a big and diverse society and a wealth of traditions. On the other hand, however, due to the various limitations that were discussed above, as well as the relative stringency of the European provisions, this was to be expected. Additionally, if one takes into account the belated start of Polish producers in their quest for regional protection, one understands the pattern.

It is to be hoped that the incentive presented by participation in the common market and the interest of European consumers will continue to work as encouraging factors for Polish entrepreneurs to organise and apply for the available European protection. It cannot be expected that the EU will recognise the particularity of the Polish situation, which is in fact quite representative of the situation of many of the new member states, and so initiate a discussion on the appropriateness of the current European protection scheme for the new member states, which could theoretically be done in the course of preparation of the reform of the EU quality protection policy announced by the Commission. Poland should, thus, concentrate on providing additional incentives for regional producers, raising awareness of the available means, and facilitating procedures so as to allow the widest possible use of the instrument for the benefit of both local producers as well as EU consumers.

2.1.6.3.2. *GM-Free Poland? EU Requirements versus Societal Expectations*

2.1.6.3.2.1. Poland vs GMOs. Polish policy towards genetically modified organisms (GMOs) can be seen as a case in point in my considerations. I will, therefore, examine in closer detail the genesis of the case and its development throughout the integration process.

The story of Poland's uneasy relationship with GMOs goes back to the roots of the Polish agricultural tradition, and to the specificity of Poland's agrarian economy. As discussed above, at the time of its EU accession, Poland's biggest liability—its simple, traditional, fragmented and obsolete agricultural system—turned out to be one of its greatest assets. Poland had exactly the traditional, natural and organic agriculture and food production system that much of Europe at that time was seeking. Despite the initial fears and propaganda, Polish farmers were the first social group to benefit from the enlargement. This was an advantage they did not want to let go of. Taking into consideration Poland's traditional approaches to farming and food production, it is hardly surprising that the farmers felt seriously threatened by the idea

[123] Situation as of 15 November 2010, according to the DOOR database maintained by the European Commission <http://ec.europa.eu/agriculture/quality/door/list.html;jsessionid=pL0hLqqLXhNmFQyFl1b24mY3t9dJQPflg3xbL2YphGT4k6zdWn34!-370879141?locale=en> accessed 15 November 2010.

that it was impossible for a member state to unilaterally reject the introduction of GM crops.

According to a survey performed in 2008, 60% of Poles are certain that consumption of genetically modified food may be harmful.[124] Fifty-five per cent want the farming of GMOs to be banned in Poland. Forty-five per cent think that Poland should forbid the farming of GM plants even if that caused a conflict with the European Commission. Forty-nine per cent go even further, agreeing that such ban should be implemented even if it led to an increase in food prices. Finally, 66% declare that they would not buy a food product containing GMOs even if its price was considerably lower than that of a comparable product that does not contain them. Eighty-seven per cent do not believe that genetically modified food can be better than traditionally produced natural foodstuffs. Poles' resistance to GMOs is equally strong irrespective of their level of education, place of residence or profession. The results of the opinion poll opened up a public debate about GMOs in the biggest Polish daily newspaper. In the course of the debate, both supporters and opponents of opening up the Polish market to transgenic products presented four types of arguments: scientific, economic, legal and emotional.

In support of biotechnology, scientists claimed that transgenic plants are simply better. It was claimed that genetic modification is just another step on the path which humanity began centuries ago, when various plant species were cross-bred for the first time. They emphasised that there is no available scientific expertise that directly and undeniably proves GMOs have harmful effects for human or animals.

The economic arguments, supported by verified figures, go to the heart of the matter. Firstly, the declarations of the Polish consumers who took part in the opinion poll were confronted by the experiences of food industry. Although almost half of Polish consumers declared that a GMO ban should be sustained even if it translated into an increase of food prices, food-industry scientists responded that this declaration should be treated with utmost caution. They claimed that, for an average consumer, only an insignificant increase of 1% to 2% would be practically acceptable in return for the 'eco' nature of the product. Anything that goes beyond that amount will, in the longer run, turn out to be problematic, while a rise of around 10% would practically erase a given product from the market. The problem was illustrated with a practical example. GMO feedstuffs, mainly transgenic soy, constitute around 95% of the overall world export of soy for feedstuffs, and have been allowed in Poland for a couple of years. Food-industry activists claim that the introduction of a ban on

[124] According to the opinion poll carried out by PBS DGA for *Gazeta Wyborcza*—the biggest Polish daily newspaper—with excerpts published in *Gazeta Wyborcza*: 'Jak ja się boję GMO' *Gazeta Wyborcza* (Warszawa 12 March 2008).

GM feedstuffs could lead to a collapse of Polish animal production, with the cost of feedstuffs rising as much as 200%.

Among legal arguments, the most important referred to an obvious fact: that unilateral national ban on transgenic plants and products constitutes a breach of European and WTO law. It was suggested that in the future it might be possible to build a coalition of member states that oppose GMOs, and thus influence the development of European legislation, but until then Poland remains in outright conflict with EU law and may expect all possible legal consequences, including a case in the ECJ, as well as a financial penalty for infringement.

Finally, the emotional arguments of GMO supporters label their adversaries as backward and radical, with some going as far as comparing the opponents of GMOs to followers of Trofim Lysenko.[125]

On the other side of the barricade, the opponents of opening the Polish market to GMOs formulated the following set of arguments. Scientists raised the problem of jeopardy to biodiversity that is connected with transgenic plants, and warned against uncontrolled cross-pollination. Even more importantly, however, their second argument pertained to the potential adverse effects of GMOs on human and animal health. Among the economic arguments, two crucial points deserve mentioning here. The first referred to possible damage to farmers who wish to continue conventional organic production. The second argument, based on American studies, tried to show that transgenic plant production creates additional costs for producers and the environment. The report quoted claims that, since the introduction of GM farming in the USA, 55,000 more tonnes of pesticide would be released into the environment, than if conventional production were kept, with use of the most popular chemical product increasing nineteen times. GMO opponents also made reference to emotional arguments, tending to use them much more than enthusiasts of modern biotechnology. These range from a lack of trust or simply a lack of willingness to take risks, to invoking a conspiracy of multinational companies that are only interested in market domination and profit-making and that disregard consumers' health and well-being.[126]

To conclude, leaving aside the national debate and looking simply at the actual facts, it has to be pointed out that since February 2006, all the sixteen

---

[125] Trofim Lysenko was a biologist and agronomist, and a leading figure of Soviet biology under Joseph Stalin. Lysenko rejected Mendelian genetics in favour of the hybridisation theories of the Russian horticulturist Ivan Michurin, moulding them into a powerful political and scientific movement later referred to as 'Lysenkoism'. His experimental research in improved crop yields earned him the strong support of the Soviet leadership, but the crop yields he promised failed to materialise. For more, see <http://en.wikipedia.org/wiki/Trofim_Lysenko> accessed 25 May 2011.

[126] Details in Gazeta Wyborcza, 'GMO, czyli nie chcę ale muszę' *Gazeta Wyborcza* (Warszawa 31 March 2008)

regions of Poland have declared themselves GMO-free. Poland therefore has joined Greece and Austria and has become the third country with a complete 'GMO-free' status. Additionally, Poland took national steps towards its GM-free status. In May 2006, a law banning the sale and registration of genetically modified seeds was signed by the President.

2.1.6.3.2.2. European GMO Regulation. Genetically modified organisms and the European regulation pertaining to them have gained substantial political and academic interest recently, and there is a large amount of literature that explores the relating legal and political questions.[127] For the sake of this volume, I will restrict myself to a simplified summary of the state of art in the field, which should make it easier to understand the case study that follows without going into the complexity and sensitivity of biotechnology regulation.

The concept of 'genetic engineering' implies the use of technology for the isolation and manipulation of genes from one organism, and their use in another organism. Genetically modified organisms (GMOs) are, thus, organisms such as plants, animals and micro-organisms whose genetic characteristics have been modified in order to give them new properties and qualities. These might include better resistance to disease, a higher tolerance, increased productivity or an improvement in nutritional value. Modern biotechnology may have many different applications in the pharmaceutical and agri-food industries. One example is the use of GMOs in the food-production chain. In order to ensure that the engagement of modern biotechnology in production of foodstuffs is properly supervised and controlled—to guarantee its safety for consumers—its production, use and marketing has been regulated both nationally and internationally. Regulatory interest in biotechnology first began in the 1970s, when it focused mainly on matters relating to the research and development of biotechnology. In Europe, this regulatory phase was conducted by the member states, and only towards the end of the 1980s did the Commission initiate efforts to develop its own regulatory agenda, which has been evolving since then. The current European legal framework for GMOs has a series of components that pertain to different aspects of the production and use of GMOs.

---

[127] For a general overview of the European GMO regulations, especially with regard to trade issues, as well as a detailed analysis of the European framework, see P Dąbrowska, *Hybrid Solutions for Hybrid Products?: EU Governance of GMOs*, PhD thesis, European University Institute, 2006; GC Schaffer and MA Pollack, 'Regulating Between National Fears and Global Disciplines: Agricultural Biotechnology in the EU' (2004) Jan Monnet Working Paper No. 10/04 <http://www.jeanmonnetprogram.org/papers/04/041001.pdf> accessed 27 May 2011; J Scott, 'European Regulation of GMOs: Thinking about "Judicial Review" in the WTO' (2004) Jean Monnet Working Paper No. 4/04 <http://www.jeanmonnetprogram.org/papers/04/040401.pdf> accessed 27 May 2011.

The placing on the market of GMOs—and, more specifically, of products containing or consisting of GMOs—for cultivation, import or processing into industrial products is subject to Directive 2001/18 on the deliberate release into the environment of genetically modified organisms.[128] The same directive also regulates the experimental release of GMOs into the environment, e.g. for field-testing. The contained use of genetically modified micro-organisms—e.g. laboratory research (in a confined environment)—is regulated separately by Directive 90/219 on the contained use of genetically modified micro-organisms.[129] Finally, unintentional movements of GMOs between member states and exports of GMOs to third countries are governed by Regulation 1946/2003 on transboundary movements of genetically modified organisms.[130]

The second regulatory component of the EU's biotech legislation is the use of GMOs for products intended for human consumption, or for the production of foodstuffs. There, the placing on the market of GMOs intended for food or feed, as well as the placing on the market of food or feed products containing, consisting of or produced from GMOs, is governed by Regulation 1829/2003 on genetically modified food and feed.[131] Moreover, GMOs and food products derived from GMOs placed on the market must also comply with labelling and traceability requirements. These requirements are to be found in Regulation 1829/2003 itself, as well as in Regulation 1830/2003 concerning the traceability and labelling of genetically modified organisms and the traceability of food and feed products produced from genetically modified organisms.[132]

Where a food product contains or consists of GMOs, the applicant has a choice either to follow the principle of 'one door, one key', where the application as a whole is subject solely to Regulation 1829/2003, in order to obtain authorisation for the deliberate release of a GMO into the environment—in accordance with the criteria laid down by Directive 2001/18—and for the use of this GMO in food products—in accordance with the criteria laid down by Regulation 1829/2003; alternatively, the applicant can apply on

---

[128] Directive (EC) 2001/18 of the European Parliament and of the Council on the deliberate release into the environment of genetically modified organisms [2001] OJ L 106/1, as amended.

[129] Council Directive (EEC) 90/219 of 23 April 1990 on the contained use of genetically modified micro-organisms [1990] OJ L 117/1.

[130] Regulation (EC) 1946/2003 of the European Parliament and of the Council of 15 July 2003 on transboundary movements of genetically modified organisms [2003] OJ L 287/1.

[131] Regulation (EC) 1829/2003 of the European Parliament and of the Council of 22 September 2003 on genetically modified food and feed [2003] OJ L 268/1.

[132] Regulation (EC) 1830/2003 of the European Parliament and of the Council of 22 September 2003 concerning the traceability and labelling of genetically modified organisms and the traceability of food and feed products produced form genetically modified organisms and amending Directive 2001/18/EC (2003) OJ L 268/24.

the basis of both Directive 2001/18 and Regulation 1829/2003. The formulation of Directive 2001/18, including the coexistence guidelines, points to the EU's intention to end the *de facto* moratorium on the production and trade of GM food, as it must be remembered that between December 1998 and March 2003 no new GM varieties received approval.[133] The new Commission proposal for reform of the cultivation policy, presented in 2010, brings a new dimension to the system, and will be evaluated later in this volume.

In order to make this overview complete, another aspect of the meeting between biotechnology and food should be mentioned. Foods and food ingredients which were not used for human consumption within the EU before 15 May 1997 fall under the common definition of 'novel foods'. Detailed rules for the authorisation of novel foods and novel-food ingredients are governed by Regulation 258/97,[134] under which, until November 2010, 115 applications for authorisation were filed, out of which almost fifty were reviewed positively, and three were refused.[135]

2.1.6.3.2.3. Poland's Attempt to Remain GM-Free. The specific case I will discuss here arose following the Polish notification of draft law implementing the deliberate release Directive, which included certain reservations on the basis of Article 114(5) TFEU (ex Article 95(5) TEC). Before the analysis of the justification of those reservations which is of particular importance here, a brief review of the procedural background and the most critical stages of the process is provided.[136]

The provisions of Article 114(5) and (6) TFEU (ex Article 95(5) and (6) TEC) allow member states to introduce, after the adoption by the Council or the Commission of a harmonisation measure, national provisions based on new scientific evidence relating to the protection of the environment or the working environment, on the grounds of a problem specific to that member state that has arisen after the adoption of the harmonised measure. The member state must notify the Commission of the envisaged provisions as well as the grounds for introducing them, then the Commission shall, within six months,

[133] For more on the historical development of European GMO regulations, see P Oosterveer, *Global Governance of Food Production and Consumption. Issues and Challenges* (Edward Elgar, Cheltenham 2007) 121–132.

[134] Regulation (EC) 258/97 of the European Parliament and of the Council of 27 January 1997 concerning novel foods and novel food ingredients (1997) OJ L 43/1.

[135] According to the List of Applications under Regulation 258/97, for authorisation of a novel food, updated 05.06.2010, available <at http://ec.europa.eu/food/food/biotechnology/novelfood/app_list_en.pdf> accessed 5 June 2010.

[136] For a detailed analysis of the case and its implications, see K Żurek, 'When Lab Results Are Not Sufficient: On the Limitations of Science in Tackling Modern Food Regulatory Concerns' (2009) SIEPS *European Policy Analysis* No. 5.

approve or reject the national provisions, having verified whether or not they are a means of arbitrary discrimination or a disguised restriction on trade between member states, and whether or not they would constitute an obstacle to the functioning of the internal market.

In a letter of 13 April 2007, Poland officially called attention to two articles of its national legislation, namely Article 111 and Article 172 of a draft Law on Genetically Modified Organisms, which were in derogation of the provisions of the deliberate release Directive.[137] On 9 July 2007, the Commission informed Poland that the notification was received, and the six-month period for examination began. Simultaneously, the Commission published in the *Official Journal*[138] an information note on the proposed Polish measures, so that all interested parties could submit their observations. Observations were issued by the government of Lithuania, a number of non-governmental organisations, as well as individuals, professionals and institutions. On 12 October 2007, the Commission issued a Decision concerning the case.[139] I first examine the particular notified provisions, the argumentation presented in support of those individual restrictions, and the Commission's response. Secondly, I will look at the general Polish argumentation for the introduction of restrictions and the wider context of the Polish approach.

The first notified provision—Article 111 of the Polish draft Law on Genetically Modified Organisms—pertains to deliberate release of a GMO for experimental purposes, and lays down the content of an application for the issuing of a decision on the deliberate release of a GMO. According to paragraph 2 of that article, the application should be accompanied by, among other things, a certification from the mayor of the municipality, confirming that, in the local spatial-development plan, with regard to the need to protect local environment, nature and cultural landscape of the area in question, a provision has been made for the possibility of deliberate release. Moreover, the application should also be accompanied by written declarations form the holders of farms neighbouring the location of the deliberate release that they do not object to the release. The legislation's objective, as presented by the Polish government in an explanatory note, is that the conditions for assessing the safety of a given field experiment, with regard to its safety for the environment, should be set as strictly as possible. As the effects of such organisms on the environment are

---

[137] Directive (EC) 2001/18 of the European Parliament and of the Council on the deliberate release ... (n 128).

[138] (2007) OJ C 173/8.

[139] Commission Decision (EC) 2008/62 of 12 October 2007 relating to Articles 111 and 172 of the Polish Draft Act on Genetically Modified Organisms, notified by the Republic of Poland pursuant to Article 95(5) of the EC Treaty as derogations from the provisions of the Directive 2001/18/EC of the European Parliament and of the Council on the deliberate release into the environment of genetically modified organisms [2008] OJ L 16/17.

unknown and could potentially be harmful, special safety conditions should be maintained, in accordance with the EU principle of precaution. This is particularly important in view of the richness of biodiversity in Poland, to which the introduction of GMOs into the environment could cause serious disturbances.

In the Commission's view, it was clear from the wording of the proposed provision as well as the explanatory note that the notified provision would have an impact on the releases of GMOs for any other purpose than for placing on the market, and primarily for field trials.[140] According to the system established by the Directive 2001/18, if a GMO receives consent for cultivation in the EU, member states are not allowed to introduce any additional restrictions on its cultivation. As a consequence, the application of Directive 2001/18 would be affected, as the Polish draft law restricted the cultivation of all GMOs, even if already approved for use in the market under EU legislation, unless designated in specific zones. Thus, the Polish provision would restrict the cultivation of GM seeds for experimental releases by establishing additional administrative requirements for the authorisation of such releases; it must, therefore, be considered as contradictory to the Directive.[141]

The second notified provision, Article 172 of the draft Law, refers to the establishment of special zones for the cultivation of GMOs, and states clearly that the cultivation of GM plants shall be prohibited, subject to the provisions of paragraph 2. Paragraph 1, for that matter, grants to the minister responsible for agriculture, in consultation with the minister responsible for environment and after the opinion of the municipality in question, the authority to issue a decision concerning the creation of a zone designated for the cultivation of GM plants in a specified area within a territory of that municipality. Furthermore, in paragraph 5, it is required that any application for the issue of a decision shall be accompanied by written declarations from the holders of land within the area of spatial isolation from the land on which it is planned to cultivate the GM plants that they do not object to the intention to create a zone designated for the cultivation of GM plants.

According to the Polish explanatory note, the rules on commercial cultivation in the national provisions are based, to a large extent, on the Commission Recommendation 2003/556 of 23 July 2003 on guidelines for the development of national strategies and best practices to ensure the coexistence of genetically modified crops with conventional and organic farming.[142] The idea of creating zones designated for the cultivation of GM plants is a development

[140] Commission Decision (EC) 2008/62 of 12 October 2007 relating to Articles 111 and 172 of the Polish Draft Act on Genetically Modified Organisms, ibid, par. 13.

[141] Ibid, par. 38.

[142] (2003) OJ L 189/36.

of paragraph 3.3 of the aforementioned Recommendation, which concerns cooperation between neighbouring farms. Additionally, account was also taken of paragraphs 2 and sub-paragraph 3.3.2 (coordinated management measures), which speaks of the voluntary clustering of fields of different farms for the cultivation of similar crop varieties (GM, conventional or organic) in a particular area, as well as sub-paragraph 3.3.3, concerning voluntary agreements among farmers on zones of a single production type. According to the draft act, the cultivation of GM plants should be limited to areas that do not contain elements of value from a nature conservation standpoint and whose agrarian structure enables the safe cultivation of transgenic plants without damaging the operations of other farmers. Such an arrangement should minimise the risks associated with the mixing of reproductive material and the crossing of GM plants with unmodified plants.

According to the Commission, this general ban is in breach of Article 19 of Directive 2001/18, which stipulates that, if written consent has been given for the placing on the market of a GMO as or in a product, that product may be used without further notification throughout the EU, insofar as the specific conditions of use and the environmental and/or geographical areas stipulated in these conditions are strictly adhered to. Furthermore, the ban is also in breach of Article 22 of the Directive, which stipulates that member states may not prohibit, restrict or impede the placing on the market of GMOs or products that comply with the requirements of the Directive. Thus, the Commission, in its Decision 2008/62 of 12 October 2007, stated outright that the national provisions notified cannot be approved in accordance with Article 114(6) TFEU (ex Article 95(6) TEC).[143]

On 12 February 2008, Poland brought an action for annulment of the Commission Decision 2008/62.[144] The action was based on a procedural argument: that the contested decision was notified to the applicant on 4 December 2007, which was after the expiry of the six-month period laid down in Article 114(6) TFEU (ex Article 95(6) TEC). In accordance with the Article, that should have meant that the provisions should have been considered to have been approved upon the expiry of that period. The applicant claimed that the fact that the Decision was adopted on 12 October 2007 was immaterial as regards observance of the time-limit, as it is the date of the notification of the Decision that should be decisive. Thus, in support of its application, Poland brought forward the following pleas: (1) breach of Article 114(6) TFEU (ex Article 95(6) TEC) in conjunction with Article 297(2) TFEU (ex Article 254(3) TEC); (2) breach of an essential procedural requirement consisting in the obligation to notify a

---

[143] (n 139).
[144] T-69/08 [2008] OJ C 92/42.

decision to those to whom it is addressed within the period laid down by law, and thus to enable them to become aware of the decision's content; (3) breach of the principle of legal certainty. With the judgement of 9 December 2010, the Court of First Instance annulled the Commission Decision.[145]

Irrespective of the outcome of that procedural dispute, the interesting aspects of the problem lay in the arguments Poland invoked to justify the introduction of the restriction, which should open the door for further deliberation. In its notification, Poland presented the following three main arguments:

a) The deliberate release of GMOs requires special safety measures in accordance with the EU precautionary principle, in view of the richness of biodiversity in Poland and the need to prevent serious disturbances to the functioning of the environment.
b) The structure of Polish agriculture is among the most fragmented in the EU, with almost two million farms and an average farm size of less than eight hectares.
c) Domestic legislation concerning the coexistence of three types of cultivations—GMOs, conventional and organic—does not exist, nor do regulations concerning compensation for damage or loss of crops in the case of uncontrolled cross-pollination.

As its main grounds for the introduction of derogations in the national provisions with regard to the restriction of cultivation of transgenic plants, Poland pointed to 'the need to fulfil the expectations of Polish society'. The provisions restricting the cultivation of GM crops, Poland explained, have the purpose of preventing potential damage that could be caused as a result of crossover of transgenes into conventional crops. Thus, the impossibility of the elimination of a risk of cross-contamination was presented as the main source of concerns associated with the cultivation of GM plants.

Another aspect of this issue was the particular structure of Polish agriculture, with its high degree of fragmentation. Additionally, Polish agriculture is characterised by a conventional production system, with an increasing interest in organic farming and production. Due to this high level of fragmentation and particular production profile, it is impossible to isolate GM crops from conventional crops, as well as from organic crops, which is thus a considerable threat to farmers, and specifically to the developing organic production profile. In such a situation, Poland argues, the uncontrolled introduction of transgenic plants into cultivation may inflict serious losses upon farmers. The aversion of Polish farmers towards GM crops is additionally increased by the fact that the Polish legal system foresees no provisions for compensation for agricultural

[145] (2011) OJ C 30/34.

losses resulting from the uncontrolled crossing of varieties, and there are no national rules on the coexistence of the three types of farming at stake.

Some additional but no less interesting justifications presented by the Polish government were based upon a number of other important aspects of the problem. The first point concerned the uncertainty surrounding the first stage of research, where the new GMO comes into contact with the environment, and where the effect of such an organism on the environment is unknown and may be harmful. Another point concentrated on the need to limit the cultivation of GM plants to areas that do not contain elements of value for nature conservation, and whose agrarian structure enables the safe cultivation of transgenic plants without damaging the nature and the operations of other farmers.

Taking into consideration the problematic nature of the conflict in question, as well as the nature of Polish argumentation, it would be interesting to know whether these arguments made any impression on the European Commission. The Commission, unfortunately, has not made much reference to them; in fact, it has not discussed the validity of the Polish concerns at all. In its decision on the notified Polish reservations, the Commission observed that no reference was made to any new information related to the protection of the environment, either in the notification or in the accompanying documents. Furthermore, no reference was made to any new scientific studies, research, findings or literature, nor was there any indication of new evidence concerning the protection of the environment or the working environment. Under those circumstances, the Commission saw no reasons to submit the Polish notification to the European Food Safety Authority for its opinion, in accordance with the Directive 2001/18, but instead took an immediate decision on the case.

As a lack of new scientific evidence constitutes a failure to fulfil one of cumulative conditions of Article 114(5) TFEU (ex Article 95(5) TEC), the Commission rejected the Polish notification without even examining the fulfilment of the other conditions. From the point of view of the case, as well as in a broader perspective, it would have been very interesting to see how the Commission would have responded to Poland's 'unconventional' arguments. Instead, however, just as the ECJ had done in the French BSE conflict a couple of years before,[146] the Commission chose to hide behind formality, without taking the trouble of addressing the critical regulatory issues at stake.[147] Hence, the overarching problem is that the Commission's avoidance—as stifling as it, in the current context of more and more critical attention being given to concerns about food safety in Europe—seems not to be the result of a single

[146] Case C-1/00 *Commission v. France* [2001] ECR I-9989.

[147] See discussion on the case, including the analysis of this issue, in: K Szawłowska, 'Risk Assessment in the European Food Safety Regulation: Who is to Decide Whose Science is Better? Commission v. France and Beyond …' (2004) 5 *German Law Journal* 1259–1274.

odd occurrence, but rather a result of the shortcomings of the EU food safety regulations themselves.

Having failed at its first attempt, the Polish government developed a new idea of how to prevent the farming of transgenic plants without formally forbidding them.[148] The plan was to circumvent the EU legislation and introduce the ban 'through the back door'. Hence, the new law would not openly ban GMO farming, but would instead leave the decision to local authorities. The internal effectiveness of this technique could not be doubted, as all Polish voivodships had already declared themselves 'GM-free zones' a couple of years before. What remained doubtful, however, was its acceptance by the European Commission.

The technique is not new in the EU. Austrian authorities had tried a similar one before, but had failed to justify it in front of the Commission. All nine Austrian regions had declared themselves 'GM-free zones'. The Commission had originally, in 2003, rejected the regional ban with the argument that it had no scientific justification.[149] The decision was appealed, but in October 2005 the Court of First Instance ruled against the request of Upper Austria to have the zone established.[150] The decision was again appealed to the ECJ, which again ruled against Upper Austria and the Republic of Austria.[151] The arguments used by Austria in their application were, in fact, for the most part very similar to those provided by the Polish government in its first attempt to be granted derogations: the protection of biodiversity, the protection of organic farming and traditional agricultural crops, a fear of contamination of natural biodiversity in ecologically sensitive areas, the prevalent structure of small farms, as well as a high percentage of organic farming in the region. The Polish arguments with regard to the local specificity were more developed, and Poland also mentioned societal preferences as a factor, which the Austrian authorities did not. Additionally, the technical, process-oriented aspect was evaluated, as the suggested regulatory solution was strongly connected with the administrative delegation of decision-making, and this opened up a wide field for procedural arguments. Despite its wider argumentation, however, the Polish attempt was criticised by the Commission, who declared that under no circumstances would such a solution be accepted under the current regulatory framework.

---

[148] Gazeta Wyborcza, 'Tu mi gen wyrośnie. Jak nie zakazać upraw transgenicznych tak by ich zakazać' *Gazeta Wyborcza* (Warszawa 25 April 2008).

[149] Commission Decision (EC) 2003/653 of 2 September 2003 relating to national provisions banning the use of genetically modified organisms in the region of Upper Austria notified by the Republic of Austria pursuant to Article 95(5) of the EC Treaty [2003] OJ L 230.

[150] Judgement in Joined Cases T-366/03 and T-235/04 *Land Oberösterreich and Republic of Austria* v *Commission of the European Communities* [2005] ECR II-4005.

[151] Judgement in Joined Cases C-439/05 P and C-454/05 P *Land Oberösterreich and Republic of Austria* v *Commission of the European Communities* [2007] ECR I–7141.

Not discouraged by these two failures, the Polish government developed a third suggestion and put it forward for the assessment of the European Commission.[152] The new draft Law uses the sole possibility left open by the European legal framework: the bottom-up approach. Under the newly drafted national rules, the GMO farming restrictions will be introduced on the basis of a voluntary declaration by farmers, who will proclaim their fields 'GM-free zones'. According to the draft, such GM-free zones will comprise neighbouring fields (as set up by the national land register). They will be established by the agreement of a group of land owners, on their own initiative.

The overarching idea behind this governmental initiative is that there are no legal obstacles for all Polish farmers to enter into such agreements. It is certainly possible that not all individual land-owners would be willing to do it, and there are no mechanisms to control this part of the process. There are detailed provisions in the draft that lay down rules for those farmers who do not wish to join the agreement and decide instead to take up GM farming. These provisions contain a number of conditions and restrictions, including a requirement for special isolation zones and the consent of neighbours. According to the Minister of the Environment, the suggested considerable size of the 'buffer zones', in conjunction with the small size of the average Polish farming field, will create a situation that could considerably reduce the likelihood of GM farming occurring, and so contribute to the protection of Poland's GM-free status.[153]

It was not an easy task to convince the European Commission to accept this solution. In the course of the technical meetings, many amendments were suggested by the Commission's officials, who also set number of requirements for the openness of the farmers' agreements, the information to be provided, as well as the ability of farmers to change their minds and take up GM farming. The most important thing, however, is that the Commission's preliminary assessment has been that the new draft law does not directly breach EU law and is, therefore, acceptable as an appropriate implementation measure. According to the Polish Minister of the Environment, the new draft was supposed to be adopted in 2010 and enter into force by the end of the year.[154] The proceeding of the draft by the Parliament, however, has caused a significant delay, which coincided in time with the first occurrences of relaxation of the European Commission standpoint on the possibility of variation of national GMO cultivation policies by member states. Consequently, although the successful

[152] New draft Law on genetically modified organisms as adopted by the Council of Ministers on the 13th of October 2009 (currently under scrutiny by the Parliament).

[153] Quoted after *Gazeta Wyborcza*: Gazeta Wyborcza, 'Tu nam gen wyrośnie' *Gazeta Wyborcza* (Warszawa 29 May 2009).

[154] Ibid.

adoption and implementation of the draft Law has not yet occurred, the proposed solution, its preliminary acceptance by the Commission as well as the indicated change of the Commission approach are very promising.

On 13th of July 2010, the Commission adopted a comprehensive proposal that provides to member states the freedom to allow, restrict or ban the cultivation of GMOs on part or all of their territory, keeping unchanged the EU's science-based GM authorisation system. The reform proposal consists of a Communication,[155] a new Recommendation on co-existence of GM crops with conventional and/or organic crops[156] and a draft Regulation proposing a change to the GMO legislation.[157] The new Recommendation on co-existence allows more flexibility to member states taking into account their local, regional and national conditions when adopting co-existence measures. The proposed regulation amends Directive 2001/18 to secure legal certainty for Member States when they decide on GMO cultivation on grounds other than those based on a scientific assessment of health and environmental risks. To this end, the Commission proposes to include a new article (26b), which would be applicable to all GMOs that will be authorised for cultivation in the EU. Member states will be able to restrict or prohibit GMO cultivation in part or all of their territory without recourse to the safeguard clause. Their decisions will not need to be authorised by the Commission, but they will have to inform other member states and the Commission one month before the adoption of the measures. They will also have to respect the general principles of the Treaties and the single market, and be consistent with the international obligations of the EU.

The proposed reform has been received with mixed feelings. Criticism has been raised as to the international consequences of its application for member states who decide to invoke the ban. It is, namely, so that member states wishing to ban or restrict national cultivation risk breaching the WTO rules.[158] The reform, however, if adopted, will constitute an important step towards a diversified approach in Europe. It has to be noted that Poland is not the only EU member state which has been making continuous attempts to block GM

---

[155] Commission (EC), Communication on the freedom for Member States to decide on the cultivation of genetically modified crops, COM (2010) 380 final, 13 July 2010.

[156] Commission (EC), Commission Recommendation of 13 July 2010 on guidelines for the development of national co-existence measures to avoid the unintended presence of GMOs in conventional and organic crops, [2010] OJ C 200/1.

[157] Commission (EC), Proposal for a Regulation of the European Parliament and of the Council amending Directive 2001/18/EC as regards the Possibility for the Member States to restrict or prohibit the cultivation of GMOs in their territory, COM (2010) 375 final, 13 July 2010.

[158] For a thorough evaluation of the proposal and its possible implications see M Weimer, 'What Price Flexibility?—The Recent Commission Proposal to Allow for National "Opt-Outs" on GMO Cultivation under the Deliberate Release Directive and the Comitology Reform Post-Lisbon' (2010) 4 *European Journal of Risk Regulation* 347–354.

farming.[159] During the last couple of months, a large group of countries, led by Germany, Austria, France and Hungary, entered into a conflict with Brussels on the question of GMOs. Thus, the number of countries that do not conform to the current European approach is growing; it is thus possible to build a strong coalition and lobby for an amendment of the EU regulations in that area. Poland's stubbornness in prioritising the national concerns may have been an important contributing factor to the development of a proposed reform envisaging more flexible approach, accommodating some level of diversity in the united European market.

3. Conclusions: Regulating Food in Enlarged European Union

In the following paragraphs I make some concluding remarks on the problems of regulation in the enlarged EU, and, in particular, in view of my detailed case studies, on the impact of the accession on Polish agri-food production and marketing. Firstly, I describe the context of Poland's accession to the common market, its adaptation to common-market regulations and the benefits it has gained by participating. Secondly, I provide some summarising ideas on the immediate discoveries and the more or less expected short-term effects of the enlargement on the Polish market. Thirdly, I close this section by briefly revisiting the two main instruments for allowing a dissenting opinion by a member state, and their application in the Polish case. Finally, I offer a couple of more general concluding thoughts about the dilemmas of regulating an enlarged and more diversified market.

3.1. *Becoming European?*

I open these concluding remarks by referring back to Dunn[160] and her idea of the Trojan pigs, which in fact is based directly on the case of Poland and the specificity of its agriculture and food production. International standards will not always create a unified playing field wherever they are applied, because they are always embedded in local social, economic and institutional circumstances. Thus, externally imposed standards can often function as 'Trojan horses', which enter specific regulatory environments and local sets of conditions and produce unintended side-effects.[161] This is partly so because

[159] The Polish determination in retaining a status of a GM-free country was confirmed openly and officially in the Framework Position of the Polish Government on Genetically Modified Organisms (GMO), adopted by the Council of Ministers on 18 November 2008.

[160] EC Dunn, 'Trojan Pig: Paradoxes of Food Safety Regulation' (2003) 35 *Environment and Planning A* 1493–1511.

[161] Ibid 1494.

international standards are more than just scientifically developed technical rules for market organisation they also intervene in particular local societal and economic situations. This is particularly the case with regard to the EU and its enlargements.

In implementing European standards, acceding states often act merely as transmitters of supranationally established norms, which are outcomes of the balancing of the variety of interests of the current member states. As a consequence, governments face a particular challenge in managing these externally imposed regulations and different local interests. Holmes, perhaps overstating the situation a little, refers to 'quasi-colonial' arrangements.[162] In the longer term, the implementation of such external regulatory regimes may, under the pressure of supranational standardisation and competition, lead to the detachment of local interest from European and global settings.[163]

Moreover, such a forced reallocation of resources away from the objectives of the greatest social/public importance in order to live up to regulatory standards developed by an external power can have detrimental consequences for the local economy as well as the society. In the case of the last two enlargements, most of the new member states had already been overburdened with the high costs of their transition reforms and the restructuring of their economies from being state-planned to becoming free-market systems. Furthermore, the first years of this adjustment process, both economically and socially, had been very costly.

This was the case particularly with regard to the social costs of transformation. In this situation, it is little wonder that the extra costs of implementing the externally imposed directives were not welcomed by the acceding states and their societies. Additionally, and unlike in previous enlargements, where the EU had focused on post-accession adjustment by new member states, the enlargements of the twenty-first century carried a requirement that compliance should have been acquired *before* the planned date of accession, which was then strengthened by strictly applied conditionality.[164] Another important point discussed in the literature is that the new member states were required to withdraw their human and economic links with countries to their east, without simultaneously being allowed to replace them or even partially compensate for them by making new human and economic contacts with countries to their west.[165]

---

[162] S Holmes, 'A European Doppelstaat?' (2003) 17 *East European Politics and Societies* 114.

[163] L Bruszt, D Stark, 'Who Counts? Supranational Norms and Societal Needs' (2003) 17 *East European Politics and Societies* 76.

[164] K Krause, 'European Union Directives and Poland: A Case Study' (2006) 27 *University of Pennsylvania Journal of International Economic Law* 163.

[165] S Holmes, 'A European Doppelstaat? …' (n 162) 115.

Thus, the lack of a complete implementation of the single-market legislation and some form of selective non-compliance could, in fact, favour the new member states and their economic and social well-being. Interesting comments in that regard can be found in literature. Just to give an example, Krause, analysed a Polish case of a lack of implementation of EU directives, where in September 2004 Poland had still failed to implement more than 250, which is around one-sixth of the total number of single-market directives. On the basis of her study, Krause makes a strong argument in favour of non-compliance.[166] Her analysis shows that the implementation of directives in new member states could be seen as an undermining of their competitive advantage. The problem is that, although the implementation of directives carries a promise of an improvement of the overall situation, it is required in all cases, irrespective of the costs involved and the real potential that a country will benefit from their adoption. Thus, in many cases, a failure to comply with certain directives could serve a nation's important long-term goals, and ultimately be beneficial.

Hence, it is important to recognise that the failure of these directives to properly address the situation of the recently admitted states suggests that a 'multi-faceted regulatory model' may have been a more useful system, rather than the current reliance on externally imposed mandatory rules. This indicates that, in many areas, current EU policies and legislation require reconsideration, and new member states might indeed be the catalysts of such reform.[167] The current EU approach towards acceding states, in Krause's reading of the disparity in the implementation of the CAP provisions, in particular, illustrates the extent to which the legislation as well as the accession criteria were driven by the old member states' self-interest and willingness to straightforwardly apply model solutions to the CEE countries. Consequently, this hindered regulatory diversity and innovation, which could have offered solutions to some ongoing European regulatory problems.

3.2. *Some Observations from the Polish Accession Story*

This section will start by drawing some conclusions from the two short case studies presented in this chapter, in order to illustrate the possibilities available to member states in their attempts to retain reservations to the *acquis* with the objective of safeguarding their important local particularities. It is undoubtedly a good thing that there are legislative measures in place which can be used by member states to allow them to retain and protect things they hold dear from the potentially destructive influence of the common market. The problem, however, is the limited impact of those measures. In Europe after

[166] K Krause, 'European Union Directives and Poland …' (n 164) 164–194.
[167] Ibid 195.

Maastricht, and after the last two enlargements, one wishes that the availability of instruments to protect national specialties was greater, so that a wider range of options could serve to protect a richer set of values and circumstances. The two instruments referred to in this chapter should be appreciated for the purposes they serve, but they also have certain important shortcomings which should be pointed out.

Firstly, the case studies have shown that the available legal means of protecting diversity can often turn out to be too inflexible. Hence, in cases where their application would be perfectly in accordance with their overarching aim and regulatory purpose, the stringency of their legal form does not allow it. This was the case with regard to many Polish products that would generally enjoy protection because of their regional origin, but which, due to the stringency of the formal requirements, were deprived of the right to apply for such protection. One illustrative example concerns a certain traditional Polish liqueur, which takes its fragrance from a herb that grows almost exclusively in one particular region of the country. However, due to a questionable decision of the communist state during the period of state monopoly and central planning, the production of the liqueur was moved to a factory located in a different region; and this, with regard to EU law, made it practically impossible for the liqueur to claim regional protection.

Secondly, it is debatable whether the catalogue of values which these diversity promoting mechanisms protect should not be reviewed. Referring to the second case study, the GMO case, it is interesting to observe that Poland's main argument—its most important justification for the introduction of a national derogation—was based on societal expectations. This argument, however, was not even discussed by the Commission in its decision. The Commission, following the old track, only reviewed the issue of the lack of new scientific evidence. Thus, it is clear that the protection offered by the reviewed EU measures, although it is highly necessary and important, is of a rather limited application and impact. In this situation, it seems necessary to look for other possible solutions. If the EU laws cannot offer them yet, a discussion should be initiated on the appropriateness of their consideration in future regulatory reforms. Until that happens, however, it will be interesting to observe how the markets and societies of new member states deal with these shortcomings and find their own ways out of the crises.

It turned out, shortly after Poland's accession that those who feared EU integration the most—farmers and food producers—in fact benefitted from it to the greatest extent. Polish agricultural and food production has found new consumers and widened its market. There was no sudden flooding of the Polish market by cheaper products from the west. Initially, there was no sudden exodus of Polish workers to the old member states, which was also expected to occur, in consequence of a serious increase of domestic unemployment rate. Hence, one can argue that, in the short term, a lot of the forecast problems and breakdowns were fixed by the self-regulating power of the market. This, however, had far-reaching long-term consequences, which have to be dealt with now, and which will remain issues for years to come.

It is interesting to observe how the market catches up and how producers manage to find their niche, redirect their focus and find new solutions in response to market demand. An illustrating example was the development of tourism, especially agro-tourism, which emerged as an alternative source of income for small-scale farmers, who would otherwise have had little chance to survive the pressures of the common market. Nevertheless, the social costs of those developments are enormous. The social costs and, in the longer run, the economic costs of large-scale Polish emigration, concerning about a million Polish citizens, are still difficult to estimate. The fact is that the phenomenon of Polish emigration ameliorated the first years after accession and had a beneficial influence on the economy. Paradoxically enough, in the receiving states, such as the United Kingdom and Ireland, despite the dread of the infamous 'Polish plumber', national economies have also benefitted tremendously. Currently, however, with development in the international financial market and the gradual reduction of the initially striking differences in income and income value, a problem with returning emigrants has emerged, as the Polish economy is no longer capable of accepting the emigrant workers back and there are no regulatory means to facilitate the process. Furthermore, due to the ties imposed by EU law, often the adoption of such facilitating mechanisms would not even be possible.

3.3. *Bigger Market—Bigger Problems?*

> … given heterogeneous policy legacies in the member states as well as the diverse preferences of national governments and other domestic actors, one-size-fits-all solutions are neither politically feasible nor normatively desirable.[168]

As the quotation suggests, the response to the question asked in the heading must be affirmative. It is not merely a question of size, but it is also a problem of more diversified market. Thus, the regulatory solutions successfully applied in the initial constellation may no longer achieve their aims. They may, in fact, even contradict some of the objectives of the common market. This is because heterogeneity implies slightly different needs and is more difficult to manage. In case of European integration, considering the post-Second World War

[168] G Falkner et al., *Complying with Europe: EU Harmonisation and Soft Law in the Member States* (Cambridge University Press, Cambridge 2005) 1.

division of the continent and its consequences for the development of states on both sides of the 'iron curtain', the growing increase in the heterogeneity of the common market after each enlargement, and especially after the 2004 enlargement, should definitely have been expected. Moreover, increased mobility and trade, which was also aggravated by the global financial crisis, has made the regulatory exercise in the 'bigger Europe' more difficult and constrained than had ever been expected.[169] With such increasing diversity, the consistent application of unified solutions will inevitably lead to a further disembedding of market regulation, and distance it from the society it serves.

A growing number of examples suggest the emergence of problems to which neither the old EU method nor the new methods of softer governance are able to respond. Those problems stem both from the increased heterogeneity of the enlarged EU, as well as from the internal development of the European project, which now encompasses a much wider set of issues than it did at the initial stage of the integration process. In my view, both those phenomena lead to a similar concern, which can most simply be described as detachment. Firstly there has been a detachment of the regulation from the market and the societies which it concerns, which, after Polanyi, has been here referred to as disembeddedness. Secondly, there has been a detachment of the economic and the social spheres of regulation, which, despite the promises of 'Social Europe', remains an unresolved issue of imbalanced integration.

Even without referring to the strong and obvious examples of the last two accessions, differences in the approach and provision of social-welfare policy and social protection were already striking among the previous fifteen member states. In fact, a harmonisation of welfare issues, as Scharpf has often pointed out, was already too difficult to negotiate when it could potentially have been recognised. Deliberating on the 'European Social Model' and the facilitation of European compromises by means of side-payments and package deals, Scharpf presents an opinion that not all sacrifices can be compensated, and that the difficulty of reaching negotiated agreements increases with the growing heterogeneity of member states' conditions, interests and preferences. Thus, he concludes that the hope of achieving the 'European Social Model' had already been destroyed with the first enlargement from the original six states, leaving alone the current situation.[170] The solution to this problem goes far

---

[169] See, for example, M Artis, A Banerjee and M Marcellino (eds), *The Central and Eastern European Countries and the European Union* (Cambridge University Press, Cambridge 2006); DC Vaughan-Whitehead, *EU Enlargement versus Social Europe? The Uncertain Future of the European Social Model* (Edward Elgar, Cheltenham 2003).

[170] FW Scharpf, 'The Joint-Decision Trap Revisited' (2006) 44 *Journal of Common Market Studies* 851.

beyond the scope of this volume, although the overarching question of what we should do with the problematic 'social' is among its main concerns.

What this volume has concentrated on instead, is the possibility of embracing 'the social' by means of market regulation, and in that way reintegrating and re-embedding it to make it more responsive to the contemporary needs of the enlarged EU. My main argument has been that methods for re-embedding European market regulation can be found in the increasing flexibility and inclusiveness of the current regulatory framework. In the food sector, which is at issue here, this framework does not seem to leave enough room for flexibility and inclusiveness. Hence, 'the social' can only marginally be reflected in the regulatory outcome. In an area such as food regulation, where the social sphere of regulation should logically be of primary concern, a growing detachment is being noticed. This is the case now more than ever before, due to the diversity of local markets within the new member states, as well as the varying concerns and preferences of their societies, which require a more appropriate regulatory response. One-size-fits-all regulatory solutions will not be able to respond to these concerns, and therefore they may no longer be able to achieve their objectives. The consequences of this will not only be of a social and political nature, such as the protests of farmers and conscious consumers, or the diverging opinions of national representatives. It may also have more far-reaching consequences for the entire EU market, such as structured non-compliance.

Finally, it should be remembered that there are ways of heeding a wider set of concerns within European regulation. As the example of the REACH regulation shows, it does not require a great revolution. Moreover, European regulatory framework can be made more flexible simply by rebalancing the patterns of use of the available regulatory instruments, favouring those that allow more flexibility and the consideration of local economic and social circumstances. With the growing needs of the larger European market, it is recommended to consider reforming in that direction, and thus opening up the system, instead of maintaining the fictitious assumption that the social sphere of regulation can simply be disregarded by the laws of the market.

CHAPTER FIVE

CONCLUSION

In the preceding chapters I have gathered critical observations on current trends in contemporary food safety regulation in Europe, approaching it from different perspectives: theoretical, evolutionary, external, and internalised. I looked, first, at the theoretical background of three regulatory mechanisms commonly used in EU market regulation, and juxtaposed their flexibility and inclusiveness, as well as the potential intended and unintended consequences of their application. Secondly, I presented an evolutionary analysis of the development of EU food regulation, tracing the application of the three regulatory mechanisms reviewed in the theoretical section. Thirdly, I looked at the regulatory issues at stake from the perspective of new member states, and, using the example of Poland's accession to the EU agri-food market, I discussed the shortcomings of the current system and presented problems whose wider socioeconomic context cannot be encompassed by the applicable regulatory mechanisms.

My main purpose has been to create a platform by which to deliberate on the need, the possibility, and the necessity of regulatory reform in the field of food safety in Europe. In this concluding chapter, then, I will revisit those observations and approach the issue of regulatory reform options before summarising my findings and recommendations.

1. Do the Current Trends in Regulation Require Reconsideration?

The overarching problem that must first be highlighted, and which has clearly emerged from my empirical study, is the unidirectional regulation of trade issues. The guiding philosophy of market regulation—which is applied systemically and almost uniformly to all types of products, ranging from coal and steel, through cars and computers, to potato chips and cheese—assigns a similar degree of social and economic sensitivity to products of diametrically opposed social and economic characters. Such an approach may have been justified in the early stages of the building of the common market, when market organisation and regulation were the overarching aims of the whole European Community. Now that the EU is different, its relations with the global market have developed. Furthermore, as the awareness of consumers and the increased sensitivity to social issues make the social impact of regulatory decisions even more problematic, such an approach can no longer be justified. The example used in this research—food regulation—illustrates very well the variety of needs and the possible unintended consequences of improvident regulatory unification.

Food safety regulation in Europe has always resulted from a certain type of trade-off, which reflects the current trends of development in EU law and policy, or is negotiated and installed as a response to an immediate need or crisis. During the first decades of its development, European food law seemed to receive very little criticism. This was probably because the market-integration tendencies which it was following were, at the same time, the point of reference against which it was evaluated. Additionally, as the entire integration process was oriented towards 'market-building', hardly any non-market issues were considered. All in all, although means and methods were sometimes discussed, adjudicated or adjusted, the fundamental issues were clear and set.

It was only after the outbreak of the BSE crisis that omissions were first admitted and a change in attitude was expected. The highly advertised 'turn towards consumers' was, at first, expected to solve all the outstanding issues and move food law away from market thinking and into the safety zone. The post-BSE reform, however, although publicised as a total refurbishment of all aspects of food law, turned out instead to be a move from one extreme to another, with many problems left overlooked. Moreover, new developments within as well as outside the EU—in particular, the progress of enlargement—revealed that the European food regulation might lack the necessary flexibility that would enable the accommodation of all new interests and concerns, and thus allow the bigger EU food market to function smoothly and to the satisfaction of both producers and consumers. Various shortcomings of the situation have been highlighted in the literature. Most of it, as discussed above, was centred on the procedural aspects of risk regulation and problems in decision-making processes.

Recently, however, more and more interesting critical voices have questioned the current status of the European food regulation, asking whether the direction of development that the EU food regulation is following is optimal. Before I move on to summarising my ideas on the issue, I would like to present the most interesting and inspiring of those critical positions.

The first novel approach I consider particularly worth mentioning here is the SAFE FOODS Project (Integrated Project SAFE FOODS: 'Promoting Food Safety Through a New Integrated Risk Analysis Approach for Foods'), which was funded by the European Commission under the 6th Framework Programme. The project undertook probably the most comprehensive study of the EU food safety regulation, and published its findings in 2009.[1] It advocated a reform of European food safety regulations that would allow decision-making to include an assessment of 'socio-political ambiguity', so that it takes account of, among other factors, the divergences in individual perceptions of risk, amplification effects in the news and media, as well as social and ethical concerns or political mobilisation. The inclusion of a 'concern assessment' could be achieved through the creation of a concern assessment panel at the European Food Safety Authority, which would possess a specific social science expertise. Concern assessment would be done by means of surveys, focus groups, social science research, hearings of relevant interests and public constituencies, as well as a transdisciplinary commission to analyse social concerns. One of the panel's key purposes would be to arrive at balanced, values-based judgements about the acceptability and tolerability of a given food safety threat or a trade-off analysis of a set of functional equivalents, which would be created using both scientific knowledge as well as political and socioeconomic expertise.

The SAFE FOODS Project itself recognised that theirs is a rather innovative and far-fetched proposal, so they also suggested a minimum basic recommendation: the establishment of an Internet Forum, managed by the European Commission which would facilitate the use of internet for consultation procedures by both EFSA and DG SANCO. The Internet Forum would act as a site for the dissemination of information associated with each of the key stages in the governance process as well as for deliberation.

It is underlined strongly that the objective of concern assessment should not be to provide for interest-representation and conflict-resolution at the assessment stage. Instead, the purpose would be to gather, through a sound scientific exercise, the necessary knowledge of the concerns, expectations and worries that individuals, groups or different cultures may have about a given food safety threat or the cause of the threat, so as to provide those conducting evaluation and management activities with a broader basis of information. The use of the assessment, however, would be restricted in a way that both concern assessment and precautionary assessment would only be required in specific circumstances. More routine cases, on the other hand, would be dealt with using a standard risk assessment procedure, so that the increased capacity is used only in specifically challenging situations.[2]

---

[1] M Dreyer and O Renn (eds), Food Safety Governance: Integrating Science, Precautions and Public Involvement (Springer-Verlag, Berlin Heidelberg 2009); to some the extent similar messages expressed by M Dreyer and O Renn, 'Some Suggestions for a Structured Approach to Participation In Food Risk Governance with a Special Emphasis on the Assessment Management Interface' in E Vos (ed), *European Risk Governance—Its Science, its Inclusiveness and its Effectiveness* (2008) CONNEX Report Series, No. 6, 89–121.

[2] Ibid 3–4.

To conclude, I wish to emphasise the unique position of the SAFE FOOD group in having an involvement with and impact on policy-makers and the EU administration. Going far beyond the academic forum, SAFE FOOD successfully created an all-inclusive consultative group and a thoroughly supported study, and reached out with its results to the key players who might actually have an impact. Thus, although I consider that their postulate overlooks certain essential aspects of the food safety decision-making process, I find their output very impressive. In fact, by presenting a modest reform option and disseminating it to the right audience, the group has managed to turn its limitation into a strength, and has actually, as a result, increased its chances of success.

A second critical voice I wish to remark on here is that of C. Macmaolain,[3] who argues that, in European food regulation, far too much emphasis has lately been placed on safety, and that this has happened at the cost of nutritional considerations. This, of course, can be explained by reference to history, especially to the food crises of the 1990s and the following regulatory trend that aimed to avoid such a situation in the future. Nevertheless, it has led to emphasis being put on 'outbreaks', 'scandals' and 'scares', while actual food-related problems escape any EU regulatory control. This is specifically the case with nutrition-related problems, such as obesity, which in turn contributes to other devastating health problems (heart diseases, blood pressure diseases, cancers and strokes), and which in practice affects a much wider population than the BSE crisis, for instance. Moreover, the nature of EU regulation on free movement makes it impossible for member states to intervene and try to counteract these developments by means of their national legislation. As a consequence, no significant action against nutritional problems or obesity is taken at any level of European governance. Hence, European regulation seems to be missing the point by overemphasising the crisis and ignoring everyday threats to health of consumers. Labelling legislation, Macmaolain argues, will remain impotent in that situation, and he argues that a general modification of the EU's regulatory approach is necessary. He foresees three aspects of such a transformation. Firstly, he suggests that the Commission's decision to cease harmonisation of standards for all food products should be reconsidered. Secondly, he claims that over-regulation of all aspects of the food production process should be relaxed. Thirdly, he advocates a move towards simpler common standards, where, instead of emphasising food safety, the high quality of food and its benefits for health should be underlined.[4]

---

[3] C Macmaolain, *EU Food Law. Protecting Consumers and Health in a Common Market* (Modern Studies in European Law, Hart Publishing, Oxford, Portland Oregon 2007) 12, 14–15, 221–239.

[4] Ibid 15.

What I find particularly interesting in Macmaolain's observations is his criticism of the focus of European activities in the sphere of food regulation. Indeed, I believe the crisis mentality seems to be shifting the European regulatory effort away from some very important aspects of the regulatory process, in particular the negative social consequences of the current approach to regulation. When combined with inability to mediate intervention by the member states in these crucial areas, it can have serious consequences, and it seems that the European regulator is not taking account of this. As a result, the current food regulatory system based on response to crisis and focusing on its anticipation is unable to fulfil its own objectives, allowing many essential problems to escape regulation. The resulting regulatory imbalance can have adverse effects not only for the important task of responding to food crises, but also with the possibly even more critical task of anticipating and preventing deterioration in the quality of the food we are producing and the food we are eating.

Especially given the many new challenges facing the European food safety architecture following the last two enlargements, the current approach should be reconsidered. The irony of the matter is that, while Western Europe still lives with a perception largely shaped by the BSE crisis, it does not perceive that future crises could successfully be avoided if traditional patterns of production and consumption were allowed to remain in place. Instead, EU enlargement might contribute to the weakening of such traditions and thus—paradoxically—to the risk of reoccurrences of crises in the future. Hence, considering those observations, it seems legitimate to suggest that many shortcomings in the EU's food safety regulation could be overcome if a more inclusive concept of food *quality* was placed alongside that of food *safety*.

I will end this section by drawing some conclusions on the basis of the two highly valid and important academic voices referred to above, confronting them with the findings of my research and my reflections presented in this volume. Without a doubt, it has to be emphasised that both SAFE FOOD and Macmaolain's approaches constitute valid steps towards new ways of thinking about food regulation, and its analysis in academic research. They also reflect a new type of bravery in the critical analysis of food regulation. At the same time, I wish to point out that, although the problems depicted by my colleagues are highly relevant, the dilemma of the Europeanisation of food-safety decision-making, as I see it, goes deeper than they show. Both suggestions, for concern assessment as well as for a re-emphasising of the nutritional quality of food, constitute responses to parts of the bigger problem. There are many more such concerns, however, which also deserve reflection and consideration. Among them, the problems of diversity, economic discrepancies and different stages of development of member states, the evolving expectations of modern consumers, the sensitivity of their social attachments and traditions, biodiversity and so on. I hope, however, that the sources quoted above, as well as my own work, will serve as starting points for discussion about the need for a changing of the direction in which the European food regulation is developing.

2. Is Risk-Regulatory Reform Possible … and Desirable?

In researching the meandering paths of the European food-safety regulation, its historical development, its global implications and the new challenges posed by the EU's enlargement, the above questions were always the guide. Is the system as functioning, efficient and coherent as we Europeans would wish it to be? Is it capable of dealing with the challenges we face? Should we simply accept it for what it is, or should we try to steer its development in a more desirable direction? In this volume, I have tried to argue that potentially better directions and solutions should be explored.

In the following paragraphs, I will discuss whether improvement could be achieved with help of the legal techniques and methodologies already used within the European market-regulatory system. I wish to explore the possibilities offered by the regulatory mechanisms analysed in the theoretical framework above, and to establish the reform potential of the system.

Secondly, and although it may seem counterintuitive, having established whether the practical possibilities exist, I will then address questions of the desirability of such reforms, and of the readiness of Europe and Europeans to undertake them.

2.1. *What Options Does the Theoretical Framework Suggest?*

2.1.1. *Mutual Recognition*

Mutual recognition, especially in its modern forms, has proved to be a very efficient self-regulating mechanism of market governance. This section recapitulates the theoretical reflections on mutual recognition, and combines them with empirical observations on its application in Europe, in order to show that this form of regulating diverse markets is worth promoting.

The principle of mutual recognition is an intermediate device that helps to reconcile tensions stemming from regulatory diversity in an integrated market.[5] Its regulatory philosophy is based on the reciprocal acceptance of an equivalence of protection granted by a foreign legal system by different

[5] See JHH Weiler, 'Mutual Recognition, Functional Equivalence and Harmonization in the Evolution of the European Common Market and the WTO' in F Kostoris Padoa Schioppa (ed), *The Principle of Mutual Recognition in the European Integration Process* (Palgrave Macmillan, Hampshire 2005) 25–26.

states participating in an integrated market. Thus, it trespasses the traditional national–international dichotomy, creating a transnational meta-norm that aims to resolve differences in the national legislations of various trade partners. The inherent value written into the principle is, thus, mutual trust among the participants of the integrated market, which leaves room for local variation in means and methods without compromising the protection of the health and safety of consumers. In contemporary circumstances, the automatic application of mutual recognition is relatively rare. Instead, various forms of managed mutual recognition apply, under which states retain some degree of their vestigial powers and some form of control over the recognition process.[6]

The most important benefit of mutual recognition, as presented in my analysis above, is that it is the most sensitive and the least intrusive mechanism of market regulation. Hence, it allows a balance to be retained between the common requirement for protection with the local preferences and circumstances of diverse societies and states. Moreover, the sensitivity of mutual recognition also applies to the economic sphere. Here, mutual recognition allows economies that are more developed and financially stronger to accept higher production costs, relying on their consumers' willingness and ability to pay for the extra quality they will gain, while allowing those states that are less well-off to retain the regulatory stage they can afford. Even more so, it allows less-developed states to take advantage of their specific economic circumstances and make use of lower labour costs or cheaper commodities. Hence, less-developed and poorer states can use those extra benefits for the betterment of their economic performance, instead of being pushed to invest in technologies for which they do not have sufficient resources.

Mutual recognition was identified as reflecting the values of flexibility, sensitivity, openness and inclusiveness. In its modern form, it manages to fulfil its regulatory role of coordinating market regulation without implying uniform regulatory practices. Consequently, it facilitates the avoidance of excessive intrusion into the legal and economic systems of states. Thus, it seems to offer a relevant model for regulatory reform.

It is a pity that in the field of food regulation, where diversity is a particularly precious virtue, the EU seems to be increasingly giving up on mutual recognition. As my empirical study has shown, in the formative decades of the common market, after the *Cassis* judgement, mutual recognition was an important regulatory principle of the EU trade in goods. Gradually, however, trends towards stricter standardisation, and—in many areas—unification of

[6] K Nikolaidis, 'Globalization with Human Faces: Managed Mutual Recognition and the Free Movement of Professionals' in F Kostoris Padoa Schioppa (ed), *The Principle of Mutual Recognition* ... ibid 129–189.

practices, pushed mutual recognition out of the regulatory architecture. There are still areas where mutual recognition applies, but its role in the regulation of the food market is now rather marginal. On the basis of my analysis of the objectives of mutual recognition and its contemporary role in global regulation, it seems that returning to some managed form of mutual recognition could be beneficial to many market sectors. It could guarantee the overall aim of consumer-protection, and at the same time leave room for a variety of methods and processes, all of which would lead to the same—safe—product. Over-standardisation in the field of food regulation frequently leads to unintended developments and produces side-effects of far-reaching impact. In many areas, the relaxation of stringent regulation and an increased reliance on trust between member states could, to my mind, be beneficial to both producers and consumers.

We must also take into account that the last decades of practising European standards have bequeathed a considerable degree of experience and institutional memory. If we allow new member states to practise and learn the tricks of the trade for some time, more trust could be put in producers and their willingness and readiness to deliver safe food. Consequently, a relaxation of legal stringency would be possible.[7] With food safety standards already very well fixed, if inspection mechanisms are kept, some degree of relaxation and a movement towards mutual recognition would not jeopardise the overall safety of European food products. Instead, it would allow Europe to retain its precious diversity of production and consumption patterns, simultaneously allowing member states to make use of their competitive advantage. It could also, as a longer-term consequence, lead to a rediscovery of the link between market regulation and markets and societies, remedying the effects of disembeddedness, and consequently, allowing a gradual withdrawal of this critical regulatory tendency.

2.1.2. *Risk Regulation beyond Science*

I now move to the findings of my research on theory, as well as on the impact of contemporary scientific risk regulation, especially regarding the objectives it is meant to fulfil and the outcomes of its application. As with the section on

[7] As a side remark, a similar development can be observed in food safety management, more specifically in safety-control, where a mutual-trust mechanism,—managed in accordance with the EU's legal provisions and guidelines and resembling the mutual-recognition logic—is applied via the HACCP system of control. Under that system, safety-checking and risk-prevention is performed by the manufacturer; as long as he fulfils the requirements, the presumption exists that his products are safe. Hence, the products enjoy 'trust' on the market, although *ex post* official control still applies and reacts in case of risk-occurrence. The same goes, although in a less stringent form, for the application of Good Hygiene Practice (GHP) and Good Manufacture Practice (GMP).

mutual recognition above, I begin by recapitulating the theoretical findings on risk regulation techniques.

In its archetypical form, risk analysis for the sake of regulation comprises three basic elements: risk assessment, risk management and risk communication. Within this typology, two constitutive phases need distinction: risk assessment, which represents the provision of technical knowledge by scientifically informed specialists, and risk management, which refers to the regulatory decisions taken by politically accountable entities on the basis of the provided assessment and taking into account other valid concerns. As repeatedly emphasised, risk analysis in practice is quite distinct. Firstly, the boundaries between the assessment and the management phases are far from clear. Secondly, and more critically, the management phase does not usually fulfil its assigned role in the process, which is to gather and weigh up the various interests and concerns against the scientific considerations. Instead, it tends to follow the recommendations of scientists, which means that other, non-scientific concerns are often overlooked in the decision-making process. At the same time, science is no longer able to respond impartially and definitively to all the questions put to its scrutiny by regulators. Not only has the universality of science been questioned, but the rapid development of new technologies in food production has also confronted scientists with questions to which they have not always been able to find unanimous answers.

The main criticism towards Europe's risk-regulatory method pertains to its one-dimensional character, which allows technical natural science to dominate regulatory decision-making and leaves it blind to other considerations. Following the logic of science, the European legislators have emphasised the need to improve the quality of the scientific assessment involved in regulatory decision-making, as well as the procedural circumstances of its inclusion, leaving aside the most consequential aspect of the process: the management phase. This naturally strengthened the assessment part of the procedure. Consequently, in the management phase, decision-makers have tended to follow the decisions of risk assessors, which are based solely on science. Thus, science can now become such a strong foundation that risk managers will find it difficult to make arguments that are based on other values and interests, which should ideally be taken into consideration in the regulatory procedure. Among these relevant values we find societal concerns, the social and economic impact of regulation, and consumer preferences. This can create a practice where non-scientific arguments—or perhaps insufficiently scienticised arguments—may not be given due consideration and recognition. Instead, established and traditional science will dominate the decision-making process to such a high degree that it becomes its only overriding rationale, despite the fact that decisions must also be made about problems that have not been exhaustively addressed by traditional science.

Naturally, this phenomenon has far-reaching consequences for market regulation, especially in such a science-intensive yet culturally sensitive area as food regulation. Risk regulation, as much as any aspect of the market, must be embedded in the social structure that gave rise to it and that contextualises its existence and development. Disconnecting risk regulation from its social basis causes a gradual disembedding of the market in which it is exercised, which in effect deprives it of social legitimacy and is generally detrimental.

In the light of my study of the application of risk analysis in the European context, one can see that the current narrow approach to risk regulation, which relies solely on science, has proved to be tainted with a number of deficiencies and concerns. Not only has science been shown to lack the qualities it was believed to possess, but the modern problems and new developments of the European common market have also brought about new concerns and problems, to which science is unable to adequately respond. Consequently, the continued application of the current approach throws into question whether the European system of food regulation can respond to the evolving challenges of the EU market and society—that is, whether it can achieve its set regulatory objectives. This aspect of the problem is emphasised by the fact that many European consumers are no longer interested only in the scientifically proven aspects of food safety. Conscious consumers now want to make choices based on other criteria, such as food quality, ecology, or animal friendliness. Some of these modern consumers' considerations are not even food-related, but are meant to promote other non-food objectives such as the greater good in international relations, fair trade, or the protection of green agriculture or biodiversity.

The Polish GMO case described above illustrates a very interesting bias with regard to the European policy of relying on science in regulatory matters. Here, Europe seems to be using double-standards. The EU is ready to go beyond scientific arguments when defending its position in transatlantic trade disputes against conflicting WTO countries, such as in the hormones and GMOs cases. At the same time, it keeps using the good old 'no new scientific expertise was provided' argumentation against its own undisciplined members, without even looking at the non-scientific argumentation.

It is promising, therefore, to see that movements towards greater inclusiveness have appeared, and are attempting to attract the attention of policymakers. The SAFE FOOD project, referred to above, is a prime example of such activity. I am convinced that it is necessary to reconsider the balance of concerns currently taken into account in European risk regulation, and that a discussion on the matter will have to take place eventually. It will then be for the policy-makers to decide what balance of incentives they want for Europe. The scheme presented by the SAFE FOOD is just one of many possibilities of accommodating non-scientific considerations in the regulatory process. It is important to point out, however, that from a legislative perspective, widening the scope of considerations in risk decision-making is possible, and may even be necessary, in order to live up to the requirements of the regulatory model.

What seems to be more complicated, however, is how to strengthen the risk management part of the regulatory procedure. This, I believe, is the biggest and the most important challenge, if Europe wants to credibly rely on risk regulation in the decision-making processes. The analysis of how to achieve this objective would make for a separate dissertation, so I will limit my observations here to a couple of points. Firstly, as the *Meroni* doctrine impedes the use of the agency solution for management purposes, this option, which seems administratively the easiest, must be ruled out. A realistic scenario must be based on the use of comitology.

Although efforts to improve the management of committees have, so far, produced rather limited results it is relevant to point out the existence of such a possibility in the EU framework. Even if I have expressed scepticism about the developments under the 'comitology' tag, I do think it has potential, if only the political will is strong enough. Again, in my opinion, it is the management phase of the risk-regulatory process which must be strengthened, and it is there where the various regulatory values should be weighed and balanced. This, in fact, is also a rationale for the comitology system of governance. It is reasonable, then, to assume that comitology committees should be able to confront the challenges of the improved management system and allow the inclusion of all types of valid interests and values in the regulatory process. The fact that this does not happen nowadays creates doubt that any legislative reform would be able to change what seems mostly to be an outcome of malpractice in the functioning of the procedures. Still, this, in my view, remains the optimal direction for the necessary future improvements to the application of the risk regulation model in Europe.

2.1.3. *Standardisation*

Standardisation is an important element of the new wave of voluntary self-constraint regulatory mechanisms, which are meant to provide a minimum level of uniformity and thus contribute to improved market efficiency. Standardisation emerged as a response to the profusion of new technologies as well as the growing dynamics of market conditions. In demanding transnational circumstances, such a coordinative private–public regulatory exercise offers a wide range of advantages.

Firstly, as it operates in an environment of advanced expertise and technical knowledge, it can rely on these to a larger extent than any public institution. Simultaneously, by operating closer to the stakeholders, standardisation can be more responsive to their needs, and be more flexible and adjustable in changing circumstances. Finally, as a private form of rulemaking, standardisation is less formalised and can therefore be expected to be more efficient.

Simultaneously, standardisation raises a number of important concerns. Firstly, its legitimacy is questionable. In fact it is contested whether delegating responsibility for the safety of citizens to private organisations can be accepted at all. Contemporarily, however, public involvement in the overall standardisation process diminishes the relevance of these concerns. Secondly, questions can be raised concerning the notion of the 'voluntariness' of standards. The notion indicates that standards are free to be observed or disregarded. In practice, however, when a society places a high value on conformity, and when a considerable part of it accepts a common standard, the rest will be almost automatically expected to follow; those who insist on diverging will, sooner or later, find themselves disadvantaged. Hence, a standard adopted voluntarily by a group of interested parties will become much less voluntary when it is implemented successfully.[8] Therefore, despite the possible first impression, the objective that standards pursue is in fact unification.

In transnational cases, such common standards are often imposed on less-developed countries without regard to their socioeconomic situation. This can have very far-reaching consequences for the markets and economies of those states, which often have no say in standard-setting and no resources for their implementation. If standards are unilaterally imposed on these poorer states without offering them some degree of moderation or support, the consequences may be twofold. The states might choose to not comply with the standards and thus risk trade restrictions, or they might implement standards that are against their national economic rationality at the cost of other sectors of the economy and its citizens.

International trade organisations such as the WTO and the EU justify their strong regulatory reliance on standards by referring to the duty to ensure that all competitors are subjected to an equal regulatory burden. They claim that standards based on universal scientific principles create such level playing field. This claim, however, must be questioned and the research presented in this volume provides contrary observations.

In view of theoretical observations as well as the empirical study, harmonised standards can only lead to the creation of regulatory homogeneity on a

[8] Compare CD Sullivan, *Standards and Standardization. Basic Principles and Application* (Marcel Dekker, New York 1983) 8–10.

limited scale. This is primarily due to the fact that international regulatory standards are always embedded in local social, economic and institutional circumstances. Moreover, externally imposed standards can often function as 'Trojan horses', entering a regulatory environment and a local set of conditions, and producing unintended side-effects.[9] This is because international standards are more than just scientifically developed technical rules of market organisation; they also intervene in particular local societal and economic situations and attempt to regulate ethical market behaviours. Hence, markets created by standards are, in fact, different from one place to another, depending on the circumstances in which they are implemented. Thus, they create many unique regulatory landscapes instead of one uniform regulatory environment.

From an economic point of view, the prospect of the creation of a level playing field for all competitors in the standardised market is also an illusion. Standards implemented in different locations impose categorically unequal burdens, creating costs that are significantly different for different producers, depending on the specific circumstances in which they operate. The long-term effects of such developments, both economic and social, should definitely be considered.

It is argued that the application of contemporary standardisation in the European context can, in certain situations, turn out to be questionable. One cannot deny that standardisation is very efficient in securing uniformity throughout a diversified market, and that the legislative means for its implementation in Europe facilitates straightforward compliance-checking. I suggest, however, that uniformity is not the best direction for the contemporary European product market. During the stage of market-building, standardisation was definitely a very welcome and effective regulatory tool and it was useful in coordinating European consumer protection levels. It does, however, have far-reaching economic implications for the weaker participants of the market, which should ideally be considered when establishing standardisation as a regulatory philosophy. Furthermore, by imposing unifying conditions on production processes, it can significantly affect the landscape of the product market, eliminating diversity and limiting consumers' choices. When applied in translational settings such as the EU without any countervailing mechanisms that would negotiate their side-effects for less-developed trade partners, standards can contribute to a gradual disembeddedness of market regulation, applying common solutions in dramatically different sets of circumstances, which were often not considered when developing the standard in question.

---

[9] EC Dunn, 'Trojan Pig: Paradoxes of Food Safety Regulation' (2003) 35 *Environment and Planning A* 1494.

All those aspects, taken together, imply that the use of standardisation as the main mechanism for regulating the European common market should be reconsidered, since the diversity of conditions and traditions in Europe tend to allow the negative effects of standardisation to flourish; in the longer term, they may even transcend its benefits. This is especially the case when a market sector becomes over-standardised. As my evolutionary analysis aimed to show, in many respects this seems to be the case with food-safety regulation. There are several recent developments that, in my opinion, encourage a fresh discussion on the use of standardisation in Europe. These are the effects of the last two enlargements and the impact that stringent EU standards have had on new member states, the growing significance of the idea of European solidarity, as well as a series of developments at the global level.

In the new member states, as is well illustrated by the Polish example, the stringent European standards, which were developed for the old members and with respect to their specific circumstances, may in fact lead to the realisation of the worst-case scenario analysed above. It has to be kept in mind, in this context, that the economies of many of the new member states are significantly different than those in Western Europe. Hence, a different reaction to the introduction of standards developed by the West and for the West could reasonably be expected. Moreover, after the 2007 enlargement, the new member states amount to twelve, which, compared to the old fifteen, makes for a significant share of the common market and should definitely not be marginalised.

Following the same line of thought, some academics have suggested that some side-effects of standards on the economies of the new member states were, to a certain extent, comprehended, if not welcomed. Dunn, among others, observes that the introduction in local rural economies of global agribusiness, which is favoured by international standards, threatens not only the agri-food producers and processors directly involved, but also the entire village communities. This is because foreign businesses impose vertical integration, which is their global practice, and thus pose challenges to the livelihood of rural communities, especially in developing countries. Dunn indicates that the EU was well aware of the effect that food safety regulations would have on economic competition within the Polish agri-food sector. She claims, moreover, that it was clear that they were meant to work as 'Trojan pigs' and facilitate a restructuring of the Polish food sector. In conjunction with the structure of SAPARD, this shows that the EU was promoting the consolidation of the Polish food industry and facilitating the promotion of larger plants and businesses.[10]

---

[10] Ibid 1499–1500.

SPS standards have been introduced in the new member states as a means to reduce or eliminate the risks of food poisoning and food-borne diseases. This, however, can be perceived as mainly a rhetorical device, offering both a problem and then an answer to it. At the same time, the SPS standards fulfil the role of 'placing consideration of the effects of those standards in wider socio-economic context out of the bounds of discussion', thus limiting deliberation on these issues.[11]

In the context of the enlargement, the problem should be regarded through yet another perspective: that of unequal treatment. As Holmes points out, accession entails that Western Europe exports its health, safety, quality and environmental standards to the East, which, although appearing neutral, is in fact prejudicially in favour of Western producers. Not only do they have better access to knowhow and the resources for the necessary investment, but they are also substantially in compliance to begin with.[12]

Looking at the problem through the lens of the historical development of food safety regulation in Europe, it can be noted that in countries such as Poland, the introduction of SPS standards may, in fact, have contradictory effects. The BSE crisis is a good example in that regard. Paradoxically, Poland's poverty and small-scale farming practices have acted as a shield that has protected the country against the spread of BSE, which was caused primarily due to the industrial practice of feeding animals with commercially produced feedstuffs containing bovine derivatives. In small Polish holdings, which constitute the great majority of its national bovine production, farmers simply could not afford such feeding practices and mainly fed cows on grass and hay collected on their own land. The forced introduction of stringent EU rules may lead to the elimination of small farmers from the market, with them replaced by large industrial cattle producers who primarily use commercially produced feedstuffs, which were the source of the disease. Additionally, the quality, as well as the health and nutritional value of the meat, decrease significantly. When one thinks of the economic and social costs of such a transformation, one wonders whether the implementation of such standards is really in the interests of Polish society.[13]

There are a couple of potential methods of dealing with (over-)standardisation in Europe that can be considered. These range from the elimination of part of the regulatory burden, to the supporting of standards implementation with additional measures that might level out their socioeconomic implications. Here, a parallel to the global developments, with special regard to the

[11] Ibid 1501.

[12] S Holmes, 'A European Doppelstaat?' (2003) 17 *East European Politics and Societies* 112.

[13] Compare similar observations in K Krause, 'European Union Directives and Poland: A Case Study' (2006) 27 *University of Pennsylvania Journal of International Economic Law* 164–194.

issue of the clash between developed and developing counties, could be very helpful.

2.2. *Which Directions of Reform Can We Conceive of in Europe?*

In the following paragraphs I try to identify, on the basis of the findings of the previous sections, suggestions for the possible direction of the development of European regulation in the field of foodstuffs.

Through the analysis of the application of the three regulatory instruments that build my theoretical framework, it is possible to discern the tendencies of regulatory development and to predict where they may lead. Thus, I would like to speculate what these tendencies are and how they might be directed and diverged. I am not trying here to generally criticise any of the three regulatory approaches analysed in this volume. What I would like to point out, rather, is the proportion of their use in European market regulation, and consequently the overall direction of regulatory development.

All three regulatory mechanisms that were theoretically analysed and empirically traced in this volume serve different purposes, promote different values and have different focal points. Most probably, all three have, at some time, been necessary in order to secure safe food for consumers and an undisturbed market for producers in the EU. It is important, however, to be aware of the implications and consequences of the application of each one. Analysis from that perspective would allow them to be applied in situations where they will bring more gain than pain. It also helps to avoid situations where one of them becomes the primary regulatory tendency, which could lead to its automatic application with regard to sectors or problems that might not in fact benefit from the regulatory approach it offers. I have, therefore, suggested a two-dimensional analysis, which looks at regulatory solutions both in terms of their theoretical value-weigh, as well as their application in concrete cases. In my opinion, the outlook offered by such an analysis suggests that developing a better framework would be possible simply by balancing the use of the available regulatory mechanisms in accordance with the needs of a given sector, paying special attention to the values and objectives of regulation. From that perspective, my evolutionary analysis of the actual regulatory structure was intended to show whether there are any signs pointing in the direction of an 'opening-up of the system', or whether, on the contrary, the *status quo* is strictly adhered to despite internal and external developments. It was also hoped that it may allow the building of some analogies and give grounds for speculation about the prospects of EU food-safety regulation in that respect.

The analysis of the EU food-legislative framework undertaken here has aimed to show, *inter alia*, how the impact of the three regulatory mechanisms developed and shifted over time. It shows clearly that all three instruments are present in the current regulatory framework for food, and have guided its development at different times. The following summary will concentrate, first, on mutual recognition and standardisation and their interplay in the EU market regulation. Secondly, it will look at scientific risk regulation and its role in decision-making.

Evolutionarily, the emergence of mutual recognition constituted the first significant turn towards value-inclusiveness in market regulation. The safeguard it offered with regard to both consumer protection and diversity created an interesting regulatory equilibrium. Mutual recognition has played a very important role in the regulation of the food market, and due to its interpretation in ECJ jurisprudence it has developed over time to take on a more modern—'managed'—form. The role of mutual recognition was seriously diminished with the growing trend towards unification following the BSE crisis. More and more areas that had previously been left to the member states became Europeanised. At the same time fields that had previously been covered by directives, leaving some room for national manoeuvring, became more and more unified as directives were gradually replaced by regulations. In the current legislative scheme, both mutual recognition and harmonisation/standardisation coexist.

There is no official Commission document specifying what percentage of the food market is harmonised and how much is covered by mutual recognition. According to the Commission official who responded to my query, such a percentage would be extremely difficult to calculate, since most food products are at least partly subject to harmonised rules and partly subject to mutual recognition.[14] This implies that, for most food products that do not fall within the scope of Annex I of the EC Treaty (now TFEU), one should calculate the value of the part of any food product covered by harmonised rules and the value of the part subject to mutual recognition. Nevertheless, although quantifying the 'market share' of both regulatory methods in question seems difficult, the initial analysis shows a growing dominance of standardisation. In my view, if we could only imagine a more flexible approach to market regulation that allowed the selective use of those mechanisms, a much better regulatory balance could be achieved. In practice, this would mean retaining standardisation in those market sectors where unification is the overarching goal, and where there are no sufficiently strong conflicting values and objectives that would collide with or override the benefits of unification. On the other hand, in sectors where the longstanding practice of the common market has allowed market participants

[14] The response quoted here is a result of email exchanges with various Commission officials employed by DG Industry and DG SANCO. I wish to point out here that the context of the conversation implies that no distinction is made between harmonisation and standardisation, and both regulatory techniques are treated under the tag of 'harmonisation'.

to gain enough experience in adhering to the core principles and practices of consumer safety, the stringency of the regulation could be relaxed, allowing more space for local considerations.

Similar logic could apply in sectors where existing national, regional or professional rules provide a sufficient guarantee of consumer safety, and where, being tailor-made for the locality in question, they do not disturb other relevant social and economic objectives. In such cases, unifying standardisation would in fact be counterproductive, destroying the existing equilibrium and creating a new fictitious state of affairs that does not respond to local concerns and which, thus, fails the embeddedness test. With regard to such situations, one could imagine that, instead of imposing a supranational unifying regulation, it would instead be advisable to resort to some form of mutual recognition. Such a selective approach would open up the system to more flexibility, and provide the ability to respect other legitimate concerns in regulation, at least in those sectors of the market that would not suffer from a lack of stringent uniform standards. I believe that, within the realm of food regulation, considerable room for such flexibility could be found.

Finally, having summarised the analysis and reform suggestions with regard to the first two regulatory mechanisms under scrutiny, let us move on to the third: scientific risk regulation. Its link with the previous two cannot be overlooked, in particular with regard to standardisation, where both regulations as well as standards are based on risk analysis. The role of risk analysis in the regulatory framework for food in the EU has also evolved over time, peaking as a result of the reforms following the BSE crisis. Although its role in the decision-making processes has always been significant in fields involving consumers' health and safety, the post-crisis reform emphasised the significance of the reliance on science and strengthened the foundation of its use in regulation. This was additionally highlighted by the creation of the EFSA, which provides scientific assessment of cases of various degrees of specificity, ranging from the approval of substances to the shape of new policies and legislation. Paradoxically, the legal reinforcement of risk analysis as a method in regulatory decision-making about food happened, in my opinion, precisely when the challenges facing the system began to outgrow the potential of the method. As I have tried to argue above, reliance only on classically framed natural science is no longer optimal for decision-making in contemporary European food regulation, because it cannot respond to the growing concerns of the sector and the market as a whole. It is, however, still an important regulatory tool, and in many instances it is probably the only possible solution for regulatory problem-solving.

I suggest, therefore, that a reform of the method should be considered. The reform should concentrate on strengthening the management phase of the risk analysis process, in order for it to be able to counteract the outcomes of the already-strengthened risk assessment phase, in cases where other legitimate values should be considered alongside science. This is especially important in cases where other legitimate concerns suggest different solutions than those implied by the scientific assessment, or when there is no credible outcome from the scientific process—for example, in the case of new technologies, when traditional natural science is as yet unable to provide the regulators with an unequivocal response to problems in question.

In conclusions, my analysis suggests that the necessary regulatory solutions are in place, but it is the challenge of finding the right equilibrium that remains to be solved. All three regulatory mechanisms reviewed here have their pros and cons when applied to an integrated market. They prove useful in some situations, while they tend to produce negative effects in others. Hence, if the choice and intensity of their application in different contexts were reconsidered, it could lead to positive developments and guide the common market closer to the ideal of embeddedness. It would allow a better balancing of regulatory intervention in the market in response to the needs of the concrete regulatory field, and, consequently, might perhaps help rediscover a middle way between *unity* and *diversity*. At the same time, it would facilitate better reflection of the values that are considered in regulatory decision-making, which may perhaps open up the possibility of including other legitimate socioeconomic considerations that currently escape scrutiny and are not properly mirrored in the regulatory process.

2.3. *Is Europe Ready for Such a Transition?*

Having established that, in theory, regulatory solutions that could enhance value-inclusiveness in the system are available, I wish now to consider whether they could come into use in practice in the foreseeable future. The rhetorical and somewhat provocative question posed in the title of this section cannot, of course, be answered here in any straightforward manner. What I would like to provide, however, are some concluding reflections on current regulatory developments in Europe and on possible directions of future progress. Thus, the objective is instead to gather ideas for my speculations than to provide concrete answers, which seem to be of a political rather than a legal nature.

In order to find material for my speculative exercise, I will go beyond the realm of food law and look at general developments in market regulation, and at reform initiatives in other sectors and disciplines. As already previously mentioned, there have been important developments in some areas of EU legislation, that point towards a relaxation of strict central regulation, and towards increased responsibility for and trust in market participants. At the same time, in some fields there are signs of gradual opening-up towards a more flexible and pluralistic approach.

Firstly, I would like to look briefly at areas where a relaxation of a previously instituted stringency can be observed. A good example can be seen in the competition law, where, under the new scheme, the enforcement of competition issues has been handed back to the member states under the assumption that, after over four decades of experience under the centralised scheme, they are now able to manage those matters themselves, and are themselves able to guarantee the proper functioning of the system.[15] Although, in this case, it is merely a question of implementation, I believe it does mark an important tendency towards decentralisation and more trust, which is exactly what I am looking for in the case of food.

Secondly, it has to be remembered that, in increasingly more areas of the European common market, some modest expressions of concern about inclusion of socioeconomic considerations can be observed both in the policy-making forum as well as within the academic debate. This applies, mainly, in areas where the interplay of science and technology with human lives is the strongest, such as in biotechnology regulation referred to above, novel foods regulation,[16] as well as in nanotechnology.[17]

Another interesting field, in this respect, is sustainable development, where socioeconomic concerns would logically seem to deserve substantial attention. In fact, in the 2006 renewed Strategy for sustainable development in Europe the Council seemed to pave the way towards greater openness.[18] It may be that relevance of socioeconomic homogeneity became apparent due to the ineffectiveness of some existing mechanisms that were not adequately adhered to by new member states, such as emissions control. It was, therefore, surprising

---

[15] Council Regulation (EC) 1/2003 of 16 December 2002 on the implementation of the rules on competition laid down in Article 81 and 82 of the Treaty [2003] OJ L 1/1, in particular the first paragraphs of the preamble.

[16] Commission (EC), Communication from the Commission to the Council, the European Parliament, the Economic and Social Committee and the Committee of the Regions. Life Sciences and Biotechnology—A Strategy for Europe, COM (2002) 27 final, 23 January 2002, especially 8 and 11–14.

[17] Commission (EC), Communication from the Commission to the Council, the European Parliament, and the Economic and Social Committee. Nanosciences and Nanotechnologies: An Action Plan for Europe 2005–2009, COM (2005) 243 final, 7 June 2005, in particular 8–9, as well as International Risk Governance Council (IRGC), 'Policy Brief: Appropriate Risk Governance Strategies for Nanotechnology Applications in Food and Cosmetics', Geneva 2009 <http://www.irgc.org/IMG/pdf/IRGC_Report_FINAL_For_Web.pdf> accessed 25 May 2011.

[18] Council of the European Union, Review of the EU Sustainable Development Strategy (EU SDS)—Renewed Strategy, 10917/06, 26 June 2006, 6–7.

that this direction of development was not reflected in the 2009 version of the Strategy.[19]

Eventually, and probably most importantly, the first indicators of flexibility awareness were observed in the debate on agricultural regulations.[20] In the Commission Communication on 'Health check' of the CAP reform, a very promising although still theoretical option is suggested: that in one particular sector—supply management and set-aside scheme—the current regulatory scheme could be replaced 'by locally targeted RD measures taking account that agri-environmental conditions are heterogeneous in space'.[21] I am aware that one swallow does not make a summer, but the mere admittance by the Commission of the possibility of a geographical diversification of instruments due to the heterogeneity of local conditions can be taken as an important step in the right direction and, at least, as an indication of the birth of its awareness that new solutions are necessary in response to new challenges.

Last but not least, also within the realm of food regulation, voices can be heard that are advocating more openness and inclusiveness in the system, so that it takes account of valid socioeconomic concerns. Some of the proponents of this direction of reforms have been referred to earlier in this volume, and the most advanced, the SAFE FOOD project, received detailed attention. I would like to emphasise here again the importance of all those initiatives, as they indicate the need for transformation as well as the growing awareness of this need among European academics and, to some extent, among policy-makers.

Finally, it is necessary to refer to the areas where a certain degree of inclusion of socioeconomic elements or diversity was foreseen in the reformed legislative framework. The most important examples are the new Commission proposal on member states' authority to decide nationally on GMO cultivation, and the reform of the regulation of chemicals that is embedded in the new REACH system. Both were discussed earlier in this volume and both should be considered as milestones in the systemic opening up. The reform of GMO regime is still in the proposal stage, but the REACH regulation is already adopted and in the phase of implementation, so can be considered a step already taken. Might we see it as an indication of a rise of new tendency in European legislation? Might we use REACH as an inspiring example for food regulation?

---

[19] Commission (EC), Communication from the Commission to the European Parliament, the Council, the European Economic and Social Committee and the Committee of the Regions. Mainstreaming Sustainable Development into EU Policies: 2009 Review of the European Union Strategy for Sustainable Development, COM (2009) 400 final, 24 July 2009.

[20] Commission (EC), Communication from the Commission to the European Parliament and the Council. Preparing for the 'Health Check' of the CAP reform, COM (2007) 722 final, 20 November 2007.

[21] Ibid 7.

I for one would definitely like to see chemicals regulation used as an example for food regulation, at least in the sense that it manifests a possible direction of regulatory development in the new, more challenging, post-enlargement circumstances. It should alert us to the need to embed regulatory framework in a complex setting of social and economic conditions, which both affect and are affected by regulatory decision-making. If, however, the path set by the chemicals regulation were to be followed for the foodstuffs framework, it would be necessary to increase the framework's ability to accommodate a wider range of socioeconomic concerns, and to look for possible ways of rebalancing the system. The chemicals regulation has proved that there are technical possibilities to introduce such an inclusive approach within the realm of European market regulation that conform to the common market rules and do not jeopardise the impartiality of the science-based regulatory approach. Irrespective of the varying characteristics of the legal framework in the case of chemicals compared to foodstuffs, the transplantation of some regulatory mechanisms could be considered, at least with regard to foodstuffs that require pre-market approval, such as novel foods.

It has to be admitted that the greater variety and complexity of foodstuffs regulation, which is a result of the wider and more differentiated nature and usage of products, probably justifies the concerns and doubts about such a cognitive opening-up of the system. Fears also exist that a systematic reform of a large volume of legislation would be necessary. In my view, however, such reform does not have to entail a revolution. It can very well be taken step by step, as with many previous EU law developments. Probably, novel foods would be the best place to start—not only because the mechanisms used in the chemicals regulation could most easily be imitated due to the nature of the pre-market approval procedures, but also because it is one of the areas with the clearest sensitivity to social and economic implications. Hence, especially now, when growing demands of the larger and increasingly diversified European market are becoming more explicit, we may wonder whether it is the legal framework that does not allow the introduction of an inclusive approach, or whether it is more a question of a lack of the political will. Considering Europe's experiences with the chemicals regulation, it seems that it may be the latter. This brings me to a further question: is the political will lacking because the socioeconomic implications in the case of food are not considered relevant, or is it rather because they are considered too problematic?

Before I conclude, a couple of general observations should be made, which pertain to the crucial question about the readiness of European society for a transition towards the inclusion of socioeconomic concerns in regulation. Again, this is not a legal question, but I am allowing myself to engage in this type of speculation in order to place my considerations in another, wider debate. What I am referring to, in particular, is the current state of understanding and application of European solidarity. Naturally, for me as a lawyer, the main source of ideas about the state of affairs of *solidarity* in the EU is an analysis of developments in the legal sphere. Unfortunately, however, this approach offers a rather pessimistic picture of the situation. Apart from some progress in GMO and chemicals regulations, which have, to varying degree, been reflected in legislative process, all the other examples reviewed in this section should be understood as more or less structured wishful thinking. Hence, their impact on the applicable reality of regulation is relatively minimal.

The same can be said about developments within the judicial sphere, which are mirrored in the ECJ jurisprudence and also do not give much cause for optimism. A number of judgements, beginning with the famous *Viking*[22] and *Laval*,[23] and followed by *Rüffert*[24] and *Luxembourg*,[25] have raised serious concern about the ECJ's approach towards sensitivity and diversity, as well as its general readiness to face the challenges and concerns of the new 'post-enlargement' EU. Although they concern a different regulatory field, those cases illustrate a phenomenon that has distinct similarities with the problems I am analysing in the field of food. More specifically, they show a striking lack of respect for diverse national circumstances, in a situation where a supranational legal system is incapable of offering a regulatory alternative.[26] The judgements also conceal a kind of misconception of *togetherness* and *solidarity*, blindly applying the logic of protecting market freedom in a situation where, due to the interplay of economic and social concerns, solidarity cannot be understood so simplistically and one-sidedly.

Bearing in mind these findings, and my speculations, in the concluding sentences I will return to the question posed in the title: is Europe ready for such a transition? As the question is meant to be rhetorical, I will limit myself to saying that it should definitely be ready. In fact, it is already slightly delayed. With the increasing diversity that Europe has developed since 2004, the consistent application of unified solutions will inevitably lead to a further disembedding of market regulation, and will distance it from the societies it is meant to serve.

---

[22] C-438/05 *International Transport Workers' Federation and Finnish Seamen's Union v Viking Line ABP and OÜ Viking Line Eesti* [2007] ECR I-10779.

[23] C-341/05 *Laval un Partneri Ltd v Svenska Byggnadsarbetareförbundet* [2007] ECR I-11767.

[24] Case C-346/06 *Dirk Rüffert v. Land Niedersachsen* [2008] ECR I-1989.

[25] Case C-319/06 *Commission v. Grand Duchy of Luxembourg* [2008] ECR I-4323.

[26] The problem is thoroughly and convincingly analysed in Ch Joerges and F Rödl, 'Informal Politics, Formalised Law and the "Social Deficit" of European Integration: Reflections after the Judgments of the ECJ in *Viking* and *Laval*' (2009) 15 *European Law Journal* 1–19. See specifically this quintessential statement on 18: 'In view of the obstacles to the establishment of a comprehensive European welfare state, the respect for the common European legacy of *Sozialstaatlichkeit* seems to require both the acceptance of European diversity and judicial self-restraint whenever European economic freedoms come into conflict with national welfare state traditions.'

Consequently, compliance problems will start piling up, causing more reasons for social discontent. Last but not least, if the trend towards unification continues, Europe risks a further loss of diversity, which will be extremely difficult to restore. In the light of my analysis, I believe that measures to protect diversity, value-inclusiveness and a balance of regulatory objectives can be found within the European framework. The examples quoted above show, additionally, that the technical possibilities are not so difficult to develop and apply. I am aware that any acknowledgement of the relevance of socioeconomic concerns in food regulation will open a Pandora's box and initiate a whole new wave of debate. The fact that it is problematic, however, should not mean that it is better to disregard it. Retaining the status quo will probably cause a further disembedding, and will distance market regulation from the market itself as well as from the societies which it serves. Delaying reform until another grand crisis occurs is, of course, not very helpful—especially since, this time, the crisis may be much less spectacular, but much more polygonal.

3. On Food and Europe—Closing Remarks

Many various ideas for the targeted development of European agriculture and food production can be imagined. In my opinion, supported by the research presented in this volume, the most important thing is to avoid applying a unified solution to the many agri-food sectors in the many different regions and societies of Europe. The goal should be, rather, to promote diverse directions of development, which might be adjusted to the needs and the capabilities of those various localities. It seems counterintuitive, for example, to try to congregate and industrialise Eastern European agri-food production, in order to apply to it a Western-developed model of regulation. Not only would such project be bound to meet with opposition and non-compliance, which are costly and inefficient. It could also be considered biased, implicitly favouring Western producers and disregarding the needs and specificity of the new member states. More importantly, however, such a regulatory attitude destroys traditional and well-functioning patterns, which have been established for centuries and which often require only a few small adjustments in order to comply with the core European requirements of consumer protection. It is sad, then, that this seems to be the direction that Europe has chosen and continues to implement.

On the other hand, at the receiving end of the food chain, consumers in regions where traditional production patterns are a part of their heritage have tended to oppose moves towards industrialisation and technological influence. Opposition towards GM farming in Poland and other new member states is a case in point. The fairly good condition of Polish farming, which has been achieved despite the accession shock, the costs of restructuring and the disadvantaged conditions of participation in the CAP, can be seen as an illustration of this tendency among consumers. It would thus seem logical and beneficial to retain traditional patterns in the new member states, without reproducing the policies that have been implemented in Western Europe, but rather limiting their scope to industrialised farming in the old member states. Moreover, it has to be borne in mind that farming and production patterns constitute an important element of societal construction. This is especially the case in countries where agriculture still employs a large segment of the population. Any intervention in those established patterns creates a serious risk to the stability of social organisation, and in the longer term can have important consequences for family patterns, demographic structures as well as the labour market.

Small, family-operated farms and food-production enterprises, which often use natural and organic methods, are now enjoying a return to favour in many developed countries of the West. Consequently, conscious and programmed steps are being taken to establish such units anew, often with heavy state financial support. In many EU member states, especially the recently acceded ones, such farms and establishments have for generations been the norm rather than the exception. Under the current European regulatory regime, however, such units have precious little chance of surviving, mainly due to the introduction of stringent norms and production standards, as well as to external pressures to change the structure of local agriculture and food. The question arises: why destroy these traditional small farms and family businesses, and then, in a couple of years or maybe decades, when the need for organic and differentiated production becomes more prominent and gains more supporters, have to establish special European support schemes in order to bring them back through regulation. Such schemes are often difficult and costly, and tend to offer a limited chance of effectiveness. Therefore, instead of risking a need for such a solution, would it not be more reasonable to act now and try to prevent the need from arising at all?

The complexity and long-term effect of the problems I have discussed are far grander than what we are used to considering. To show just one more of those aspects, let me place my analysis in the context of the wider debate on biodiversity. In order to provide an illustrative example, let me ask a provocative question: does the fact that McIntosh is the most productive and pest-resistant apple variety mean that we should give up on cultivating all the other less-yielding but more characteristic varieties? The intuitive answer would, of course, be negative, as it does not present us with a welcomed scenario. The EU agricultural and food policy, however, seems to be developing in exactly that direction, and apples are just a small and trivial example. The promotion of large-scale agriculture, as well as the unification of production methods in the name of consumer safety and economic efficiency, are leading to a gradual restructuring of production patterns towards 'more of the same'. This, especially in countries whose production is largely dependent on foreign investment, may lead to a reduction in the variety of species traditionally cultivated and the replacement of them with more universal and more standardised varieties. Additionally, with the increasing use of GMOs, whose impact on the environment is still uncertain, all this might, to take a long perspective, pose a significant threat to biodiversity. Although the thought may seem far-fetched or exaggerated, the tendency has in fact been noticed by scientists; the figures, in Europe as well as elsewhere, are alarming.[27]

Thus, it is advisable to let food and Europe develop harmoniously, side by side, creating the necessary legal guarantees in order to protect the market and consumers, but at the same time preserving diversity and variety, and the way that these reflect the uniqueness of the different regions and societies within the EU. This will allow the EU to stay true to its founding notion of 'unity in diversity'. It will also allow European food products to survive and maintain the wealth of their traditions and circumstances, because although we are definitely not facing a Europe without food, we may be facing *food* without *Europe*.

[27] According to the FAO, it is estimated that about three-quarters of the genetic diversity found in agriculture has been lost over the last century, and the genetic decline continues. See, for example, FAO, The State of the World's Plant Genetic Resources for Food and Agriculture, Rome, 1997; see also the Convention on Biological Diversity website, available at <http://www.cbd.int/agro> accessed 27 May 2011.

BIBLIOGRAPHY

A) Documents

a) *EU Documents*

Regulations

Regulation 25/62 on the financing of the common agricultural policy, OJ *30, 20.4.1962;*

Council Regulation 2092/91/EEC of 24 June 1991 on organic production of agricultural products and indications referring thereto in agricultural products and foodstuffs, OJ L 198, 22.7.1991;

Regulation 258/97/EC of the European Parliament and of the Council of 27 January 1997 concerning novel foods and novel food ingredients, OJ L 43, 14.2.1997;

Council Regulation 1257/1999/EC of 17 May 1999 on support for rural development from the European Agricultural Guidance and Guarantee Fund (EAGGF) and amending and repealing certain Regulations, OJ L 160, 26.6.1999;

Council Regulation 1259/1999/EC of 17 May 1999 establishing common rules for direct support schemes under the common agricultural policy, OJ L 160, 26.6.1999;

Regulation 178/2002/EC of the European Parliament and of the Council of 28 January 2002 laying down the general principles and requirements of food law, establishing the European Food Safety Authority and laying down procedures in matters of food safety, OJ L 31, 1.2.2002;

Commission Regulation 445/2002/EC of 26 February 2002 laying down detailed rules for the application of Council Regulation 1257/1999 on support for rural development from the European Agricultural Guidance and Guarantee Fund (EAGGF), OJ L 74, 15.3.2002;

Regulation 1/2003/EC of 16 December 2002 on the implementation of the rules on competition laid down in Article 81 and 82 of the Treaty, OJ L 1, 4.1.2003;

Council Regulation 58/2003 of 19 December 2002 laying down the statute for executive agencies to be entrusted with certain tasks in the management of Community programmes, OJ L 11/1, 16.1.2003;

Regulation 1829/2003/EC of the European Parliament and of the Council of 22 September 2003 on genetically modified food and feed, OJ L 268, 18.10.2003;

Regulation 1830/2003/EC of the European Parliament and of the Council of 22 September 2003 concerning the traceability and labelling of genetically modified organisms and the traceability of food and feed products produced form genetically modified organisms and amending Directive 2001/18/EC, OJ L 268, 18.10.2003;

Regulation 1946/2003/EC of the European Parliament and of the Council of 15 July 2003 on transboundary movements of genetically modified organisms, OJ L 287, 5.11.2003;

Regulation 460/2004/EC of the European Parliament and of the Council of 10 March 2004 establishing the European Network and Information Security Agency, OJ L 2004/77/1;

Commission Regulation 817/2004/EC of 29 April 2004 laying down detailed rules for the application of Council Regulation 1257/1999 on support for rural development from the European Agricultural Guidance and Guarantee Fund (EAGGF), OJ L 153, 30.4.2004;

Regulation 852/2004/EC of the European Parliament and of the Council of 29 April 2004 on the hygiene of foodstuffs, OJ L 226, 25.6.2004;

Regulation 853/2004/EC of the European Parliament and of the Council of 29 April 2004 laying down specific hygiene rules for food of animal origin, OJ L 226, 25.6.2004;

Regulation 854/2004/EC of the European Parliament and of the Council of 29 April 2004 laying down specific rules of official controls on products of animal origin intended for human consumption, OJ L 226, 25.6.2004;

Regulation 882/2004/EC of the European Parliament and of the Council of 29 April 2004 on official controls performed to ensure the verification of compliance with feed and food law, animal health and animal welfare rules, OJ L 191, 28.5.2004;

Regulation 1935/2004/EC of the European Parliament and of the Council of 27 October 2004 on material and articles intended to come into contact with food and repealing Directives 80/590/EEC and 89/109/EEC, OJ L 338, 13.11.2004;

Regulation 183/2005/EC of the European Parliament and of the Council of 12 January 2005 laying down requirements for feed hygiene, OJ L 35, 8.2.2005;

Regulation 396/2005/EC of the European Parliament and of the Council of 23 February 2005 on maximum residue levels of pesticides in or on food and feed of plant and animal origin and amending Council Directive 91/414/EEC, OJ L 70, 16.3.2005;

Council Regulation 509/2006/EC of 20 March 2006 on agricultural products and foodstuffs as traditional specialties guaranteed, OJ L 93, 31.3.2006;

Council Regulation 510/2006/EC of 20 March 2006 on the protection of geographical indications and designations of origin for agricultural products and foodstuffs, OJ L 93, 31.3.2006;

Regulation 1080/2006/EC of the European Parliament and of the Council of 5 July 2006 on the European Regional Development Fund and repealing Regulation 1783/1999/EC, OJ L 210/1, 31.7.2006;

Regulation 1081/2006/EC of the European parliament and of the Council of 5 July 2006 on the European Social Fund and repealing Regulation 1784/1999/EC, OJ L 210/12, 31.7.2006;

Regulation 1082/2006/EC of the European Parliament and of the Council of 5 July 2006 on a European grouping of territorial cooperation (EGTC), OJ L 210/19, 31.7.2006;

Council Regulation 1083/2006/EC of 11 July 2006 laying down general provisions on the European Regional Development Fund, the European Social Fund and the Cohesion Fund and repealing Regulation 1260/1999/EC, OJ L 210/25, 31.7.2006;

Council Regulation 1084/2006/EC of 11 July 2006 establishing a Cohesion Fund and repealing Regulation 1164/94/EC, OJ L 210/79, 31.7.2006;

Regulation 1907/2006/EC of the European Parliament and of the Council of 18 December 2008 concerning the Registration, Evaluation, Authorisation and Restriction of Chemicals (REACH), establishing a European Chemicals Agency, amending Directive 1999/45/EC and repealing Council Regulation (EEC) No 793/93 and Commission Regulation (EC) No 1488/94 as well as Council Directive 76/769/EEC and Commission Directives 91/155/EEC, 93/67/EEC, 93/105/EC and 2000/21/EC, OJ L 396, 30.12.2006;

Commission Regulation 642/2007/EC of 11 June 2007 registering a name in the Register of protected designations of origin and protected geographical indications Bryndza Podhalańska (PDO), OJ L 150, 12.6.2007;

Commission Regulation 127/2008/EC of 13 February 2008 entering in the register of protected designations of origin and protected geographical indications (Oscypek (PDO)), OJ L 40, 14.2.2008;

Regulation 767/2009/EC of the European Parliament and of the Council of 13 July 2009 on the placing on the market and use of feed, amending European Parliament and Council Regulation (EC) No 1831/2003 and repealing Council Directive 79/373/EEC, Commission Directive 80/511/EEC, Council Directives 82/471/EEC, 83/228/EEC, 93/74/EEC, 93/113/EC and 96/25/EC and Commission Decision 2004/217/EC, OJ L 229, 1.9.2009;

Regulation (EU) No 182/2011 of the European Parliament and of the Council of 16 February 2011 laying down the rules and general principles concerning mechanisms for control by Member States of the Commission's exercise of implementing powers, OJ L 55/13, 28.2.2011;

Directives

Council Directive 90/219/EEC of 23 April 1990 on the contained use of genetically modified micro-organisms, OJ L 117, 8.5.1990;

Council Directive 93/43/EEC of 14 June 1993 on the hygiene of foodstuffs, *OJ L 175, 19.7.1993;*

Directive 2001/18/EC of the European Parliament and of the Council of 12 March 2001 on the deliberate release into the environment of genetically modified organisms and repealing Council Directive 90/220/EEC, OJ L 106, 17.4.2001;

Decisions

Council Decision 69/414/EEC of 13 November 1969 setting up a Standing Committee for Foodstuffs, OJ L 291, 19.11.1969;

European Commission, Decision 74/234/EEC of 16 April 1974 relating to the institution of a Scientific Committee for Food, OJ L 136, 20.5.1974;

European Commission, Decision 75/420/EEC of 26 June 1975 setting up an Advisory Committee on Foodstuffs, OJ L 182, 12.7.1975;

Council Decision 87/373/EEC of 13 July 1987 laying down the procedures for the exercise of implementing powers conferred on the Commission, OJ L 197, 18.7.1987;

European Parliament, Decision setting up a temporary committee of inquiry, (1996) OJ C 261, 9.9.1996;

European Commission, Decision 97/579/EC of 23 July 1997 setting up Scientific Committees in the field of consumer health and food safety, OJ L 237, 28.8.1997;

Council Decision 1999/468/EC of 28 July 1999 laying down the procedures for exercise of implementing powers conferred on the Commission, OJ L 184, 17.7.1999;

European Commission, Decision 2000/374/EC of 5 June 2000 amending Decision 98/272/EC on epidemio-surveillance for transmissible spongiform encephalopathies, OJ L 135, 08.6.2000;

European Commission, Decision 2000/418/EC of 29 June 2000 regulating the use of material presenting risks as regards transmissible spongiform encephalopathies and amending Decision 94/474/EC, OJ L 158, 30.6.2000;

European Commission, Decision 2000/639/EC of 13 October 2000 on the list of programmes for the monitoring of BSE qualifying for a financial contribution from the Community in 2001, OJ L 269, 21.10.2000;

Council Decision 2000/766/EC of 4 December 2000 concerning certain protection measures with regard to transmissible spongiform encephalopathies and the feeding of animal protein, OJ L 306, 07.12.2000;

European Commission, Decision 2000/773/EC of 30 November 2000 approving the programmes for the monitoring of BSE presented for 2001 by the Member States and fixing the level of the Community's financial contribution, OJ L 308, 08.12.2000;

Commission Decision 2003/653/EC of 2 September 2003 relating to national provisions banning the use of genetically modified organisms in the region of Upper Austria notified by the Republic of Austria pursuant to Article 95(5) of the EC Treaty, OJ L 230, 16.09.2003;

Commission Decision 2004/458/EC of 29 April 2004 amending Appendix B to Annex XII of the 2004 Act of Accession to include certain establishments in the meat, milk and fish sectors in Poland in the list of establishments in transition, OJ L 156, 30.4.2004;

Council Decision 2006/512/EC of 17 July 2006 amending Decision 1999/468/EC laying down the procedures for the exercise of implementing powers conferred on the Commission, OJ L 200, 22.7.2006;

Commission Decision 2008/62/EC of 12 October 2007 relating to Articles 111 and 172 of the Polish Draft Act on Genetically Modified Organisms, notified by the Republic of Poland pursuant to Article 95(5) of the EC Treaty as derogations from the provisions of the Directive 2001/18/EC of the European Parliament and of the Council on the deliberate release into the environment of genetically modified organisms, OJ L 16, 19.1.2008;

Other Documents

European Commission, Communication from the Commission concerning the consequences of the judgment given by the Court of Justice on 20 February 1979 in case 120/78 ('Cassis de Dijon'), OJ C 256, 03.10.1980;

European Commission, The Agricultural Policy of the European Community, 3rd Edition, 1982;

European Commission, The New Approach to Technical Harmonization and Standardization, COM (85) 19 final, 31.1.1985;

European Commission, Completing the Internal Market: White Paper from the Commission to the European Council, COM (85) 310 final, 14.06.1985;

European Commission, Completion of the Internal Market: Community Legislation on Foodstuffs, COM (85) 603 final, 8.11.1985;

The Single European Act, OJ L 169, 29.6.87;

European Commission, Communication on the Free Movement of Goods within the Community, OJ C 217, 1989;

European Commission, Commission interpretative communication concerning the free circulation of foodstuffs within the Community, COM (89) 256, OJ C 271, 24.10.1989;

European Commission, White Paper: European Social Policy—A Way Forward for the Union, COM (94) final, 333, 27.07.1994;

European Parliament, Report on alleged contraventions or maladministartion in the implementation of Community law in relation to BSE, without prejudice to the jurisdiction of the Community and national courts, 7 January 1997, A4-0020/97;

European Commission Communication from the Commission, Action Plan for the Single Market, SEC (97) 1 final;

European Commission, Green Paper on The General Principles of Food Law in the European Union, COM (97) 176 final;

European Commission, Communication to the Council and the European Parliament: Mutual Recognition in the Context of the Follow-up to the Action Plan for the Single Market, COM (99) 299 final, 16.06.1999;

European Commission, White Paper on Food Safety, COM (1999) 719 final;

Presidency Conclusions, Lisbon European Council, 23 and 24 March 2000, 100/1/00, available at: http://www.consilium.europa.eu/ueDocs/cms_Data/docs/pressData/en/ec/00100-r1.en0.htm;

Scientific Steering Committee, Final Opinion of the Scientific Steering Committee on the Geographical Risk of Bovine Spongiform Encephalopathy (GBR) of 6 July 2000, available at: http://www.europa.eu.int/comm/food/fs/sc/ssc/out113_en.pdf;

SAPARD Operational Programme, proposal as of 12 September 2000, Ministry of Agriculture and Rural Development, available at: http://ec.europa.eu/agriculture/external/enlarge/countries/poland/plan/plan_en.pdf;

Presidency Conclusions, Nice European Council Meeting, 7, 8 and 9 December 2000, SN 400/1/00, available at: http://www.consilium.europa.eu/ueDocs/cms_Data/docs/pressData/en/ec/00400-r1.%20ann.en0.htm;

European Commission, European Governance. A White Paper, COM (2001) 428 final, 25.7.2001;

European Commission, Communication from the Commission to the Council, the European Parliament, the Economic and Social Committee and the Committee of the Regions. Life Sciences and Biotechnology—A Strategy for Europe, COM (2002) 27 final, Brussels, 23.1.2002;

European Commission, Report from the Commission to the Council, the European Parliament and the Economic and Social Committee, Second Biennial Report on the Application of the Principle of Mutual Recognition in the Single Market, COM (2002) 419 final, 23.7.2002;

European Commission, Communication from the Commission on the Collection and Use of Expertise by the Commission: Principles and Guidelines—"Improving the knowledge base for better policies", COM (2002) 713 final, 11.12.2002;

European Commission, Communication from the Commission, The Operating Framework for the European Regulatory Agencies, COM (2002) 718 final, 11.12.2002;

European Commission, Communication from the Commission, Towards uniform and effective implementation of the Common Fisheries Policy, COM (2003) 130 final, 21.3.2003;

European Commission, Commission Recommendation 2003/556/EC of 23 July 2003 on guidelines for the development of national strategies and best practices to ensure the coexistence of genetically modified crops with conventional and organic farming, OJ L 189, 29.7.2003;

Proposal for a Regulation concerning the Registration, Evaluation, Authorization and Restriction of Chemicals, establishing a European Chemicals Agency and amending Directive 1999/45 and Regulation on Persistent Organic Pollutants, COM (2003) 644 final of 29.10.2003;

European Commission, Commission interpretative communication on facilitating the access of products to the markets of other Member States: the practical application of mutual recognition, OJ C 256/2, 4.11.2003;

Act concerning the conditions of accession of the Czech Republic, the Republic of Estonia, the Republic of Cyprus, the Republic of Latvia, the Republic of Lithuania, the Republic of Hungary, the Republic of Malta, the Republic of Poland, the Republic of Slovenia and the Slovak Republic and the adjustments to the Treaties on which the European Union is founded, OJ L 236, 23.9.2003;

Comprehensive Monitoring Report of the European Commission on the State of Preparedness for EU Membership of the Czech Republic, Estonia, Cyprus, Latvia, Lithuania, Hungary, Malta Poland, Slovenia and Slovakia, 5 November 2003, COM (2003) 675 final—C5-0532/2003;

European Commission, Communication from the Commission to the Council, the European Parliament, and the Economic and Social Committee. Nanosciences and Nanotechnologies: An Action Plan for Europe 2005-2009, COM (2005) 243 final, Brussels, 7.6.2005;

Council of the European Union, Review of the EU Sustainable Development Strategy (EU SDS)—Renewed Strategy, 10917/06, Brussels, 26.6.2006;

Publication of an application in accordance with Article 6(2) of Council Regulation (EC) No 510/2006 on the protection of geographical indications and designations of origin for agricultural products and foodstuffs (2006/C 180/09); Application for registration in accordance with Articles 5 and 17(2), 'OSCYPEK', No EC: PL/0451/21.02.2005, OJ C 180, 2.8.2006;

Publication of an application pursuant to Article 6(2) of Council Regulation (EC) No 510/2006 on the protection of geographical indications and designations of origin for agricultural products and foodstuffs (2006/C 230/02); Application for registration pursuant to articles 5 and 17(2), 'BRYNDZA PODHALAŃSKA', EC No: PL/PDO/005/0450/18.02.2005, OJ C 230, 23.9.2006;

European Commission, Fact Sheet: European Policy for Quality Agricultural Products, KF-76-06-383-EN-C, January 2007, available at: http://ec.europa.eu/agriculture/publi/fact/quality/2007_en.pdf;

European Commission, Notification pursuant to Article 95, paragraph 5 of the EC Treaty, 2007/C 173/05, Polish Draft Act on Genetically Modified Organisms, including derogations from the provisions of the Directive 2001/18/EC of the European Parliament and of the Council on the deliberate release into the environment of genetically modified organisms, OJ C 173, 26.07.2007;

European Commission, Communication from the Commission to the European Parliament and the Council. Preparing for the "Health Check" of the CAP reform, COM (2007) 722 final, Brussels, 20.11.2007;

European Commission, List of Applications under Regulation 258/97, for authorisation of a novel food, updated 16.1.2008, available at: http://ec.europa.eu/food/food/biotechnology/novelfood/app_list_en.pdf;

Proposal for a Regulation of the European Parliament and of the Council on the provisions of food information to consumers, COM (2008) 40 final, 30.1.2008;

European Commission, Single market for goods—Information pack 2008, available at: http://ec.europa.eu/enterprise/regulation/goods/index_en.htm;

European Commission, Communication for the Commission to the European Parliament, the Council, the European Economic and Social Committee and the Committee of the Regions on agricultural product quality policy, COM (2009) 234 final, 28.5.2009;

European Commission, Communication from the Commission to the European Parliament, the Council, the European Economic and Social Committee and the Committee of the Regions.

Mainstreaming Sustainable Development into EU Policies: 2009 Review of the European Union Strategy for Sustainable Development, COM (2009) 400 final, Brussels, 24.7.2009;

Proposal for a Regulation of the European Parliament and of the Council amending Directive 2001/18/EC as regards the possibility for the Member States to restrict or prohibit the cultivation of GMOs in their territory, COM (2010) 375 final, 13.7.2010;

Case Law

9/56, *Meroni v. High Authority*, [1957-1958], ECR 133;

5/67, *Beus v. Hauptzollamt München*, [1968], ECR 83;

5/73, *Balkan-Import-Export GmbH v. Hauptzollamt Berlin Packhof*, [1973], ECR 1091;

8/74, *Procureur du Roi v. Dassonville*, [1974], ECR 837;

114/76, *Bela-Mühle Josef Bergmann KG v. Grows-Farm GmbH and Co. KG*, [1977] ECR 1211;

C 120/78, *Rewe-Zentral AG v. Bundesmonopolverwaltung für Branntwein*, [1979], ECR 649;

C 138/79, *Roquette*, [1980], ECR 3333;

C 178/84, *Commission v. Germany*, [1987], ECR 1227;

C 265/87, *Schräder*, [1989], ECR 2237;

C 25/88, *Esther Renée Bouchara, née Wurmser, and Norlaine SA*, [1989], ECR 1105;

C-267 and 268/91, Criminal Proceedings against Keck and Mithouard, [1993], ECR I-6097;

C-1/00, *Commission v. France*, [2001], ECR I-9989;

T-366/03 and T-235/04, *Land Oberösterreich and Republic of Austria v Commission of the European Communities*, [2005], ECR II-4005;

C-341/05, *Laval un Partneri Ltd v Svenska Byggnadsarbetareförbundet*, [2007], ECR I-11767;

C-438/05, *International Transport Workers' Federation and Finnish Seamen's Union v Viking Line ABP and OÜ Viking Line Eesti*, [2007], ECR I-10779;

C-439/05 P and C-454/05 P, *Land Oberösterreich and Republic of Austria v Commission of the European Communities*, [2007], ECR I-7141;

C-319/06, *Commission v. Grand Duchy of Luxembourg*, [2008], ECR I-4323;

C-346/06, *Dirk Rüffert v. Land Niedersachsen*, [2008], ECR I-1989;

T-69/08, OJ C 92, 12.4.2008, p.42;

b) *International Documents*

Agreement on Sanitary and Phytosanitary Measures, 15 April 1994, Marrakesh Agreement Establishing the World Trade Organization, Annex 1A;

Joint FAO/WHO Consultation, Risk Management and Food Safety, FAO Food and Nutrition Paper 65, Rome, 1997;

FAO, The State of the World's Plant Genetic Resources for Food and Agriculture, Rome, 1997;

European Communities—Measures Concerning Meat and Meat Products (Hormones), Report of the Appellate Body adopted 13 February 1998, WT/DS26/AB/R, WT/DS48/AB/R;

OECD, "Compendium of National Food Safety Systems and Activities" of 15 May 2000, SG/ADHOC/FS(2000)5/ANN/FINAL;

OECD, Processes and Production Methods (PPMs): Conceptual Framework and Considerations on the Use of PPM-based Trade Measures, OCDE/GD (97) 137, 11.08.1997;

Codex Alimentarius Commission, Criteria for Consideration of the Other Factors Referred to in the Second Statement of Principle, Decision of the 24th Session of the Commission, 2001, ALINORM 01/41;

Panel Report, *European Communities—Protection of Trademarks and Geographical Indications for Agricultural Products and Foodstuffs*, Complaint by the United States, adopted 15 March 2005, WT/DS174/R;

Panel Report, *European Communities—Protection of Trademarks and Geographical Indications for Agricultural Products and Foodstuffs*, Complaint by Australia, adopted 20 April 2005, WT/DS290/R;

European Communities—Measures Affecting the Approval and Marketing of Biotech Products, Panel Report adopted 29 September 2006, United States (WT/DS291/R), Canada (WT/DS292/R), and Argentina (WT/DS293/R);
Codex Alimentarius Commission, Procedural Manual of the Codex Alimentarius Commission, 15th edition, available at: http://www.codexalimentarius.net;
Confederation of the Food and Drink Industries of the EU, CIIA Annual Report 2009, available at: http://www.ciaa.be/asp/documents/brochures_form.asp?doc_id=75;
Confederation of the Food and Drink Industries of the EU, The EU Food and Drink (F&D) Industry in Figures' available at: http://www.ciaa.be/documents/brochures/CIAA%20key%20figures%20bookmarkV6.pdf;
World Trade Organisation, WTO report, 'International Trade Statistics 2007', available at: http://www.wto.org/english/res_e/statis_e/its2007_e/its07_toc_e.htm;

c) *Polish Documents*

Law of 14 March 1985 on State Sanitary Inspection, Journal of Laws No 90, Item 575, 1998;
Europe Agreement establishing an association between the European Communities and their Member States, of the one part, and the Republic of Poland, of the other part, of 16th December 1991, OJ L 348, 31.12.1993;
National Program of Preparation for Membership in the EU, adopted by the Council of Ministers as a governmental document on 23rd June 1996;
Law of 8 August 1996 on the Committee for European Integration, Journal of Laws of 30 August 1996;
Regulation of the Chairman of the Council of Ministers of 2 October 1996 on the assignment of status to the Office of the Committee for European Integration, Journal of Laws of 3 October 1996;
Constitution of the Republic of Poland of 2nd April 1997, Journal of Laws, No 78, Item 483, 1997;
Law of 24 April 1997 on control of infectious diseases of animals, examinations of slaughter animals and meat, and on the Veterinary Inspection, Journal of Laws No 66, Item 752, 1999 as amended;
Law of 21 August 1997 on animal welfare, unified text in Journal of Laws No 106, Item 1002, 2003;
Ordinance of the Minister of Health modifying competences of the General Sanitary Inspectorate of 30 December 1999, Official Journal of the Ministry of Health, No 111, Item 1315, 1999;
Law of 15 December 2000 on the Protection of Competition and Consumer, Journal of Law No 86, Item 804, 2003;
Law of 21 December 2000 on Commercial Quality of Agricultural and Food Products, Journal of Laws No 5, Item 44, 2001;
Law of 11 May 2001 on Health Conditions of Food and Nutrition, unified text in Journal of Laws No 31, Item 265, 2005;
Law of 22 June 2001 on genetically modified organisms, unified text in Journal of Laws No 36, Item 233, 2007;
Law of 23 August 2001 on animal feedstuffs, Journal of Laws No 123, Item 1350, 2001;
Food Safety Strategy in Poland, Warsaw 11 February 2002;
Regulation of the Chairman of the Council of Ministers of 28 June 2002 on specific range of tasks of the Minister of Health, Journal of Laws No 93, Item 833, 2002;
Ordinance of the Minister of Health of 9 September 2002 on the establishment of a Group on Food Safety, Official Journal of the Ministry of Health No 9, Item 49, 12.09.2002;
Law of 25 June 2003 on seed material, unified text in Journal of Laws No 41, Item 27, 2007;
Law of 27 August 2003 on border veterinary control, Journal of Laws No 165, Item 1500, 2003;
Law of 10 December 2003 on veterinary control of trade, Journal of Laws No 16, Item 145, 2004;
Law of 18 December 2003 on Plan Protection, Journal of Laws No 11, Item 94, 2003, unified text in Journal of Laws No 133, Item 849, 2008;
Law of 29 January 2004 on the Veterinary Inspection, Journal of Laws No 33, Item 287, 2004;

Law of 29 January 2004 on veterinary requirements for products of animal origin, Journal of Laws No 33, Item 288, 2004;
Law of 11 March 2004 on protection of animal health and eradication of contagious animal diseases, Journal of Laws No 69, Item 625, 2004;
Law of 2 April 2004 on the system of identification and registration of animals, Journal of Laws No 91, Item 872, 2004;
Law of 20 April 2004 on organic farming, Journal of Laws No 93, Item 898, 2004;
Law of 25 August 2006 on safety of food and feed, Journal of Laws No 171, Item 1225, 2006;
Framework Position of the Polish Government on Genetically Modified Organisms (GMO), adopted by the Council of Ministers on 18th November 2008;
New draft Law on genetically modified organisms as adopted by the Council of Ministers on the 13th of October 2009 (currently under scrutiny by the Parliament).

B) Literature

Adamowicz, M., Rytko, A., "Polish Agro-Food Trade with European Countries Before and After Joining EU", paper prepared for presentation at the 98th EAAE Seminar "Marketing Dynamics within the Global Trading System: New Perspectives", Crete, Greece, 29 June—2 July 2006;
Alter, K. J., Meunier-Altsahalia, S., "Judicial Politics in the European Community: European Integration and the Pathbreaking Cassis de Dijon Decision", *Comparative Political Studies*, Vol.26, 1994, p. 535;
Andenaes, M., Türk, A. (eds.), *Delegated Legislation and the Role of Committees in the EC*, Kluwer Law International, 2000;
Andreosso—O'Callaghan, B., *The Economics of European Agriculture*, Palgrave Macmillan, 2003;
Ansell, A., Vogel, D. (eds.), *What's the beef? The Contested Governance of European Food Safety*, Cambridge MA, The MIT Press, 2006;
Arnull, A., Wincott, D. (eds.), *Accountability and Legitimacy in the European Union*, Oxford University Press, 2002;
Artis, M., Banerjee, A., Marcellino, M. (eds.), *The Central and Eastern European Countries and the European Union*, Cambridge University Press, 2006;
Balcerowicz, E., "The Impact of EU Accession on Poland's Economy", CASE E-brief, Center for Social and Economic Research, 2007/5;
Bański, J., "Selected Aspects of Present-Day Changes in Polish Rural Space", *Geographia Polonica*, Vol. 76, No. 1, Spring 2003, pp. 73–96;
Battaglia, A., "Food Safety: Between European and Global Administration", *Global Jurist Advances*, Vol.6, Issue 3, 2006, pp. 1–14;
Beck, U., *Risk Society. Towards a New Modernity*, London, Sage Publications, 1986, 1992;
Bergström, C. F., *Comitology—Delegation of Powers in the European Union and the Committee System*, Oxford University Press, 2005;
Bermann, G., Pistor, K. (eds.), *Law and Governance in an Enlarged European Union*, Hart Publishing, Oxford and Portland, Oregon, 2004;
Bernauer, T., Aerni, P., "Trade Conflict over Genetically Modified Organisms", in: K. Gallagher (ed.), *Handbook on Trade and the Environment*, Edward Elgar Publishing, 2008;
Bertram, C., "Decision-making in the EEC: the management committee procedure", *Common Market Law Review*, Vol. 68, 1967, pp. 246–265;
Bieber, R., Dehousse, R., Pinder, J., Weiler, J. (eds.), *1992: One European Market?*, Nomos, 1988;
Blind, K., *The Economics of Standards. Theory, Evidence, Policy*, Edward Elgar Publishing, 2004;
Bradley, K., "Comitology and the Law: Through a Glass Darkly", *Common Market Law Review*, Vol. 29, 1992, pp. 693–721;
Braithwaite, J., Drahos, P., *Global Business Regulation*, Cambridge University Press, 2000;
Broberg, M. P., "Transforming the European Community's Regulation of Food Safety", SIEPS Report 2008:5, April 2008;
Bronckers, M., Quick, R. (eds.), *New Directions in International Economic Law: Essays in Honour of John H. Jackson*, the Hague: Kluwer Law International, 2000;

Bronzini, G., "The European Social Model and the Constitutional Treaty of the European Union", in: C. Joerges, B. Stråth, P. Wagner (eds.), *The Economy as a Polity: The Political Constitution of Contemporary Capitalism*, UCL Press, 2005;
Brouwer, O., "Free Movement of Foodstuffs and Quality Requirements: Has the Commission Got it Wrong?", *Common Market Law Review*, Vol. 25, 1988, pp. 237–262;
Brunsson, N., Jacobsson, B., "The Pros and Cons of Standardisation—An Epilogue", in: N. Brunsson, B. Jacobsson *et al.*, *A World of Standards*, Oxford University Press, 2000;
Brunsson, N., Jacobsson, B., et al., A *World of Standards*, Oxford University Press, 2000;
Bruszt, L., Stark, D., "Who Counts? Supranational Norms and Societal Needs", *East European Politics and Societies*, Vol. 17, No. 1, 2003, pp. 74–82;
Buonanno, L., "The Creation of the European Food Safety Authority", in: C. Ansell, D. Vogel, *What's the Beef? The Contested Governance of European Food Safety*, Cambridge MA, The MIT Press, 2006;
Buonanno, L., Zablotney, S., Keefer, R., "Politics versus Science in the Making of a New Regulatory Regime for Food in Europe", *European Integration online Papers*, Vol. 5, No. 12, 2001;
Button, C., *The Power to Protect. Trade, Health and Uncertainty in the WTO*, Hart Publishing, 2004;
Cardwell, M., *The European Model of Agriculture*, Oxford University Press, 2004;
Carson, M., *From Common Market to Social Europe? Paradigm Shift and Institutional Change in European Policy on Food, Asbestos and Chemicals, and Gender Equality*, Acta Universitatis Stockholmiensis, Stockholm Studies in Sociology N.S. 22, 2004;
Chalmers, D., "Deliberative Supranationalism and the Reterritorialization of Authority", in Joerges, Ch. "Rethinking European Law's Supremacy" (with comments by D. Chalmers, R. Nickel, F. Rödl and R. Wai), EUI Working Paper Law No. 12/2005, pp. 29–44;
Chalmers, D., "'Food for Thought': Reconciling European Risks and Traditional Ways of Life", *Modern Law Review*, Vol. 66, July 2003, pp. 532–562;
Chalmers, D., and Lodge, M., *The Open Method of Co-ordination and the European Welfare State*, CARR, LSE, 2003;
Chiti, E., "On European Agencies", in: E. O. Eriksen, C. Joerges, J. Neyer (eds.), *European Governance, Deliberation and the Quest for Democratisation*, ARENA Report No 02/2003;
Chiti, E., "The Emergence of a Community Administration: The Case of European Agencies", *Common Market Law Review*, Vol. 37, 2000, pp. 309–343;
Cohen, M. J. (ed.), *Risk in the Modern Age. Social Theory, Science and Environmental Decision-Making*, Palgrave, 2001;
Craig, P., de Burca, G., *EU Law. Texts, Cases and Materials*, Third Edition, Oxford University Press, 2003;
Cremona, M., "Accession to the European Union: Membership Conditionality and Accession Criteria", *Polish Yearbook of International Law*, Vol. 25, 2002, pp. 219–240;
Cremona, M. (ed.), *The Enlargement of the European Union, The Collected Courses of the Academy of European Law*, Vol. XII/1, Oxford University Press, 2003;
Czechowski, P., *Proces Dostosowania Polskiego Prawa Rolnego i Żywnościowego do Prawa Unii Europejskiej*, Twigger, Warszawa, 2001;
Czyżewski, A., "Macroeconomic Interdependencies in the Process of Transformation of Agriculture", in: P.-Ch. Müller-Graff, A. Stępniak (eds.), *Poland and the European Union—Between Association and Membership*, European Community Studies Association Series, Vol. 4, Nomos, 1997;
Czyżewski, A., Pawelczak, L., "The Association Agreement between Poland and the European Union in the agribusiness sector—experience and first evaluations", in: P.-C. Müller-Graff, A. Stępniak, (eds.), *Poland and the European Union—Between Association and Membership*, European Community Studies Association Series, Vol. 4, Nomos, 1997;
Dąbrowska, P., *Hybrid Solutions for Hybrid Products?: EU Governance of GMOs*, PhD thesis, European University Institute, 2006;
Daugbjerg, C., "Policy Feedback and Paradigm Shift in EU Agricultural Policy: The Effects of the MacSharry Reform on Future Reform", *Journal of European Public Policy*, Vol. 10, No. 3, June 2003, pp. 421–437;

de Burca, G. (ed.), *EU Law and the Welfare State. In search of Solidarity*, Oxford University Press, 2005;

de Burca, G., Scott, J. (eds.), *Constitutional Change in the EU From Uniformity to Flexibility?*, Hart Publishing, 2000;

Dehousse, R., "Completing the Internal Market: Institutional Constraints and Challenges", in: R. Bieber, R. Dehousse, J. Pinder, J. Weiler (eds.), *1992: One European Market?*, Nomos, 1988;

Dehousse, F., Coussens, W., Grevi, G., "Integrating Europe. Multiple Speeds—One Direction?", EPC Working Paper, No. 9, April 2004;

de Frahan, B. H., Vancauteren, M., "Harmonisation of Food Regulations and Trade in the Single Market: Evidence from Disaggregated Data", *European Review of Agricultural Economics*, Vol. 33, No. 3, 2006, pp. 337–360;

de la Porte, C., "Is the Open Method of Coordination Appropriate for Organising Activities at European Level in Sensitive Policy Areas?", *European Law Journal*, Vol. 8, No. 1, 2002, pp. 38–58;

de Schutter, O., Lebesis, N., Patterson, J., *Governance in the European Union*, Luxembourg, European Commission 2001;

Dougan, M., "Minimum Harmonization and the Internal Market", *Common Market Law Review*, Vol. 37, 2000, pp. 853–885;

Dreyer, M., Renn, O. (eds), Food Safety Governance: Integrating Science, Precautions and Public Involvement, Springer-Verlag, Berlin Heidelberg, 2009;

Druesne, G., *La Politique Agricole Commune devant la Cour de Justice des Communautés Européennes 1958-1978*, Paris, Éditions techniques et économiques, 1980;

Dunn, E. C., "Trojan Pig: Paradoxes of Food Safety Regulation", *Environment and Planning A*, Vol. 35, 2003, pp. 1493–1511;

Echols, M. A., *Food Safety and the WTO. The Interplay of Culture, Science and Technology*, Kluwer Law International, 2001;

Edelstein, M. E., "'Outsiders Just Don't Understand': Personalization of Risk and the Boundary Between Modernity and Postmodernity", in: M. J. Cohen (ed.), *Risk in Modern Age. Social Theory, Science and Environmental Decision-Making*, Palgrave, 2001;

Editorial Comment, *Common Market Law Review*, Vol. 43, 2006, pp. 1243–1250;

Egan, M. P., *Constructing a European Market: Standards, Regulation and Governance*, Oxford University Press, 2001;

EPC, Egmont and CEPS Joint Study, "The Treaty of Lisbon: Implementing the Institutional Innovations", November 2007;

Eriksen, E. O., Joerges, C., Neyer, J. (eds.), *European Governance, Deliberation and the Quest for Democratisation*, ARENA Report No 02/2003;

European Farmers' Coordination, "For a Legitimate, Sustainable and Supportive CAP" available at: http://www.cpefarmers.org/positions/en/17_171103.pdf;

Everson, M., "Independent Agencies: Hierarchy Beaters?", *European Law Journal*, Vol. 2, No. 1, 1995, pp. 180–204;

Everson, M., "The Constitutionalization of European Administrative Law", in: Ch. Joerges, E. Vos (eds.), *EU Committees: Social Regulation, Law and Politics*, Oxford Hart Publishing, 1999;

Everson, M., Joerges, Ch, "Consumer Citizenship in Postnational Constellations?", EUI Working Paper LAW No. 2006/47;

Falke, J., "Achievements and Unresolved Problems of European Standardization: The Ingenuity of Practice and the Queries of Lawyers", in: C. Joerges, K.-H. Ladeur, E. Vos, *Integrating Scientific Expertise into Regulatory Decision-Making. National Traditions and European Innovations*, Nomos, 1997;

Falkner G., et al., *Complying with Europe: EU Harmonisation and Soft Law in the Member States*, Cambridge University Press, 2005;

Farrell, J., Saloner, G., "Competition, Compatibility and Standards: The Economics of Horses, Penguins and Lemmings", in: H. Landis Gabel (ed.), *Product Standardisation and Competitive Strategy*, Elsevier Science Publishers B.V., 1987;

Fernandez-Armesto, F., *Food: A History*, Macmillan, 2001;

Fisher, E., *Risk Regulation and Administrative Constitutionalism*, Hart Publishing, 2007;

Fredman, S., "Transformation or Dilution: Fundamental Rights in the EU Social Space", *European Law Journal*, Vol. 12, No. 1, 2006, pp. 41–60;
Frewer, L., Salter, B., "Public Attitudes, Scientific Advice and the Politics of Regulatory Policy: The Case of BSE", *Science and Public Policy*, Vol. 29, No. 2, 2002, pp. 137–145;
Gaines, S. E., "Processes and Production Methods: How to Produce Sound Policy for Environmental PPM-Based Trade Measures?", *Columbia Journal of Environmental Law*, Vol. 27, 2002, pp. 383–432;
Gallagher, K. (ed.), *Handbook on Trade and the Environment*, Edward Elgar Publishing, 2008;
Garland, D., *Risk and Morality*, University of Toronto Press, 2003;
Garland, D., "The Rise of Risk", in: D. Garland, *Risk and Morality*, University of Toronto Press, 2003;
Gazeta Wyborcza, "Pierwsza piekarnia z certyfikatem HACCP nie straszy", 12.08.2003;
Gazeta Wyborcza, "GMO, czyli nie chcę ale muszę", 31.03.2008;
Gazeta Wyborcza, "Jak ja się boję GMO", 12.03.2008;
Gazeta Wyborcza, "Tu mi gen wyrośnie. Jak nie zakazać upraw transgenicznych tak by ich zakazać", 25.04.2008;
Gazeta Wyborcza, "Jak podbiliśmy unijny rynek", 3.05.2009;
Gazeta Wyborcza, "Rzeźnie i Mleczarnie jak Laboratoria", 4.05.2009;
Gazeta Wyborcza, "Tu nam gen wyrośnie", 29 May 2009;
Geradin, D., Muñoz, R., Petit, N. (eds.), *Regulation through Agencies in the EU. A New Paradigm of European Governance*, Edward Elgar Publishing, 2005;
Geradin, D., Petit, M., "The Development of Agencies at EU and National Levels: Conceptual Analysis and Proposals for Reform", Jean Monnet Working Paper 1/4;
Giddens, A., "Risk and Responsibility", *Modern Law Review*, Vol. 62, No. 1, January 1999, pp. 1–10;
Goetz, S., Jaksh, T., Siebert, R. (eds.), *Agricultural Transformation and Land Use in Central and Eastern Europe*, Ashgate, 2001;
Goody, J., *Cooking, Cuisine and Class. A Study in Comparative Sociology*, Cambridge University Press, 1982;
Gormley, L. W., "Cassis de Dijon and the Communication from the Commission", *European Law Review*, Vol. 6, 1981, pp. 454–9;
Grochowska, M., *Bezpieczeństwo Żywności i Żywienia. Komentarz do Ustawy oraz Przepisów Wspólnotowych*, ODDK, Gdańsk, 2007;
Gronowska-Senger, A., Izdebski, H., Trochimczuk, G., Czarnecki, J., *Prawo Żywnościowe i Strategia Bezpieczeństwa Żywności, Stanowisko Polskiej Federacji Producentów Żywności*, 2002;
Hagenmeyer, M., "Modern food safety requirements—according to EC Regulation No 178/2002", *Zeitschrift für das gesamte Lebensmittelrecht*, Vol. 4, 2002, pp. 443–459;
Hardacre, A., Keading, M., "Delegated and Implementing Acts. The New Comitology. EIPA Essential Guide", European Institute of Public Administration, 2011;
Hasselgard, M., *Playing Games with Values of Higher Importance? Dealing with 'Risk Issues' in the Standing Committee on Foodstuffs*, ARENA Report No. 2003/01;
Herwig, A., *Taking Pluralism Seriously—How the WTO should Regulate Food Safety and Consumer Choice Aspects of Trade in Genetically Modified Foods*, Thesis submitted for the JSD degree at New York University School of Law, September 2005;
Heyvaert, V., "The EU Chemicals Policy: Towards Inclusive Governance?", in: E. Vos (ed.), *European Risk Governance—Its Science, its Inclusiveness and its Effectiveness*, CONNEX Report Series, No. 6, February 2008;
Hodson, D., Maher, I., "The Open Method as a New Mode of Governance: The Case of Soft Economic Policy Coordination", *Journal of Common Market Studies*, Vol. 39, No. 4, 2001, pp. 719–746;
Hofmann, H. C. H., Türk, A. H. (eds.), *EU Administrative Governance*, Edward Elgar Publishing, 2006;
Hoffmann, H. C. H., Türk, A. H., "Policy Implementation" in: H. C. H. Hoffmann, A. H. Türk (eds.), *EU Administrative Governance*, Edward Elgar Publishing, 2006,
Holland, D., Pope. H., *EU Food Law and Policy*, Kluwer Law International, 2004;

Holmes, P., "Trade and 'Domestic' Policies: the European Mix", *Journal of European Public Policy*, Vol. 13, No. 6, September 2006, pp. 815–831;

Holmes, S., "A European Doppelstaat?", *East European Politics and Societies*, Vol. 17, No. 1, 2003, pp. 107–118;

Hood, C., Rothstein, H., Baldwin, R., *The Government of Risk. Understanding Risk Regulation Regimes*, Oxford University Press, 2001;

Hooghe, L., Marks, G., "The Making of a Polity: The Struggle over European Integration", *European Integration Online Papers*, Vol. 1, No. 4, 1997;

Houdec, R. E., "The Product-Process Doctrine in GATT/WTO Jurisprudence", in: M. Bronckers, R. Quick (eds.), *New Directions in International Economic Law: Essays in Honour of John H. Jackson*, the Hague: Kluwer Law International, 2000;

Howse, R., "Adjudicative Legitimacy and Treaty Interpretation in International Trade Law: The Early Years of WTO Jurisprudence", in: J. H. H. Weiler (ed.), *The EU, the WTO and the NAFTA: Towards a Common Law of International Trade*, Oxford University Press, 2000;

Howse, R., "Democracy, Science, and Free Trade: Risk Regulation on Trial at the World Trade Organization", *Michigan Law Review*, Vol. 98, 2000, pp. 2329–2357;

Howse, R., Horn, H., "European Communities—Measures Affecting the Approval and Marketing of Biotech Products", *World Trade Review*, Vol. 8, No. 1, 2009, pp. 49–83;

Howse, R., Regan, D., "The Product/Process Distinction—An Illusory Basis for Disciplining 'Unilateralism' in Trade Policy", *European Journal of International Law*, Vol. 11, No. 2, 2000, pp. 249–289;

Inglis, K., "Implications of Enlargement for EC Agri-Food Law: The Accession Treaty, its Transitional Arrangements, and Safeguard Clauses", *European Law Journal*, Vol. 10, No. 5, 2003, pp. 595–612;

Inglis, K., "The Europe Agreements Compared in the Light of their Pre-accession Reorientation", *Common Market Law Review*, Vol. 37, 2000, pp. 1173–1210;

Instituto di dritto agrario internazionale e comparato (IDAIC), "La sicurezza alimentare nell'Unione europea", *Le Nuove Leggi Civili Comentate*, N.1-2, Gennaio-Aprile 2003;

International Risk Governance Council (IRGC), "Policy Brief: Appropriate Risk Governance Strategies for Nanotechnology Applications in Food and Cosmetics", Geneva 2009;

Jackson, J. H., "Comments on Shrimp/Turtle and the Product/Process Distinction", *European Journal of International Law*, Vol. 11, 2000, pp. 303–307;

James, P., Kemper, F., Pascal, G., "A European Food and Public Health Authority. The future of scientific advice in the EU", European Commission, December 1999;

Jasiecki, K., *Postrzeganie Polskiej Marki w Krajach Unii Europejskiej. Raport z Badań*, Polska Agencja Rozwoju Przedsiębiorczości, 2004;

Jaskiernia, J., "Badanie Zgodności Projektów Ustaw z Prawem Unii Europejskiej w Sejmowym Postępowaniu Ustawodawczym", *Państwo i Prawo*, No. 7, 1999, pp.19–33;

Jepsen, M., Pascual, A. S., "The European Social Model: An Exercise in Deconstruction", *Journal of European Social Policy*, Vol. 15 (3), 2005, pp. 231–245;

Joerges, Ch., "Constitutionalism in Postnational Constellations: Contrasting Social Regulation in the EU and in the WTO", in: Ch. Joerges, E. -U. Petersmann, *Constitutionalism, Multilevel Trade Governance and Social Regulation*, Hart Publishing, 2006;

Joerges, Ch., "'Deliberative Supranationalism'—A Defence", *European Integration online Papers*, Vol. 5, No. 8, 2001, available at: http://eiop.or.at/texte/2001-008a.htm;

Joerges, Ch., "'Deliberative Supranationalism'—Two Defences", *European Law Journal*, Vol. 8, No. 1, 2002, pp. 133–151;

Joerges, Ch., "Free Trade with Hazardous Products? The Emergence of Transnational Governance with Eroding State Government", *European Foreign Affairs Review*, Vol. 10, No. 4, Winter 2005, pp. 553–574;

Joerges, Ch., "'Good Governance' Through Comitology?", in: Ch. Joerges, E. Vos, *EU Committees: Social Regulation, Law and Politics*, Oxford Hart Publishing, 1999;

Joerges, Ch., "Integrating Scientific Expertise into Regulatory Decision-Making. Scientific Expertise in Social Regulation and European Court of Justice: Legal Framework for Denationalized Governance Structures", EUI Working Paper RSC No. 96/10;

Joerges, Ch., "Rethinking European Law's Supremacy" (with comments by D. Chalmers, R. Nickel, F. Rödl and R. Wai), EUI Working Paper Law No. 12/2005, pp. 29-44;

Joerges, Ch., "The Idea of Three-Dimensional Conflicts Law as Constitutional Form", RECON Online Working Paper 2010/5;

Joerges, Ch., "The Market without the State? The 'Economic Constitution' of the European Community and the Rebirth of Regulatory Politics", *European Integration online Papers*, Vol. 1, No. 19, 1997;

Joerges, Ch., Dehousse, R. (eds.), *Good Governance in Europe's Integrated Market*, Oxford University Press, 2002;

Joerges, Ch., Falke, J., Micklitz, H. W., Brüggemeier, G., "European Product Safety, Internal Market Policy and the New Approach to Technical Harmonisation and Standards", EUI Working Papers LAW, Nos. 91/10-14;

Joerges, Ch., Ladeur, K.-H., Vos, E. (eds.), *Integrating Scientific Expertise into Regulatory Decision-Making: National Traditions and European Innovations*, Nomos, 1997;

Joerges, Ch., Neyer, J., "'Deliberative Supranationalism' Revisited", EUI Working Papers, Law No. 2006/20;

Joerges, Ch., Neyer, J., "From Intergovernmental Bargaining to Deliberative Political Process: The Constitutionalisation of Comitology", *European Law Journal*, Vol. 3, 1997, pp. 273–299;

Joerges, Ch., Petersmann, E.-U. (eds.), *Constitutionalism, Multilevel Trade Governance and Social Regulation*, Hart Publishing, 2006;

Joerges, Ch., Rödl, F., "Informal Politics, Formalised Law and the 'Social Deficit' of European Integration: Reflections after the Judgments of the ECJ in *Viking* and *Laval*", *European Law Journal*, Vol. 15, No. 1, 2009, pp. 1–19;

Joerges, Ch., Rödl, F., "Reconceptualising the constitution of Europe's post-national constellation—by dint of conflict of laws", in: I. Lianos and O. Odudu (eds.), *Regulating Trade in Services in the EU and the WTO: Trust, Distrust and Economic Integration*, Cambridge University Press, 2010;

Joerges, Ch., Sand, I.-J., Teubner, G. (eds.), *Transnational Governance and Constitutionalism*, Hart Publishing, 2004;

Joerges, Ch., Schepel, H., Vos, E., "The Law's Problems with the Involvement of Non-governmental Actors in Europe's Legislative Process: The Case of Standardisation under the 'New Approach'", EUI Working Paper LAW No. 99/9;

Joerges, C., Stråth, B., Wagner, P. (eds.), *The Economy as a Polity: The Political Constitution of Contemporary Capitalism*, UCL Press, 2005;

Joerges, Ch., Vos, E., *EU Committees: Social Regulation, Law and Politics*, Oxford Hart Publishing, 1999;

Josling, T., Roberts, D., Orden, D., *Food Regulation and Trade. Towards Safe and Open Global System, Institute for International Economics*, Washington, DC, 2004;

Jurcewicz, A., "Legal problems Resulting from the Assignment of New Tasks to the Agricultural Sector in Poland", in: P.-Ch. Müller-Graff, A. Stępniak (eds.), *Poland and the European Union—Between Association and Membership*, European Community Studies Association Series, Vol. 4, Nomos, 1997;

Kjaer, P., "Rationality within REACH? On Functional Differentiation as the Structural Foundation of Legitimacy in European Chemicals Regulation", EUI Working Paper LAW No. 2007/18;

Klinke, A., Renn, O., "A New Approach to Risk Evaluation and Management: Risk-Based, Precaustion-Based, and Discourse-Based Strategies", *Risk Analysis*, Vol. 22, No. 6, 2002, pp. 1071–1094;

Konecka-Matyjek, E., Turlejska, H., Pelzner, U., Szponar, L., "Actual situation of implementing quality assurance systems GMP, GHP and HACCP in Polish food production and processing plants", *Food Control*, Vol. 16, 2005, pp. 1–9;

Kostoris Padoa Schioppa, F., "The Cultural Foundation of Mutual Recognition", in: F. Kostoris Padoa Schioppa (ed.), *The Principle of Mutual Recognition in the European Integration Process*, Palgrave Macmillan, 2005;

Kostoris Padoa Schioppa, F. (ed.), *The Principle of Mutual Recognition in the European Integration Process*, Palgrave Macmillan, 2005;

Krapohl, S., "Risk Regulation in the EU between Interests and Expertise—The Case of BSE", *Journal of European Public Policy*, Vol. 10. No. 2, 2003, pp. 189–207;

Krapohl, S., "Thalidomide, BSE and the single market: An historical-institutionalist approach to regulatory regimes in the European Union", *European Journal of Political Research*, Vol. 46, Issue 1, 2007, pp. 25–46;

Krapohl, S., Żurek, K, "The Perils of Committee Governance: Intergovernmental Bargaining During the BSE Scandal in the European Union", *European Integration online Papers*, Vol. 10, No. 2, 2006;

Kraus, P. A., "Legitimacy, Democracy and Diversity in the European Union", *International Journal of Multicultural Societies*, Vol. 8, No. 2, 2006, pp. 203–224;

Krause, K., "European Union Directives and Poland: A Case Study", *University of Pennsylvania Journal of International Economic Law*, Vol. 27, 2006, pp. 155–204;

Kreher, A., "Agencies in the European Community—a step towards administrative integration in Europe", *Journal of European Public Policy*, Vol. 2, No. 4, 1997, pp. 225–245;

Kritikos, M., "Traditional Risk Analysis and Releases of GMO's into the European Union: Space for Non-Scientific Factors?", *European Law Review*, Vol. 34, No. 3, 2009, pp. 420–423;

Kurbas, S., De Clerck-Sachsse, J., Torreblanca, J.I., Ricard-Nihoul, G., "From Threat to Opportunity: Making Flexible Integration Work", EPIN Working Paper, No. 15/September 2006;

Kysar, D. A., "Preferences for Processes: the Process/Product Distinction and the Regulation of Consumer Choice", Cornell Law School Legal Studies Research Paper Series, Paper 8, 2004;

Ladeur, K. -H. (ed.), *Public Governance in the Age of Globalization*, Ashgate Publishing Company, 2004;

Ladeur, K.-H., "The Introduction of the Precautionary Principle into the EU Law: a Pyrrhic Victory for Environmental and Public Health Law? Decision-Making under Conditions of Complexity in Multi-Level Political Systems", *Common Market Law Review*, Vol. 40, 2003, pp. 1455–1479;

Lafond, F. D., "The creation of the European Food Authority. Institutional implications of risk regulation", *European Issues*, No. 10, November 2001, pp. 1–31;

Landis Gabel, H. (ed.), *Product Standardisation and Competitive Strategy*, Elsevier Science Publishers B.V., 1987;

Lang, T., Heasman, M., *Food Wars. The Global Battle for Mouths, Minds and Markets*, Earthscan, 2004;

Lash, S., Szerszynski, B., Wynne, B.,(eds.), *Risk, Environment and Modernity: Towards a New Ecology*, London, Sage, 1996;

LaVia Campesina and the People's Food Sovereignty Network, "People's Food Sovereignty. Food and Agriculture Statement";

Łazowski, A., "Adaptation of the Polish legal system to European Union law: Selected Aspects", Sussex European Institute Working Paper No 45, 2001;

Leibfried, S., "Social Policy. Left to the Judges and the Markets?", in: H. Wallace, W. Wallace, and M. A. Pollack (eds.), *Policy-Making in the European Union*, Fifth Edition, Oxford University Press, 2005;

Leibfried, S., Pierson, P. (eds.), *European Social Policy: Between Fragmentation and Integration*, Brookings, 1995;

Lenaerts, K., Verhoeven, A., "Towards a Legal Framework for Executive Rule-making in the EU? The Contribution of the New Comitology Decision", *Common Market Law Review*, Vol. 37, No. 3, 2000, pp. 645–686;

Lien, M. E., Nerlich, B. (eds.), *The Politics of Food*, Berg, 2004;

Lister, C., *Regulation of Food Products by the European Community*, Butterworths, 1992;

Little, G., "Reports. BSE and the Regulation of Risk", *Modern Law Review*, Vol. 64, 2001, pp. 730–756;

Luhmann, N., *Law as a Social System*, Oxford University Press, 2004, (translated by K. A. Ziegert, original title: Das Recht der Gesellschaft, Suhrkamp Verlag Frankfurt am Main, 1993);

Luhmann, N., *Risk. A Sociological Theory*, Aldine Transaction, A Division of Transaction Publishers, 2005;

MacMaolain, C., *EU Food Law. Protecting Consumers and Health in a Common Market*, Modern Studies in European Law, Hart Publishing, Oxford—Portland Oregon, 2007;

MacMaolain, C., "Free movement of foodstuffs, quality requirements and consumer protection: have the Court and the Commission both got it wrong?", *European Law Review*, Vol. 26, 2001, pp. 413–428;
Maduro, M. P., *We the Court. The European Court of Justice and the European Economic Constitution*, Hart, 1998;
Mahiou, A., Snyder, F. (eds.), *La Sécurité Alimentaire. Food Security and Food Safety*, Martinus Nijhoff Publishers, 2006;
Majone, G., "Cross-national Sources of Regulatory Policy-Making in Europe and the United States", *Journal of Public Policy*, Vol. 11, Part 1, 1991, pp. 76–106;
Majone, G., *Dilemmas of European Integration. The Ambiguities and Pitfalls of Integration by Stealth*, Oxford University Press, 2005;
Majone, G., "European Regulatory Agencies: The Dilemma of Delegation of Powers in the European Union", in G. Majone (eds.), "Risk Regulation in the European Union: Between Enlargement and Internationalization", RSCAS Working Paper, 2003.
Majone, G., *Regulating Europe*, London: Routledge, 1996;
Majone, G. (ed.), *Risk Regulation in the European Union: Between Enlargement and Internationalization*, RSCAS, Florence, 2003;
Majone, G., "The New European Agencies: Regulation by Information", *Journal of European Public Policy*, Vol. 4, 1997, pp. 262–275;
Majone, G., "The Rise of the Regulatory State in Europe", *West European Politics*, Vol. 17, 1994, pp. 77–101;
Majone, G., Everson, M., "Institutional Reform: Independent Agencies, Oversight, Coordination and Procedural Control", in: O. de Schutter, N. Lebesis, J. Patterson, *Governance in the European Union*, Luxembourg, European Commission 2001;
Marks, G., Scharfp, F. W., Schmitter. P. C., Streeck, W., *Governance in the European Union*, Sage Publications, 1996;
Masson-Matthee, M, D., *The Codex Alimentarius Commission and Its Standards*, the Hague: TMC Asser Press, 2007;
Mattera, A., "The Principle of Mutual Recognition and Respect for National, Regional and Local Identities and Traditions", in: F. Kostoris Padoa Schioppa (ed.), *The Principle of Mutual Recognition in the European Integration Process*, Palgrave Macmillan, 2005;
McMahon, J. A., *Law of the Common Agricultural Policy*, European Law Series, Longman, Pearson Education Limited, 2000;
Millstone, E., "Recent developments in EU food policy: institutional adjustments or fundamental reforms?", *Zeitschrift für das gesamte Lebensmittelrecht*, Vol. 27, No. 6, 2000, pp. 1–15;
Millstone, E., van Zwanenberg, P., "Politics of Expert Advice: Lessons from the Early History of the BSE Saga", *Science and Public Policy*, Vol. 28, 2001, pp. 99–112;
Mohan Reddy, N., "Technology, Standards, and Markets: A Market Institutionalization Perspective", in: H. Landis Gabel (ed.), *Product Standardisation and Competitive Strategy*, Elsevier Science Publishers B.V., 1987;
Moroz, M. (ed.), *Sprawy Rolnictwa i Gospodarki Żywnościowej w Umowach Polski ze Wspólnotami Europejskimi*, Fundacja im. Mikołaja Rataja, Warszawa 1992;
Müller-Graff, P. C., "East Central Europe and the European Union: From Europe Agreements to a Member Status", in: P. C. Müller-Graff (ed.), *East Central Europe and the European Union: From Europe Agreements to a Member Status*, Nomos, 1997;
Müller-Graff, P. C., Stępniak, A. (eds.), *Poland and the European Union—Between Association and Membership*, European Community Studies Association—Europe Series, Vol. 4, Nomos, 1997;
National Resrearch Council, *Science and Judgment on Risk Assessment*, National Academy Press, Washington DC, 1994;
Nestle, M., *Food Politics. How the Food Industry Influences Nutrition and Health*, University of California Press, 2002;
Neyer, J., "The Regulation of Risk and the Power of the People: Lessons from the BSE Crisis", European Integration online Papers, Vol. 4, No. 6, 2000;
Nikolaidis, K., "Globalization with Human Faces: Managed Mutual Recognition and the Free Movement of Professionals", in: F. Kostoris Padoa Schioppa (ed.), *The Principle of Mutual Recognition in the European Integration Process*, Palgrave Macmillan, 2005;

Nicolaidis, K., "Mutual Recognition of Regulatory Regimes: Some Lessons and Prospects", Jean Monnet Working Paper, No. 7/97;

Nicolaidis, K., Shaffer, G., "Transnational Mutual Recognition Regimes: Governance without Global Government", *Law and Contemporary Problems*, Vol.62, Summer/Autumn 2005, pp. 263–317;

Nicolaidis, K., Howse R. (eds.), *The Federal Vision. Legitimacy and Levels of Governance in the United States and the European Union*, Oxford University Press, 2001;

Noiville, Ch., "Compatibility or Clash? EU Food Safety and the WTO", in: C. Ansell and D. Vogel (eds.), *What's the Beef? The Contested Governance of European Food Safety*, Cambridge MA, The MIT Press, 2006;

Nugent, N., *The Government and Politics of the European Union*, Fifth Edition, Palgrave Macmillan, 2003;

Offe, C., "The European Model of 'Social' Capitalism. Can it Survive European Integration?", *Journal of Political Philosophy*, Vol. 11, No. 4, 2003, pp. 437–469;

Ogus, A., *Regulation. Legal Form and Economic Theory*, Hart Publishing, 2004;

Oliver, P., "Some Further Reflections on the Scope of Articles 28-30 (ex 30-36)", *Common Market Law Review*, Vol. 36, 1999, pp. 783–806;

Oosterveer, P., *Global Governance of Food Production and Consumption. Issues and Challenges*, Edward Elgar, 2007;

O'Rourke, R., *European Food Law*, Palladian, 1998;

Pedler, R. H., Schaefer, G. F., (eds.), *Shaping European Law and Policy: The Role of Committees and Comitology in the Political Process*, European Institute of Public Administration, 1996;

Pelkmans, J., "Mutual Recognition in Goods and Services: An Economic Perspective", in F. Kostoris Padoa Schioppa (ed.), *The Principle of Mutual Recognition in the European Integration Process*, Palgrave Macmillan, 2005;

Pelkmans, J., "The New Approach to Technical Harmonization and Standardization", *Journal of Common Market Studies*, Vol. 25, 1987, pp. 249–269;

Philippart, E., Sie Dhian Ho, M., "From Uniformity to Flexibility. The Management of Diversity and its Impact on the EU System of Governance", in: G. de Burca, J. Scott (eds.), *Constitutional Change in the EU From Uniformity to Flexibility?*, Hart Publishing, 2000;

Polanyi, K., *The Great Transformation The Political and Economic Origins of our Time*, Beacon Press, 1957, Second Paperback Edition 2001;

Post, D. L., "Diffusion of International Food Safety Standards: Developing Country Experiences", WP of the Centre on Regulation and Competition, Paper No. 58, June 2004;

Post, D. L., "Standards and Regulatory Capitalism: The Diffusion of Food Safety Standards in Developing Countries", *Annals of the American Academy of Political and Social Science*, Vol. 598, March 2005, pp. 168–183;

Purcell, K., Clarke, L., Renzulli, L., "Menus of Choice: the Social Embeddedness of Decisions", in: M. J. Cohen (ed.), *Risk in the Modern Age. Social Theory, Science and Environmental Decision-Making*, Palgrave, 2001;

Renn, O., Jaeger, C. C., Rosa, E. A., Webler, T., "The Rational Actor Paradigm in Risk Theories: Analysis and Critique", in M. J. Cohen (ed.), *Risk in the Modern Age. Social Theory, Science and Environmental Decision-Making*, Palgrave, 2001;

Rieger, E., "Protective Shelter or Straitjacket: An Institutional Analysis of the Common Agricultural Policy of the European Union", in: S. Leibfried and P. Pierson (eds.), *European Social Policy: Between Fragmentation and Integration*, Brookings, 1995;

Rieger, E., "The Common Agricultural Policy: External and Internal Dimensions", in: H. Wallace, W. Wallace (eds.), *Policy-making in the European Union*, Oxford University Press, 1996;

Rieger, E., "The Common Agricultural Policy. Politics Against Market", in: H. Wallace and W. Wallace (eds.), *Policy-Making in the European Union*, Fourth Edition, Oxford University Press, 2000;

Rodrigues, M. J., "The Open Method of Coordination as a New Governance Tool", in: Telo, M. (ed.), *L'Evoluzion della Governance Europea*, special issue of *Europa/Europe*, Rome, No. 2–3, 2001, pp. 96–107;

Rodrik, D., *Has Globalization Gone Too Far?*, Institute for International Economics, Washington DC, 1997;

Rollo, J., "Agriculture, the Structural Funds and the Budget after Enlargement", in: Neuwahl, N. (ed.), *European Union Enlargement. Law and Socio-Economic Changes, Les Editions Themis*, Universite de Monteral, 2004, pp. 117–131;

Rosset, P. M., *Food is Different. Why We Must Get the WTO out of Agriculture*, The Global Issues Series, Zed Books Ltd, 2006;

Rowiński, J., "Adjustments of the Polish Agro-food Sector in the Course of the Association Process", in: P.-C. Müller-Graff, A. Stępniak (eds.), *Poland and the European Union—Between Association and Membership*, European Community Studies Association—Europe Series, Vol. 4, Nomos, 1997;

Rowiński, J., "Integracja Polski z Unia Europejska—Niezbędne Procesy Dostosowawcze Polskiej Gospodarki Żywnościowej", in: M. Moroz (ed.), *Sprawy Rolnictwa i Gospodarki Żywnościowej w Umowach Polski ze Wspólnotami Europejskimi*, Fundacja im. Mikołaja Rataja, Warszawa, 1992;

Rudolf, B., Simons, J., "European Governance of Food Safety", in C. H. Hofmann, A. H. Türk (eds.), *EU Administrative Governance*, Edward Elgar Publishing, 2006;

Rytko, A., "Analysis of Trade Relations between Poland and the European Union and their Impact on Volume and Structure of Agro-Food Articles Trade", *Electronic Journal of Polish Agricultural Universities*, Vol. 8, Issue 4, 2005, available at http://www.ejpau.media.pl/volume8/issue4/art-06.html;

Sapir, A., "Globalization and the Reform of European Social Models", *Journal of Common Market Studies*, Vol. 44, No. 2, 2006, pp. 369–390;

Schaffer, G. C., Pollack, M. A., "Regulating Between National Fears and Global Disciplines: Agricultural Biotechnology in the EU", Jean Monnet Working Paper, No. 10/04, 2004;

Scharpf, F. W., "Democratic Legitimacy under Conditions of Regulatory Competition: Why Europe Differs from the United States", in: K. Nicolaidis, R. Howse (eds.), *The Federal Vision. Legitimacy and Levels of Governance in the United States and the European Union*, Oxford University Press, 2001;

Scharpf, F. W., *Governing in Europe: Effective and Democratic?*, Oxford University Press, 1999;

Scharpf, F. W., "Legitimacy in the Multilevel European Polity", *European Political Science Review*, Vol. 1, No. 2, 2009, pp. 173–204;

Scharpf, F. W., "The European Social Model: Coping with the Challenges of Diversity", *Journal of Common Market Studies*, Vol. 40, No. 4, 2002, pp. 645–670;

Scharpf, F. W., "The Joint-Decision Trap Revisited", *Journal of Common Market Studies*, Vol. 44, No. 4, 2006, pp. 845–864;

Schepel, H., The Constitution of Private Governance. Product Standards in the Regulation of Integrating Markets, Oxford: Hart Publishing, 2005;

Schillhorn van Veen, T. W., "International Trade and Food Safety in Developing Countries", *Food Control*, Vol. 16, 2005, pp. 491–496;

Scott, J., "European Regulation of GMOs: Thinking about 'Judicial Review' in the WTO", Jean Monnet Working Paper, No. 4/04, 2004;

Scott, J., *The WTO Agreement on Sanitary and Phytosanitary Measures. A Commentary*, Oxford: Oxford University Press, 2007;

Scott, J., Vos, E., "The Juridification of Uncertainty: Observations on the Ambivalence of the Precautionary principle within the EU and the WTO", in: Ch. Joerges, R. Dehousse, *Good Governance in Europe's Integrated Market*, Oxford University Press, 2002;

Senior Nello, S., "Food and Agriculture in an Enlarged EU", EUI Working Paper RSC No. 2002/58;

Slovic, P., "Perceived Risk, Trust and Democracy", *Risk Analysis*, Vol. 13, No. 6, 1993, pp. 675–682;

Smith, K. E., "The Evolution and Application of EU Membership Conditionality", in: M. Cremona (ed.), *The Enlargement of the European Union*, The Collected Courses of the Academy of European Law, Vol. XII/1, Oxford University Press, 2003;

Smoter, B., "Polish Agriculture within the Common Agricultural Policy", *The Polish Foreign Affairs Digest*, Issue 3(12), 2004, pp. 81–119;

Snyder, F., "A Regulatory Framework for Foodstuffs in the Internal Market", EUI Working Paper LAW, No. 94/4;

Snyder F., *Law of the Common Agricultural Policy*, London, Sweet and Maxwell, 1985;
Stawarska, R., "EU Enlargement from the Polish Perspective", *Journal of European Public Policy*, Vol. 6, No. 5, 1999, pp. 822–838;
Steele, J., *Risks and Legal Theory*, Hart Publishing, 2004;
Steiner, J., "Drawing the Line: Uses and Abuses of Article 30 EEC", *Common Market Law Review*, Vol. 29, 1992, pp. 749–780;
Stephanou, C. A. (ed.), *Adjusting to EU Enlargement. Recurring Issues in a New Setting*, Edward Elgar, 2006;
Streeck, W., "Solidarity: Rethinking the 'European Social Model'", MPIfG Working Paper No 99/8, 1999;
Sullivan, C. D., *Standards and Standardization. Basic Principles and Application*, Marcel Dekker, Inc., 1983;
Sunstein, C. R., *Free Markets and Social Justice*, Oxford University Press, 1997;
Sunstein, C. R., *Laws of Fear. Beyond the Precautionary Principle*, Cambridge University Press, 2005;
Sunstein, C. R., *Risk and Reason. Safety, Law, and the Environment*, Cambridge University Press, 2002;
Sunstein, C. R., Pildes, R., "Experts, Economists, and Democrats", in: C. R. Sunstein, *Free Markets and Social Justice*, Oxford University Press, 1997;
Surdej, A., "Enlarging the EU Food safety Regime: Selected Problems in Adjusting the Polish Food Safety Regime to the EU Food Safety Requirements", in: G. Majone (ed.), *Risk Regulation in the European Union: Between Enlargement and Internationalization*, RSCAS Working Paper, 2003;
Surdej, A., Żurek, K., "The Polish Regulatory System on Food", in: E. Vos, M. Everson (eds.), *Uncertain Risks Regulated: Facing the Unknown in National, EU and International Law*, Routledge-Cavendish Publishing, Series: Law, Science and Society, 2009;
Szawłowska, K., "Risk Assessment in the European Food Safety Regulation: Who is to Decide Whose Science is Better? Commission v. France and Beyond…", German Law Journal, Vol. 5, No. 10, October 2004, pp. 1259–1274;
Szponar, L., Traczyk, I., Stoś, K. (eds.), *System Bezpieczeństwa Żywności w Polsce—Wybrane Zagadnienia*, Prace IŻŻ 104, Warszawa 2003;
Szponar, L., Turlejska, H., Traczyk, I., Gielcinska, I., "Rola urzędowej kontroli żywności w Polsce w realizacji strategii bezpieczeństwa żywności", in: L. Szponar, I. Traczyk, K. Stoś (eds.), *System Bezpieczeństwa Żywności w Polsce—Wybrane Zagadnienia*, Prace IŻŻ 104, Warszawa 2003;
Szyszczak, E., "Social Policy in the Post-Nice Era", in: A. Arnull & D. Wincott (eds.), *Accountability and Legitimacy in the European Union*, Oxford University Press, 2002;
Teubner, G., "Societal Constitutionalism: Alternatives to State-Centred Constitutional Theory", in: Ch. Joerges, I.-J. Sand, G. Teubner (eds.), *Transnational Governance and Constitutionalism*, Hart Publishing, 2004;
Trachtman, J. P., "Embedding Mutual Recognition at the WTO", *Journal of European Public Policy*, Vol. 14, No. 5, 2007, pp. 780–799;
Trachtman, J. P., "International Trade as a Vector in Domestic Regulatory Reform: Discrimination, Cost-Benefit Analysis, and Negotiations", in: K. -H. Ladeur (ed.), *Public Governance in the Age of Globalization*, Ashgate Publishing Company, 2004;
Trubek, D. M., Trubek, L. G., "Hard and Soft Law in the Construction of Social Europe: the Role of the Open Method of Co-ordination", *European Law Journal*, Vol. 11, No. 3, 2005, pp. 343–364;
Trumbull, G., *Consumer Capitalism. Politics, Product Markets, and Firm Strategy in France and Germany*, Cornell University Press, Ithaca and London, 2006;
Turlejska, H., Pelzner U., Konecka-Matyjek, E., "System Kontroli Wewnętrznej w zakładach produkcji, przetwórstwa i obrotu żywnością ze szczególnym uwzględnieniem sytemu HACCP", in: L. Szponar *et al.*, *System Bezpieczeństwa w Polsce—Wybrane Zagadnienia*, Prace IŻŻ 104, Warszawa 2003;
Ugland, T., Veggeland, F., "Experiments in Food Safety Policy Integration in the European Union", *Journal of Common Market Studies*, Vol. 44, No. 3, 2006, pp. 607–624;

Urwin, D., *The Community of Europe: A History of European Integration*, 2nd edition, Longman, 1995;
Urząd Komitetu Integracji Europejskiej, *4 lata Członkostwa Polski w UE. Bilans Kosztów i Korzyści Społeczno-Gospodarczych*, UKIE, Departament Analiz i Strategii, Warszawa, 2008, available at: www. ukie.gov.pl;
Usher, J. A., *EC Agricultural Law*, 2nd Edition, Oxford EC Law Library, Oxford University Press, 2001;
van der Heijden, K. A., Miller, S., *International Food Safety Handbook: Science, International Regulation, and Control*, Marcel Dekker Inc, 1999;
van der Meulen, B., van der Velde, M., *Food Safety Law in the European Union: An Introduction*, Wageningen Academic Publishers, 2004;
van Waarden, F., "Taste, Traditions, Transactions, and Trust: The Public and Private Regulation of Food", in: C. Ansell and D. Vogel (eds.), *What's the Beef? The Contested Governance of European Food Safety*, The MIT Press, 2006;
Vaughan-Whitehead, D. C., *EU Enlargement versus Social Europe? The Uncertain Future of the European Social Model*, Edward Elgar, 2003;
Veggeland, F., Borgen, S. O., "Negotiating International Food Safety Standards: The World Trade Organization's Impact on the Codex Alimentarius Commission", *Governance: An International Journal of Policy, Administration, and Institutions*, Vol. 18, No. 4, 2005, pp. 675–708;
Vincent, K., "'Mad Cows' and Eurocrats—Community Responses to the BSE Crisis", *European Law Journal*, Vol. 10, No. 5, 2004, pp. 499–517;
von Heydebrand, H.-Ch., "Free Movement of Foodstuffs, Consumer Protection and Food Standards in the European Community: Has the Court of Justice Got it Wrong?", *European Law Review*, Vol. 16, 1991, pp. 391–413;
Vos, E., "Agencies and the European Union", in T. Zwart, L. Verhey (eds.), *Agencies in European and Comparative Law*, Intersentia, 2003;
Vos, E. (ed.), *European Risk Governance—Its Science, its Inclusiveness and its Effectiveness*, CONNEX Report Series, No. 6, February 2008;
Vos, E., "EU Food Safety Regulation in the Aftermath of the BSE Crisis", *Journal of Consumer Policy*, Vol. 23, 2000, pp. 227–255;
Vos, E., "The Rise of Committees", *European Law Journal*, Vol. 3, No. 3, 1997, pp. 210–229;
Vos, E., Everson, M. (eds.), *Uncertain Risks Regulated: Facing the Unknown in National, EU and International Law*, Routledge-Cavendish Publishing, Series: Law, Science and Society, 2009;
Vos, E., Wendler, F., "Food Safety Regulation at the EU Level", in: E. Vos, F. Wendler, *Food Safety Regulation in Europe. A Comparative Institutional Analysis*, Intersentia, 2006;
Vos, E., Wendler, F. (eds.), *Food Safety Regulation in Europe. A Comparative Institutional Analysis*, Intersentia, Antwerpen—Oxford, 2006;
Wallace, H., Wallace, W. (eds.), *Policy-Making in the European Union*, Oxford University Press, 1996;
Wallace, H., Wallace, W., Pollack, M. A. (eds.), *Policy-Making in the European Union*, Fifth Edition, Oxford University Press, 2005;
Weatherill, S., Beaumont, P., *EU Law*, Third Edition, London, Penguin Books, 1999;
Weiler, J. H. H., "A Constitution for Europe? Some Hard Choices", in: G. Bermann, K. Pistor (eds.), *Law and Governance in an Enlarged European Union*, Hart Publishing, Oxford and Portland, Oregon, 2004;
Weiler, J. H. H., "Mutual Recognition, Functional Equivalence and Harmonization in the Evolution of the European Common Market and the WTO", in: F. Kostoris Padoa Schioppa (ed.), *The Principle of Mutual Recognition in the European Integration Process*, Palgrave Macmillan, 2005;
Weiler, J. H. H. (ed.), *The EU, the WTO and the NAFTA: Towards a Common Law of International Trade*, Oxford University Press, 2000; Weiler, J. H. H., "The Transformation of Europe", *Yale Law Journal*, Vol. 100, 1991, pp. 2403–2483;
Weimer, M., "What Price Flexibility?—The Recent Commission Proposal to Allow for National "Opt-Outs" on GMO Cultivation under the Deliberate Release Directive and the Comitology Reform Post-Lisbon", *European Journal of Risk Regulation*, Vol. 4, 2010, pp. 347-354.

White, E., "In Search of the Limits of Article 30 of the EEC Treaty", *Common Market Law Review*, Vol. 26, 1989, pp. 235–280;
Wils, W. P. J., "The Search for the Rule in Article 30 EEC: Much Ado about Nothing", *European Law Review*, Vol. 18, 1993, pp. 475–492;
Wouters, J., Verhoeven, S., "Regulation and Globalization: Interactions between International Standards-setting Agencies and the European Union", in: D. Geradin, R. Muñoz, N. Petit (eds.), *Regulation through Agencies in the EU. A New Paradigm of European Governance*, Edward Elgar Publishing, 2005;
Young, A. R., "The Single Market. A New approach to Policy", in: H. Wallace, W. Wallace, M. A. Pollack, *Policy-Making in the European Union*, Fifth Edition, Oxford University Press, 2005;
Young, A. R., Holmes, P., "Protection or Protectionism? EU Food Safety and the WTO", in: C. Ansell and D. Vogel (eds.), *What's the Beef?The Contested Governance of European Food Safety*, Cambridge MA, The MIT Press, 2006;
Zeitlin, J., "Social Europe and Experimentalist Governance: Towards a New Constitutional Compromise?", in: G. de Burca (ed.), EU *Law and the Welfare State. In search of Solidarity*, Oxford University Press 2005;
Żurek, K., "When Lab Results Are Not Sufficient: On the Limitations of Science in Tackling Modern Food Regulatory Concerns", SIEPS, *European Policy Analysis*, No. 5, 2009;
Zwart, T., Verhey, L. (eds.), *Agencies in European and Comparative Law*, Intersentia, 2003.

INDEX

www.ingramcontent.com/pod-product-compliance
Lightning Source LLC
LaVergne TN
LVHW081515300926
849161LV00006B/1181